BASIC DOCUMENTS
OF
ASIAN REGIONAL ORGANIZATIONS

Edited by
MICHAEL HAAS

Volume II

1974
Oceana Publications, Inc. Dobbs Ferry, New York

Library of Congress Cataloging in Publication Data

Haas, Michael, 1938-   comp.
  Basic documents of Asian regional organizations.

  Includes bibliographies.
  1. Asia--Foreign relations. 2. Regionalism (international organization) I. Title.
JX1569.A2H33   341.24'7   74-2248
ISBN 0-379-00177-2

Manufactured in the United States of America

PREFACE

This volume is the second of four volumes to be completed by
Oceana Publications on <u>Basic Documents of Asian Regional
Organizations</u>. For a discussion of the organizational scheme,
including a key to the numbering system for references, see
the Introduction, published in Volume I.

Chapter III

ASIAN-AFRICAN ORGANIZATIONS

Chapter III

ASIAN-AFRICAN ORGANIZATIONS

A. INTRODUCTORY NOTE

In the years after the formation of the United Nations, issues involving the conflict between Western countries and the Soviet Union and its allies tended to eclipse the attention and energies of delegates to UN bodies. An effort was made to mobilize the resources of countries outside this arena so that there would be a united bloc of states in Asia and Africa. India, with cooperation from Egypt and Indonesia and other countries, assumed leadership in advancing the interests of the Third World not only in the United Nations but also in efforts to establish new international organizations outside the great-power framework. Several NGOs were set up, and some IGOs of this sort were headquartered in Asian and African locations. Only two IGOs were organized with headquarters in Asia--the Asian African Legal Consultative Committee (AALCC) and the Afro-Asian Rural Reconstruction Organization (AARRO). These are the subject of this chapter.

i. Asian African Legal Consultative Committee (AALCC)

Origins. Each year Asian and African countries attend conferences on international law of various sorts. At many of the early sessions, the Third World delegates were insufficiently briefed in advance and tended to cast votes in conformity with their erstwhile colonial mentors in view of the latters' long tradition of expertise in the field. It occurred to representatives of India, however, that national interests in the Third World would be better served by a different method for determining which measures to support. Accordingly, an Asian Legal Conference was convened in New Delhi during 1954, where it was decided that an Asian Legal Consultative Committee should be formed. During a follow-up meeting of plenipotentiaries on November 15, 1956, Statutes of the Committee (1;3001) were adopted. The Committee held its inaugural session from April 18 to 27, 1957. When it became clear that several African countries were also interested in joining the organization, Prime Minister Nehru of India suggested that the scope of the organization should enlarge; the Statutes were amended on April 19, 1958, and the name of the

353

organization was changed to Asian African Legal Consultative Committee. Although the Committee was established to function for an initial period of five years, it was continued after this period for successive five-year terms.

Purposes. AALCC provides a forum for an exchange of views on legal matters. Its purposes are enumerated in the Statutes (Article 3):

"(a) to examine questions that are under consi-
      deration by the International Law Commis-
      sion and to arrange for the views of the
      Committee to be placed before the Commis-
      sion; to consider the reports of the Com-
      mission and to make recommendations thereon...

"(b) to consider legal problems that may be re-
      ferred to the Committee...and to make...
      recommendations...

"(c) to exchange views and information on legal
      matters and to make recommendations thereon...

"(d) to communicate...points of view of the Com-
      mittee on international legal problems...to
      the United Nations, other institutions and
      international organizations."

Constitutional Framework. The basic constitutional docu-ment is called the Statutes of the Committee (1;3001), which is 8 Articles in length. Provisions therein are expanded in further detail in the Statutory Rules of the Committee (2; 3002), which were adopted at the 1st AALCC Session in 1957; there are 11 Rules in this document, with several subsections in each Rule. Articles on the Immunities and Privileges of the Committee (3;3003) provide the juridical basis for the Secretariat in its location at New Delhi; there are 7 Articles in this third document, which was not approved until the 6th AALCC Session in 1958. Each of these documents has been re-vised from time to time.

Structure. The supreme organ of AALCC is the Committee, which meets in annual Sessions. The Committee is assisted by the Secretariat, which is located in New Delhi. A Secretary-General is the principal officer of the Secretariat; there is a Deputy Secretary-General, a Director of Research, 2 Assist-ant Directors, 5 legal officers, and a French Translation Sec-tion. The Secretariat is aided by an Administrative Panel, which meets 4 to 5 times each year. In addition, each coun-try appoints a representative as Liaison Officer to act as a channel of communication between the Secretariat and the member countries; the Liaison Officers meet as necessary during the year. Working Groups are established at times by the Committee to prepare recommendations on various legal questions to be discussed at the following Session. Sub-Committee meetings are also held between sessions.

Members. A country may acquire membership if it receives a two-thirds vote from the Committee, provided those in favor include two-thirds of the original participating countries. As of 1962 countries may join as Associate Members at reduced assessments, but they are not entitled to vote. Members are as follows:

Arab Republic of Egypt	(original member)
Burma	(original member)
Ceylon	(original member)
India	(original member)
Indonesia	(original member)
Iraq	(original member)
Japan	(original member)
Syria	(original member; in 1958, when it merged with Egypt, its seat was occupied by the latter; re-admitted in 1970)
Sudan	(admitted October 1, 1958; later withdrew)
Pakistan	(admitted January 1, 1959)
Morocco	(admitted February 24, 1961; later withdrew)
Thailand	(admitted December 6, 1961)
Ghana	(admitted October 28, 1963)
Jordan	(admitted January 1, 1968)
Sierra Leone	(admitted October, 1969)
Philippines	(admitted as Associate Member in 1969; full Member in 1971)
Iran	(admitted in 1970)
Kuwait	(admitted in 1970)
Malaysia	(admitted in 1970)
Nigeria	(admitted in 1970)
Korea	(admitted as Associate Member in 1970)
Kenya	(admitted in 1970)
Nepal	(admitted in 1971)
Mauritius	(admitted as Associate Member in 1972)
Tanzania	(admitted in 1973)

Observers from many other countries, both from Asia and Africa and from other regions of the world, have attended Sessions of the Committee from time to time, depending upon the topics under discussion.

Finances. Full Members pay a contribution varying between ₤900 and ₤1,400 (US $2,160 and $3,360) each year, according to a formula adopted by the Committee; this formula takes relative GNP figures into account. Associate Members pay a fixed contribution of ₤437.50 (US $1,050). These amounts total to approximately US $60,000 per annum, and they are used to pay the expenses of the Secretariat. The country that hosts an annual Session of the Committee pays local costs for the meeting. In addition, AALCC staff are sometimes seconded from their respective governments.

Projects. Each year the Committee authorizes studies to be undertaken on legal topics. The Secretariat assembles pertinent materials and background information. A Working Group may be selected to provide a summary and set of recommendations for discussion by the Committee. If there is sufficient consensus within the Committee, a draft formulation (such as a treaty or statute) may be prepared for adoption as a recommendation from the Committee. Texts of the more important reports finalized at the various Sessions of the Committee are contained with the documents reprinted below in this chapter (4-14).

In addition, the Secretariat has prepared studies on economic laws (3019;3020) and has assembled the Constitutions of African (3018) and Asian (3017) countries into two volumes, with annotations. The Secretariat also is on call for consultation in legal matters by the member countries.

The Secretariat operates a training program in international law for officials from Foreign Ministries. This is a recent innovation.

Relations with Other International Organizations. The Statutes of the Committee explicitly link AALCC with the International Law Commission and the United Nations. Rule 11 in the Statutory Rules of the Committee directs the Secretary-General of AALCC to effect communication with other international bodies, and he has presented his views in person from time to time.

Officials relations are maintained with these two organizations, along with the Hague Conference on Private International Law, League of Arab States, Organization of African Unity (OAU), UN Commission on International Trade Law (UNCITRAL), UN Conference on Trade and Development (UNCTAD), and the UN High Commissioner for Refugees. These bodies all send

356

observers to AALCC Sessions, and the Committee is invited to meetings of these organizations as well. AALCC Sessions also have been attended by representatives from the International Institute for the Unification of Private Law (UNIDROIT), the International Law Association (ILA), and the South Pacific Commission (SPC). Decisions at these bodies are considered by AALCC during its deliberations, and reports and recommendations of AALCC are placed before these organizations on a regular basis.

Several international organizations have requested that AALCC prepare studies on specific topics.

ii. Afro-Asian Rural Reconstruction Organization (AARRO)

Origins. One of the central problems of development is to enable rural communities to change from subsistence agriculture to accept farming as a business in which crops are grown for consumption in the industrial regions of a country. "Rural reconstruction" is the term applied to the process of mobilizing the rural population to assume its role as an integral part of a market-oriented national economy. In 1961 India convened the 1st Afro-Asian Rural Reconstruction Conference in New Delhi to discuss common problems among nearly 50 countries, approximately half from Africa and half from Asia. The following year, from March 19 to 31, 1962, Cairo was the location of the 2nd Afro-Asian Rural Reconstruction Conference, where the Constitution (15;4001) of the Afro-Asian Rural Reconstruction Organization was adopted.

Purposes. The objective behind the formation of AARRO is to "launch concerted and, wherever possible, coordinated action to reconstruct the economy of...rural people and revitalize their social and cultural life," according to the Preamble to the AARRO Constitution. Functions are set forth in detail in Article I:

   (a) "To develop understanding...of each other's problems and to explore, collectively, opportunities for coordination of efforts for promoting welfare and eradication of hunger and poverty amonst rural people"

   (b) "To assist the member countries in obtaining financial and technical assistance for their

Rural Development Programs"

(c) "To collaborate with the appropriate...organizations and agencies...for the purpose of taking such action as may accelerate the pace of Rural Development"

(d) "To lay the views of the Organization before any Committee, Commission or Organization"

(e) "To assist in the formation and development of ...organizations of farmers and the establishment of healthy relationship between them and the governmental agencies responsible for agricultural development and rural reconstruction"

(f) "To promote principles of cooperation and cooperative activities in the various phases of the life of the rural people"

(g) "To promote exchange of farmers and experts from one country to the other"

(h) "To organize international and regional meetings, seminars, conferences, exhibitions and fairs and produce literature and undertake publicity"

(i) "To initiate studies on subjects of common interests and collect, analyze, interpret and disseminate data, statistics and information"

(j) "To consider the possibilities of and assisting in, if necessary, the disposal or exchange of surplus agricultural commodities"

(k) "To raise funds by contributions and donations and hold property"

(l) "To do all things incidental to and take all actions calculated to achieve the objects of the Organization."

Constitutional Framework. The Constitution (15;4001) is the basic constitutional document of AARRO. It was adopted at the 2nd Afro-Asian Rural Reconstruction Conference in 1962, and it has been revised subsequently to bring its provisions up to date. It contains a Preamble, 16 Articles, and 2 Annexures. In addition, AARRO is governed by Rules of Pro-

358

cedure of the Organization (16;4002), which contains 6 parts
--The Conference, consisting of 65 Rules; The Executive Committee, with 32 Rules; President and Vice-Presidents, containing 9 Rules; Secretary General, 21 Rules; Financial
Rules, which number 49; and Staff Regulations, which are 37
in number.

Structure. AARRO functions through 3 organs--the General Conference, the Executive Committee, and the Secretariat.
The General Conference is the plenary body; it meets once
every 3 years, alternating between Asian and African venues.
The Executive Committee meets at least 3 times in between
General Sessions of the AARRO Conference; it is composed of
the President, the 2 Vice Presidents (one for Asia, the other for Africa) of the Conference, with representatives from
9 other countries, such that the overall composition of the
body is half Asian and half African. The Secretariat, located in New Delhi, is headed by a Secretary General. A Sub-
Committee of Experts functions to review technical aspects of
AARRO programs. A Liaison Committee, established at the 10th
Session of the Executive Committee in 1970, operates at the
consular level and handles policy questions in between meetings of the Executive Committee.

Because of the geographic expanse of the membership in
AARRO, the 7th Executive Committee Session decided in March,
1967, that Regional Offices of AARRO shall be established.
There are 4 such Regional Offices. The Middle East is served
by a Regional Office in Amman; Far East, in Seoul; West Africa, Accra; East and Central Africa, Addis Ababa. These function under Honorary Representatives of AARRO to assist in implementing programs and in making recommendations to the Head
Office for new programs.

In addition, Centers of AARRO have been established to
function in specialized fields. During 1967 the Research and
Education Center (RECA) was established in Tokyo. Other Centers include a Small Scale Extension Training Institute in
Hyderabad and a Training Institute for Community Development
in Alexandria. A new Center for youth activities has been
proposed.

Members. Membership is open to any of the 49 countries
that were invited to the Afro-Asian Rural Reconstruction Conferences in 1961 and 1962; countries not represented at these
conferences are eligible, provided they are Members or Associate Members of the UN or any of its Specialized Agencies
and so long as they are included as regional members of the
African, East African, Near East, and Asia and the Far East
regions demarcated by the UN Food and Agriculture Organiza-

tion (FAO). Some 64 countries in all are eligible. Australia
and New Zealand or any other Australasian country are eligible
to join as Associate Members. New members may apply directly
to the AARRO Secretariat; if there is no objection raised
while the Secretary General circulates notice of the application, the country is admitted, pending ratification at the
next General Session of the AARRO Conference.

Membership has fluctuated somewhat over the years, and
a complete chronology on the subject is not available. Present members are the following:

Algeria
Ceylon
China
Ethiopia
Ghana
India
Indonesia
Iran
Iraq
Japan
Jordan
Kenya
Korea
Laos
Lebanon
Libya
Malaysia
Morocco
Philippines
Sierra Leone
Singapore
Sudan
Syria
Tunisia
United Arab Republic
Vietnam

Finances. Every member is required to pay a contribution
calculated at 8.5 percent of its current FAO assessment. This
amount pays the cost of the Secretariat in New Delhi and its
various operational activities. Facilities of RECA, the Center in Alexandria, and Indian agricultural institutes participating in the training program are open to trainees free of
charge, provided their home governments pay their international travel costs. AARRO does not accept funds from outside the
region of Africa and Asia. In 1968 AARRO spent US $92,500.24.
Contributions were $72,342.73 for 1969, and some countries
were in arrears on payments. The Central Union of Agricultur-

al Cooperatives of Japan, which operates RECA, pays $37,000 annually as a membership contribution.

Projects. AARRO operates with relation to rural community development, rural cooperatives, and farmers' professional organizations. Research and surveys have been conducted in all three areas, with publications (4020-4023) summarizing the results.

Pilot projects in community development have been undertaken in Jordan with AARRO assistance. Similar efforts have been provided to Iraq, Lebanon, Tanzania, and Uganda in the field of rural cooperatives.

RECA provides training in the field of community development and rural cooperatives. RECA also has facilities for research in these fields, and several studies have been published (4027-4033). Training arrangements are available to Afro-Asians in various institutions in India. Among these is the Small Scale Extension Training Institute, which offers a 10-week course. Seminars have been held at the offices in Alexandria, New Delhi, and Tokyo (4017-4019).

In 1969 AARRO inaugurated an exchange program, wherein a study team of farmers from India visited their counterparts in Hongkong, the Philippines, and Taiwan (4024). The program was continued in 1970 (4025).

Relations with Other International Organizations. AARRO clearly operates in an area close to the work of the Food and Agriculture Organization of the United Nations (FAO). At the time when AARRO was set up there were no substantial operational programs with a regional focus functioning out of any of the FAO Regional Offices in Asia or Africa. FAO, thus, was pleased to learn of the formation of AARRO, and in August, 1965, a formal collaborative relationship was established between the two organizations, as ratified at the 2nd General Session of AARRO in Nairobi on January, 1966. FAO permits AARRO full latitude in serving as an extension field agent in assisting national farmers' organizations and thus does not duplicate its efforts. In addition, the UN Conference on Trade and Development (UNCTAD), at its 2nd Session, granted AARRO a permanent observer status.

AARRO has had dealings over the years with the Afro-Asian Organization for Economic Cooperation (AFRASEC), the UN's Economic Commissions for Africa (ECA) and for Asia and the Far East (ECAFE), International Cooperative Alliance (ICA), International Federation of Agricultural Producers (IFAP), International Labor Organization (ILO), League of

Arab States (LAS), Organization of African Unity (OAU), UN Children's Fund (UNICEF), UN Educational, Scientific, and Cultural Organization (UNESCO), World Assembly of Youth (WAY), and the World Health Organization (WHO). AARRO invites these and other organizations to attend its various meetings, and vice versa. It has been decided that joint projects will be undertaken with AFRASEC, ECA, and LAS, and the latter organization has entered into a formal agreement with AARRO--Agreement for a Program of Mutual Collaboration and Assistance Between the League of Arab States and the Afro-Asian Rural Reconstruction Organization (17;4003), which has a preamble and 5 Articles.

Article I of the AARRO Constitution charges the organization with the task of obtaining financial and technical assistance for member countries from the African Development Bank (ADB), Asian Development Bank (ADB), the World Bank, and UN organs and Specialized Agencies, as well as national and governmental agencies throughout the world. AARRO, in turn, has supplied assistance to other bodies. A conference on agricultural cooperatives in 1969 was held in conjunction with ICA (4019). AARRO collaborated with AFRASEC in organizing the 1st Afro-Asian Conference on the Development of Small Industries, which was held in Cairo in March 24-27, 1969, and the 1st Afro-Asian Tobacco Industry and Trade Conference in March, 1971. AFRASEC has nominated a trainee for AARRO's Hyderabad center. It has been proposed that all Colombo Plan aid concerned with rural development be routed through AARRO. Recipient countries are free to do so at their option.

B. SELECTED BIBLIOGRAPHY

1. Books

1001.   GHANEM, Hafez. <u>The Asian-African Legal Consultative Committee</u> (Cairo, 1958). NC.

2. Articles

1961

2001.   JAHN, E. "The Work of the Asian-African Legal
        Consultative Committee on the Legal Status of
        Refugees," <u>Zeitschrift fur Auslaudisches Offen-
        tliches Recht und Volkerrecht</u>, XXVII (July 2). NC.

1967

2002.   JAGOTA, S. P. "A Review of the Work of the Asian-
        African Legal Consultative Committee." [Paper read
        in the Seminar on Asian States and the Development
        of Universal International Law, New Delhi, November
        6-9.] NC.

2003.   WILSON, Robert R. "A Decade of Legal Consultation--
        Asian-African Collaboration," <u>American Journal of
        International Law</u>, LXI (October), pp. 1011-1015.

3. Documents of the Asian-African Legal Consultative
Committee (AALCC)

a. Basic Documents

3001. Statutes of the Committee. [Adopted in New Delhi on
November 15, 1956, by the Asian Legal Consultative
Committee. Original text is published in ASIAN LEGAL
CONSULTATIVE COMMITTEE, First Session (New Delhi,
April 18-27, 1957), pp. 7-8. Subsequently revised
on several occasions. The most up-to-date version
is published in AFRO-ASIAN LEGAL CONSULTATIVE COM-
MITTEE, Basic Facts (New Delhi, 1969), pp. 31-33.]

3002. Statutory Rules of the Committee. [Adopted in New
Delhi on April 18-27, 1957, at the 1st Session of
the Asian Legal Consultative Committee. Original
text is published in ASIAN LEGAL CONSULTATIVE COM-
MITTEE, First Session (New Delhi, April 18-27, 1957),
pp. 9-17. Subsequently revised on several occasions.
The most up-to-date version is published in ASIAN-
AFRICAN LEGAL CONSULTATIVE COMMITTEE, Basic Facts
(New Delhi, 1969), pp. 37-46.]

b. Supplementary Documents

3003. Articles on the Immunities and Privileges of the
Committee. [Adopted in Cairo on October, 1958,
at the 6th Session of the Asian-African Legal Con-
sultative Committee. Original text in ASIAN-
AFRICAN CONSULTATIVE COMMITTEE, 6th Session (Cairo,
October, 1958), pp. 24-28. Subsequently revised.
The most up-to-date version is in ASIAN-AFRICAN
CONSULTATIVE COMMITTEE, Basic Facts (New Delhi, 1969),
pp. 47-52.]

c. Conference Proceedings

3004.   ASIAN LEGAL CONSULTATIVE COMMITTEE. First Session
(New Delhi, April 18-27, 1957), 20 pp. [History
of the organization, agenda for the 1st session,
texts of the Statutes and Statutory Rules.]

3005.   ASIAN-AFRICAN LEGAL CONSULTATIVE COMMITTEE. Second
Session (Cairo, October 1-13, 1958), 63 pp. [Pro-
ceedings of the session, including 2 reports--on
Diplomatic Immunities (pp. 11-28) and on Immunity
of States in Respect of Commercial Transactions (pp.
29-51), with 2 appendices, containing texts of the
revised Statutes and Statutory Rules.]

3006.   ASIAN-AFRICAN LEGAL CONSULTATIVE COMMITTEE. Third
Session (Colombo, 20 January-4 February, 1960, iii +
247 pp. [Proceedings of the session, including 5
reports--on Diplomatic Immunities and Privileges
(pp. 15-54), Immunity of States in Respect of
Commercial Transactions (pp. 55-81), Status of Aliens
(pp. 82-158), Extradition (pp. 159-225), Arbitral
Procedure (pp. 226-232)--and 2 appendices, containing the Statutes and Statutory Rules of the Committee.]

3007.   ASIAN-AFRICAN LEGAL CONSULTATIVE COMMITTEE. Fourth
Session: Report (Tokyo, February, 1961), ii + 428
pp. [Proceedings of the session, including 2 reports
--on Legal Aid (pp. 199-375) and Recognition and Enforcement of Foreign Decrees in Matrimonial Matters
(pp. 376-428).]

3008.   ASIAN-AFRICAN LEGAL CONSULTATIVE COMMITTEE. Report
of the Fifth Session (Rangoon, January 17th-30th,
1962), iii + 189. [Proceedings of the session, including reports-- on Dual Nationality (pp. 21-178), Legality
of Nuclear Tests (pp. 179-183), Arbitral Procedure (pp.
184-188).]

3009.   ASIAN-AFRICAN LEGAL CONSULTATIVE COMMITTEE. Report
of the Sixth Session (Cairo, 24th February-6th March,
1964), iii + 47 + 286 pp. [Proceedings of the session,
including 3 reports--on Immunities and Privileges of
the Committee (pp. 21-28), Dual Nationality (pp. 29-
36), and the Legality of Nuclear Tests (pp. 37-42)--
followed by "The Legality of Nuclear Tests: Report
of the Committee and Background Material," 286 pp.]

3010.   ASIAN-AFRICAN LEGAL CONSULTATIVE COMMITTEE. Report
         of the Seventh Session (Baghdad, March 23-April 1,
         1965), iii + 58 + 205 pp. [Proceedings of the Session,
         including 3 reports--Rights of Refugees (pp. 23-34),
         Double Taxation and Fiscal Evasion (pp. 35-44), The
         Recognition and Enforcement of Foreign Judgments,
         Service of Process, and Recording of Evidence, Both
         in Civil and Criminal Cases (pp. 45-53)--followed by
         "The Recognition and Enforcement of Foreign Judgments,
         Service of Process, and Recording of Evidence, Both in
         Civil and Criminal Cases: Report of the Committee &
         Background Materials," 205 pp.]

3011.   ASIAN-AFRICAN LEGAL CONSULTATIVE COMMITTEE. Report
         of the Eighth Session (Bangkok, 1966), iv + 97 + 409
         pp. [Proceedings of the Session, including reports--
         on the Rights of Refugees (pp. 29-54), Relief Against
         Double Taxation and Fiscal Evasion (pp. 55-69), Codi-
         fication of the Principles of Peaceful Coexistence
         (pp. 71-80), World Court Judgment on South West Africa
         Cases (pp. 81-97)--followed by "The Rights of Refugees:
         Report of the Committee and Background Materials,"
         409 pp.]

3012.   ASIAN-AFRICAN LEGAL CONSULTATIVE COMMITTEE. Report
         of the Ninth Session (New Delhi, 18th-29th December,
         1967), iv + 59 + 414 + 291 pp. [Proceedings of the
         session, including 2 reports--Law of Treaties (pp.
         27-48) and Law of International Rivers (pp. 49-59)--
         followed by "South West Africa Cases: Report of the
         Committee & Background Materials," 414 pp., and
         "Relief Against Double Taxation & Fiscal Evasion:
         Report of the Committee & Background Materials,"
         291 pp.]

3013.   ASIAN-AFRICAN LEGAL CONSULTATIVE COMMITTEE. Report
         of the Tenth Session (Karachi, 21st-31st January,
         1969), 412 pp. [Proceedings of the session, includ-
         ing reports--on the Law of International Rivers
         (pp. 29-40), the Rights of Refugees (pp. 41-64), the
         Law of Treaties (pp. 65-412.]

3014.   ASIAN-AFRICAN LEGAL CONSULTATIVE COMMITTEE. Report
         of the Eleventh Session (Accra, 19th-29th January,
         1971), 377 pp. [Proceedings of the session, includ-
         ing reports--on the Rights of Refugees (pp. 25-188),
         the Law of International Rivers (pp. 189-258), the
         Law Relating to International Sale of Goods (pp.
         259-282), International Legislation on Shipping
         (pp. 283-377).]

3015. ASIAN-AFRICAN LEGAL CONSULTATIVE COMMITTEE.
       Report of the Twelfth Session (1971). NA.

3016. ASIAN-AFRICAN LEGAL CONSULTATIVE COMMITTEE.
       Report of the Thirteenth Session (1972). NA.

d. Technical Publications

i. Constitutions

3017. ASIAN-AFRICAN LEGAL CONSULTATIVE COMMITTEE,
       Constitutions of Asian Countries (Bombay, 1968),
       viii + 1171 pp. [A second edition is in prepara-
       tion.]

3018. ASIAN-AFRICAN LEGAL CONSULTATIVE COMMITTEE.
       Constitutions of African Countries. NA.

ii. Economic Laws Series

3019. ASIAN-AFRICAN LEGAL CONSULTATIVE COMMITTEE.
       Laws & Regulations Relating to Control of Import
       & Export Trade in Member Countries (New Delhi,
       1965), 85 pp. [Economic Laws Series, No. 1.]

3020. ASIAN-AFRICAN LEGAL CONSULTATIVE COMMITTEE.
       Foreign Investment Laws and Regulations of Member
       Countries (New Delhi, c. 1965 [n.d.]), 91 pp.
       [Economic Laws Series, No. 2.]

iii. Reports (Reprints from Conference Proceedings)

3021. ASIAN-AFRICAN LEGAL CONSULTATIVE COMMITTEE.
       The Legality of Nuclear Tests: Report of the
       Committee and Background Materials (New Delhi,
       c.1966 [n.d.]), ii + 286 pp. [Reprinted from
       ASIAN-AFRICAN LEGAL CONSULTATIVE COMMITTEE,
       Report of the Sixth Session (Cairo, 24th February-
       6th March, 1964.]

3022. ASIAN-AFRICAN LEGAL CONSULTATIVE COMMITTEE.
       Reciprocal Enforcement of Foreign Judgments,
       Service of Process and Recording of Evidence Both
       in Civil and Criminal Cases: Report of the Com-
       mittee and Background Materials (New Delhi, c.
       1966 [n.d.]), ii + 205 pp. [Reprinted from ASIAN-
       AFRICAN LEGAL CONSULTATIVE COMMITTEE, Report of the
       Seventh Session (Baghdad, 1965).]

3023.   ASIAN-AFRICAN LEGAL CONSULTATIVE COMMITTEE.
        Relief Against Double Taxation and Fiscal Evasion:
        Report of the Committee and Background Materials
        (New Delhi, 1968), iii + 291 pp.   [Reprinted from
        ASIAN-AFRICAN LEGAL CONSULTATIVE COMMITTEE, Report
        of the Seventh Session (Baghdad, 1965).]

3024.   ASIAN-AFRICAN LEGAL CONSULTATIVE COMMITTEE.
        The Rights of Refugees: Report of the Committee
        and Background Materials (New Delhi, 1967), ii + 409 pp.
        [Reprinted from ASIAN-AFRICAN LEGAL CONSULTATIVE
        COMMITTEE, Report of the Eighth Session.]

3025.   ASIAN-AFRICAN LEGAL CONSULTATIVE COMMITTEE.
        South West Africa Cases: Report of the Committee
        and Background Materials (New Delhi, c. 1967), 414
        pp.   [Reprinted from ASIAN-AFRICAN LEGAL CONSULTA-
        TIVE COMMITTEE, Report of the Ninth Session (New
        Delhi, 18th-29th December, 1967).]

e.   Other Publications

3026.   ASIAN AFRICAN LEGAL CONSULTATIVE COMMITTEE.
        Basic Facts (New Delhi, 1969), iii + 76 pp.
        [Describes the history, structure, operations of
        AALCC, including texts of the basic and supple-
        mentary documents.]

4. Documents of the Afro-Asian Rural Reconstruction
Organization (AARRO)

a. Basic Documents

4001. Constitution. [Adopted in Cairo on March 19-31,
1962, at the 2nd Afro-Asian Rural Reconstruction
Conference. Published in AFRO-ASIAN RURAL RECON-
STRUCTION ORGANIZATION, EXECUTIVE COMMITTEE, 10th
Session Report (New Delhi, November, 1970), pp.
171-181.]

4002. Rules of Procedure for the Organization. [Adopted in
Cairo on March 19-31, 1962, at the 2nd Afro-Asian
Rural Reconstruction Conference. Published in AFRO-
ASIAN RURAL RECONSTRUCTION ORGANIZATION, EXECUTIVE
COMMITTEE, 10th Session Report (New Delhi, November,
1970), pp. 182-212.]

b. Supplementary Documents

4003. Agreement for a Program of Mutual Collaboration and
Assistance Between the League of Arab States and the
Afro-Asian Rural Reconstruction Organization. [Adopted
in New Delhi on November 20-22, 1970, at the 10th
Session of the Executive Committee. Published in
AFRO-ASIAN RURAL RECONSTRUCTION ORGANIZATION, EXECUTIVE
COMMITTEE, 10th Session Report (New Delhi, November,
1970), pp. 32-36.]

c. Conference Proceedings

4004. AFRO-ASIAN RURAL RECONSTRUCTION ORGANIZATION,
EXECUTIVE COMMITTEE. 1st Session Report. NA.

4005. AFRO-ASIAN RURAL RECONSTRUCTION ORGANIZATION,
EXECUTIVE COMMITTEE. 2nd Session Report. NA.

4006. AFRO-ASIAN RURAL RECONSTRUCTION ORGANIZATION,
EXECUTIVE COMMITTEE. 3rd Session Report. NA.

4007. AFRO-ASIAN RURAL RECONSTRUCTION ORGANIZATION,
EXECUTIVE COMMITTEE. 4th Session Report. NA.

4008. AFRO-ASIAN RURAL RECONSTRUCTION ORGANIZATION,
EXECUTIVE COMMITTEE. 5th Session Report. NA.

4009. AFRO-ASIAN RURAL RECONSTRUCTION ORGANIZATION,
EXECUTIVE COMMITTEE. 6th Session Report. NA.

4010. AFRO-ASIAN RURAL RECONSTRUCTION ORGANIZATION,
EXECUTIVE COMMITTEE. 7th Session Report. NA.

4011. AFRO-ASIAN RURAL RECONSTRUCTION ORGANIZATION,
EXECUTIVE COMMITTEE. 8th Session Report. NA.

4012. AFRO-ASIAN RURAL RECONSTRUCTION ORGANIZATION,
EXECUTIVE COMMITTEE. 9th Session Report. NA.

4013. AFRO-ASIAN RURAL RECONSTRUCTION ORGANIZATION,
EXECUTIVE COMMITTEE. 10th Session Report
(New Delhi, November, 1970), 226 pp.

4014. AFRO-ASIAN RURAL RECONSTRUCTION ORGANIZATION,
EXECUTIVE COMMITTEE. 11th Session Report
(Accra, October 6-7, 1971). NA.

4015. AFRO-ASIAN RURAL RECONSTRUCTION ORGANIZATION,
EXECUTIVE COMMITTEE. 12th Session Report
(Accra, October 16-17, 1971). NA.

d. Periodicals

4016. AFRO-ASIAN RURAL RECONSTRUCTION ORGANIZATION.
Rural Reconstruction (New Delhi), 1966- (quarterly).
[Reports on activities of AARRO or its member
countries related to rural reconstruction. Also
available in French.]

e. Colloquia and Seminars (Reports)

4017. AFRO-ASIAN RURAL RECONSTRUCTION ORGANIZATION,
RESEARCH AND EDUCATION CENTER. First Seminar on
The Role of Agricultural Cooperatives in Develop-
ing Rural Communities: Seminar Report (Tokyo,
March 11-April 13, 1968), 36 pp.

4018. AFRO-ASIAN RURAL RECONSTRUCTION ORGANIZATION.
Planning for Rural Development: First Arab Seminar
(Alexandria, May, 1970), ii + 64 pp.

4019. AFRO-ASIAN RURAL CONSTRUCTION ORGANIZATION.
The Role of Cooperatives in Agricultural Development
(New Delhi, October, 1970), 57 pp. [Jointly published
with the International Cooperative Alliance Regional
Office & Education Center for South and East Asia,
Delhi. Report of a conference held in Kathmandu,
November 16-21, 1969.]

f. Research and Studies (Reports)

4020. AFRO-ASIAN RURAL RECONSTRUCTION ORGANIZATION.
       Comparative Study of Community Development Programmes
       in Afro-Asian Countries (ARRC-III/CO/I (ii), New Delhi,
       c. 1968 [n.d.]), 35 pp. [Originally circulated at the
       3rd General Session of the AARRO Conference, Seoul,
       April 22-29, 1968. The Conference approved and adopted
       the study and directed that it be printed and circulated.]

4021. AFRO-ASIAN RURAL RECONSTRUCTION ORGANIZATION.
       Comparative Study of Professional Organizations of
       Farmers in Afro-Asian Countries (ARRC-III/CO/I (ii),
       New Delhi, c. 1968 [n.d.]), 28 pp. [Originally cir-
       culated at the 3rd General Session of the AARRO Con-
       ference, Seoul, April 22-29, 1968. The Conference
       approved and adopted the study and directed that it
       be printed and circulated.]

4022. AFRO-ASIAN RURAL RECONSTRUCTION ORGANIZATION.
       Cooperative Movements in Afro-Asian Countries
       (ARRC-III/RC-1(i), New Delhi, c. 1968 [n.d.]),
       203 pp. [Originally circulated at the 3rd General
       Session of the AARRO Conference, Seoul, April 22-29,
       1968. The Conference approved and adopted the study
       and directed that it be printed and circulated.
       Survey of 19 countries.]

4023. AFRO-ASIAN RURAL RECONSTRUCTION ORGANIZATION.
       Directory of Professional Organizations of Farmers
       in Afro-Asian Countries (ARRC-III/CO/2, New Delhi,
       c. 1968 [n.d.]), 128 pp. [Originally circulated at
       the 3rd General Session of the AARRO Conference,
       Seoul, April 22-29, 1968. The Conference approved
       and adopted the study and directed that it be printed
       and circulated. Covers 10 countries.]

4024. CHEEMA, A. S. Report of the Study Team of Agricul-
       tural Experts of Rice-Growing States on Their Visit
       to Philippines, Taiwan & Hong Kong (from 5th to 13th
       Oct., 1969), vii + 208 + XXVII pp. [The visit, spon-
       sored by AARRO, was made by experts from 6 rice-
       growing states of India. The report consists of a
       summary of various programs in operation in each
       country, with a set of recommendations for imple-
       mentation. The report was prepared by a team headed
       by A. S. Cheema, Agricultural Commission, Department
       of Agriculture, Ministry of Food, Agriculture, Com-
       munity Development and Cooperation, New Delhi.]

4025.   AFRO-ASIAN RURAL RECONSTRUCTION ORGANIZATION.
"Report of the Team of Indian Farmers Who Visited
Philippines & Taiwan" (24 August-3rd September 1970),
46 pp. [Presented by Mrs. K. Lakshmi Raghu Ramaiah,
Vice President, Bhartiga Gramin Mahila Sangh, New
Delhi. Observations, remarks, and recommendations.]

g. Technical Publications

4026.   AFRO-ASIAN RURAL RECONSTRUCTION ORGANIZATION.
Directory on International Trade in Agricultural
Commodities (New Delhi, c. 1970), 2 vols. [Covers
60 countries.] NC.

4027.   AFRO-ASIAN RURAL RECONSTRUCTION ORGANIZATION,
RESEARCH AND EDUCATION CENTER. "Agricultural
Cooperative Finance in Japan" (Tokyo, c. 1970). NC.

4028.   AFRO-ASIAN RURAL RECONSTRUCTION ORGANIZATION,
RESEARCH AND EDUCATION CENTER. "The Agricultural
Cooperative Society Law" (Tokyo, c. 1970). NC.

4029.   AFRO-ASIAN RURAL RECONSTRUCTION ORGANIZATION,
RESEARCH AND EDUCATION CENTER. "Business Practice
of Cooperative Marketing" (Tokyo, c. 1970). NC.

4030.   AFRO-ASIAN RURAL RECONSTRUCTION ORGANIZATION,
RESEARCH AND EDUCATION CENTER. "Compiled Laws
Relating to Agricultural Cooperatives" (Tokyo,
c. 1970). NC.

4031.   AFRO-ASIAN RURAL RECONSTRUCTION ORGANIZATION,
RESEARCH AND EDUCATION CENTER. "Farm Guidance
Activities and Cooperative Farming Complex in
Japan" (Tokyo, c. 1970). NC.

4032.   AFRO-ASIAN RURAL RECONSTRUCTION ORGANIZATION,
RESEARCH AND EDUCATION CENTER. "Japan's Agri-
culture and Tasks of Agricultural Cooperatives"
(Tokyo, c. 1970). NC.

4033.   AFRO-ASIAN RURAL RECONSTRUCTION ORGANIZATION,
RESEARCH AND EDUCATION CENTER. "Summary Account
of Amendments Worked into Japanese Compensation
Against Agricultural Loss System" (Tokyo, c. 1970).
NC.

4034. AFRO-ASIAN RURAL RECONSTRUCTION ORGANIZATION.
"Education & Training" (AARRC-IV/P-II/3, New
Delhi, c. 1971 [n.d.]), 8 pp. [Proposed seminars
and training programs at specific centers.]

4035. AFRO-ASIAN RURAL RECONSTRUCTION ORGANIZATION.
"Exchange Programme" (AARRC-IV/P-II/4, New Delhi,
c. 1971 [n.d.]), 5 pp. [Proposed exchange of farmers
and rural leaders.]

4036. AFRO-ASIAN RURAL RECONSTRUCTION ORGANIZATION.
"Integrated Rural Development" (AARRC-IV/P-II/1,
New Delhi, c. 1971 [n.d.]), 25 pp. [Principles under-
lying AARRO training program for 1972-1973.]

4037. AFRO-ASIAN RURAL RECONSTRUCTION ORGANIZATION.
"Research & Publications" (AARRC-IV/P-II/5,
New Delhi, c. 1971 [n.d.]), 5 pp. [Proposed
research and publications of AARRO.]

4038. AFRO-ASIAN RURAL RECONSTRUCTION ORGANIZATION.
"Youth Activities" (AARRC-IV/P-II/2, New Delhi,
c. 1971 [n.d.]), 6 pp. [Role of youth training in
AARRO program, with a report on a "Young Farmers'
Training" Pilot Program by Aberra Maltot, Honorary
Representative of AARRO for the Regional Office for
East and Central Africa.]

h. Other Publications

4039. AFRO-ASIAN RURAL RECONSTRUCTION ORGANIZATION.
Informative Pamphlet (New Delhi, c. 1968 [n.d.]),
32 pp. [Describes the history, structure, and
operations of the organization.]

C. DOCUMENTS OF THE ASIAN-AFRICAN LEGAL CONSULTATIVE COMMITTEE

A. BASIC DOCUMENTS

(1) STATUTES OF THE COMMITTEE, 1956

Adopted in New Delhi on November 15, 1956, by the Asian Legal Consultative Committee.

Text from ASIAN-AFRICAN LEGAL CONSULTATIVE COMMITTEE, Basic Facts, pp. 31-33.

Article 1

The Asian-African Legal Consultative Committee shall consist of members nominated by the Governments of the original participating countries of Burma, Ceylon, India, Indonesia, Iraq, Japan, and the United Arab Republic. The Committee may from time to time admit to membership persons nominated by the Governments of other Asian-African countries.

Article 2

The government of each of the participating countries shall nominate a legal expert to serve on the Committee as Member. An alternate member may also be nominated if considered necessary.

*Article 2A

(1) The Committee may admit as associate member a person nominated by the Government of any other Asian-African country.

(2) The terms of admission of an associate member shall be prescribed by rules to be framed by the Committee under Article 8.

*Article 3

The Committee shall function for an initial period of five years and its purpose shall be as follows:

   (a) to examine questions that are under consideration by the International Law Commission and to arrange for the views of the Committee to be placed before the Commission; to consider the reports of the Commission and to make recommendations thereon to the Governments of the participating countries;

(b) to consider legal problems that may be referred to the Committee by any of the participating countries and to make such recommendations to governments as may be thought fit;

(c) to exchange views and information on legal matters of common concern and to make recommendations thereon, if deemed necessary;

(d) to communicate with the consent of the governments of the participating countries, the points of view of the Committee on international legal problems referred to it, to the United Nations, other institutions and international organisations.

Article 4

The members of the Committee may exchange views by correspondence either directly or through the Secretariat on matters that are under consideration. The Committee shall normally meet once every year and such meetings shall be held in the participating countries by rotation.

Article 5

The Committee shall have a permanent Secretariat at such place as may be determined by the Committee for facilitating mutual consultation between the members and for achieving the purposes of the Committee generally. The Committee shall appoint a qualified person as its Secretary who may be authorised to act on its behalf on such matters as the Committee may determine and until the Secretary is appointed by the Committee, the Secretary to the International Legal Conference at New Delhi shall perform the functions of the Secretary to the Committee with a temporary Secretariat at New Delhi.

Article 6

The expenses incurred in connection with the meetings of the Committee other than the cost of travel of the members for the purpose of attending the meetings shall normally be met by the participating country in which the meeting is held; the expenditure incurred on the Secretariat shall be borne by the participating countries in such proportions as may be agreed and the amount shall be paid annually in advance in the account to be maintained in the name of the Committee.

Article 7

The Committee may enter into arrangements for consultations with such international organisations, authorities and bodies as may be considered desirable.

Article 8

The Committee may from time to time frame such rules as may be considered necessary for carrying into effect the purposes of the Committee.

Article 1.   The title of the organization was originally
"Asian Legal Consultative Committee".   In 1958 it was changed
to "Asian African Legal Consultative Committee".   "Syria" was
changed to "United Arab Republic" in the listing of the seven
original members.   In 1962 the phrase "shall consist of seven
original members nominated by the Governments of" was changed
to "shall consist of members nominated by the Governments of
the original participating countries of".

Article 2A.   This was added to the Statutes at the 5th
Session in Rangoon, 1962.

Article 3(a).   The word "said," which appeared before
"Commission" on the last line, was deleted in 1962.   The
phrase "to consider the reports of the Commission and to
make recommendations thereon to the Governments of the
participating countries" was added in 1962.

Article 3(c).   The phrase "and to make recommendations
thereon, if deemed necessary" was added in 1962.

Article 3(d).   This was added in 1958.

(2) STATUTORY RULES OF THE COMMITTEE, 1957

Adopted in New Delhi at the First Session of the
Asian Legal Consultative Committee, April 18-27, 1957.

Text from ASIAN-AFRICAN LEGAL CONSULTATIVE COMMITTEE,
Basic Facts, pp. 37-46.

STATUTORY RULES OF THE COMMITTEE

1. Short Title

These rules shall be called the Asian-African Legal
Consultative Committee Statutory Rules.

2. Interpretation

In these Rules unless the context otherwise requires:

(a) "Committee" means the Asian-African Legal Consultative Committee.

(b) "Liaison Officer" means a person appointed by the
government of a participating country under the
provisions of these rules.

(c) "Member" means a person who is so nominated
by the government of a participating country under
the provisions of Article 2 of the Statutes and except
for purposes of clause (1) of Rule 10, includes an
Alternate Member.

(d) "Original Member" means a Member nominated by
the government of any of the countries enumerated
in Article 1 of the Statutes.

(e) "Participating country" means a country the government of which has accepted the Statutes and whose
nominee has been admitted to the membership of
the Committee.

(f) "President" means the person who has been elected
as such under the provisions of these rules and
includes any other person temporarily performing
the functions of the President.

(g) "Secretariat" means collectively the staff appointed
by the Committee.

(h) "Secretary" means the person so appointed by
the Committee and includes any person temporar-

ily performing the functions of the Secretary.

3. Election and Functions of President

(1) The Committee shall at each Annual Session elect a member in his representative capacity as the President of the Committee and the person so elected shall hold office until the election of another President.

(2) The President shall perform such functions as are specified in these rules.

(3) The Committee shall elect a member in his representative capacity to be the Vice-President of the Committee and the Vice-President shall perform all the functions of the President if the latter for any reason is unable to perform them.

4. Admission of Members

The Committee may by a decision supported by a two-thirds majority inclusive of two-thirds of the original members admit to membership a person nominated by the Government of an Asian or African country, if such a Government by a written communication addressed to the Secretary of the Committee intimates its desire to participate in the Committee and its acceptance of the Statutes and the Rules framed thereunder. Such decision may be taken either by circulation or by means of a resolution adopted in any of its Sessions.

5. Nomination of Members

(1) Each of the participating countries shall nominate a legal expert to serve on the Committee as a Member and may at its discretion also nominate an Alternate Member. Intimation of such nomination shall be given forthwith to the Secretary of the Committee.

(2) A person nominated as Member or Alternate Member shall hold office until his nomination is revoked by his Government and intimation to that effect is received by the Secretary of the Committee.

*5A Terms of admission of Associate Members

(a) The Government of the country desiring to nominate an associate member should, by a written communication addressed to the Secretary of the Committee, intimate such desire and its acceptance of the Statutes and the Statutory Rules for the time being in force;

(b)   Such Government should pay a fixed contribution of Indian Rupees 5000/- per annum* in advance to the Secretariat of the Committee at New Delhi;

(c)   The associate member may attend the Sessions of the Committee and address the Committee but shall not be entitled to vote;

(d)   The associate member will be furnished with the Proceedings of the meetings of the Committee as well as Briefs of Documents usually furnished to the members;

(e)   The Committee would endeavour to consider any specific legal problem suggested by the Government of such country;

and

(f)   The Committee will take note of any comments made by the associate member on the topics under discussion of the Committee.

6.   Functions of the Committee

(1)   The Government of a participating country by communication addressed to the Secretary may refer for the opinion of the Committee any legal problem together with a memorandum setting out the questions on which the views of the Committee are sought.

(2)   The legal problem so referred under clause (1) shall be placed by the Secretary on the provisional agenda of the next Session of the Committee and the Committee shall, subject to the question of priority to be attached to the subject, consider the problem and shall make such recommendations as the Committee may determine.

(3)   Notwithstanding anything contained in clause (2) if, a problem referred for consideration of the Committee under clause (1) in the opinion of the Government referring the problem is of an urgent nature, the Secretary shall at the request of the Government concerned after informing the President obtain by correspondence the individual opinions of the members on the problem so referred. He shall then transmit the views so obtained to the President, the Government concerned, and the Governments of all the participating countries.

(4)   The Committee may at the request of the Government of any of the participating countries or on the motion of

any of the members take up for consideration any legal matter of common concern and may express such views or make such recommendations as may be thought fit.

(5) (a) At each annual Session of the Committee the Secretary shall place before it a report containing the work done by the International Law Commission of the United Nations at its Session immediately preceding the Session of the Committee together with any memoranda that may be received by the Secretary on this subject from the Governments of the participating countries.

(b) The Secretary may, at each annual Session of the Committee, submit reports on the work done in the year immediately preceding the Session of the Committee by other institutions and international osganisations with whom consultative arrangements have been concluded.

(6) The Committee shall consider the report submitted to it and make such recommendations or send their views to the Governments of the participating countries as the Committee may determine.

(7) The Committee may at any of its Sessions finally dispose of a subject placed on the Agenda or may reserve it for further consideration, or may postpone its consideration.

(8) The Committee may in respect of a subject reserved for further consideration adopt an interim report setting forth its provisional views or interim recommendations on the subject, and may appoint a member as Rapporteur on the subject. The Rapporteur so appointed shall at the subsequent meeting of the Committee place before it his provisional or final report on the subject. The Rapporteur may seek the views of the other members of the Committee and consult them in the preparation of his report.

(9) The members of the Committee may by correspondence consult one another on any matter that is under consideration of the Committee.

7. Sessions of the Committee

(1) The Committee shall normally meet once annually in the participating countries by rotation.

(2) The date and place of such Sessions shall either be determined by the Committee at its previous Session or

be left to the Secretary after consulting the Governments of the participating countries.

(3) At each Session of the Committee the Government of a participating country may at its discretion in addition to its member and alternate member send such number of advisers as it thinks fit.

(4) The Committee may at its discretion admit to its Sessions observers from non-participating countries and from such inter-Governmental or non-Governmental organisations with whom consultative arrangements have been made by the Committee under Article 7. Such observers shall not address the meeting or take part in the discussions unless invited to do so by the Committee. The Committee may, however, declare any of its meetings during a Session to be a closed meeting to which observers shall not be admitted.

(5) The Committee may also at its discretion invite a recognised expert to attend any of its meetings and assist in its deliberations. The expert so invited shall act in his individual capacity.

(6) The Committee may, if it thinks fit, appoint sub-committees for detailed consideration of the subjects.

(7) All the meetings of the Committee shall be presided over by the President and in his absence by the Vice-President.

(8) All decisions or recommendations of the Committee shall be by a simple majority except in cases specified under the rules. The dissenting views expressed by any member or members shall also be recorded. An alternate member shall not vote on the resolutions if the member is present.

(9) The proceedings of all the meetings of the Committee together with resolutions and dissenting opinions shall be furnished forthwith to the Governments of the participating countries.

8. Secretariat

(1) The Committee shall have a permanent Secretariat at such place as may from time to time be determined by the Committee.

(2) The Committee shall, as soon as may be, appoint as its Secretary a national of the participating countries who is a legal expert with administrative experience.

(3) The Committee may, if for financial or any other reason considers it expedient so to do, keep the post of the Secretary in abeyance, and appoint a person qualified to be the

Secretary under the preceding clause to perform the functions of the office. A person so appointed shall be known as the Acting Secretary.

(4) The Secretary or the Acting Secretary shall receive such salaries, travelling and other allowances and such other emoluments as may be determined by the Committee.

(5) The Committee may authorise the Secretary to appoint such technical and other staff as may be necessary on such remuneration as may be determined from time to time by the Committee.

(6) The Secretary shall be responsible to the Committee in respect of the work of the Secretariat.

(7) The Secretary shall have the right to address the meetings of the Committee on all administrative and organisational matters and he may make statements and furnish information during deliberations of the Committee or of a Sub-Committee if called upon to do so. The Secretary may be represented by a member of the Secretariat for this purpose.

(8) The Secretary shall be authorised to act on behalf of the Committee in all correspondence, to take decisions on all administrative matters and to perform such other functions as are specified in these rules.

(9) The Secretary shall, however, in the performance of his duties act in consultation with the Liaison Officers appointed under Rule 9 except in routine and administrative matters. The Secretary shall report to the Liaison Officers at their meetings any action taken by him in this regard.

9. Liaison Officer

(1) Each of the participating countries shall appoint an officer to act as Liaison Officer.

(2) The Liaison Officer shall act as the channel of communication between the Secretariat of the Committee and the Governments of the participating countries.

(3) The Liaison Officers shall meet as often as necessary and all decisions of Liaison Officers shall be taken at meetings by a simple majority of the total number of Liaison Officers.

10. Finance and Expenditure

(1)   The participating country in which the Session of the Committee is held shall be responsible for all expenses in connection with the organisation of the Session including the cost of board and lodging of the Members during the Session of the Committee.

(2)   The cost of travel of the Member, Alternate Member and Advisers shall be the concern of each participating country.

(3)   The expenditure incurred on the Secretariat shall be met by the participating countries in such proportions as may be agreed on the recommendations of the Committee subject to minimum contribution per year of 10,000/- Indian Rupees or equivalent thereof.   Such contribution shall be paid in advance annually.

(4)   The cost of travel and other expenses incurred by the Secretary or the staff of the Secretariat shall be met out of the funds placed at the disposal of the Committee for the purposes of the Secretariat under clause (3).

(5)   The Committee shall maintain an account in a recognised bank in its name at the place where the Secretariat is situated and the contributions of each of the participating countries under clause (3) shall be deposited in this account. The account so maintained shall be operated by the Secretary or such other person as may be authorised by him in consultation with the Liaison Officers.

(6)   The Secretary shall be authorised to incur such expenditure on the Secretariat and for other purposes of the Committee as may be necessary provided that any item of expenditure over one thousand Indian Rupees or equivalent thereof shall require to be sanctioned at a meeting of the Liaison Officers.

(7)   The account of the Committee shall be audited once annually by an Auditor appointed by the Liaison Officers and the accounts so audited shall require to be passed at a meeting of the Liaison Officers.

11. Consultations with other Organisations

(1)   The Committee may from time to time direct the Secretary to communicate with such international, regional, inter-Governmental or non-Governmental organisations or committees engaged in legal work with a view to enter into suitable arrangements for consultations.

(2) (a) The Committee may nominate as observer any of its members or the Secretary or a member of the Secretariat as the case may be to attend the meetings of such organisations or committees with whom arrangements for consultations may have been entered into.

(b) When the Committee is not in session such nomination may be made by the Liaison Officers.

(c) The Committee or the Liaison Officers may in the event of non-availability of a person specified in sub-clause (a) nominate a member of the mission of any of the participating countries to attend such meetings.

* ANNOTATIONS

Rule 1.   The name was originally "Asian Legal Consultative Committee".

Rule 2a.   Note the name change.

Rule 2c.   The phrase "except for purposes of clause (1) of Rule 10" was added in 1962.

Rule 4.   The phrase "of African" was added in 1958.

Rule 5A.   Added at the 5th Session, 1962. At the 9th Session it was decided that the value of the Indian Rupee will be calculated on the basis of its 1961 value. This means that the fixed contribution was in 1969 approximately Ŀ 450 sterling, the rupee equivalent at the 1969 rate of exchange.

Rule 6.   In 1958 and 1960 the words "Session", "Agenda", and "Annual" were capitalized with more consistency. "Report" was changed to lower case in 1960.

Rule 7(8). In 1958 "recommendation" was changed to "recommendations".

Rule 9(2). In 1960 "officers" was changed to "Officer".

Rule 10(3). The value of the Indian Rupee is to be calculated on the basis of its value in 1961, as decided at the 9th Session. In 1969 this meant that the minimum contribution was Ŀ 873 sterling, the rupee equivalent at the 1969 rate of exchange.

Rule 10(5). "Account" was reduced to lower case, as was "Recognized Bank", as decided in 1960.

SUPPLEMENTARY DOCUMENTS

(3) ARTICLES ON THE IMMUNITIES AND PRIVILEGES OF THE COMMITTEE, 1958

Adopted in Cairo on October, 1958, at the Sixth Session of the Asian-African Legal Consultative Committee.

Text from ASIAN-AFRICAN LEGAL CONSULTATIVE COMMITTEE, Basic Facts, pp. 47-52.

Article I

Privileges and immunities are accorded under this Instrument, not to benefit individuals but to ensure the efficient performance of the functions of the Committee. Consequently, the Committee and the participating governments have not only the right but also a duty to waive the immunity in any case where in their opinion the immunity would impede the course of justice and where it can be waived without prejudice to the purpose for which the immunity is accorded.

Article II

Juridical Personality

The Committee shall possess juridical personality and shall have the capacity to contract, to acquire and dispose of immovable and movable property and to institute legal proceedings in its name.

Article III

Property, Funds and Assets

(a) The Committee, its property and assets wherever located and by whomsoever held, shall enjoy immunity from every form of legal process, except insofar as in any particular case the Committee has expressly waived its immunity. It is, however, understood, that no waiver of immunity shall extend to any measure of execution.

(b) The Committee, its property and assets as also its archives shall be inviolable and shall be immune from search, requisition, confiscation, expropriation and any other form of interference whether by executive, administrative, juridical or legislative action in any of the participating countries. The premises occupied by the Committee for its Secretariat shall be likewise inviolable and immune from search provided the said premises are solely used for the purposes of the Committee.

(c) The Committee shall be immune from the regulations relating to exchange control in the matter of holding or transfer of its funds from one participating country to another. In exercising this right, the Committee shall pay due regard to any representations made by the Government of any participating country, insofar as it is considered that effect can be given to such representations without detriment to the interests of the Committee. However, the Committee shall not take out of any participating country more than what the Committee has brought in.

(d) The Committee, its assets, income and other property whether owned or occupied by it, shall be exempt from all direct taxes; it is understood, however, that the Committee will not claim exemption from taxes which are in fact no more than charges for public utility services.

(e) The Committee shall be exempt from payment of customs duty as also prohibitions and restrictions on imports and exports in respect of articles or publications imported or exported by it for its official use. It is understood that articles imported under such exemption will not be sold in the country to which they are imported except under such conditions as have been agreed upon with the Government of that country, which in any case shall not exceed those extended to similar inter-governmental organisations.

Article IV

Facilities in respect of Communications

(a) The Committee and its Secretariat shall enjoy in each of the participating countries freedom of communication and no censorship shall be applied to the official correspondence of the Committee certified as such and bearing the official seal of the Committee.

(b) Nothing in this article shall be construed to preclude the adoption of appropriate security precautions to be determined by agreement between the participating Governments and the Committee.*

Article V

Representatives of the Participating Countries,

1. Representatives of the participating countries designated as members, alternate members, and advisers as also Observers and the Secretary or the Acting Secretary of the Committee shall during their stay in the country in which the Session of the Committee is held and also during their journey to and from that country, enjoy the following :

(a) Immunity from personal arrest or detention and from seizure of the personal baggage and immunity from legal procedure in respect of words spoken or written and all acts done by them in their official capacity ;

(b) Inviolability of all papers and documents ;

(c) The right to receive papers or correspondence in sealed covers;

(d) Exemption in respect of themselves and their spouses from immigration restrictions, aliens registration or national service obligations in the country in which the Session of the Committee is held and in the participating countries through which they are in transit for the purpose of attending the Session of the Committee;

(e) The same facilities in respect of currency or exchange restrictions as are accorded to temporary diplomatic missions ;

(f) The same immunities and privileges in respect of their personal baggage as are accorded to diplomatic agents. The words 'personal baggage' in this section shall not be interpreted to include an automobile and other means of transportion. Personal baggage shall not, however, be sold in the country in which the Session of the Committee is held without an express authorisation from the Government of that country ;

(g) Such other privileges and immunities and facilities not inconsistent with the foregoing as the diplomatic agents enjoy, except that they shall have no right to claim exemption from customs duties on goods imported (otherwise than as part of their personal baggage) or from excise duties or sales-taxes ;

Provided always that the immunities specified in the foregoing clauses can be waived in any individual case in regard to a member of the delegation, by the Government of the participating country which the individual represents, and in case of the Secretary by the Committee itself.

2. The provisions of Article V are not applicable as between a representative and the authorities of the country of which he is a national or of which he is or has been the representative.

3. Where the incidence of any form of taxation depends upon residence, the periods during which the representatives of participating countries to the Committee and to conferences convened by the Committee are present in a participating country for the discharge of their duties, shall not be considered as periods of their residence.

Article VI

Officials of the Secretariat

1. Officials of the Committee shall:

(a) Be immune from legal process in respect of words spoken or written and all acts performed by them in their official capacity;

(b) Enjoy the same exemptions from taxation in respect of the salaries and emoluments paid to them by the Committee and on the same conditions as are enjoyed by officials of the United Nations;

(c) Be immune, together with their spouses and relatives dependent on them from immigration restrictions and aliens registration;

(d) Be accorded the same privileges in respect of exchange facilities as are accorded to officials of comparable rank of diplomatic missions;

(e) Be given, together with their spouses and relatives dependent on them, the same repatriation facilities in time of international crises as officials of comparable rank of diplomatic missions;

(f) Have the right to import free of duty furniture and effects within one year of the time when they first take up their posts in the country in question; the term "effects" in this section shall not be interpreted to include an automobile or other means of transportation;

(g) Be exempt from national service obligations.

2. The immunities and privileges except those specified in clause 1 (a) above shall not be applicable to the nationals of the country in question unless expressly extended by the participating country.

3. The Secretary of the Committee, with the approval of the Committee, shall communicate to the Governments of participating countries the categories of the officials to whom the provisions of this Article shall apply.

4. The immunities specified in the foregoing clauses can be waived in any individual case, in regard to an official of the Secretariat by the Secretary of the Committee.

5. The Committee shall co-operate at all times with the appropriate authorities of participating countries to facilitate the proper administration of justice, secure the observance of police regulations and prevent the occurrence of any abuses in connection with the privileges, immunities and facilities mentioned in this Article.

Article VII

Settlement of Differences

If any participating country considers that there has been an abuse of any privilege or immunity conferred by this Instrument, consultations shall be held between that country and the Committee to determine whether any such abuse has occurred, and if so to attempt to ensure that no repetition occurs.

*ANNOTATIONS

Article IV(b).   Indonesia reserved its position on this
provision.

(4) FINAL REPORT OF THE COMMITTEE ON FUNCTIONS, PRIVILEGES AND IMMUNITIES OF DIPLOMATIC ENVOYS OR AGENTS, 1960

Adopted in Colombo on January-February, 1960, at the Third Session of the Asian-African Legal Consultative Committee.

Text from ASIAN-AFRICAN LEGAL CONSULTATIVE COMMITTEE, Report of the Third Session, pp. 34-54.

1. The Committee at its second, third, fourth and fifth meetings of the Cairo Session held on Thursday, Friday and Saturday the 2nd, 3rd and 4th of October, 1958, considered item 1 of Part III of the Agenda—Functions, Privileges and Immunities of Diplomatic Envoys or Agents—which had been referred by the Governments of India and Japan.

2. The Committee had before it the two memoranda on the subject presented by the Governments of India and Japan during the First Session, as also the draft articles on Diplomatic Immunities adopted by the International Law Commission during its 9th and 10th sessions. The Harvard Draft Convention, the Havana Convention on Diplomatic Officers, and the Report prepared by the Rapporteur were also placed before the Committee.

3. The Committee had considered this subject during its First Session in New Delhi on the basis of the three questions formulated in the Indian memorandum which were in the following terms :

(1) Whether it is desirable to undertake legislation to provide for immunities to foreign diplomatic missions and officers so as to incorporate in the municipal law of a state the principles of international law in this regard ;

(2) if it is considered desirable to have recourse to legislation in the matter of immunity, whether such legislation should merely be declaratory of the principles of international law or should it be a comprehensive piece of legislation ;

(3) whether in cases where disputes arise regarding the extent of the immunity, the matter should be left to the decision of the courts of a country or whether it should be decided by the Foreign Office and its decision given by means of a certificate be regarded as conclusive,

4. The Committee drew up an interim report at that session in the light of discussions. The conclusions which could be drawn from the discussions held during the First Session were as follows :

(i) There was agreement in principle among the delegations of Burma, Ceylon, India, Indonesia and Iraq on the need for domestic legislation on this subject but at the same time it was agreed that it would be difficult to undertake comprehensive legislation at present. The view of the delegation of Japan, however, was that domestic legislation on this subject was undesirable as it may lead to confusion. The delegation considered that the proper course to adopt was to have a convention or a multilateral treaty between states which would specify the agreed extent of diplomatic immunities and privileges.

(ii) There was general agreement between the delegations of Burma, India, Indonesia and Japan that a communication from the Foreign Office as regards the privileges and immunities of diplomatic personnel ought in practice to be regarded as conclusive and binding on the courts and other authorities. The delegation of Ceylon whilst agreeing that such a communication ought to be conclusive in criminal matters felt that the position needed to be further examined with respect to enforcement of civil rights by private persons against diplomatic personnel.

(iii) It was agreed between all delegations that before any legislation or international convention could be undertaken, it would be necessary to collect more data.

5. The Committee recommended a further study of the subject and appointed the Member for Japan as Rapporteur to collect information and materials and prepare a draft of a convention on diplomatic immunities and privileges.

6. The first question which the Committee considered during the Second Session (Cairo) was the necessity or otherwise of having a Convention between the participating countries in the Committee on the subject of diplomatic

immunities. It was generally agreed between the various delegations that as long as the immunities and privileges were accorded to the diplomatic agents in the participating states it was not of much consequence as to the method by which such immunities and privileges were granted. It was unanimously decided that the Committee should formulate the principles dealing with the nature and extent of diplomatic immunities and privileges in the form of a draft convention, but the question as to whether a country should adopt these principles by means of a convention or domestic legislation should be left to the Government of the participating country itself.

7. The draft of a convention containing the principles on the nature and extent of diplomatic immunities and privileges as approved by the Committee was set out in the annexure to the Committee's report.

8. The Committee decided to make no recommendation regarding the method to be adopted for settlement of disputes between states in the matter of diplomatic immunities. Article 45 of the Draft prepared by the International Law Commission was considered as being inappropriate for adoption since the Governments held divergent views on the matter and it was difficult to reach agreement and make an agreed recommendation on the question.

9. Three questions were specifically raised in the course of discussions. These were :

(a) Whether the concept of reciprocity should be adopted in regard to immunities and privileges of a diplomatic agent.

(b) Whether a distinction should be made between a home—based national of the sending State and a locally recruited person who is also a national of the sending state employed as a member of the subordinate staff in a diplomatic mission.

(c) Whether and to what extent a certificate of the Foreign Office should be treated as conclusive and binding in matters of diplomatic immunity.

10. As regards the first question, the delegation of India was of the view that the immunity of a diplomat was absolute

under international law and as such the concept of reciprocity should not enter on the question of diplomatic immunity. The delegation was for discouraging the present trend in restricting immunity of diplomats on the basis of reciprocity. The delegation was, however, in favour of having reciprocity in the matter of privileges as it felt that privileges were not essential to performance of diplomatic functions and was a matter of comity. The delegation of Indonesia supported the views of the delegation of India. The other delegations were however, of the view that immunities and privileges both should be granted on the basis of reciprocity.

11. The delegations were of the view that no specific answer was required on the second question since articles 36 and 37 of the draft convention (Annex) sufficiently dealt with the principles relating to immunities and privileges of subordinate staff of diplomatic missions.

12. As regards the third question, the delegations were of the view that a certificate of the Foreign Office in so far as questions of fact were concerned such as the status of the person or the extent of immunities or privileges admissible to the diplomatic agent concerned under the practice followed by the state should be conclusive and binding since these were matters within the particular knowledge of the Foreign Office. In so far as questions of law were concerned, the majority of the delegations were in favour of leaving the matter to the courts.

13. The Report of the Committee as adopted in the Cairo Session was circulated among the Governments of the participating countries for their comments and the subject was further discussed in the Colombo Session in the light of the observations received from the Governments. The Verbatim Reports of the discussions are appended to this Report.*

14. The Committee endorsed its earlier recommendations contained in paragraphs 6, 8, 11, and 12 above. As regards the point mentioned in paragraph 10 the Delegations could not reach agreement on the question whether the grant of Diplomatic Immunities should be on the basis of reciprocity. The Delegates of India, Indonesia, Japan and the United Arab

*Verbatim reports are omitted from the Printed Summary Edition.

Republic were of the view that the concept of reciprocity should not enter into the question of Diplomatic immunities as Diplomatic Envoys were entitled to immunity as a matter of right under International Law. The Delegate of Ceylon was of the view that there was no question of reciprocity in respect of immunities as enumerated in these Articles which were considered to be the minimum necessary for the performance of Diplomatic functions. Any grant of Immunities to Diplomatic Agents other than those enumerated in these Articles should be on the basis of reciprocity. The Delegates of Burma maintained that the grant of immunities shall be on the basis of reciprocity. The Delegates of Iraq and Pakistan had no particular views in the matter. All the delegates were, however, agreed that reciprocity was a proper basis on the question of grant of privileges.

15. The Committee also made alterations in some of the Articles in the Draft Convention in the light of the comments received from the Governments. The Draft convention incorporating the amendments is annexed hereto and the provisions of the Convention shall be regarded as the final recommendations of the Committee on the subject in so far as principles are concerned.

16. The Delegate of Pakistan whilst taking part in the deliberations and endorsing the Committee's recommendations clarified that he did so in his individual capacity as he could not express the views of his Government since they did not have sufficient time to consider the matter.

B. Sen.
Secretary to the Committee.

ASIAN – AFRICAN LEGAL CONSULTATIVE COMMITTEE.

DRAFT OF A CONVENTION

Concerning Diplomatic Immunities & Privileges

(As adopted in the Colombo Session)

Preamble

Recalling that the peoples of all nations have long had the practice and conviction of respecting the status of diplomatic envoys;

Considering that an international convention regarding the rights and duties of diplomatic agents would contribute greatly to the promotion of good neighbourly relations among the States;

Considering that the immediate purpose is to reach an agreement on general provisions embodying the well-defined trend in international relations, taking into account the special usages and practices of the various states;

The States participating in the Asian-African Legal Consultative Committee have agreed upon the following principles on the immunities and privileges of Diplomatic Agents :—

Definitions

Article 1

For the purpose of the present draft convention, the following expression shall have the meaning hereunder assigned to them :

(a) The 'head of the mission' is the person charged by the sending State with the duty of acting in that capacity;

(b) The 'members of the mission' are the head of the mission and the members of the staff of the mission;

(c) The 'members of the staff of the mission' are the members of the diplomatic staff, of the administrative and technical and the services staff of the mission;

(d) The 'diplomatic staff' consists of the members of the staff of the mission having diplomatic rank;

(e) A 'diplomatic agent' is the head of the mission or a member of the diplomatic staff of the mission;

(f) The 'Administrative and technical staff consists of the members of the staff of the mission employed in the administrative and technical service of the mission;

(g) The 'service staff' consists of the members of the staff of the mission in the domestic service of the mission;

(h) A 'private servant' is a person in the domestic service of the head or of a member of the mission.

Establishment of Diplomatic Relations and Missions

Article 2

The establishment of diplomatic relations between States, and the permanent diplomatic missions, takes place by mutual consent.

Functions of A Diplomatic Mission

Article 3

The functions of a diplomatic mission consist inter alia in :—

(a) Representing the sending State in the receiving State;

(b) Protecting the interests of the sending State and of its nationals in the receiving State;

(c) Negotiating with the Government of the receiving State;

(d) Ascertaining by all lawful means conditions and developments in the receiving State, and reporting thereon to the Government of the sending State;

(e) Promoting friendly relations between the sending State and the receiving State;

(f) Developing economic, cultural and scientific relations.

Appointment of the Head and Staff of the Mission.

Article 4.

The sending State must make certain that the agreement of the receiving State has been given for the person it proposes to accredit as head of the mission to that State.

Appointment to more than one State

Article 5.

Unless objection is offered by any of the receiving states concerned, a head of mission to one State may be accredited as head of mission to one or more other States.

Article 6.

Subject to the provisions of Article 7, 8 and 10, the sending State may freely appoint the other members of the staff of the mission.

Appointment of Nationals of the Receiving State

Article 7.

Members of the diplomatic staff of the mission may not be appointed from among persons having the nationality of the receiving State except with the express consent of that State, which may be withdrawn at any time.

Reservation :

In the view of the Government of the United Arab Republic it is necessary to have the express consent of the receiving State to appoint any person having the nationality of the receiving State to any of the offices of a foreign Diplomatic Mission whether Diplomatic or otherwise.

Persons Declared 'Persona non Grata'

Article 8.

1. The receiving State may at any time notify the sending State that the head of the mission, or any member of the staff of the mission, is 'persona non grata' or not acceptable. In such a case, the sending state, according to circumstances, shall not send such person, or shall recall him or shall terminate his functions with the mission.

2. If a sending State refuses or fails within a reasonable time to comply with its obligations under paragraph 1, the

receiving State may refuse to recognise the person concerned as a member of the mission.

Notification of Arrival and Departure.

Article 9.

The arrival and departure of the members of the staff of the mission, and also of members of their families, and of their private servants, shall be notified to the Ministry of Foreign Affairs of the receiving State. A similar notification shall be given whenever members of the mission and private servants are locally engaged or discharged.

Limitation of Staff

Article 10.

1. In the absence of any specific agreement as to the size of the mission, the receiving State may refuse to accept a size exceeding what is reasonable and customary, having regard to the circumstances and conditions in the receiving State, and to the needs of the particular mission.

2. The receiving State may also, within similar bounds and on a non-discriminatory basis, refuse to accept officials of a particular category.

3. The receiving State may decline to accept any person as military, naval, or air attache, or any person performing such functions without previous agreement.

Offices away from the Seat of the Mission

Article 11.

The sending State may not, without the consent of the receiving State, establish offices in towns other than those in which the mission itself is established.

Commencement of the functions of the head of the mission.

Article 12.

The head of the mission is considered as having taken up his functions in the receiving State either when he has notified his arrival and a true copy of his credentials has been presented to the Ministry of Foreign Affairs of the receiving State, or when he has presented his letters of credence, according to the practice prevailing in the receiving State, which shall be applied in a uniform manner.

Charge d'Affaires Ad Interim.
Article 13.

1. If the post of the head of the mission is vacant or if the head of the mission is unable to perform his functions, the affairs of the mission shall be handled by a charge d'affaires ad interim whose name shall be notified to the government of the receiving State.

2. In the absence of notification, the member of the mission placed immediately after the head of the mission on the mission's diplomatic list shall be presumed to be in charge.

Classes of Heads of the Mission
Article 14.

1. Heads of mission are divided into three classes, namely :

   (a) That of ambassadors ; or nuncios accredited to heads of State ; or High Commissioners exchanged between Commonwealth Countries.

   (b) That of envoys, ministers, inter nuncious and other persons accredited to heads of State ;

   (c) That of charges d'affaires accredited to Ministers for Foreign Affairs.

2. Except as concerns precedence and etiquette, there shall be no differentiation between heads of mission by reason of their class.

Article 15.

States shall agree on the class to which the heads of their missions are to be assigned.

Precedence
Article 16.

1. Heads of mission shall take precedence in their respective classes in the order of date either of the official notification of their arrival or of the presentation of their letters of credence, according to the rules of the protocol in

the receiving State, which must be applied without discrimination.*

2. Any change in the credentials of a head of mission shall not affect his precendence in his class.

3. The present regulations are without prejudice to any existing practice in the receiving State regarding the precedence of the representative of the Pope.

Mode of Reception.

Article 17.

A uniform mode shall be established in each State for the reception of heads of mission of each class.

Use of Flag and Emblem

Article 18.

The mission and its head shall have the right to use the flag and emblem of the sending State on the premises of the mission, and on the residence and the means of transport of the head of the mission.

Accommodation.

Article 19.

The receiving State shall either permit the sending State to acquire on its territory the premises necessary for its mission, or ensure adequate accommodation in some other way.

Inviolability of the Mission Premises

Article 20.

1. The premises of the mission shall be inviolable. The agents of the receiving State may not enter them, save with the consent of the head of the mission.

---

*1. In the view of the Government of the United Arab Republic it would be desirable to have uniformity of practice in the matter of precedence of Heads of Missions among the participating countries in the Committee and that precedence should date from the presentation of a copy of the letter of credence to the Ministry of Foreign Affairs of the Receiving State,

2. In the case of High Commissioners exchanged between Commonwealth Countries the letter of Introduction should be considered to be letter of Credence for the purposes of this Article.

2. The receiving State is under a special duty to take all appropriate steps to protect the premises of the mission against any intrusion or damage and to prevent any disturbance of the peace of the mission or impairment of its dignity.

3. The premises of the mission and their furnishings shall be immune from any search, requisition, attachment or execution.

Reservation by India and Japan :

Nothing in this Article shall prevent the receiving State from entry into the premises of the Mission for taking appropriate steps to ensure the safety of human life jeopardised by civil commotion, aerial bombardment, fire or other natural calamity.

Further Reservation by India :

Nor shall it affect the right of the receiving State to enter the premises to apprehend its nationals who are fugitives from local justice and have taken shelter therein.

Exemption of Mission Premises from Taxes.

Article 21

The sending State and the head of the mission shall be exempt from all national, regional or municipal dues or taxes in respect of the premises of the mission, whether owned or leased, other than such as represent payment for specific services rendered.

Reservation by Ceylon and Iraq :

The exemption from taxation shall not extend to cases where premises are leased to foreign States.

Inviolability of the Archives.

Article 22

The archives and documents of the mission shall be inviolable.

Facilities.

Article 23

The receiving State shall accord full facilities for the performance of the mission's functions.

Free Movement.

Article 24

Subject to its laws and regulations concerning zones entry into which is prohibited or regulated for reasons of national security, the receiving State shall ensure to all members of the mission freedom of movement and travel in its territory.

Freedom of Communication.

Article 25

1. The receiving State shall permit and protect free communication on the part of the mission for all official purposes. In communicating with the Government and the other missions and consulates of the sending state, wherever situated, the mission may employ all appropriate means, including diplomatic couriers and messages in code or cipher, provided that in the case of installation and use of a wireless transmitter for purposes of such communication the permission of the receiving State shall be necessary.

2. The official correspondence of the mission shall be inviolable.

3. The diplomatic bag may not be opened or detained.

4. The diplomatic bag may contain only diplomatic documents or articles intended for official use.

5. The diplomatic courier shall be protected by the receiving State. He shall enjoy personal inviolability and shall not be liable to arrest or detention, whether administrative or judicial. The diplomatic courier shall at all times have on his person a document testifying to his status. The diplomatic bag shall bear a conspicuous mark to show its quality as such.

Exemption from Taxation, Fees and Charges Levied by a Mission.

Article 26

The fees and charges levied by the mission in the course of its official duties shall be exempt from all dues and taxes.

Personal Inviolability

Article 27.

The person of a diplomatic agent shall be inviolable. He shall not be liable to any form of arrest or detention. The receiving State shall treat him with due respect and shall take all reasonable steps to prevent any attack on his person, freedom or dignity.

Inviolability of Residence and Property

Article 28.

1. The private residence of diplomatic agent shall enjoy the same inviolability and protection as the premises of the mission.

2. His papers, correspondence and, except as provided in paragraph 3 of article 29, his property, shall likewise enjoy inviolability.

Immunity from Jurisdiction.

Article 29.

1. A diplomatic agent shall enjoy immunity from the criminal jurisdiction of the receiving State. He shall also enjoy immunity from its civil and administrative jurisdiction save in the case of :

> (a) A real action relating to private immovable property situated in the territory of the receiving State, unless he holds it on behalf of his Government for the purposes of the mission ;

> (b) An action relating to a succession in which the diplomatic agent is involved as executor, administrator, heir or legatee ;

> (c) An action relating to a professional or commercial activity exercised by the diplomatic agent in the receiving State, and outside his official functions.

2. A diplomatic agent is not obliged to give evidence as a witness.

3. Measures of execution may be taken in respect of a diplomatic agent only in the cases coming under sub-para-

graphs (a), (b) and (c) of paragraph 1. Such measures should, however, be taken without infringing upon the inviolability of his person or of his residence.

4. The immunity of a diplomatic agent from the jurisdiction of the receiving State does not exempt him from the jurisdiction of the sending State.

5. The provisions contained in clauses (1) to (4) of this article shall be subject to the provisions of Article 37.

Waiver of Immunity

Article 30

1. The immunity of its diplomatic agents from jurisdiction may be waived by the sending State.

2. In criminal proceedings. waiver must always be express.

3. In civil or administrative proceedings, waiver may be express or implied. A waiver is presumed to have occurred if a diplomatic agent appears as defendant without claiming any immunity. The initiation of proceedings by a diplomatic agent shall preclude him from invoking immunity of jurisdiction in respect of counter-claims directly connected with the principal claim.

4. Waiver of immunity of jurisdiction in respect of civil or administrative proceedings shall not be held to imply waiver of immunity in respect of the execution of the judgement for which a separate waiver must be made.

Exemption from Social Security Legislation.

Article 31

The members of the mission and the members of their families who form part of their households, shall, if they are not nationals of the receiving State, be exempt from the social security legislation in force in that State except in respect of servants and employees if themselves subject to the social security legislation of the receiving State. This shall not exclude voluntary participation in social security schemes in so far as this is permitted by the legislation of the receiving State.

Exemption from Taxation

Article 32

A diplomatic agent shall be exempt from all dues and taxes, personal or real, national, regional or municipal, save :—

   (a) Indirect taxes incorporated in the price of goods or services;

   (b) Dues and taxes on private immovable property situated in the territory of the receiving State, unless, he holds it on behalf of his Government for the purpose of the mission.

Reservation by Ceylon and Iraq.

The exemption from taxation shall not extend to cases where premises are leased to foreign States.

   (c) Estate, succession or inheritance duties levied by the receiving State, subject, however, to the provisions of Article 38 concerning estates left by members of the family of the diplomatic agent;

   (d) Dues and taxes on income having its source in the receiving State;

   (e) Charges levied for specific services rendered.

   (f) Subject to the provisions of article 21, registration, court or record fees, mortgage dues and stamp duty.

Exemption from personal services and contributions.

Article 33

The diplomatic agent shall be exempt from all personal ervices or contributions.

Exemption from customs duties and inspection.

Article 34

1. The receiving State shall, in accordance with the regulations established by its legislation, grant exemption from customs duties on :—

   (a) Articles for the use of a diplomatic mission;

   (b) Articles for the personal use of a diplomatic agent or members of his family belonging to his household, including articles intended for his establishment.

2. The personal baggage of a diplomatic agent shall be exempt from inspection, unless there are serious grounds for presuming that it contains articles not covered by the exemption mentioned in paragraph 1, or articles the import or export of which is prohibited by the law of the receiving State. Such inspection shall be conducted only in the presence of the diplomatic agent or in the presence of his authorised representative.

Acquisition of Nationality

Article 35

Members of the mission, not being nationals of the receiving State, and members of their families forming part of their household, shall not, solely by the operation of the law of the receiving State, acquire the nationality of that State.

Persons entitled to Privileges and Immunities

Article 36

1. Apart from diplomatic agents, the members of the family of a diplomatic agent forming part of his household and likewise the administrative and technical staff of a mission, together with the members of their families forming part of their respective households, shall if they are not nationals of the receiving State, enjoy the privileges and immunities specified in Articles 27 to 35.

2. Members of the service staff of the mission who are not nationals of the receiving State shall enjoy immunity in respect of acts performed in the course of their duties and exemption from dues and taxes on the emoluments they receive by reason of their employment.

3. Private servants of the head or members of the mission shall, if they are not nationals of the receiving State, be exempt from dues and taxes on the emoluments they receive by reason of their employment. In other respects, they may enjoy privileges and immunities only to the extent admitted by the receiving State. However, the receiving State must exercise its jurisdiction over such persons in such a manner as not to interfere unduly with the conduct of the business of the mission.

Diplomatic Agents who are Nationals of the
Receiving State.

Article 37.

1. A diplomatic agent who is a national of the receiving State shall enjoy inviolability and also immunity from jurisdiction in respect of official acts performed in the exercise of his functions. He shall enjoy such other privileges and immunities as may be granted to him by the receiving State.

2. Other members of the staff of the mission and private servants who are nationals of the receiving State shall enjoy privileges and immunities only to the extent admitted by the receiving State. However, the receiving State should exercise the jurisdiction over such persons in such a manner as not to interfere unduly with the conduct of the business of the mission.

Duration of Immunities and Privileges.

Article 38.

1. Every person entitled to diplomatic privileges and immunities shall enjoy them from the moment he enters the territory of the Receiving State on proceeding to take up his post or, if already in its territory, from the moment when the appointment is notified to the Ministry of Foreign Affairs.

2. When the functions of a person enjoying privileges and immunities have come to an end, such privileges and immunities shall normally cease at the moment when he leaves the country or on expiry of a reasonable period in which to do so, but shall subsist until that time, even in case of armed conflict. However, with respect to acts performed by such a person in the exercise of his functions as a member of the mission, immunity shall continue to subsist.

3. In the event of the death of a member of the mission not a national of the Receiving State or of a member of his family, the receiving State shall permit the withdrawal of the movable property of the deceased, with the exception of any property acquired in the country, and the export of which was prohibited at the time of his death. Estate, succession and inheritance duties shall be levied only on immovable property, situated in the receiving State.

Duties of third States

Article 39.

    1. If a diplomatic agent passes through or is in the territory of a third State while proceeding to take up or to return to his post, or when returning to his own country the third State shall accord him inviolablity and such other immunities as may be required to ensure his transit or return. The same shall apply in case of any member of his family enjoying diplomatic privileges or immunities who are accompanying the diplomatic agent, or travelling separately to join him or to return to their country.

    2. In circumstances similiar to those specified in paragraph 1, third States shall not hinder the passage of members or administrative, technical or service staff of a mission, and of members of their families through their territories.

    3. *Third States shall accord to official correspondence and other official communication in transit, including messages in code or cipher, the same freedom and protection as is accorded by the receiving State. They shall accord to diplomatic couriers in transit the same inviolability and protection as the receiving State is bound to accord.

Conduct of the Mission and its Members towards the Receiving State

Article 40.

    1. Without prejudice to their diplomatic privileges and immunities, it is the duty of all persons enjoying such privileges and immunities to respect the laws and regulations of the receiving State. They also have a duty not to interfere in the internal affairs of that State.

    2. Unless otherwise agreed, all official business with the receiving State entrusted to a diplomatic mission by its Government, shall be conducted with or through the Ministry for Foreign Affairs of the Receiving State.

    3. The premises of a diplomatic mission must not be used in any manner incompatible with the functions of the mission as laid down in the present convention or by other rules of general international law, or by any special agreements in force between the sending and the receiving State.

*The Indonesian Delegation reserved their position on this clause.

412

End of the Function of a Diplomatic Agent-
modes of termination.

Article 41

The function of a diplomatic agent comes to an end, inter alia :

(a) If it was for a limited period, then on the expiry of that period, provided there has been no extention of it ;

(b) On notification by the Government of the sending State to the Government of the receiving State that the Diplomatic agent's functions has come to an end (recall) ;

(c) On notification by the receiving State, given in accordance with Article 8, that it considers the diplomatic agent's functions to be terminated.

Facilitation of Departure

Article 42

The receiving state must, even in case of armed conflict grant facilities in order to enable persons enjoying privileges and immunities to leave at the earliest possible moment, and must, in particular, in case of need, place at their disposal the necessary means of transport for themselves and their property.

Protection of Premises, Archives and Interests

Article 43

If the diplomatic relations are broken off between two States, or if a mission permanently or temporarily recalled :

(a) The receiving State must, even in case of armed conflict, respect and protect the premises of the mission, together with its property and archives ;

(b) The sending State may entrust the custody of the premises of the mission, together with its property and archives, to the mission of a third State acceptable to the receiving State.

Reciprocity in respect of Immunities and Privileges.

Article 44

The privileges of a diplomatic agent shall be accorded on the basis of reciprocity.*

Non-discrimination.

Article 45

1. In the application of the present rules, the receiving State shall not discriminate as between States.

2. However, discrimination shall not be regarded as taking place :

(a) Where the receiving State applies one of the present rules restrictively, because of a restrictive application of that rule to its mission in the sending state ;

(b) Where the action of the receiving State consists in the grant, on the basis of reciprocity, of greater privileges and immunities than are required by the present rules.*

---

*The delegations could not reach agreement on the question whether the grant of Diplomatic Immunities should be on the basis of reciprocity. The Delegates of India, Indonesia, Japan and the United Arab Republic were of the view that the concept of reciprocity should not enter into the question of Diplomatic Immunities as Diplomatic Envoys were entitled to immunity as a matter of right under International Law. The Delegate of Ceylon was of the view that there was no question of reciprocity in respect of immunities as enumerated, in these Articles which were considered to be the minimum necessary for the performance of Diplomatic functions. Any grant of immunities to Diplomatic Agents other than those enumerated in these Articles should be on the basis of reciprocity. The Delegate of Burma maintained that the grant of immunities shall be on the basis of reciprocity. The Delegates of Iraq and Pakistan had no particular views in the matter. All the Delegates were, however, agreed that reciprocity was a proper basis on the question of grant of privileges.

(5) FINAL REPORT OF THE COMMITTEE ON IMMUNITY OF STATES IN RESPECT OF COMMERCIAL AND OTHER TRANSACTIONS OF A PRIVATE CHARACTER, 1960

Adopted in Colombo on January-February, 1960, at the Third Session of the Asian-African Legal Consultative Committee.

Text from ASIAN-AFRICAN LEGAL CONSULTATIVE COMMITTEE, Report of the Third Session, pp. 66-69.

This subject was referred for the opinion of this Committee by the Government of India during its First Session. The question referred was whether a Foreign State or a State Trading Organization should be regarded as immune from jurisdiction of the Courts in respect of commercial and other transactions which do not strictly fall within the ambit of "Governmental Activities" as traditionally understood.

2. It is observed that many of the states today do not confine their activities to the traditional functions of a State. Some of them not only own and control means of production and distribution inside the state but also enter into trading contracts with merchants in foreign countries in the exercise of their state functions. Such contracts are usually entered into on behalf of the state or a government department or a state trading organization. It is being increasingly realised that the doctrine of sovereign immunity of foreign states was not meant to include these new and extended functions which are being assumed by the governments at present. The State Department of the U.S.A. declared in 1952 that they would advise that immunity of foreign states and sovereigns should not be granted in respect of activities of this nature. The majority judgment of the U. S. Supreme Court delivered by Justice Frankfurter in the Republic of China case in 1955 gave expression to this modern trend in restricting sovereign immunity. A similar view was expressed by Lord Justice Denning in Rahimtullah *versus* the Nizam of Hyderabad—an English House of Lords decision of 1957. Judge Lauterpacht in the 1955 edition of "Oppenheim's International Law" also lends support to this view. Professor A. G. Hanbury, writing in "Current Legal Problems" in 1955 was also of the view that the traditional doctrine of sovereign immunity is getting out of date. The views taken by courts in Egypt, France, Germany and Switzerland (as set out in the Memorandum presented by the Government of India) appear to go even further along this modern trend. In these circumstances it was thought to be opportune for the Asian African Nations to consider if they

should also place restrictions on the immunity granted to foreign states in respect of such activities.

3. The question was generally considered by the delegations of the participating countries during the First Session. A brief summary of the views expressed by the several delegations was given in the interim report of the Committee. As the majority of the delegations were favourably inclined to consider a restriction on the immunity of foreign states in respect of commercial transactions, a detailed questionnaire on the various aspects of the subject was prepared by the Secretariat. During this session delegations have expressed their views in the form of answers to the various questions posed in the questionnaire. A summary of the discussion on the basis of the questionnaire is annexed to this Report.

4. All the delegations except that of Indonesia were of the view that a distinction should be made between different types of state activity and immunity to foreign states should not be granted in respect of their activities which may be called commercial or of private nature. The Indonesian delegate, however, adhered to the view that immunity should continue to be granted to all the activities of the foreign state irrespective of their nature provided they were carried on by the government itself.

5. All the delegations were agreed that a state trading organisation which is part of the government and is not a separate juristic entity should be treated on the same footing as the government proper. All the delegations were also agreed that where a state trading organisation has an entity of its own under the Municipal Laws of the state, immunity should not be available to it.

6. The majority of the delegations were agreed that the trade representative of a government would not be entitled to immunity for the same reason and on the basis that a foreign government would not be so entitled. The Indonesian delegation was, however, of a contrary view.

7. Regarding the method of claiming immunity by sovereign states the majority were of the view that the certificate of the Foreign Ministry should be given considerable weight. The minority took the view that a certificate of the

Foreign Office, if given, should be conclusive and binding on the courts.

8. It was recognised by all delegations that a decree obtained against a foreign state could not be executed against its public property. The property of a state trading organisation which has a separate juristic entity may, however, be available for execution.

9. The Committee having taken the view of all the delegations into consideration decided to recommend as follows :-

(i) The State Trading Organisations which have a separate juristic entity under the Municipal Laws of the country where they are incorporated should not be entitled to the immunity of the state in respect of any of its activities in a foreign state. Such organisations and their representative could be sued in the Municipal Courts of a foreign state in respect of their transactions or activities in their State.

(ii) A State which enters into transactions of a commercial or private character, ought not to raise the plea of sovereign immunity if sued in the courts of a foreign state in respect of such transactions. If the plea of immunity is raised it should not be admissible to deprive the jurisdiction of the Domestic Courts.

10. The Committee noted that the Government of the United Arab Republic are of the opinion :-

(a) That a foreign State should not enjoy immunity, except in public transactions undertaken by it in its capacity as an international entity, excluding any legal transaction similiar to the usual civil activities undertaken by individuals and private entites.

(b) That neither a commercial representative of a foreign government, nor any State Trading Organisation belonging to it, which have an independent juridical entity, may enjoy immunity in commercial transactions.

(c) That all questions of immunity of a foreign State, its representatives or State Trading Organisation belonging to it, should be left to the decision of courts, sufficiently considering certificates issued by ministries for Foreign Affairs in compliance with the courts demand.

(d) The foreign judgments should not be enforced on the State's public property, in an absolute manner. Nevertheless, the State Trading organisations belonging to the State, and having an independent juridical entity are not immune, and law suits against them and their representatives may be brought to the courts of a foreign State, concerning their transactions and activities of the last mentioned State.

(e) That although the plea of immunity should be left to the decision of national courts alone, yet, litigations relating to commercial transactions of the State, may be referred to arbitration.

(f) That a multilateral convention on enforcement of judgement against a foreign State is premature.

11. The memorandum presented by the Government of India on the subject, the Interim Report of the Committee adopted during the First Session and a summary of Discussions on the subject during the Cairo Session as edited by the Secretariat shall form Annexes to this report.

12. The recommendation contained in clause (1) of paragraph 9 was adopted unanimously. The Delegation of Indonesia dissented on the recommendation contained in clause (ii) which was agreed upon by all other Delegations.

B. SEN
Secretary to the Committee.

(6) FINAL REPORT OF THE COMMITTEE ON EXTRADITION OF FUGITIVE OFFENDERS, 1961

Adopted in Tokyo on February 25, 1961, at the Fourth Session of the Asian-African Legal Consultative Committee.

Text from ASIAN-AFRICAN LEGAL CONSULTATIVE COMMITTEE, <u>Report of the Fourth Session</u>, pp. 18-42.

1. The subject of extradition of fugitive offenders, namely, the principles concerning extradition of offenders in one State taking refuge in the territory of another, including questions relating to desirability of conclusion of extradition treaties and simplification in the procedure for extradition was referred to this Committee for consideration by the Government of the Union of Burma. The government, in its memorandum referring this subject for consideration of this Committee, had stated :

> "Extradition in most countries was based on either specific enactments or upon treaties. These vary in their list of extraditable offences, depending upon the relationship between the States concerned. In Asian States, which have only recently regained their independence, the extradition laws of colonial days have continued and at the present juncture it is necessary to examine the position. It is most desirable that as between the Member States of the Asian-African Legal Consultative Committee, definite arrangements should exist for the extradition of fugitive criminals. Each Member State should see that it has adequate statutory laws for this purpose and then enter into relations with Member States either bilateral or multilateral".

2. The Government of India had also, by a separate reference, referred to this Committee for its opinion the following questions relating to the subject of extradition, that is :

   (a) Whether and on what principle should a State voluntarily extradite fugitive criminals even in the absence of an extradition treaty?

   (b) Whether a State should extradite its own nationals and nationals of States other than the requesting State?

   (c) What should be the procedure to be followed in the matter of extradition?

   (d) What offences should properly be regarded as extraditable and whether attempts to commit such offences should also make a person liable to be extradited?

   (e) What principles ought to be followed in determining the question as to whether a crime is of a political

419

nature?

3. The Indian memorandum in referring these questions for consideration of the Committee had set out a summary of the views of text-writers on international law and the prevailing practice in various countries of the world on these questions.

4. The Government of Japan also submitted a memorandum on this subject dealing with the various questions raised in the Indian and Burmese memoranda, and generally on the subject.

5. The Committee considered this subject at its first Session held in New Delhi in April 1957 on the basis of the three memoranda presented by the Governments of Burma, India and Japan. The discussion at that Session was mainly confined to the five questions raised in the Indian memorandum as set out above. The conclusions which could be drawn from the discussions of the Committee at that Session on those five specific questions were as follows :

(1) There was agreement in principle among the Delegations of Burma, Ceylon, India, Indonesia and Japan that the conclusion of extradition treaties between various States was desirable so that fugitive criminals could be surrendered to the State in whose territory the crime had been committed. The Indian and the Japanese Delegations were of the opinion that there was no objection to the voluntary surrender of criminals even in the absence of a treaty. The Indonesian Delegation considered such voluntary surrender to be desirable only in respect of crimes of a serious character. The Delegations of Burma and Ceylon were not in favour of such voluntary surrender.

(2) On the question of extradition by a State of its own nationals, whilst the Indian Delegation was of the view that there was not sufficient justification in refusing to extradite its own nationals and the Indonesian Delegation favoured surrender of one's own nationals in respect of crimes of a serious character, the Delegations of Burma and Japan were opposed to such surrender of its own nationals by a State. The position taken by the Delegation of Ceylon was that surrender of its own nationals ought to be on a reciprocal basis between the States, but such reciprocity need not be insisted upon in all cases. On the question of surrender of nationals of a third State, the Burmese Delegation was of the view that such extradition ought to be through the State of origin of the offender which should be approached by the requesting State. The other Delegations saw no objection to direct surrender of offenders to the

requesting State in such cases.

(3) The Delegations of Burma, Ceylon, India, Indonesia and Japan were agreed that a **prima facie** case of guilt in respect of an extraditable offence ought to be established before a fugitive offender could be handed over to the requesting State.

(4) The Delegations of Burma, Ceylon, India, Indonesia and Japan were agreed that extraditable offences should be determined by the States themselves by means of extradition treaties on the question; as to whether attempts to commit extraditable offences should themselves be extraditable, the Delegations expressed varying opinions.

(5) The Delegations of Burma, Ceylon, India, Indonesia and Japan were agreed that no particular text or formula could be evolved to determine the question as to whether a particular crime could be regarded as one of a political nature.

The Committee having considered the statements and views put forward by various Delegations represented at that Session was of the opinion that it was necessary for the Committee to collect further material and make a study of the question of voluntary surrender of fugitive criminals and the questions of extradition of its own nationals and those of third States before making its recommendations to the governments of the participating countries. The Committee, however, submitted an interim report on the three other questions on which there was agreement between the five Delegations (the Delegations of Syria and Iraq having reserved their position). The recommendations of the Committee were in the following terms :

(1) The Committee favours the view that before a State surrenders a fugitive criminal to a requesting State, a **prima facie** case of guilt ought to be established to show :

(i) that an extraditable offence was committed;

(ii) that the offence was committed in the territory of the requesting State;

(iii) that the crime was committed by the person who is sought to be extradited; and

(iv) that the crime is not of a political nature.

(2) The Committee is of the view that no specific procedure need be laid down in respect of establishment of such a **prima facie** case and this should be governed in accordance with the rules of criminal procedure as prevailing in the country where the offender

421

has taken refuge.

(3) The Committee is of the view that extradition treaties ought to be concluded between the participating countries and that the list of extraditable offences should be set out in such treaties.

(4) The Committee is of the opinion that it is not feasible to formulate any specific text to determine the question as to whether a crime is of a political character or not and has to be judged in the facts and circumstances of each case.

6. This subject was again taken up at the Second Session of the Committee held in Cairo in October 1958 and a second interim report was drawn up. At the Cairo Session the entire subject concerning principles of extradition as referred by the Government of Burma was discussed on the basis of a detailed questionnaire prepared by the Secretariat and a memorandum submitted by the Delegation of the United Arab Republic. The second interim report adopted at the Cairo Session stated "As there appears to be a fair measure of agreement on most of the questions discussed in this Session, it is for consideration whether an attempt should be made to embody the agreed principles into a draft of a convention at a later stage."

7. The Secretariat of the Committee accordingly prepared a draft incorporating the agreed principles on the subject in the form of Articles for consideration of this Committee. This draft prepared by the Secretariat together with the Draft of an Agreement submitted by the Delegation of the U.A.R. was considered by the Committee at its Colombo Session and the Committee at that Session drew up certain Draft Articles containing the principles on the subject which were submitted to the governments for their comments. The subject was placed before this Session for final consideration of the Draft Articles prepared at the Colombo Session in the light of the comments received from the governments of the various participating countries in this Committee, and the comments made by the Delegations present at this Session.

8. The Committee having considered all the materials placed before it and having taken note of the views expressed by the Delegations of the participating countries present at this Session decides to present its final report in the form of draft articles embodying the principles on the subject of extradition of fugitive offenders. These Articles are annexed to and form part of this Report.

9. There was no unanimity in the Committee on the question as to whether the arrangements for extradition between the participating countries and other Asian-African countries should be made by means of bilateral treaties or by means of a multi-

lateral convention between a group of States. The Delegations of Burma, Ceylon, India, Pakistan and Japan are in favour of conclusion of separate bilateral treaties whilst the Delegations of Iraq and U.A.R. prefer adoption of a multilateral convention. The Delegation of Indonesia was not in a position to indicate its views as to its preference between bilateral treaties and a multilateral convention. Consequently it was not possible to reach unanimity on the provisions of all the Articles embodying the principles on this subject and the views expressed by various Delegations wherever they are divergent have been embodied in alternative drafts in the Articles.

10. The Committee takes the view that it is a matter for each State to decide as to whether it would enter into bilateral arrangements with other States on the question of extradition of fugitive offenders or whether it should be a party to a multilateral convention among a group of States. The Committee, however, is of the opinion that whether a State enters into bilateral arrangements or becomes a party to a multilateral convention certain principles would need to be observed on the question of extradition of fugitive offenders.

11. The Committee having examined the entire position on the subject as requested by the Governments of the Union of Burma and India has formulated the principles on the subject in the light of State practice prevailing in various countries and particularly in the Member States participating in this Committee.

(Sd.) R. W. Prodjodikoro,   Chairman.

(Sd.) B. Sen,   Secretary.

25-2-1961

ARTICLES CONTAINING THE PRINCIPLES CONCERNING EXTRADITION OF FUGITIVE OFFENDERS

Article 1

The Contracting Parties undertake to surrender to each other, in the present Treaty/Convention, persons who are within the jurisdiction of one party and are being prosecuted or have been convicted by the judicial authorities of the other party.

Note : (1) The Delegation of Iraq was in favour of adoption of the words "in the territory" in place of the words "within the jurisdiction".

(2) Burma, Ceylon, India, Japan and Pakistan were in favour of the view that extradition arrangements should be made by means of bilateral treaties,

whilst Iraq and the United Arab Republic favoured adoption of a multilateral convention. The Delegation of Indonesia did not express any specific view.

Commentary

At the Cairo Session of the Committee there appeared to be a fair measure of agreement among the delegations of the participating countries on the general principles relating to the extradition of fugitive criminals, although some differences of opinion were expressed on certain aspects. It was agreed that "no legal duty is imposed by customary international law on States to extradite fugitive offenders". The majority of the delegations was, however, of the opinion that "extradition may, in the absence of a treaty, be effected by way of international co-operation in suppression of crimes on a reciprocal basis". India was of the opinion that "international law imposes no obligation to extradite criminals, but States do recognise it even in the absence of treaties". The U.A.R. expressed the view that "extradition is a moral obligation based on the principles of solidarity and co-operation between nations" and Japan stated that although international law imposes no obligation, "extradition is made even in the absence of treaties". Some delegations, however, thought that extradition could be effected only in pursuance of a treaty. Ceylon stated that her law recognised extradition but only with countries with which she had a treaty and Sudan expressed the view that "there should be a treaty regarding extradition because otherwise things would be fluctuating". Although it has been asserted by some writers on international law that there is a legal duty to extradite even in the absence of a treaty, this doctrine has not become an established rule of international law and there was agreement in principle among the delegations to the Cairo Session that there is no legal duty of extradition under customary international law. These Articles, therefore, commence with an Article which states that the contracting parties undertake to surrender fugitive offenders only "in the circumstances and under the conditions stipulated in the present Treaty/Convention". The words "Treaty/Convention" have been inserted because there is a divergence of view as to whether extradition arrangements should be made between States by separate bilateral treaties or by a multilateral convention between a group of States.

Article 2

Alternative 'A'

Extradition shall not be granted unless the act constituting the offence for which the person sought is being prosecuted or has been convicted is punishable at least by three years' imprisonment under the laws of both the requested and requesting States.

Alternative 'B'

(1) Extradition may be granted if the person whose extradition is requested, is accused as a principal or as an accessory, of committing or attempting to commit an offence, within the jurisdiction of the requesting State, punishable at least by one year's imprisonment under the laws of both the requesting and the requested States.

(2) If this person has been already convicted for such an offence, he should not be extradited unless he was condemned for at least two months' imprisonment.

Alternative 'C'

Extradition shall not be granted under Article 1 except in respect of offences enumerated in the Schedule to the present Treaty.

Note : The Delegations of Burma and Japan accepted alternative "A" of the draft. The Delegation of Pakistan wished to leave the position open as to whether to accept alternative "A" with an amendment or to accept alternative "C". The amendment suggested by the Delegation of Pakistan to Alternative "A" was that the period of one year should be substituted in place of three years. The Delegations of Ceylon and India were in favour of accepting alternative "C". The Delegation of Indonesia accepted paragraph (1) only of alternative "B". The Delegations of Iraq and the U.A.R. accepted alternative "B" of the draft.

Commentary

Every convention or treaty on extradition has to choose between two methods of qualifying extraditable offences, namely, the enumerative method and the eliminative method. The enumerative method, which specifies each offence for which extradition may be granted, has been adopted by most extradition treaties in the nineteenth and early twentieth centuries. This system has also been adopted in municipal legislation by the United Kingdom (Extradition Acts 1870, 1873, 1906 and 1932), Belgium (Law of 1933), and countries such as India, who have based their Extradition Acts on the British model. Until recently the practice among most of the Member Countries of this Committee has been to enumerate the offences which are to be extraditable in treaties as also in the municipal legislations relating to extradition. The modern trend, in both extradition treaties and municipal legislation, is to adopt the eliminative method, which defines extraditable offences by reference to the maximum or minimum penalty which may be imposed. Modern bilateral treaties, such as Extradition Treaty of 12th June 1942 between Germany and Italy, and the Treaty of 29th November 1951 between France and the Federal Republic of Germany, have adopted the eliminative method in preference to the enumerative method. The recent treaty between Iraq and Turkey provides that the offence must be punishable in both countries with at least one year's imprisonment. The eliminative method has also been adopted in municipal legislation by countries such as France (Law of 1927) and Germany (Law of 1929). Recently concluded multilateral conventions, such as the Extradition Agreement of 14th September 1952 between the Member States of the League of Arab States and the Extradition Convention of 5th May 1954 adopted by the Legal Committee of the Council of Europe, have adopted the eliminative method. The eliminative method has also been adopted by the well-known Harvard Research Draft on Extradition and by the Draft Convention of Extradition adopted by the Inter-American Council of Jurists at its Third Session in the Mexico City in February 1956.

Although the majority of the delegates in this Committee appeared to favour the eliminative method, there was no unanimity on the specific provisions to be included regarding this matter and the Committee has finally adopted 3 alternative Articles on this question. The laws and treaties of most of the Member Countries of the Committee have adopted the principle of double criminality, namely, that the act should be punishable as an offence in both the requesting and requested States. All the delegations appeared to be in agreement on this question.

Article 3

Extradition shall not be granted for political offences. The requested State shall determine whether the offence is political.

Note : This Article is adopted by a majority. The Delegations of Ceylon and Indonesia dissented (See Commentary).

Commentary

The majority of the delegations at the Cairo Session were of the opinion that extradition should not be granted for political offences. The Delegation of Ceylon, however, observed that "although this principle has been accepted in Ceylon at present, in future legislations she would reserve the right to extradite persons who commit serious types of mixed crimes, such as crimes which are both of a political and ordinary nature." The Delegation of Indonesia urged consideration by the Member States of the principle that "no offence should be considered as being of a political character by the Member States if it was committed in any of these States by a foreigner." In the view of Indonesia, a political crime can only be committed by persons exercising political rights in the State in which the crime has been committed; in other words, it can be committed only by a citizen of that State within the boundaries of the State concerned. Thus, in the view of Indonesia, a political crime can only be committed against one's own State within its boundaries and foreigners cannot be regarded as having committed a political crime against a State other than his own.

426

At the Colombo Session, the Delegations of Burma, India, Iraq, Japan, Pakistan and the United Arab Republic were in agreement that extradition should not be granted for political offences. The Delegation of Ceylon was of the opinion that in the matter of extradition no distinction should be made between ordinary crimes and crimes which amount to political offences or which are of a political nature, and as such Ceylon was not in a position to accept the provisions of this Article. The Delegation of Indonesia stated that the Article went must beyond the hitherto accepted notions in the matter of non-extradition of political offenders. The Delegation was of the view that the difficulties in determining whether a crime is of a political character or not may lead to complications and if the principle of non-extradition of political offenders was accepted it would be difficult to determine in each case whether a person should be extradited or not, especially in the case of mixed offences. The Delegation was also of the opinion that aliens or foreigners have no right to meddle in the internal affairs of a foreign country and if such a person did so, he should not be given asylum. The Delegation of Indonesia therefore felt that the principles behind this Article should not be applicable to the cases of persons who are not the nationals of the States where the political crime is committed since foreign nationals do not enjoy any political rights. The Delegation also drew attention to the provisions of the Harvard Draft Convention on the subject and stated that the Article should begin with the words "unless otherwise provided by a treaty". The Draft suggested by the Indonesian Delegation was in the following terms :

(a) Unless otherwise provided by a treaty, extradition shall not be granted for political offences.

(b) An offence shall not be considered as political if it is committed by a person who does not exercise political rights in the aggrieved State.

(c) An offence shall not be considered as of a political nature if there is a preponderance of the features of a common crime over the political motives or objectives of the offender.

At the Tokyo Session of the Committee the Delegation of Ceylon also accepted this draft of the Article. Extradition treaties do not usually contain a definition of the term "political offence". A similar situation prevails in most systems of municipal law. Although the Japanese Law of Extradition has adopted the principle of non-extradition of political criminals, no definition of a political crime is given in either the Ordinance or the Law of Extradition. With regard to the United Arab Republic, neither the Syrian Penal Code nor the Laws of the Egyptian Region contain a definition of political offences for the purposes of extradition. A similar position prevails in the municipal legislations of the other Member Countries. This is true of almost all systems of municipal law. The difficulty of defining a political crime is no less reflected in the writings of text-book writers among whom there is much controversy. Some writers consider a crime "political" if committed from a political motive, whereas others call "political" any crime committed for a political purpose; again others recognise such a crime only as "political" as was committed both from a political motive and at the same time for a political purpose; and finally, some writers confine the term "political crime" to certain offences against the State only, such as high treason. In view of the paucity of legislative precedents and the failure of text-book writers to formulate a satisfactory definition of the term, the feasibility of defining a political crime has always been doubted and in most countries the question is left to the discretion of the authorities exercising jurisdiction in the matter. English law, for instance, merely refers to "offences of a political character" and does not attempt a precise definition. A similar position prevails in French law, with the exception that in France an offence committed during an insurrection or civil war is always regarded as a political offence. Belgian law recognises the so-called "fait connexe a un crime au delit politique" and Swiss law, the "systeme de la predominance". At the Colombo Session, the Delegations agreed that no particular test or formula could be evolved to determine what is a political offence. Article 3 accordingly provides that the decision as to whether an offence is political or not, shall be left to the discretion of the requested State. Such a provision is in accordance with the State practice in the Member Countries. A similar provision has been adopted by the League of Arab States in its Extradition Agreement of 1952, and by the Inter-American Council of Jurists in its Extradition Convention of 1956.

Article 4

Extradition may be refused, if the person in question is a national of the requested State.

Commentary

The municipal laws of most countries provide that nationals shall not be extradited, but there are some countries which are prepared to extradite their own nationals on the basis of reciprocity. Belgium, Denmark, France, Germany, Greece, Italy, Spain, Switzerland and almost all other continental European States have provisions in their laws and Constitutions that nationals may not be extradited. On the other hand, the United Kingdom and the United States do not make any distinction in their extradition laws between their own nationals and foreign citizens; presumably the United Kingdom and the United States are prepared on principle to surrender their own nationals, but in practice this policy is not always followed on account of the difficulty of securing reciprocity. Most of the treaties between the United States and foreign countries either disclaim any obligation to surrender citizens of the asylum State or make their surrender discretionary with that State. Simi-

428

larly, it is not unusual for the United Kingdom when concluding extradition treaties with countries which prohibit the extradition of their own nationals to insert a clause which leaves it to the discretion of the United Kingdom to grant or refuse the extradition of United Kingdom nationals. With regard to the Member States of this Committee, India, Ceylon, Iraq, Sudan and Indonesia appear to be in favour of the extradition of their own nationals on a reciprocal basis but Burma, Japan and the United Arab Republic have expressed a contrary view. This Article accordingly leaves it to the discretion of the Contracting Party whether to grant or refuse extradition of its own nationals.

Article 5

Extradition shall not be refused on the ground that the person sought to be extradited is not a national of the requesting State.

Note : This Article was adopted by a majority. The Delegations of Burma and India did not accept the provisions of this Article. The Delegation of Pakistan reserved its position.

Commentary

The practice of States as evidenced in various extradition treaties appears to favour the extradition of persons who are not nationals of the requesting State. The majority of the delegations of the Member Countries agreed that extradition of nationals of third States could not be refused. The Delegation of Pakistan reserved their position on this Article as the Government of Pakistan did not have an opportunity of considering this matter fully. The Delegations of Burma and India could not accept the provisions of this Article.

Article 6

Extradition shall not be granted for purely military offences.

Note : This Article was adopted by a majority. The Delegations of Burma, Indonesia and Pakistan were of the view that this Article should be deleted. The Delegation of Indonesia was of the opinion that the principle of non-extradition of military offences is not an accepted notion of international law.

Explanation: The expression "purely military offences" means acts or omissions which are punishable only under the military laws of a State and do not fall within the scope of ordinary penal laws of the State. This Article will have no application to offences i.e., acts or omissions which are punishable both under the military laws and ordinary penal laws of a State.

Commentary

Most extradition treaties exclude military offences but the exemption is intended to be granted only for offences of an exclu-

429

sively military character. The Agreement between Egypt and Iraq of 1931, for instance, expressly prohibits extradition for "purely military offences" and the Franco-German Treaty of 1951 provides that extradition shall not be granted if the offence "consists exclusively of a violation of military duties." The Inter-American Draft Convention of 1956 similarly excludes "essentially military crimes". The exemption is for offences of an exclusively military character and not for those which are also offences under general criminal law. At the Cairo Session, Japan, Indonesia, India and Ceylon stated that there were no provisions in their extradition laws relating to military offences. Iraq stated that under her law there was an express provision excluding military offences from extradition and the United Arab Republic said that the "Egyptian Military Code defines military offences as being offences committed by any member in the rank and file of the Armed Forces in violation of military duties and discipline imposed on him by his military status."

At the Colombo Session, the Delegations of Burma, Ceylon, India, Iraq and the United Arab Republic agreed that extradition should not be granted for purely military offences and accepted the provisions of Article 6. The expression "purely military offences" was defined as "acts or omissions which are punishable only under the military laws of the State and do not fall within the scope of ordinary penal laws of the State." This Article would, therefore, have no application to offences which are punishable both under the military laws and the ordinary penal laws of a State.

Article 7

(1) The requested State has the right to seek information and clarification from the requesting State as to the nature of the offence for which extradition has been requested in order to determine whether the offence is of a political character or not.

(2) In cases where the person sought to be extradited submits prima facie evidence that his offence is of a political character the burden of proving the opposite lies on the requesting State.

Note : The Delegations of Ceylon and Japan were in favour of deletion of the whole Article whilst Delegations of Burma, India and Indonesia wished paragraph 2 of the Article to be deleted. The Delegations of Iraq and the U.A.R. accepted the Article as it stood. The Delegation of Pakistan was prepared to accept the provisions of this Article but had no objection to deletion of paragraph 2 of this Article.

Article 8

Extradition shall be granted only if the offence for which the person sought is being prosecuted or has been convicted, has been committed within the jurisdiction of the requesting State.

Note : The provisions of this Article will be unnecessary if the alternative (B) to Article 2 is adopted.

Commentary

Most extradition treaties provide that extradition shall be granted only if the offence was committed within the jurisdiction of the requesting State. The Anglo-American Extradition Treaty of 1931, for instance, provides that extradition shall be granted only if the crime was "committed within the jurisdiction of one party". The Extradition Treaty between Japan and the United States contains a similar provision in Article 1. The Inter-American Draft Convention also provides that the offence "must have been committed within the jurisdiction of the requesting State". The provisions of this Article were accepted unanimously. It may be stated that under the penal laws of Japan certain crimes committed outside the territorial jurisdiction are punishable in Japan. The position is also the same under the penal laws of Indonesia.

Article 9

The requesting State shall not try or punish the person extradited except for the offence for which he was extradited and with the consent of the requested State for offences directly connected with it.

Note : The Delegation of Indonesia did not accept the provisions of this Article and suggested retention of the text of the Draft Article as adopted in the Colombo Session which was as follows :

"The requesting State shall not, without the consent of the requested State, try or punish the person extradited except for the offence for which he was extradited, offences directly connected with it and committed for the same purpose and the offences he might have committed after his extradition".

Commentary

The rule of speciality is usually embodied in extradition treaties but there is no universally recognised rule of customary international law in this matter and State practice is widely divergent. The extradition laws of some countries such as the United Kingdom do not permit the trial of the person extradited "on facts other than those on which the surrender is based". Section 19 of 1870 Extradition Act of the United Kingdom provides that a person "shall not . . . . . be tried for any offence committed prior to the surrender other than such of said crimes (described in the First Schedule) as may be proved by the facts on which the surrender is grounded". German law, on the other hand, permits the consideration at the trial of "new facts" which have subsequently been revealed, provided that these "new facts" leave unaffected the general factual situation underlying the offence when viewed as a whole. Belgian law permits the prosecution of the person extradited for all offences committed prior to extradition, provided such offences fall within the category of extraditable crimes under the treaty in question. At the Cairo Session, India, Burma, Ceylon, Indonesia, Japan and Iraq were of the opinion that a person may be tried only for the offence in respect of which extradition was granted. Burma observed that "international custom seems to be that when extradition is requested by the requesting State for a particular offence, then the person can be tried only for that offence and cannot be tried for an offence other than that mentioned in the extradition report unless there was an elapse of time and permission was obtained from the requested State." Indonesia and Iraq stated that their extradition laws contained no provisions relating to this matter and Japan observed that "theoretically the person must be tried for the offence in respect of which extradition was granted". The United Arab Republic agreed that "treaties and custom usually prevent trial for any offence other than that for which extradition was granted" but raised the question of certain exceptions to this rule of speciality. Most treaties provide that the rule may be waived with the consent of the requested State. At the Colombo Session, the Committee decided to adopt a draft providing that the requesting State shall not try the person extradited for any other offence without the consent of the requested State. Such a provision has been included in most of the recently concluded conventions on extradition such as the European Draft Convention of 1956 and it also forms part of the well-known Harvard Research Draft on Extradition. The Draft adopted at the Colombo Session was revised in the light of the comments made by the Governments of the Participating Countries.

Article 10

A person who has been extradited may be tried for an offence other than those referred to in Article 9 where the person after being given an opportunity of leaving the territory of the State to which he had been surrendered fails to do so within a period of sixty days after being given that opportunity provided that notice in writing of the fact of such opportunity being afforded is given to the State of which such person is a national at or about the time when such opportunity is afforded to such person.

Commentary

The Extradition laws of some countries provide that the rule of speciality may be waived by the surrendered person himself. At the Colombo Session, the Delegations of Burma, India, Indonesia, Iraq and the United Arab Republic adopted a Draft Article containing provisions regarding this matter. The Delegations of Ceylon and Japan, however, did not accept the provisions of that Article. The Delegation of Pakistan had also reserved its position. At the Tokyo Session, however, unanimity was reached on the present text of this Article.

Article 11

Extradition shall be refused if the offence in respect of which extradition is sought is under investigation in the requested State or the person sought to be extradited has already been tried and discharged or punished or is still under trial in the requested State for the offence for which extradition is sought.

Commentary

The laws and/or treaties of most of the member countries of this Committee contain provisions providing against double jeopardy for the same act. There is, for instance, a provision in the Criminal Procedure Code of Iraq prohibiting double jeopardy and treaties concluded by Iraq with other countries, such as the Iraqi-Egyptian Treaty of 1931, contain provisions to this effect. The principle of "Non Bis In Idem" is also observed by the United Arab Republic and the agreement signed by Egypt and Iraq in 1931 stipulates that the requested person may not be surrendered if he has been previously tried for the offence for which his surrender is requested, so that punishment may not be repeated for the same offence. The extradition agreement concluded between the countries of the League of Arab States contains a stipulation to this effect. The principle of "Non Bis In Idem" is also recognised by Japan and Indonesia. Though all the Delegations at the Colombo Session were in agreement with the principle of providing against double jeopardy for the same act, there was disagreement with regard to the precise wording of the provisions to be included. At the Tokyo Session this Article was, however, unanimously adopted.

Article 12

If the person sought to be extradited is on trial in the requested State for an offence other than that for which his extradition is requested, his extradition shall be postponed until his trial is terminated and the penalty has been undergone.

Article 13

Extradition shall not be granted if the person in question has become immune by reason of lapse of time from prosecution or punishment according to the laws of either the requesting or the requested State.

Commentary

Although all extradition treaties contain a provision to the effect that extradition may be refused on the ground of lapse of time, some treaties provide that the request may be refused if the offence is time-barred under the law of the requested State, while others provide that the request may be refused only if the offence is time-barred under the laws of both the requested and requesting

States. Most treaties have in the past regarded the law of the requested State as decisive, but the modern tendency, as exemplified in the Franco-German Treaty of 1951, the European Draft Convention of 1954 and the Inter-American Draft Convention of 1956, appears to favour the refusal of extradition when the offence has become time-barred under the laws of either the requested or requesting State. At the Colombo Session the Committee followed the modern tendency and provided that extradition should be refused when the trial or punishment of the offence has become barred by lapse of time according to the laws of either the requesting or requested State. All the delegations at the Colombo and Tokyo Sessions accepted the provisions of this Article.

Article 14

The requisition for extradition shall be made in writing and shall be submitted normally through diplomatic channels to the competent authority of the requested State.

Commentary

There was a good deal of discussion at the Colombo and Tokyo Sessions regarding the proper channel through which requests for extradition should be made. It was agreed that where diplomatic posts were maintained the request should be forwarded through diplomatic channels. But if a country had no diplomatic mission in the State from whose territory it wished to extradite a criminal the request could be sent through its consular representatives and in the absence of a consular post the request could be sent directly from the Ministry of Foreign Affairs of one State to the Foreign Ministry of the other. All the delegations were agreed on the text of this Article.

Article 15

(1) The requisition for extradition shall be accompanied by the original or a certified copy of the sentence of the warrant of arrest or other document having the same validity issued by a competent judicial authority.

(2) The nature of the offence for which the requisition for extradition is made, the time and place of its commission, its legal classification or description, and the legal provisions applicable to it, should be specified as precisely as possible.

(3) The requisition shall also be accompanied by a copy of the criminal law provisions that are applicable to the case, together with a description of the person claimed and any other particulars which may serve to establish his identity and nationality.

(4) The requisition shall also be accompanied—

  (i) where the person claimed is proposed to be prosecuted, by the original or certified copies of the evidences recorded by competent judicial authorities of the re-

434

questing State establishing **prima facie** that the person concerned has committed an extraditable offence within the jurisdiction of the requesting State; and

(ii) where the person claimed is already convicted of an offence in the requesting State, by original or certified copies of documents establishing that the conviction was recorded by competent judicial authorities of the requesting State in respect of an extraditable offence committed by the person concerned within the jurisdiction of the requesting State and that he has not served his sentence in accordance with the laws of the requesting State.

Commentary

In all the member countries the procedure for extradition is substantially similar. Some differences of opinion were, however, expressed at the Colombo Session with regard to the provisions of this Article and the Committee had decided to provisionally adopt alternative Draft Articles. At the Tokyo Session, however, unanimity was reached on the text of this Article.

Article 16

Extradition shall not be granted unless the competent authorities of the requested State are satisfied that the material furnished under Paragraph 4 of Article 15 establishes—

(i) where the person claimed is proposed to be prosecuted that he has **prima facie** committed an extraditable offence within the jurisdiction of the requesting State; and

(ii) where the person claimed is already convicted for an offence in the requesting State, that he was convicted by competent judicial authorities in respect of an extraditable offence committed by him within the jurisdiction of the requesting State and that he has not served his sentence in accordance with the laws of the requesting State.

Article 17

All measures to carry out extradition shall be taken in accordance with the provisions of the laws of the requested State, and the person sought shall have the right to utilise all remedies and relief available to him according to the laws of the requested State.

Commentary

In all the member countries a fugitive offender would be discharged if a **prima facie** case is not made out against him and no question of extradition would then arise. This question would, of course, be decided according to the laws of the requested State and the final decision would be left to the discretion of the executive. The person sought would, however, have the right to utilise all resources available to him according to the laws of the requested State. All the Delegations at the Colombo and Tokyo Sessions accepted the provisions of Articles 16 and 17.

Article 18

If requests for extradition are made concurrently by several States, in respect of the same person, the requested State shall have the discretion to decide thereon taking into consideration all the circumstances of the case and, in particular, the priority of the request, the gravity of the offence and the penalty to be imposed therefor.

Commentary

Concurrent requests for the extradition of the same person may arise in instances where the person sought has committed crimes in different States. The Inter-American Convention, for instance, states that "when several States request the extradition of a person, preference shall be given to the first formal request". The European Draft Convention adopts, as additional factors to be taken into account, the possibility of subsequent extradition taking place as between the requesting States, severity of the offence, the place where the offence has been committed and the nationality of the person whose extradition is sought. At the Colombo Session, the delegations were agreed that in the event of conflicting requests, the requested State shall decide to which of the requesting States the person shall be surrendered. This principle forms a part of most extradition treaties. The delegations were also in agreement that if such a situation should arise, the requested State should exercise its discretion taking into consideration the priority of the claim, the gravity of the crime and the penalty to be imposed. This Article accordingly provides that the requested State shall decide thereon, taking particularly these three factors into consideration.

Article 19

The requested State shall inform the requesting State in writing and through diplomatic channel of its decision on the requisition for extradition. If the request for extradition is rejected, the reasons shall be stated.

Article 20

The competent authorities of extraditing State shall take the necessary steps to enable the agents of the requesting State to take away the extradited person.

Commentary

The provisions of Articles 19 and 20 relating to the performance of extradition are in conformity with existing international practice and are contained in most extradition treaties and conventions. Wherever diplomatic relations between the States have not been opened, the Committee decided that the requests for extradition may be made directly by one Government to another, or through consular channels if desirable.

Article 21

If a person is abducted from a State by the agents of another State which wishes to prosecute or enforce judgment on him, the State from which he was abducted shall be entitled to demand his return.

Commentary

This Article relates to the problem of the recovery of fugitives. At the Colombo Session all the Delegations were agreed that the State from whose territory the abduction took place should be entitled to demand the return of the abducted person. At the Tokyo Session the text of the Article was modified and adopted.

Article 22

If the person whose extradition is requested is not a national of the requesting State, the requested State shall notify the State of which that person is a national, of that request as soon as it is received in order to enable the said State to defend him if necessary.

Note : The Delegations of Burma, India and Pakistan did not accept the provisions of this Article in view of their position on the provisions of Article 5.

Article 23

The person whose extradition is sought may be provisionally arrested and kept under supervision until the question of extradition is decided upon.

Note : The Delegations of Ceylon, India and Pakistan did not accept the provisions of Article 23.

Article 24

(1) In urgent cases requests for extradition may be made by post, telegram or telephone, provided that such requests include a short account of the offence, a notification that a warrant of arrest has been issued by the competent authority and that extradition shall be requested through diplomatic channels. In such cases the requested State shall take the necessary precautions to keep the person in question under supervision until it receives the written extradition request. The requested State may, if necessary, arrest and detain the said person for a period not exceeding thirty days, after which he shall be released if the written request accompanied by the necessary documents, or a request for the renewal of his detention for a period of thirty days at the most, has been

received. At the expiry of the renewal period, the person in question is immediately released if the written request accompanied by the necessary documents has not been received.

(2) The period of detention shall be deducted from the period of imprisonment to which he is sentenced in the requesting State.

(3) If the request is made by post, telegram or telephone, the competent authorities in the requested State may, if necessary, communicate with the competent authorities in the requesting State, to ascertain the request.

Note : (i) The Delegations of Iraq and the United Arab Republic accepted the whole of this Article.

(ii) The Delegations of Indonesia and Japan accepted Clauses (1) and (3) of this Article.

(iii) The Delegations of Burma, Ceylon, India and Pakistan did not accept the provisions of this Article.

Article 25

Articles seized which were in the possession of the person being extradited, at the time of his arrest, and which may be used as proof of the offence shall be delivered to the requesting State when extradition takes place, and that in so far as the laws of the extraditing State permit.

Note : The Delegation of Pakistan reserved its position on this Article.

Article 26

The requesting State shall bear all expenses incurred in the execution of the request, and if the extradited person is discharged or acquitted, the said State shall bear the expenses necessary for his return to the State from which he was extradited.

Article 27

The State which granted extradition may release the person in question, if the requesting State does not take him away within a period of one month from the date of its notification of the order of extradition to the requesting State.

Article 28

If extradition takes place as a result of fraud, deceit or misrepresentation or any similar fault on the part of the requesting State or its agents, the State which extradited the person may demand his return.

Note : The Delegation of India did not accept the provisions of this Article as in its view it would be difficult to determine as to which should be the competent authority to decide as to whether the extradition had taken place as a result of fraud, deceit or misrepresentation.

Article 29

Each contracting party shall upon presentation of a copy of the extradition order, grant facilities for the transit through their territories, of persons surrendered by one of them to the other and ensure their safe custody.

Note : This Article would apply only in cases where a multilateral convention is drawn up, and was accepted only by the Delegations of Iraq and the United Arab Republic. The Delegations of Burma, Ceylon, and India did not wish to comment on this Article as they had expressed preference for extradition agreements being made through bilateral treaties. The Delegates of Pakistan and Indonesia reserved their position on this Article. The Delegate of Japan suggested, deletion of the words "and ensure their safe custody".

Article 30

If the provisions of this agreement are in conflict with those of any bilateral agreement between two signatory States, those two States shall apply the provisions most suitable for facilitating extradition.

Note : This Article which would be applicable only in the case of a multilateral convention was accepted by the Delegations of Iraq and the United Arab Republic. The Delegations of Indonesia and Japan suggested the following Draft of this Article :

APPENDIX

ILLUSTRATIVE LIST OF EXTRADITABLE OFFENCES

(Suggested by the Delegation of India)

1. Culpable homicide.

2. Attempt to murder.

3. Causing miscarriage and abandonment of child.

4. Kidnapping, abduction, slavery and forced labour.

5. Rape and unnatural offences.

6. Theft, extortion, robbery and dacoity.

7. Criminal misappropriation and criminal breach of trust.

8. Cheating.

9. Mischief.

10. Forgery, using forged documents and other offences relating to false documents.

11. Offences relating to coins and stamps.

12. Piracy by law of nations committed on board or against a vessel of a foreign State.

13. Sinking or destroying a vessel at sea or attempting or conspiring to do so.

14. Assault on board a vessel on the high seas with intent to destroy life or to do grievous bodily harm.

15. Revolt or conspiracy to revolt by two or more persons on board a vessel on the high seas against the authority of the master.

16. Smuggling of gold, gold manufactures, diamonds and other precious stones or of any narcotic substances.

17. Immoral traffic in women and girls.

18. Any offence which may, from time to time, be specified by the Central Government by notification in the Official Gazette either generally for all States or specially for one or more States.

"The provisions of the present convention shall not affect the existing bilateral agreements concerning extradition between the contracting parties or shall not prevent the conclusion of such agreements in the future".

The Delegates of Burma, Ceylon, India and Pakistan did not comment on this Article due to the fact that the Article would be applicable only to multilateral conventions.

(7) FINAL REPORT OF THE COMMITTEE ON THE STATUS OF ALIENS, 1961

Adopted in Tokyo on February 25, 1961, at the Fourth Session of the Asian-African Legal Consultative Committee.

Text from ASIAN-AFRICAN LEGAL CONSULTATIVE COMMITTEE, Report of the Fourth Session, pp. 43-45, 52-180.

1. The subject of Status of Aliens was referred to this Committee for consideration by the Government of Japan. The Ministry of Foreign Affairs of the Government of Japan in its memorandum dated the 20th February 1957, had stated that this question was one of common concern to Asian African countries and enumerated the various topics which arise for consideration on this subject. The topics listed are as follows :

Status of Aliens

I. Definition of the term "alien".

II. Entry of Aliens.

    (1) Restriction on entry.

    (2) Entry of fugitives.

        Extradition—Kinds of extraditable crimes—Refusal to extradite—Right of Asylum.

III. Status of alien residents.

    A. Status under public laws.

        (1) Obligation to register.

        (2) Personal duties—obligatory military service—Compulsory education—Liability to taxes.

        (3) Suffrage—Status to be public officials.

    B. Status under private laws.

        (1) Respect of human rights and fundamental freedoms —Freedom of religion—Freedom to choose and change one's residence.

        (2) Protection of person and property.

            (i) Extent of protection.

                National treatment—Most-favoured-nation treatment.

441

(ii) In case of nationalisation of property.

(iii) State responsibility for damages.

(iv) Protection of nationals abroad by home State.

(3) Restriction on business activities.

IV. Departure of aliens.

(1) Freedom of departure—The case when departure is not admitted.

(2) Enforcement of departure.

(i) Conditions of expulsion.

(ii) Proceedings of expulsion.

2. The subject was generally discussed at the Second Session of this Committee held in Cairo and the views of various Delegations were ascertained on the basis of a questionnaire prepared by the Secretariat of the Committee. The Committee at that Session decided that the subject, having regard to its importance, needed further study and directed the Secretariat to prepare a report in the light of discussions held at the Cairo Session. The Secretariat accordingly collected the relevant material and drew up a report in the form of draft articles containing the principles on the subject. The matter was discussed in detail during the Third Session of the Committee held in Colombo in January 1960. At that Session it was decided to separate the topics relating to Diplomatic Protection of Citizens Abroad and State Responsibility for Maltreatment of Aliens from the other topics on the Status of Aliens as in the opinion of the Committee those two topics did not relate to the substantive rights of aliens regarding their status and treatment. The Committee decided at the Session to consider separately these two topics at its future Sessions. The Committee was able to consolidate its provisional views on the other topics.

3. The draft articles containing the provisional views of the Committee on the subject of Status and Treatment of Aliens as adopted in the Colombo Session were submitted to the Governments of the participating countries for their comments, and the subject was placed on the Agenda of this Session for reconsideration in the light of the comments received from the Governments.

4. The subject was fully discussed at the present Session. The Committee having taken note of the comments made on the draft articles adopted at the Colombo Session and having heard the views of the Delegations of the participating countries present at this Session decides to draw up its final report in the form of draft articles containing the principles regarding the Status and Treatment of Aliens or Foreign Nationals. The Committee directs the

Secretariat to prepare the commentaries to these articles in the light of discussions held at the present Session and thereafter to submit the report together with the commentaries to the Governments of the participating countries.

5. The Committee is separately considering the topics relating to Diplomatic Protection of Citizens Abroad and State Responsibility for Maltreatment of Foreign Nationals on which some progress has been made. The Committee shall submit its report on these two topics to the Governments of the participating countries in due course.

(Sd.) R. W. Prodjodikoro.

Chairman

(Sd.) B. Sen.

Secretary

25-2-1961

PRINCIPLES CONCERNING ADMISSION AND
TREATMENT OF ALIENS

(Text of the Articles drawn up by the Committee together with the commentaries proposed by the Secretariat in the light of discussions in the Committee)

Article 1

Definition of the term "Alien"

An alien is a person who is not a citizen or national of the State concerned.

Note : In a Commonwealth country the status of the nationals of other Commonwealth countries shall be governed by the provisions of its laws, regulations and orders.

Commentary

Article 1 embodies a general though not a comprehensive definition of the term "alien". The national legislations of most of the States including the Participating Countries in this Committee do not appear to include a comprehensive statutory definition of this term, nor have the text-writers been able to define this term satisfactorily. According to the Institute of International Law, "all those are considered aliens who have no actual right of nationality in a State, without distinction as to whether they are simply passing through or are resident or domiciled, or whether they are refugees or have entered the country of their own free will."[1] The question whether an individual is an alien or not, therefore, must be determined by the laws and regulations of each State. The term "alien" generally includes not only foreign nationals but also stateless persons.

The note appended to this article takes into account the fact that owing to historical reasons the citizens of the Commonwealth Countries and those of Eire are not regarded as aliens in the United Kingdom, and in some of the other Commonwealth Countries. This is a special feature of the British Nationality Law and may be regarded as an exception to the general definition of the term "alien".

Article 2

(1) The admission of aliens into a State shall be at the discretion of that State.

---

1 Scott : Resolutions of the Institute of International Law (New York, 1916), 109; Year-book of the International Law Commission, A/CN. 4,111. Vol. II. 73.

(2) A State may—

    (i) prescribe conditions for entry of aliens into its territory;

    (ii) except in special circumstances, refuse admission into its territory of aliens who do not possess travel documents to its satisfaction;

    (iii) make a distinction between aliens seeking admission for temporary sojourn and aliens seeking admission for permanent residence in its territory; and

    (iv) restrict or prohibit temporarily the entry into its territory of all or any class of aliens in its national or public interest.

Note : (1) The Delegation of Japan is of the view that in Subclause (iv) of Clause (2) of this Article the words "in times of or during armed conflicts or national emergency" should be substituted in place of the words "in its national or public interest."

(2) The Delegation of Indonesia stated that it preferred Clause (2) of Article (2) as adopted by the Committee at its Third Session in Colombo, which reads as follows: "A State admitting aliens into its territory may lay down by law, regulations or executive orders conditions for entry of aliens into its territory."

Commentary

Admission of aliens is a matter of discretion

Article 2 which deals with the regulation of admission of aliens embodies a well accepted concept of international jurisprudence, according to which no State is legally bound to admit foreign nationals into its territory, and that it may impose such conditions as it deems fit concerning such admission. This competence emanates from the basic concepts of territorial supremacy and self preservation of States.[2] Clause (1) of Article 2 establishes a rule of traditional international law and the practice adopted by several States whereby a State is under no duty to admit aliens and that admission of aliens is a matter of unfettered discretion of the State concerned. Following the general trend and considerations

---

2 Nishimura Ekiu v. United States of America, 142 U.S. 651, 659;   The Chinese Exclusion Case, 130 U.S. 581, 606-611.
Moore : A Digest of International Law Vol. IV, 67-96.

embodied in Clause (1) of Article 2, Clause (2) sets out in detail the right of a State to authorize entry of aliens on whatever conditions it may choose to impose and the right to refuse admission if its vital interests so require.

Conditions regulating admission of aliens

Under Sub-clause (i) of Clause (2) if a State decides to admit aliens within its domain it has the right to impose such conditions as it may deem fit.

Sub-clause (ii) of Clause (2) gives expression to the modern State practice on the admission of aliens. Though normally individuals wishing to visit foreign countries are provided, in accordance with the law of the State, with passports for the purpose, these are not normally granted to stateless persons and refugees who have themselves been admitted into the host State on humanitarian grounds. When these persons wish to visit or emigrate to another State, the State of temporary residence may provide them with some kind of travel documents which in a limited way take the place of passports. Under this sub-clause although normally an alien seeking admission into a State must be in possession of a valid passport yet as a State enjoys unrestricted discretion in regard to the admission of aliens it may at its discretion admit an alien, even if he does not possess a valid passport or travel document. Such cases are, however, exceptional as in the case of stateless persons or political refugees.

Sub-clause (iii) of Clause (2) incorporating a rule of State practice, establishes the right of the host State to make a distinction between an alien on a visit of short duration and the one who seeks admission into the State for purposes of permanent settlement i.e., an immigrant. Most States generally make a distinction between such foreign nationals as intend to settle down within their borders and such persons as intend merely to come for temporary stay in the country e.g., students, tourists, artists, etc. Normally States do not permit aliens to take up permanent residence on their territories without having asked for and having been granted the appropriate authorization therefor. But in the case of visitors, States generally permit their entrance provided they carry valid passports and comply with the applicable police and visa regulations relating to such class of foreigners. Even in the latter case, States have the competence to impose conditions embracing the terms of permitted sojourn or temporary residence. These may even be exemplified by a statutory stipulation requiring aliens staying on its territory for and after a specified period of time to apply for registration or comply with other requirements.[3]

Denial of Entry

Sub-clause (iv) of Clause (2) is an extension of another acknowledged rule of customary international law which empowers a State to restrict or even prohibit temporarily the admission of all aliens, or certain categories of foreigners during armed conflicts or national emergency such as internal revolt. The Committee has extended the rule to cover cases of national and public interest even apart from cases of national emergency especially taking into account the particular needs of the newly independent countries of Asia and Africa. This, however, is an exceptional provision intended to safeguard the peace and tranquillity as well as integrity of a State during certain contingencies. Since by virtue of its territorial supremacy a State possesses the competence to forbid the entrance of aliens into its territory, this sub-clause is in no way in conflict with the general principles of international law.

Opinions of Writers

Vattel observes: "A sovereign may prohibit entrance into its territory, either to all foreigners in general or to certain persons, or in certain cases or for certain purposes. according as the welfare of the State may require."[4] In the view of Oppenheim, "Apart from special treaties of commerce, friendship and the like, no State can claim the right for its subjects to enter into and reside on the territory of a foreign State. The reception of aliens is a matter of discretion and every State is by reason of its territorial supremacy competent to exclude aliens from the whole or any part of its territory."[5] According to Hackworth, "in the absence of treaty obligations, a State is under no duty to admit aliens into its territory. If it does admit them it may do so on such terms and conditions as may be deemed by it to be consonant with its national interests."[6] McNair says: "Apart from treaty stipulations to the contrary a State has a right to exclude all aliens including stateless persons or particular categories of such persons."[7]

---

3 Hines v. Davidowitz. 312 U.S. 52; Oppenheim : International Law Vol. I, 8th Ed., (1955), 676.
   Weis : Nationality and Statelessness in International Law, London, (1956), 219-236.
4 Vattel : International Law. Vol. I. s. 125, 231.
5. Oppenheim: International Law, op. cit., 675-678.
6 Hackworth: Digest of International Law. Vol. III, 717-718.
7 McNair International Law Opinions, (1956) Vol. II, 105.

Practice of Member States of the Committee

According to the relevant laws and regulations of the Member Countries of the Committee, in the absence of treaty obligations to the contrary, a State is not bound to admit aliens into its territory but if it does so, it may do so at its discretion on terms and conditions of its choosing. For instance, according to the Indonesian practice the State has the right to lay down by law or executive orders the conditions for the entry of aliens into its territory. The practice of these States reveals that an alien is not permitted to enter a State unless he is armed with a valid passport with the necessary visa endorsement thereon. A State enjoys absolute discretion in the matter of granting visas to foreign nationals. In this regard Japan follows a policy of reciprocity. Entry of foreigners into Japan is regulated by the Immigration Control Order III of April 1951, and matters relating to admission of aliens fall under the jurisdiction of the Immigration Office and the Ministry of Justice. In the Egyptian and Syrian Regions of the United Arab Republic the admission of aliens is regulated by the Egyptian Law No. 74 of 1952 and the Decree No. 54 of January 12 of 1952 respectively.

Generally all these States make a distinction between aliens seeking admission for temporary sojourn and those coming as immigrants into the country. They take the view that the State has the right to restrict or prohibit temporarily the admission of all aliens or certain class of aliens, if such course of action is considered necessary in its national or public interest. According to the practice of Japan, a State enjoys the right to forbid entrance of all aliens or any class of aliens in times of armed conflict or national emergency.

Practice of States other than Member States of the Committee

The Canadian practice has been indicated by the Supreme Court of New Brunswick in 1906 in the case of **Papageorgiou v. Turner,** in which Justice Barker declared that "the power of prohibiting aliens' entrance into a country is one which is recognized and acted upon by all civilized countries." The above view was elaborated in subsequent leading case in 1919, in which it was held that the Parliament of Canada, acting well within its right, has the right to prescribe the conditions upon which an alien may enter or be permitted to remain in Canada.[8]

In the United Kingdom, as in several other States, the right to admit, exclude or deport aliens is regarded as an incident of ter-

---

8 Rex v. Alamazoff (1919), 47 D.L.R. 533-535; Order in Council P.C. 2115 of Sept. 16, 1930, as amended by Order in Council P.C. 6229 (1951) S.C.R. 19 Dec. 28, 1950; Re Leon Ba Chai (1952) 4 D.L.R. 715.

ritorial sovereignty. The British practice reveals that apart from treaty stipulation to the contrary a State has the right to exclude aliens including stateless persons or particular categories of such persons from its territory.9 In the leading case of **Attorney-General of Canada v. Cairn** (1896), Lord Atkinson delivering the judgment of the Privy Council, quoted with approval the following passage from Vattel's Law of Nations: "One of the rights possessed by the supreme power in every State is the right to refuse to permit an alien to enter that State, to annex what conditions it pleases to the permission to enter it, and to expel or deport from the State, at pleasure, even a friendly alien especially if it considers his presence in the State as opposed to its peace, order and good government, or to its social or material interests."10

The regulations of the United States relating to the admission and exclusion of aliens are laid down in 8 United States Code,11 which declare that in the absence of treaty obligations to the contrary a State is under no duty to admit aliens into its territories. The Legal Adviser of the State Department stated that "a State is under no duty, in the absence of treaty obligations, to admit aliens to its territory. If it does admit them, it may do so on such terms and conditions as may be deemed by it to be consonant with its national interests." He added, that this is one of the incidents of sovereignty. Emphasizing this right of a State Mr. Justice Gray of the Supreme Court of the United States in the leading case of **Nishimura Ekiu v. United States** (1892) stated that "it is an accepted maxim of of international law, that every sovereign nation has the power, as inherent in sovereignty, and essential to self-preservation, to forbid the entrance of foreigners within its dominions, or to admit them only in such cases and upon such conditions as it may see fit to prescribe."12 In the **United States Ex. Rel, Knauff v. Shaughnessy** (1950), Mr. Justice Minton delivering the opinion of the court stated: "At the outset we wish to point out that an alien who seeks admission to this country (i.e., U.S.) may not do so under any claim of right. Admission of aliens to the U.S. is a privilege granted by the sovereign U.S. Government. Such privilege is granted to an alien only

---

9 McNair: International Law Opinions, Vol. II, 195;
Vattel: Law of Nations S. 125.

10 Musgrove v. Chun Teeong Toy, (1891) A.C. 272; 7 T.L.R. 378; 64 L.T. 378; Rex V. Home Secretary (1942), 1 All. E.R. 574; 2 All E.R. 232; Ex. part Greenberg and others (1947) 2 All. E.R. 550.

11 U.S. Code, SS. 100-299 & 1101-1362.

12 142 U.S. 651, 659; Fong Yue Ting v. United States, 149 U.S. 698, 705-707, Lem Moon Sing v. United States, 158 U.S. 538. Turner v. Williams, 194 U.S. 279.
Moore: Digest, op. cit., Vol. IV 71-80; Hyde: International Law, Vol. I, 216.

upon such terms and conditions as the U.S. shall prescribe. It must be exercised in accordance with the procedure which the U.S. provides."13 Further Mr. Justice Clark of the United States Supreme Court reaffirming the above view stated in the case of **Shaughnessy v. United States ex rel Mezei (1953)** that "Courts have long recognized the power to expel or exclude aliens as a fundamental sovereign attribute exercised by the government's political departments largely immune from judicial control . . . (alien's) right to enter the United States depends on the Congressional will. . . ."14 Article 5 of the French Regulation of November 2, 1945 provides that, "any alien must, in order to enter France, bear the document and visas required by international conventions and regulations in force." In carrying out the provisions of Article 1 of the decree of June 30, 1946, establishing the conditions of entry and· residence of aliens in France, the Ministries of Foreigners and of the Interior have promulgated an order on January 9, 1949 which by its Article 1 requires that any alien seeking entry into French Continental territory must "hold a national passport, or travel document in lieu of passport, valid and bearing a French visa." However, Article 2 of the same order provides that "nationals of States having entered into a reciprocal agreement with France for the waiver of this formality are exempted from the visa for days not exceeding three months in length at a time." The acknowledged right of the Minister of the Interior in France broad as it may be, is not absolutely discretionary and can only be used in the interests of "public security". The Conseil d'Etat (Council of State) will check the accuracy and materiality of the reasons given in support of the decision denying entry into French territory.15 In the **Residence of Alien Trader Case (1954),** the Administrative Court of Appeal at Münster (W. Germany) held that there was no rule of international law which conferred a right of residence on aliens as every State was entitled in its discretion to restrict or refuse the admission of aliens. The courts of most other States have also taken the same view on the question of admission.16 In, **in re Di Cesare,** the Federal Supreme

---

13 338 U.S. 537; 70 S. Ct. 309 (1950).
14 Hackworth: Digest of International Law, Vol. III, 717; 289 U.S. 422, 425; 345 U.S. 206; 96 L. Edn. 73 S. Ct. 625.
15 Marcon, Conseil D'Etat, France, (1952), Katz & Brewster: The Law of International Transactions & Relations, (London 1960) 18-21.
16 The State (At the prosecution of Hermann Goortz) v. The Minister of State (1947), Irish Law Times (1948), 34. In re Carles Wunchs (1935), 46 Semanarie Judicial 5· Epcca 3799; In re Wong (1949), Semanarie Judicial de la Federation 5a Epoca vol. 99, part 3, 2254. In Lay v. La Nacion (1939), 37 Registro Judicial 22. Van In Resenburg v. Ballinger, (1950) 4 S.A.R. 427. Mohamed v. Principal Immigration Officer (1951) 3 S.A.R. 884; Hoosain v. Van Der Merwe, N.O. and others (1935) 3 S.A.R. 535; Harneker v. Gaol Supdt., (1951) 3 S.A.R. 430 (c) Annuaire de l'Institute de Droit International, XII, 226; Scott: Resolutions of the Institute of International Law, 104.

Court of Argentina took the view that the political authorities have exclusive responsibility and power with respect to the entry of aliens.[17] Several international agreements and conventions concluded since 1920 relating to the admission of refugees are based on the principle that a State has the discretion in the matter of reception of aliens on its territory. In a number of cases the Governing Body Committee on Freedom of Association, one of the Committees of the International Labour Organisation has been confronted with questions relating to the admission and expulsion of aliens. The Committee has taken the view that the admission and expulsion of aliens are matters within national discretion.[17a]

Principles embodied in certain Conventions

Incorporating the above view, the draft Convention relating to the "International Regulation on the Admission and Expulsion of Aliens", adopted in 1892 by the **Institute of International Law** provides as follows: "The law of nations has not yet forbidden a State to exercise the largest discretion in establishing tests of undesirability of aliens seeking admission to its territory, and to that end, to enforce discrimination of its own devising." The **Havana Convention on the Status of Aliens,** signed in 1928, provides in Article 1 that "States have the right to establish by means of laws the conditions under which foreigners may enter and reside in their territory". The **International Conference on "Treatment of Foreigners"** held at Paris in 1929 approved the following provision in this regard: "Each of the High Contracting Parties remains free to regulate the admission of foreigners to its territory and to make this admission subject to conditions limiting its duration, or the rights of foreigners to travel, sojourn, settle, choose their place of residence, and move from place to place."[18]

Article 3

A State shall not refuse to an alien entry into its territory on the ground only of his race, religion, sex or colour.

Commentary

Discriminations against aliens

This article rules out discrimination by a State in the matter of admission of aliens into its territory. Refusal of admission to an alien must not be only on account of his race, religion, sex or colour. Although under international law, the reception of aliens is

---

17 Annual Digest (1938-1940) Case No. 119, 364.
17a Jenks, C.W.: The International Protection of Trade Union Freedom, (New York, 1957), 438-442.
18 League of Nations Doc. C.I.T.E. 62, 1930, II. 5, 419-421.

451

a matter of discretion and every State is by reason of its territorial supremacy competent to exclude aliens from the whole or any part of its territory, discrimination in this regard on the basis of the alien's race, religion, sex or colour has been condemned by States as immoral and as not being consonant with the concept of human dignity.

Opinions of Writers

National legislations that mark discrimination against aliens residing in or emigrating from particular geographical areas, or against those belonging to a particular race, are in the view of **Hyde**, "tokens of arrogance that defy explanation and produce resentment on the part of the States whose nationals happen to be signed out for exclusion."[19] **Fenwick** says: "the exclusion of certain races as being unassimilable is, ... a political rather than a legal question."[20] Broadly, in the view of publicists, since international law does not forbid a State to exercise the largest discretion in formulating tests of undesirability of aliens seeking admission into its territory, discriminatory exclusion laws could be challenged merely on grounds of policy rather than on those of legality. Discrimination on account of race, colour and religion is also condemned by civilized nations as an anachronism in the present day world. In the view of **Hudson** and **Brierly**, respect for human rights is an important element in securing peaceful and friendly relations among nations.[21]

Practice of Member States of the Committee

In the matter of admission of aliens, the States participating in the Committee do not appear to practise any discrimination merely on account of the individual's religion, sex or colour. But Japan takes the view that such discriminatory treatment may be called for towards a State which indulges in such practice.

Practice of States other than Member States of the Committee

Generally foreign visitors and those who seek admission for temporary stay are permitted to enter into a State. Taking advantage of the fact that the law of nations has not as yet forbidden a State to exercise largest discretion in establishing tests of undesirability of aliens seeking entrance into its territory, several Western States have been excluding certain classes of aliens as undesirable for purposes of immigration. Originally the United States permitted unfettered immigration and it was only after World War I that

---

19 Hyde: International Law, Vol. I, 218.
20 Fenwick: International Law, Vol. I, 3rd ed., 269.
21 Lauterpacht: International Law and Human Rights, (London 1950), 154.

quantitative legislative restrictions were introduced. In 1921 as a rule of emergency, and in 1924 as a definitive legislative policy of selective immigration the number of immigrants was limited by the establishment of quotas for the various countries. Thereafter restrictions became increasingly stringent culminating in the provisions of the Immigration and Nationality Act of 1952 (popularly known as Mc Carren Act). According to this Act only the alien applicant who fulfils the legal prerequisites and comes within the quota is entitled to admission. The quotas were computed by means of a complicated method, taking into account the respective numbers of immigrants prior to 1920.[22] Generally, aliens who are ineligible for American citizenship have been excluded. The practical effect of such a scheme according to Secretary Hughes was to single out Japanese immigrants for exclusion. Likewise, the matter of Chinese and Asiatic immigration has been regulated by the so-called "barred-zone" provisions of the immigration laws which with exceptions exclude foreign nationals of the Asiatic barred zone including natives of certain islands near Asia and a portion of the Asiatic mainland defined in the law as lying between specified parallels of latitude and meridians of longitude. The 'barred zone' includes the eastern portions of Baluchistan and Afghanistan, all but the extreme northern portion of Oman, most of India, Turkestan, Nepal, Bhutan, Siam, former French Indo-China and the Malaya Peninsula. It also includes the islands of Ceylon, Sumatra, Java, Borneo, Celebes, Timor, and New Guinea.[23] But natives of the barred zone in certain enumerated occupations of status together with their legal wives and children below the age of 16 accompanying them or following to join them are exempt from the above excluding provision.[24]

The laws and regulations of Australia, Canada and South Africa exclude aliens of the Asiatic races from their territories as prohibited immigrants. Also the laws of Brazil and Canada, as those of the United States of America, have adopted the quota system regulating the entry of alien immigrants. It appears that Panama imposes a heavier re-entry tax on the nationals of some States, especially the Chinese.[25]

---

22 Nussbaum: American-Swiss Private International Law, (New York, 1958). 13.

23 Moore: Digest, op. cit., Vol. IV,
Clement L. Bouve: Exclusion and Expulsion of Aliens in the United States. 85-111.

24 Hyde: International Law, op. cit., 224-25.

25 Re Munshi Singh, British Columbia Court of Appeal, 1914 20 B.C.R. 243; Mackenzie, Norman and Laing; Canada and the Law of Nations (1938) 269-272. The Immigration Restriction Act 22 of 1913 of South Africa. The Australian Immigration Acts 1901-1930; Ex parte Gurwitz (1937) Netal P.D. 185; Lay v. La Nacion (1939), 37 Registre Judicial 227.

It may be observed that to exclude all aliens impartially raises no issue of discrimination whereas the exclusion of the citizens of a particular State or region or race unjustifiably denies to that State a right or privilege accorded to others. Such discriminatory exclusions and immigration policies which have been of late showing reversion to the practice of excluding aliens for political, economic or racial reasons, are regarded as violative of the spirit of international law and are not in keeping with that State's membership in the international community. Further, the total exclusion of nationals of one particular State might diplomatically be regarded as an affront or as an unfriendly act towards the State concerned.

Article 4

Admission into the territory of a State may be refused to an alien:

(1) who is in a condition of vagabondage, beggary, or vagrancy;

(2) who is of unsound mind or is mentally defective;

(3) who is suffering from a loathsome, incurable or contagious disease of a kind likely to be prejudicial to public health;

(4) who is a stowaway, a habitual narcotic user, an unlawful dealer in opium or narcotics, a prostitute, a procurer or a person living on the earnings of prostitution;

(5) who is an indigent person or a person who has no adequate means of supporting himself or has no sufficient guarantee to support him at the place of his destination;

(6) who is reasonably suspected to have committed or is being tried or has been prosecuted for serious infractions of law abroad;

(7) who is reasonably believed to have committed an extraditable offence abroad or is convicted of such an offence abroad;

(8) who has been expelled or deported from another State; and

(9) whose entry or presence is likely to affect prejudicially its national or public interest.

Commentary

Excludable Aliens

Article 4 incorporates a widely recognised rule of State practice regarding the exclusion of certain undesirable aliens. Under

Clause (1), a State may exclude certain socially unfit persons who are generally excluded by the immigration laws of most States. This category includes among others, paupers, professional beggars, and persons who have no settled homes, etc. Similarly Clause (2) entitles a State to refuse admission to aliens who are mentally defective. This category generally comprises idiots, imbeciles, insane persons, epileptics etc., as these are regarded as physically and socially unfit. Normally an individual who has been certified by the medical officer at the port of entry as being mentally defective is denied admission into the State concerned. Clause (3) empowers a State to exclude individuals afflicted with loathsome or virulently contagious disease such as tuberculosis, cholera, trachoma etc. In the interests of the health of the nation and in order to avoid their becoming a public charge these persons are not permitted to enter the State. Under Clause (4), a State has the right to exclude certain morally unfit persons such as stowaways, drug addicts, persons engaged in illegal opium trade, individuals seeking admission into the State for purposes of prostitution, persons procuring or attempting to procure or import prostitutes and persons who generally live on the earnings of prostitution. Clause (5) excludes from admission persons who have no financial support or who have no other means of supporting themselves after reception into the State, lest they should become a public charge. By way of exception to this rule certain unaccompanied children, if otherwise unobjectionable, are admitted by some States if they are not likely to become a public charge in the State of residence. Clause (6) establishes the right of a State to exclude an alien criminal who has served his sentence and also a person who is reasonably suspected to have perpetrated a crime or one who has escaped from jail or police custody before being convicted of a crime involving moral turpitude. Under Clause (7), those who are suspected to have committed extraditable offences abroad or those who have been already convicted of such offences and who have undergone their punishments could be refused admission. It may be added that persons convicted of or those who admit having committed certain well defined political crimes are excluded from the ambit of this rule. Clause (8) incorporating another rule of State practice lays down that an alien who has been previously deported from a State may not be received in a State. This sub-clause includes foreign nationals arrested and deported in pursuance of the applicable laws of the land and aliens who have been formally ordered to be deported. Clause (9) establishes the right of a State to refuse admission to an alien if his presence on its territory is most likely to endanger its national interests, including disturbance to its peace and tranquillity. Generally most States deny admission to anarchists, members of illegal organisations and other undesirable individuals of like character.

Practice of Member States of the Committee

As in other States, Iraq and India claim unlimited discretion in the matter of exclusion of aliens from their territories, without assigning any reasons therefor. Only unobjectionable non-immigrant aliens are admitted into the countries of the Committee. The Participating Countries of the Committee claim the right to deny admission to certain categories of aliens for political, economic, health, moral and other reasons, but not on merely racial grounds. Burma and Egypt exclude the entry of unskilled labourers, and those likely to endanger public security and the general morality of the respective States. Undesirable persons are not allowed to enter Ceylon, Indonesia, Iraq and Japan. Indigent people, those suffering from incurable disease, those who are guilty of extraditable crimes, those who have been previously expelled from Syria, those who are likely to endanger the security of the country, prostitutes and their collaborators and the smugglers of opium, hashish and other narcotic drugs are denied admission into the Syrian Region of the United Arab Republic. But aliens seeking entry into Syria for purposes of medical treatment are normally received provided that they have adequate means to support themselves and that they have obtained the necessary prior permission for the purpose from the Ministry of Foreign Affairs.

Practice of States other than Member States of the Committee

Practice of States gives expression to the maxim that a sovereign nation has the broadest right as inherent in sovereignty and indispensable to self-preservation to refuse admission to all aliens into its territory at will and that a State is under no duty to admit all aliens. No State can question its authority to determine as to what aliens or categories of aliens are undesirable and excludable. Most States have on their statute books immigration laws which contain provisions concerning excludable aliens. From an international point of view the immigration laws generally contain two features: (1) the broad definition of the term immigrant and (2) the mode and extent of the restriction placed upon immigration generally.

The immigration laws of the United States generally exclude the following aliens: insane individuals, paupers or vagrants, diseased persons, criminals, polygamists, anarchists, members of unlawful organisations, prostitutes and procurers, indentured labourers, persons likely to become a public charge, persons previously deported, persons excluded from admission, persons financially assisted to come to the United States, stowaways, children unaccompanied, natives of the Asiatic barred zone, illiterates and accompanying aliens in certain cases.[25a]   Under the laws of the United Kingdom undesirable foreigners are not permitted to enter her territories. The undesirable aliens, according to her laws and regulations, are those who had been convicted of a felony or misdemeanour or had been in receipt of parochial relief.   They also exclude alien immigrants who are afflicted with disease and who have not the means of decently supporting themselves or their dependents. The laws and regulations of most of the States exclude more or less similar classes of aliens from admission for the same reasons set out above. Further, in times of war or national emergency in the interests of public safety, exceptional restrictions if not prohibitions in addition to normal restrictions, are imposed upon the entry of aliens into the State concerned, which include withholding of immigration visas, passport or tourist visas and documents of like character.

Article 5

A State may admit an alien seeking entry into its territory for the purpose of transit, tourism or study, on the condition that he is forbidden from making his residence in its territory permanent.

Commentary

Visits of short duration are to be permitted

This Article embodies a principle which States mostly follow in actual practice. Generally, States make a distinction between aliens who intend to settle down permanently in the country and those who intend only to travel as tourists, students or trainees.[26]   The latter category of aliens are not subjected to stringent restrictions and qualifications.

Practice of Member States of the Committee

Burma and Iraq permit the entry of both the classes of foreigners without any distinction but India and Indonesia differentiate between tourists and permanent settlers. Broadly, the laws relating to entry of non-immigrant aliens are less stringent. Although immigration to Ceylon is generally not permitted, her laws make no distinction between the tourists, whether they are for a short or for a prolonged visit. In India admission for permanent settle-

---

25a Hyde: International Law, Vol. I, 221-226.
26 Oppenheim: International Law, Vol. I, op. cit., 676.

457

ment is generally not feasible. In Indonesia and in the Egyptian Region of the United Arab Republic foreigners seeking admission for permanent settlement are granted permission for the purpose only if the latter are considered to be capable of contributing to the culture or wealth of the country concerned. Aliens are admitted into the Syrian Region of the United Arab Republic on condition that they will not seek employment during their stay in Syria. Once they obtain the authorization for permanent residence they are at liberty to look for a job therein. Japan makes a distinction between the permanent residents, the aliens who enter for prolonged visit and those who enter as mere tourists for short stay. In the Egyptian Region of the United Arab Republic a distinction is generally made between ordinary visitors and immigrants. Its immigration policy favours foreigners who are likely to contribute to the national wealth either culturally or financially. Further, in order to attract more and more tourists to the country it has rationalized its visa and customs regulations and other formalities as well.

Practice of States other than Member States of the Committee

The generality of State practice establishes the rule that an alien is not allowed to settle down in a country without having asked for it and having obtained the necessary authorization for the purpose. Tourists are normally admitted into a State if they satisfy the routine police and visa regulations of the State concerned. Some States permit the entry of aliens for permanent settlement only if they are specialists and skilled technicians. For instance, the Mexican Immigration Law admits technicians, and Singapore permits the entry of foreign specialists for specified periods. Normally entry permits are granted to such foreign specialists only when suitable nationals are not available.[27] Immigrants to the United States are required to comply with the terms and conditions laid down in the Immigration Law of 1924. Non-immigrants are generally required to comply with the applicable police and visa regulations which are less cumbersome and stringent than those that are applicable to immigrants.[28] The term immigrant is defined in these terms— " . . . Any alien departing from any place outside the United States destined for the United States, except (1) a government official, his family, attendants, servants, and employees, (2) an alien visiting the United States temporarily as a tourist or temporarily for business or pleasure, (3)

---

27 The Hindustan Times, Delhi, February 23, 1959.
28 The United States has recently eased its visa restrictions to encourage more foreign tourists. Under the new regulations, a foreigner can have an existing United States visa renewed instead of having to apply for a new one when his old visa expires. The Times, London, May 15, 1961.

an alien in continuous transit through the United States, (4) an alien lawfully admitted to the United States who later goes in transit from one part of the United States to another through foreign continuous territory, (5) a bona fide alien seaman serving as such on a vessel arriving at a port of the United States and seeking to enter temporarily the United States solely in pursuit of his calling as a seaman, and (6) an alien entitled to enter the United States solely to carry on trade between the United States and the foreign State of which he is a national under and in pursuance of the provisions of a treaty of commerce and navigation, and his wife, and his unmarried children under twenty-one years of age, if accompanying or following to join him."[29] Further, the United States like most States admits freely into its territory those American residents who are returning to the United States from a temporary visit abroad. It may be added that although Immigration Law of the United States normally prohibits immigration of the aliens of the Asiatic barred zone. certain categories of individuals from the barred zone are nevertheless permitted to enter. These persons include **inter alia,** government officials, religious teachers including missionaries, lawyers, chemists, civil engineers, medical practitioners, teachers, students, artists, merchants and travellers for curiosity and pleasure.[30]

Article 6

A State shall have the right to offer or provide asylum in its territory to political refugees or to political offenders on such conditions as the State may stipulate as being appropriate in the circumstances.

Commentary

The right of asylum

This Article establishes the right of a State to grant asylum on its territory to foreign nationals fleeing from political, racial or religious persecution in their own State. Just as a State possesses the undoubted right to grant or refuse admission to political refugees into its territory, it has also the right to stipulate conditions which a political fugitive is expected to comply with after his entrance into the host State. Under international law it is the duty of every State to prevent all individuals including fugitive aliens living on its territory from endangering the territorial integrity of

---

29 Hyde: International Law. op. cit.. Vol. I. 226-227; Secitons 3. 43 Stat 153, 154, as amended on July 6, 1932, 47 Stat 607, 8 U.S.C.A. E. 203.
30 Hyde: Internationa Law, op. cit., Vol. I, 225-227.

another State by organizing expeditions or by preparing common crimes against that State.[31]

Practice of Member States of the Committee

While the laws of Indonesia, Iraq and the U.A.R. have specifically provided for the grant of asylum to political refugees, those of Burma, Ceylon, India and Japan are silent in this regard. But Burma and Japan have in fact been granting asylum to political offenders. According to Iraq and the U.A.R. asylum to political refugees is a well established institution under customary international law. The Participating Countries of the Committee are of the view that the right of asylum is nothing more than the liberty of every State to grant a political refugee asylum requesting for it, that the fugitive has no legal right at international law to demand such asylum and that the only international legal right involved herein is that of the State of refuge itself to grant asylum at will.

Universal Declaration of Human Rights and Asylum

Article 14(1) of the Universal Declaration of Human Rights, approved by the General Assembly of the United Nations in 1948, which provides that "Every one has the right to seek and to enjoy in other countries asylum from persecution", does not, in the view of the Participating Countries of the Committee, impose any legal obligation on a State to grant asylum to political offenders and to receive persecuted aliens on its domain.

Vigilant Supervision of the political refugee

As regards the duty of surveillance of a political refugee by the receiving State there does not appear to be unanimity among the Member Countries of the Committee. While the laws of Burma and Ceylon are silent in this regard, the law of Japan does not admit of such surveillance at all. Both India and the U.A.R. are not in favour of surveillance of political refugees by the host State. Iraq and Indonesia take the view that this may be resorted to only if it becomes necessary. Where a political refugee misuses the hospitality of the host State, Burma, Ceylon and Japan are inclined to the view that he may be deported, but according to Indonesia and Iraq, he could be tried and punished just like any other criminal offender. On the other hand, the U.A.R. takes the view that the State concerned should forthwith draw his attention to such impropriety before a decision in favour of other appropriate action could be taken. But if he still presisted in such objectionable poli-

31 Oppenheim: International Law, Vol. I, op. cit., 678

tical activities, such refractory alien could be deported. In any case the deportation should not amount to extradition in disguise.

Practice of States other than Member States of the Committee

The right of political asylum has been developed during the 19th century largely under the influence of the Belgian practice. Belgium incorporated the principle of non-extraditability of political offenders in its Extradition Law in 1833. This principle has been embodied in course of time in the extradition laws of several other States. Further, several countries began incorporating the Belgian principle into their extradition treaties either verbatim or with minor variations.[32] As this right has always been upheld by the practice of States since the 19th century, it has crystallized into a rule of customary international law according to which, in the absence of extradition treaties stipulating to the contrary, a State is under no legal duty to refuse admission to a fugitive alien into its territory or in case he has been admitted, to expel or deliver him up to the prosecuting State. Moreover, States have always been upholding their competence to grant asylum if they choose to do so. In re Fabijan, it was held that if in the matter of the grant of asylum the jurisdiction of a territorial State was restricted, such a restriction could be possible only from the relevant provision of a treaty between the parties concerned.[33] The so-called right of asylum according to general State practice is nothing more than the freedom of a State to grant or refuse at its discretion asylum to an alien requesting for it. It may be added that the right of a State to grant asylum has been recognized as an institution of humanitarian character.[34] To sum up, the right of asylum does not mean that the individual has any right to claim the favour of asylum from a State. nor does it connote that a State is under any semblance of legal duty to grant it when sought for since under international law a State has the unlimited discretion to decide whether or not to grant such asylum to an alien.

Asylum in modern Constitutions

From the fact that Constitutions of several States contain provisions for the grant of asylum to political offenders, one cannot deduce that the granting of this privilege has become a general principle of law recognized by civilized nations. However, this so-called right belongs to the State and not to the refugee concerned.

---

32 Oppenheim: International Law, op. cit., Vol. I (1957), 679.
33 In re Fabijan, Annual Digest and Report of Public International Law Cases, 1933-34, 360-372.
   Oppenheim: International Law, Vol. I, op. cit., 677.
34 Article 3 of the Convention on Political Asylum adopted in 1933 by the Pan American Conference.

In the United States, although normally a distinction is made between individuals who voluntarily seek refuge in its territory from political persecution in their own country, and those who are compelled to emigrate to the United States under compulsion exercised by the authorities of their Government, the practice reveals that she grants refuge to persons whose lives are believed to be in actual jeopardy by reason of their political activities in their home State, and that such individuals applying for sanctuary therein are customarily admitted for a reasonable period under a liberal interpretation of the immigration laws, provided they can establish to the satisfaction of the competent authorities that their personal safety is actually in danger, and that the offences for which they have been indicted are not such as would render them inadmissible under the regulations or orders of the United States.[35]

Article 7

(1) Subject to the conditions imposed for his admission into the State, and subject also to the local laws, regulations and orders, an alien shall have the right—

(i) to move freely throughout the territory of the State; and

(ii) to reside in any part of the territory of the State.

(2) The State may, however, require an alien to comply with provisions as to registration or reporting or otherwise so as to regulate or restrict the right of movement and residence as it may consider appropriate in any special circumstances or in the national or public interest.

Note : The Delegation of Indonesia expressed preference for the text adopted at the Colombo Session in Clause (1) of this Article, which reads as follows : (1) "Without prejudice to the competence of a State to regulate the right of sojourn and residence which shall include the liberty to compel an alien to comply with its requirements as to registration, an alien shall be entitled to travel freely, sojourn, or reside in the territories of the State in conformity with the laws and regulations in force therein".

Commentary

Alien's freedom of movement

Under this Article although the host State has, in the absence of treaty obligations to the contrary, the undoubted right to regu-

---

35 Hackworth: Digest of International Law, Vol. III. 734;
   Hyde: International Law, op. cit., Vol. I, 229.

late the admission of aliens to its territory by imposing such terms and conditions as may be deemed by it to be consonant with its national interests and also it has the authority to regulate his movement during his sojourn or stay within its borders, the alien shall have, subject to the applicable local laws, regulations and executive orders, the right to move about freely therein and shall have the freedom to reside in any part of the host State.

Registration of aliens

Further, as it is not uncommon for a State to require the registration of foreign nationals sojourning or residing in its territory, this Article establishes the right of the host State to demand from the alien compliance with its laws and regulations relating to alien registration, periodical reporting, etc., which are intended to keep track of the aliens within its borders. Furthermore, as under clause (2) of this Article, the State of residence, if its national interests so require, has the right to restrict the alien's right of movement and of residence, clause (2) when read clause (1) of the Article serves to limit the ambit of the alien's freedom to choose the place of residence, his right to move from place to place etc., depending upon the peace and tranquillity of the host State as well as the discretion of that State to decide for itself whether or not it can allow such freedom of action to the alien after the latter's reception. This Article gives expression to the general State practice on this subject.

Opinions of writers

Affirming the normal practice of States in this regard, **Oppenheim** states : "A State can . . . as Great Britain did in the former times and again during the First World War and since, compel them to register their names for the purpose of keeping them under control."[36] The views of several other writers are to the same effect.

Practice of the Member Countries of the Committee

Subject to exigencies or emergencies aliens in the Member Countries of the Committee are permitted to travel about or to reside in any part of the State they visit. Registration of aliens is required in all the countries participating in the Committee. Under the Aliens Registration Law, an alien entering Japan must notify his presence to the mayor of the city concerned within 60 days after his arrival, and this is done in the form of a request for permission to stay. Any change of address will have to be

---

36 Oppenheim: International Law, Vol. I, op. cit., 689.

notified to the authorities within 15 days of such change. Foreigners in the Egyptian Region of the U.A.R. are required to notify their arrival to the Foreigner's Department. They are expected to furnish the authorities with all the relevant information required by the latter, including the purpose and the possible duration of the visit. A Residence Card must be obtained in case the stay is likely to last more than six months. As regards the alien's obligation to register at every town he visits in the host State, there is no unanimity in the practice of the Member States of the Committee. For instance, while an alien in the U.A.R. is normally expected to notify the authorities of any change of address, he is not required to do so in Burma, Ceylon, Iraq and Japan. Even in the U.A.R. exceptions to the general rule are permissible, for instance, tourists are not required to notify the change of address. Although an alien in India is not enjoined to register his arrival or presence at each and every place of his visit, he is nevertheless expected to keep the authorities informed of his movements in the country. Despite the requirement that a visitor to Indonesia is bound to register only at the place of entry, the managers of hotels or boarding houses are under a duty to maintain registers of all aliens staying in their hotels or boarding houses as the case may be. Normally, the duty of the alien to register emanates from the State's right to regulate or restrict the movement and residence of aliens within its borders. Thus Indonesia, like most other States takes the view that a State possesses the right to regulate the alien's right of sojourn or residence on its territory. An alien's right to travel about freely in the country or to reside anywhere within her borders must be subject to his complying with the applicable laws and regulations including those relating to registration therein.

Practice of States other than Member States of the Committee

It is not uncommon for a State to require registration of foreign nationals sojourning or residing within its borders. Some States compel aliens to register their names only in times of national emergency such as war or internal disturbances merely for the purpose of keeping track of them. This power is inherent in the sovereignty of the State and is deemed essential for its self-preservation.

During 1917-1918, several States of the United States of America passed suitable laws empowering the governor to require registration of aliens as and when the United States becomes a belligerent or when public necessity requires such a step.[37] Some States of the United States have passed registration laws during 1939-1940, e.g., the Pennsylvania Alien Registration Act of 1939 provides for the limitation, regulation and registration of aliens as a distinct group for reasons of security of the nation. Moreover, in several States of the United States of America even the municipalities imposed the duty of registration on aliens residing within their jurisdiction. Aliens need not carry cards and may only be punished for wilful failure to register. Section 31 of the United States Act of Congress approved on June 28, 1940 makes it obligatory on the part of every alien "now or hereafter in the United States 14 years of age or older, who remains in the United States for 30 days or longer, to apply for registration and to be finger-printed." Provision is also made in the same section for the registration by parents or legal guardians of alien children under 14 years of age. The Supreme Court of the United States of America has on several occasions reaffirmed the undoubted right of the United States Congress "to provide a system of (alien's) registration and identification . . . and to take all proper means to carry out the system which it provides" in this regard.[38]

In the United Kingdom normally the Secretary of State is empowered to make regulations relating to the landing and embarking of aliens and the conditions to be imposed upon them. In addition to or in substitution for the general restrictions, an alien or a class of aliens could be subjected to such special restrictions as the Secretary of State may deem fit in the public interest to order [Aliens Order, 1920, Art. (II) (1)]. Such special restrictions relate to residence, reporting to the police, registration, occupation, employment, the use or possession of any machine, apparatus, arms and explosives, or other articles, as well as other matters deemed necessary. The Aliens Order of 1920 deals with the following subjects: duty of a householder with whom an alien stays, alien's registration, certain particulars to be supplied by the alien, his exemption from registration, issue of registration certificate and the duties of keepers of premises.[39] In September 1939

---

37 Conn. Gen. Stats. (1930), Tit. 59. Sec. Fla Comp. Gen., Laws (1927), Sec. 2078; Iowa Code (1938), Sec. 503; La. Gen. Stats. (DART, 1939), tit. 3, Sec. 282; Me. Rev. Stats. (1930), ch. 34. Sec. 3; N. H. Pub. Laws. (1926) Ch. 154; N.Y. Cons. Laws. (Executive Law), Sec. 10.

38 142. U.S. 651, 459; 149. U.S. 698. 705-707.

39 Halsbury's Laws of England. Third Revised Edition. Vol. XV London 1950. 256-257.

an additional restriction requiring an alien to furnish particulars about his business address to the registration officer was imposed[40]

Principles embodied in certain Conventions

The same principle has been adumbrated in the Inter-American Convention on the Status of Aliens (1928), Article 2 of which declares that "Foreigners are subject as are nationals to local jurisdiction and laws, due consideration being given to the limitations expressed in conventions and treaties".[41] The International Conference on Treatment of Foreigners held in Paris in 1929, excluded from its consideration problems relating to the admission of aliens, although the proceedings indicate approval of an unperfected text which provided, in part in these terms: "Each of the High Contracting Parties remains free to regulate the admission of foreigners to its territory and to make this admission subject to conditions limiting its duration, or the rights of foreigners to travel, sojourn, settle, choose their place of residence, and move from place to place".[42]

Article 8

Subject to local laws, regulations and orders, an alien shall have the right—

    (1) to freedom from arbitrary arrest;

    (2) to freedom to profess and practise his own religion;

    (3) to have protection of the executive and police authorities of the State;

    (4) to have access to the courts of law; and

    (5) to have legal assistance.

Note : (a) The Delegation of Ceylon was of the view that in clause (2) the expression "to freedom of religious belief and practice" should be substituted;

(b) The Delegations of Burma and Indonesia suggested retention of clause (2) of the Draft adopted at the Colombo Session which provides that :

"Aliens shall enjoy on a basis of equality with nationals protection of the local laws".

The Delegations of Iraq and Japan had no objection to the retention of this clause.

---

40 Order dated September 18, 1939, S.R. & O. 1939 No. 1059.
41 Hudson: International Legislation, Vol. IV, 2374.
   Briggs: The Law of Nations, op. cit., 530.
42 League Document C.I.T.E. 62, 1930, II, 5, 419-421.
   Briggs: The Law of Nations, op. cit., 536.

Alien's rights to liberty, freedom of religion and protection for his person and property

Following the general trend and considerations of Articles 7, 11 and 12, Article 8 guarantees to aliens certain essential rights relating to their liberty, freedom of conscience, protection from executive and judicial organs of the State of residence. All these four articles, generally speaking, aim to secure to an individual certain "essential rights" which Mr. Garcia Amador describes as "fundamental human rights"[43] According to the jurisprudence of the General Claims Commissions, established under bilateral agreements between the United States and certain Latin American States, these were known as the "Minimum Standards of International Law" which every State must normally guarantee to foreign nationals on its territory. A vast majority of the modern written Constitutions have incorporated these provisions, among others, as "Fundamental Rights" of the citizens. Broadly, the rights and freedoms set out in these four articles are made available to citizens and non-citizens alike in conformity with the applicable local laws, regulations and orders. From the fact that these rights and freedoms are usually subject to such limitations and restrictions as the laws, regulations and orders expressly prescribe for reasons of internal security, public order, health and morality of the State of residence, it is clear that they are not absolute rights. Further, it may be added that although the leading Western nations had all along been asserting that these essential rights of aliens flowed from the duty of States to alien residents under customary international law, scores of bilateral treaties and agreements have been, at the same time, concluded by these nations providing for the enjoyment of these rights and privileges for the nationals of the contracting parties within the territories of the other contracting party in accordance with the standards of reciprocity and national treatment.[44]

Freedom from arbitrary arrest

Under clause (1) of Article 8, the alien has the right to freedom from arbitrary arrest. The term "freedom from arbitrary arrest" indicates that an alien cannot be arrested unless he has acted in violation of a valid local law. In

---

43 Yearbook of International Law Commission, 1958, Vol. II, 71.
44. Neer Claim (1928).
   Schwarzenberger: International Law, Vol. I, 3rd ed., 200-205.
   Per Judge Black in Hines v. Davidewitz et al. (1941) 312, U.S., 52.

case of arrest, he has the right to be informed of the grounds of such arrest, or the reasons for such arrest. He must be produced before the appropriate authorities of the State within a reasonable period of time after his arrest for adjudication of the alleged offence. He has the right to choose and employ a counsel for purposes of his defence. Finally, the appropriate rules of procedure must have been complied with by the authorities concerned. Deviation from the rules of natural justice may give rise to a claim for damages as under international law failure to fulfil an international obligation gives rise to international responsibility of the State concerned.

Freedom of religion

Subject to the local laws, regulations and orders, clause (2) secures for the alien the right to profess and practise his own religion. Normally, the right to profess connotes the right to talk freely about one's own religion and the right to practise the same indicates the right to give expression to one's faith by means of private or public religious pursuits.

Alien's protection by the State organs

Incorporating a well established rule of customary international law, clause (3) guarantees to the alien the protection of the administrative or executive organs of the State of residence. Since an alien after his entry into a State falls under the territorial jurisdiction of that State, international law imposes on the latter the duty of affording reasonable protection for his life, liberty and property. Experience has shown that international controversies of the gravest moment have arisen in the past from the wrongs to another's subjects inflicted, or permitted by a government.[45] Failure to safeguard adequately the life, freedom, human dignity or property of aliens has given rise to international responsibility of the State concerned.[46] According to modern State practice, aliens normally enjoy the protection of the State organs on a footing of equality with the nationals.

Right of access to courts of law

Giving expression to practice of States and a rule of traditional international law, clause (4) specifically lays down that an alien is entitled to have the right of access to the local courts of law for the vindication of his legal rights. As in the absence of a provision of this character, the alien's essential rights may tend to

---

45 Hines v. Davidowitz et Al (1941), 312 U.S. 52.
46 Schwarzenberger: International Law, Vol. I, op. cit., 200-201.

diminish in importance, this right is regarded as indispensable for the benefit of aliens. In order to enjoy the freedom of access to the courts of law, the alien, just like the nationals, must comply with the requirements prescribed by the local law.

Right to employ counsels

Following the general trend and considerations of the preceding clauses, clause (5) establishes the right of the alien to choose and employ lawyers both for purposes of pursuit and defence of his rights and interests in the State of residence on terms of equality with the nationals.

Opinions of writers

Borchard says: "The resident alien does not derive his rights directly from international law, but from the municipal law of the State of residence, though international law imposes upon that State certain obligations which under the sanction of responsibility to the other States of the international community is compelled to fulfil . . . The establishment of the limit of rights which the State must grant to alien is the result of the operation of custom and treaty, and is supported by the right of protection of the alien's national State. This limit has been fixed along certain broad lines by treaties and international practice. It has secured to the alien a certain minimum of rights necessary to the enjoyment of life, liberty and property, and so controlled the arbitrary action of the State."[47]

Oppenheim says: "In consequence of the right of protection over its subjects abroad which every State enjoys, and the corresponding duty of every . . . State to treat aliens on its territory with a certain consideration, an alien . . . must be afforded protection for his person and property . . . Every State is by the Law of Nations compelled to grant to aliens at least equality before the law with its citizens, as far as safety of person and property is concerned. An alien must in particular not be wronged in person or property by officials and courts of a State. Thus the police must not arrest him without just cause . . . "[48]

Practice of Member States of the Committee

According to the law and practice of the Member Countries of the Committee an alien is normally permitted to enjoy personal liberty on a par with the nationals. Broadly, the law of each State

---

47 Borchard: The Diplomatic Protection of Citizens abroad, (1915), 25-39.
48 Oppenheim: International Law (London, 1937), 5th edn. 547-548.
 Moore: Digest, op. cit., Vol. IV, 2-28.

provides for protection against arrest and detention in certain cases. For instance, Article 22 of the Constitution of India confers four rights upon an individual, citizen or non-citizen, who has been arrested. He shall not be detained in custody without being informed as soon as practicable, of the grounds of his arrest. He shall have the right to consult and to be represented by a legal practitioner of his choice. He has the right to be produced before the nearest magistrate within a period of 24 hours of such arrest. Normally, he shall not be detained in custody beyond the period of 24 hours without the authority of a magistrate. An alien enemy and an individual detained under the provisions relating to preventive detention are not entitled to the rights enumerated above.[49] Similarly, Article 9 of the Constitution of Indonesia confers upon every individual the right of freedom of movement and residence within the borders of Indonesia; and Article 12 lays down that no individual shall be arrested or detained unless by order of the competent authority and in the cases and the manner prescribed by law.[50] Likewise, Article 31 of the Constitution of Japan declares that no person shall be deprived of life or liberty, nor shall any other criminal penalty be imposed except in accordance with the procedure prescribed by law; Article 33 provides that no arrest shall be effected except upon a valid warrant therefor clearly indicating the offence for which the arrest is being made unless the individual has been apprehended redhanded committing the alleged offence, and Article 34 lays down that no person shall be arrested or detained without being at once informed of the charges against him nor shall he be detained without adequate cause.[51] Under Article 5 of the Constitution of Pakistan "no person will be deprived of life or liberty save in accordance with law". Articles 6 and 7 lay down the safeguards relating to arrest and punishment for an act which was not punishable by law when the act was done, nor may a person be subjected to a punishment greater than that prescribed by law for an offence when that offence was committed. A person arrested shall not be detained in custody without being informed, as soon as may be of the grounds for such arrest; and such person shall not be denied the right of legal consultation and defence. Further, a person arrested or detained in custody is given the right to be produced before the nearest magistrate within a period of twenty-four hours and no further detention is allowed except on the order of a magistrate. These safeguards are, how-

---

49 Shukla: Commentaries on the Constitution of India, (Lucknow, 1960) 3rd ed., 77-85.
50 Peaslee: Constitutions of Nations (Netherlands, 1956), Vol. II. 2nd ed., 373.
51 Peaslee. ibid., 514.

ever, not applicable to an enemy alien or to any person who is arrested or detained under any law providing for preventive detention.[52]

Moreover, besides the insertion of provisions relating to essential rights in the Constitutions or public laws of the Member Countries of the Committee, there is also an effective and easy procedure for enforcing them. The Constitutions or public laws of Burma, Ceylon, India and Pakistan give this right to the judiciary. In these countries the Supreme Court and the High Courts have been empowered to issue certain judicial writs for the enforcement of any rights guaranteed in the Constitutions. If an individual is subjected to arrest, imprisonment or any other physical coercion in a manner that does not admit of legal justification, with the aid of a writ of **habeas corpus** he can obtain his release from such detention. Similarly, in Indonesia liberty could be regained by means of appropriate petitions to the judicial or executive authorities as the case may be and in Iraq and the United Arab Republic, it is the procedure of "objections against provisional detainment" that is being used for the same purpose.[53]

Normally, an alien is entitled to freedom of conscience and the right freely to profess and practise his own religion. As in the case of nationals, the alien's right to freedom of religion is subject to public order, morality and health. For instance, Article 20 of the Constitution of the Union of Burma, Article 25 of the Constitution of India, Articles 18 and 43 of the Provisional Constitution of the Republic of Indonesia and Articles 19 and 20 of the Constitution of Japan provide for the right to freedom of religion to all individuals within the borders of their respective territories subject to the above qualifications.[54] In Iraq too, the alien's right to freedom of conscience is subject to public order, discipline and public morality as determined by the executive authorities of the State. In the United Arab Republic an alien has this freedom on a footing of equality with the national minorities.[55]

Every Member State of the Committee grants to aliens equal protection of laws. This right of protection is subject to applicable

---

52 Choudhuri: Constitutional Development in Pakistan (Lahore, 1951), 233-234.

53 Report of the Asian African Legal Consultative Committee, Third Session (Colombo) 1960, 113.

54 Peaslee: Constitutions of Nations, op. cit., Vol. I, 281-282, Vol. II, 374 & 376.
Basu: Commentary on the Constitution of India, Vol. I, (Calcutta, 1955); Third ed., 318-322.

55 Report of Asian African Legal Consultative Committee, Third Session, 113.

laws, regulations and orders. An alien in these countries is entitled to the protection of the executive and judicial organs of the State, and more particularly the protection of the local police force on a footing of equality with the nationals. For instance, Article 8 of the Constitution of Indonesia guarantees to all persons within the territory of Indonesia equal protection of person and property.

As the aliens are entitled to equality before the law, they have the concomitant rights of access to local courts of law and judicial protection for their persons and property. For instance, Article 13 of the Constitution of Indonesia lays down that every one is entitled in full equality to a fair and just hearing by an impartial judge for the determination of his rights and obligations and of any criminal charge against him. Under Article 14 of the Constitution of India, the guarantee of equality before the law extends to all persons, citizens as well as aliens, within the territory of India.[56] Article 5 of the Constitution of Pakistan incorporating the concept of equality before the law guarantees to all individuals the equal protection of laws.[57] In the United Arab Republic aliens enjoy the right of equal protection of law. Denial of justice is a punishable offence, and a judicial officer could be punished for this offence.[58]

Moreover, an alien has the right of legal consultation and defence in all the Member Countries of the Committee. This right is very important for the enjoyment of an individual's right to life, liberty and property. For instance, the Constitutions of India and Pakistan specifically provide that an individual shall have the right to choose and employ legal practitioners of his choice. This right and privilege is available to an alien on a footing of equality with the nationals of the State concerned.

Practice of States other than Member States of the Committee

Britain, France, Germany and the United States of America have been upholding the view that under customary international law, a State is bound to safeguard the life and property of aliens on its territory in accoradnce with the requirements of the minimum standard of international law. Several awards of the international arbitral tribunals have upheld the existence of such a minimum standard of international law. Certain South American States were held liable for having failed to safeguard adequately the life, free-

---

56 Peaslee: Constitutions of Nations. op. cit., Vol. II. 373-374; Anand: Constitution of India, New Delhi (1957), 70 & 145.

57 Chowdhuri: Constitutional Development of Pakistan, op. cit., 232.

58 Report of the Asian African Legal Consultative Committee, Third Session, 113.

dom, human dignity or property of aliens on their territories.[59] Some publicists criticise the minimum standard of international law as being vague and imprecise and that "powerful States have at times exacted from weak States a greater degree of responsibility than from States of their own strength. Further, they maintain that even those international tribunals which had accepted and applied this standard could not define the term "minimum standard of international law."[60] Vehemently opposing the minimum standard of international law, the Latin American States have been asserting that aliens who establish themselves in a country are entitled to enjoy all civil rights on a footing of equality with the nationals and that they cannot claim any greater measure of protection than that accorded by a State to its own nationals.[61]

The modern State practice concerning the nature and extent of an alien's essential rights has been set out in Guerrero's Report in 1926. He takes the view that although "customary law lays down certain rules which clearly express the definite will of States regarding the rights which they agree to accord to foreigners (and) the manner in which foreigners are to be treated", and that "the right to life, the right to liberty and the right to own property" are recognised by the international community "as being the minimum which a State should accord to foreigners in its territory", it cannot be maintained that the international community has recognized "the right to claim for the foreigners more favourable treatment than is accorded to nationals." Moreover in his view, "the maximum that may be claimed for a foreigner is civil equality with nationals" and that "this does not mean that a State is obliged to accord such treatment to foreigners unless that obligation has been embodied in a treaty."[61a] In view of the fact that the resident alien does not derive his essential rights directly from international law but from the municipal law of the host State concerned, several bilateral treaties have been concluded between States which provide inter alia that the nationals of either contracting party within the territories of the other contracting party, shall be permitted to travel therein freely and to reside at places of their choice, to enjoy liberty of conscience, to hold both private and public religious services, to

---

59 United States (Neer Claim) v. Mexico; Briggs: The Law of Nations, op. cit., 613-614.
   Walter A. Noyes Claim (United States v. Panama).
   Katz & Brewster: The Law of International Transactions and Relations, op. cit., 76-78.
60 Borchard: The Diplomatic Protection of Citizens Abroad. op. cit., 178; Amador, F. V. Garcia-Report on International Responsibility, A/CN. 4/96, 20, January 1956, 74-76.
61 Amador, F. V. Garcia: Report on International Responsibility, ibid., p. 75.
61a Briggs: The Law of Nations, op. cit., 564.

enjoy full protection and security for their persons and property; to enjoy freedom of access to the courts of justice, to administrative tribunals and agencies in all degrees of jurisdiction established by law both in pursuit and in defence of their rights, and last but not least, to choose and employ lawyers and representatives in the prosecution and defence of their rights before such courts, tribunals and agencies. Further, these treaties provide that the individuals accused of crime shall be brought to trial promptly, shall enjoy all the rights and privileges which are accorded by the applicable laws and regulations and that while within the custody of the authorities they shall receive reasonable and humane treatment. Moreover, these treaties provide that the nationals of either contracting party shall be permitted to exercise all the above rights and privileges, in conformity with the applicable laws and regulations, upon terms no less favourable than are or may thereafter be accorded to the nationals of the other contracting party and no less favourable than are or may hereafter be accorded to the nationals of any third country. However, they contain provisions to the effect that the above rights and privileges shall be subject to the right of each party to apply measures that are necessary to maintain public order and to protect the public health, morals and safety.[62] More recently, even multilateral conventions have been concluded by nations for the same purpose.[63] Further, the law and practice of most States establish the fact that foreign nationals are normally granted a minimum of rights, which in specific terms mean a modicum of respect for the life, liberty, dignity and property of foreign nationals as well as the availability of unhindered access to the national courts of law and reasonable means of redress in the case of manifest denial, delay or abuse of justice.[64] For instance, under Article 128 of the Constitution of Belgium "every foreigner within the territory of Belgium shall enjoy protection of his person and property, except as otherwise established by law;"[65] and Article 141 of the Constitution of Brazil "assures Brazilians and foreigners

---

62 Treaty of Friendship, Commerce and Navigation, concluded between the United States and the Italian Republic (1948); United States Treaties and other International Agreements, list No. 1965; Treaty of Friendship, Commerce and Navigation entered into between the United States of America and Japan (1953), United States Treaties and other International Agreements, Vol. 4, list No. 2065.

63 European Convention for the Protection of Human Rights and Fundamental Freedoms (1950); European Treaty Series, No. 5, European Yearbook, Vol. I (1955), 317-341; Robertson: "The European Court of Human Rights," The American Journal of Comparative Law (1960), Vol. 9, No. 1, 1-28.
The Treaty Establishing the Benelux Economic Union (1958); Katz & Brewster: The Law of International Transactions and Relations, op. cit., 82.

64 Schwarzenberger: A Manual of International Law, 4th ed., Vol. I (London, 1960), 99.

65 Peaslee: Constitutions of Nations, op. cit., Vol. I, 168.

residing in the country the inviolability of the rights respecting life, liberty, individual security and property."66 Similarly, under the first ten amendments and the Fourteenth Amendment to the Constitution of the United States of America, aliens enjoy the same rights as American citizens.67 In **Wong Wing v United States** (1876), Mr. Justice Shiras stated that the provisions of the Fourteenth Amendment to the Constitution of the United States "are universal in their application to all persons within the territorial jurisdiction without regard to any difference of race, of colour, or of nationality, and equal protection of the laws is a pledge of the protection of equal laws. Applying this reasoning to the Fifth and Sixth Amendments, it must be concluded that all person within the territory of the United States are entitled to the protection guaranteed by those amendments, and that even aliens shall not be held to answer for a capital or other infamous crime, unless on a presentment or indictment of a grand jury, nor he be deprived of life, liberty or property without due process of law."68

The term "alien's freedom from arbitrary arrest", as interpreted and applied by various national courts and international tribunals and also according to outstanding writers on international law connotes the following rights of an alien as a matter of international law: There must be some grounds for his arrest; in cases of arrest, suspicions must be verified by a serious inquiry; an arrested person must be given an opportunity to communicate with the consul of his State if he requests for it; he is entitled to be brought before a judge within a reasonable period following his arrest; he must be treated in a manner fitting his station, and which conforms to the standard habitually practised among civilized nations during such detention; he is entitled to be informed of all the charges against him; he must be enabled to defend himself with the aid of counsel; he is entitled not to be exposed to undue delay in the proceedings; he is entitled to a fair trial before an impartial tribunal; the provisions of the local law must not be disregarded and the same is true with respect to relevant treaty provisions; he must be given opportunity sufficiently to confront the witnesses against him; he must be given opportunity to summon witnesses in his own behalf and to interrogate them and he must not be exposed to cruel and inhuman treatment during the proceedings nor

---

66 Peaslee: ibid; 234.
67 Orfield & Re: Cases and Materials on International Law (London) 1956, 495.
68 163 U.S. 228; 16 S. ct. 977 (1876) Yick Wo v. Hopkins, 118 U.S. 356, 369; 6 S. ct., 1064, 1070.

by way of punishment after the proceedings.[69]   Thus according to the decision of U.S.-Mexican General Claims Commission in   the **Chattin Claim (1927)**   the following acts and omissions would give rise to international responsibility of a State: illegal arrest of an alien, irregularity of court proceedings such as absence of proper investigations, insufficiency of   confrontations, with-holding from the accused the opportunity to know all of the charges brought against him, undue delay of the proceedings, making the hearing in open court a mere formality, a continued absence   of seriousness on the part of the court, insufficiency of the evidence against the accused, intentional severity of the punishment flowing from the unfairmindedness of the judge and mistreatment of the alien in prison.[70]   In the **Tribolet case (1930),** the U.S.-Mexican General Claims Commission held that the execution of an   alien   without trial, without having been accorded the right   of   being   heard, without having given at any time an opportunity to defend himself, or to present   evidence   to establish his innocence and in short, without having been proven   guilty of any crime would result in grave injustice to the alien concerned.[71]   In the case of **Michael J. Malamatnis et al** (United States v. Turkey) (1957)   Fred   K. Nielsen, American Commissioner, took the view that "International law requires that, in connection with the execution of penal laws, an alien must be accorded rights such as are guaranteed under the law of civilized countries generally both to aliens and nationals. Most important among these are the requirements that there must be some grounds for arrest and trial, or as is said in domestic law, probable cause. A person is entitled to be informed of the charge against him. He must be given a reasonably prompt opportunity to defend himself. He must not be mistreated during his period of imprisonment.[72]

Broadly, a State has the undoubted right to regulate the religious teachings or practices of the individuals on its territory. This

---

69 Orfield: "What constitutes fair criminal procedure under municipal and international law," 12 University of Pittsburgh Law Review (1950) 35-44. Briggs: The Law of Nations. op. cit., 566-567. Faulkner Claim (1926) (United States v. Mexico), Roberts Claim (1926) (United States v. Mexico) Boliggs—ibid; 549-552. Chattin Claim (1927) (United States v. Mexico) Briggs: ibid; 666-674 Tribolet Claim (1930) (United States v. Mexico) Briggs: ibid; 547-548 Chevreau Claim (1933) (France v. United Kingdom) Birggs: ibid ., 566-567.

70 Chattin Claim (United States v. Mexico.) Katz & Brewster: The Law of International Transactions and Relations. op., cit., 68-73.

71 Tribolet Claim (United States v. Mexico): Briggs: The Law of Nations, op. cit., 547-548.

72 Hackworth: Digest of International Law, Vol. III, 640.

right emanates from its competence to determine its own internal policy.[73]   The United States of America took the following view in this regard—"It is fundamental that sovereign States have the right to control the internal order of their affairs in such manner as they deem to be to their best interests, free from unwarranted interference by other powers.[74]   From the above it follows that the State has the right even to forbid the religious teachings   or practices of foreigners, if in its opinion they are likely to disturb public order, public morals or its political institutions.   However, so widespread has become the habit of tolerance among the members of the international community that any attempt to curtail the freedom of worship of resident aliens would be   regarded as being out of accord with the spirit of the modern world and contrary to the practice of civilized nations.   Even States having certain State religions do not normally deny aliens the right to freedom of religion, in so far as their religious practices do not disturb law and order within their domains.   The Constitutions of several nations contain provisions which guarantee to aliens the right to freedom of religion almost on a footing of equality with the nationals.   Clause (7) of Article 141 of the Constitution of Brazil, for example, assures Brazilians and foreigners residing in the country the inviolability of the liberty of conscience and creed, and also the free exercise of religious sects as long as they are not contrary to public order or good morals of the State. Further, under clause 8 of Article 141, no one shall be deprived of any of his rights by reason of religious, philosophic or political convictions, unless he shall invoke it in order to exempt himself from   any   obligation, duty, or service required by the law of   Brazilians in general. or shall refuse those which the same law may establish as substitutes for those duties in order to meet a conscientious excuse."[75]   Mr. Buchanan, the United State's Secretary of State, sets out the religious policy of his country in these terms: "I would pray to God that the Governments of all countries like that of our own happy land, might permit knowledge of all kinds to circulate freely   among the people.   It is our glory that all men in the United States enjoy the inestimable right of worshipping God according to the dictates of their own conscience."[76]   According to the Universal Declaration of Human Rights, adopted by the General Assembly of the United Nations in 1948. freedom of religion should be granted to all in-

---

73 Moore: A Digest of International Law. Vol. II, 171.
   Hyde: International Law, Vol. I, op. cit., 702.
74 View of the U.S. Department of State dated February 12, 1935;
   Hackworth: Digest of International Law, Vol. III, 647.
75 Peaslee: Constitutions of Nations, Vol. 1 op. cit., 234-235.
76 Moore: A Digest of International Law, Vol. II, 171.

dividuals, whether aliens or nationals.[77] By the terms of the European Convention for the Protection of Human Rights and Fundamental Freedoms, adopted in 1950, the Contracting Parties guarantee to all persons within their jurisdiction, several rights including the freedom of thought, conscience and religion.[78] By reason of the fact that a State has the right to regulate the religious training and worship of all the inhabitants on its territory, nations have been entering into treaties of friendship and commerce which normally guarantee to their nationals the right to freedom of conscience, free profession and practice of their own religions during their stay or sojourn within the territories of the other party to such treaty or arrangements. The Treaty of Friendship, Commerce and Consular Rights concluded between the United States of America and Norway (1928) and the treaty that was entered into between the United States of America and Poland on June 15, 1931 could be given as examples of such treaties. More recently, the same purpose is being achieved mostly by means of bilateral treaties of friendship, commerce and navigation. The treaty between the United States of America and the Italian Republic concluded on February 2, 1948 and that between the United States of America and Japan entered into on April 2, 1953 could be cited as examples. These treaties normally provide that the nationals of each contracting party shall within the territories of the other contracting party, be permitted to exercise freedom of conscience and of worship, that they may whether individually, collectively or in religious corporations or associations conduct freely their religious services, provided that their religious teachings or practices are not contrary to public morals or public order. Moreover, they also set out that each of the contracting parties shall have the right to apply such measures as may be deemed necessary to maintain public order and protect the public health, morals and safety.[79]

The term "religious freedom of aliens" as interpreted and applied by nations appear to include the following rights and privileges:—The right to enjoy liberty of conscience. and religious worship, protection from all kinds of disabilities or persecution on account of their religious faith, belief or worship and the right to

---

77 The Universal Declaration of Human Rights does not impose any legal obligation on the members of the international community, but it appears to have considerable moral force.
78 Robertson: The European Court of Human Rights, op. cit., 1.
79 Article 9 of the Treaty of Friendship, Commerce and Navigation, concluded between the United States of America and Italian Republic (1948); Clauses 2 and 3 of Article 1 of the Treaty of Friendship and Navigation and Commerce entered into between the United States of America and Japan.

hold or conduct, without annoyance or molestation of any kind, both private and public religious services and rites of a ceremonial nature in their national language or any other language which is customary in their religion, either within their own houses or within any other appropriate buildings, provided that their teachings or practices are not contrary to public morals or public order; the right and opportunity to lease, erect or maintain in convenient situations buildings appropriate for religious purposes; the right to collect from their co-religionists voluntary offerings for religious purposes; the right to impart religious instructions to their children either singly or in groups or to have such instructions imparted by persons whom they may employ for such purpose; and the right to bury their dead in accordance with their religious practices or customs in suitable and convenient burial-grounds established and maintained by them with the approval of the competent authorities, subject to applicable mortuary and sanitary laws and regulations.[80] Moreover, most of the treaties provide that the nationals of each contracting party shall be granted rights with reference to freedom of conscience and the free exercise of religion which shall not be less favourable than those enjoyed in each contracting State by the nationals of the nations most favoured in this respect.[81]

Generally speaking, as a result of customary international law, treaties and the exercise of the right of diplomatic protection of the alien's home-State, States have been granting aliens within their territories the same measure of protection for their persons and property as are possessed and enjoyed by their own nationals. In the absence of such executive and judicial protection, the alien's right to life, liberty, dignity and property may be jeopardized.[82] Justice Black of the United States describes the source of the rights of aliens and the corresponding duty of every State in the following terms: "Apart from treaty obligations, there has grown up in the field of international relations a body of customs defining with more or less certainty the duties owing by all nations to alien residents—duties which our State Department (i.e., of the

---

80 Note from Mr. Litvinov, People's Commissar for Foreign Affairs of the Union of Soviet Socialist Republics to the Government of the United States, dated Nov. 16. 1933.

81 Article 9 of the Treaty between Germany and the Union of Soviet Socialist Republics signed at Moscow on Oct. 12. 1925. Hackworth: Digest of International Law. Vol. III. Articles XI (1) & (2) of the Treaty of Friendship, Commerce and Navigation concluded between the United States and Italian Republic; Hackworth: Digest of International Law. 1948, Vol. III, 649.

82 Oppenheim: International Law, Vol. I. op. cit., 689-690. Schwarzenberger: A Manual of International Law, Vol. I, op. cit., 90 & 99.

United States) has often successfully insisted foreign nations must recognize as to our nationals abroad. In general, both treaties and international practices have been aimed at preventing injurious discriminations against aliens".[83] Moreover, if an alien suffers an injury in consequence of the failure of a State to provide the necessary protection and security for his person and property as required by international customary or conventional law, that State incurs international responsibility; and such a lapse has been regarded by the international community as an international delinquency.[84] One of the most important and delicate of all international relationships recognized immemorially as a responsibility of government, has to do with the protection of the just rights and interests of a country's own nationals when those nationals are in another country. Experience has shown that international controversies of the gravest moment may arise from wrongs to another's subjects inflicted or permitted by a government.[85] In the **Neer Case** (1926) the duty of protection was set out by the General Claims Commission as follows:—"The treatment of an alien, in order to constitute an international delinquency, should amount to an outrage, to bad faith, to wilful neglect of duty, or to an insufficiency of governmental actions, so far short of international standards that every reasonable and impartial man would readily recognize its insufficiency. Whether the insufficiency proceeds from deficient execution of an intelligent law or from the fact that the laws of the country do not empower the authorities to measure up to international standards is immaterial."[86]

Moreover, international arbitral tribunals have repeatedly awarded indemnities in favour of aliens because of the wanton killing of aliens by local officials,[87] and the failure of the local administration to apprehend, prosecute and punish the persons who had committed wrongs against aliens.[88] They have founded international responsibility on account of the failure of the local

---

83 Hines v. Davidowitz et Al (1941), 312 U.S. 52;
   Borchard: The Diplomatic Protection of Citizens Abroad, op. cit., 25, 37, 73 & 104.

84 Oppenheim: International Law, Vol. I, op. cit., 330.
   "A State is responsible for any failure on the part of its organs to carry out the international obligations of the State which cause damage to the person or property of a foreigner in the territory of the State"; League of Nations, Acts of the Conference, Minutes of the Third Committee, 1930 V, 26-32, 236.

85 Per Justice Black in Hines v. Davidowitz et Al.
86 General Claims Commission established under bilateral agreements between the United States of America and Mexico.
   Schwarzenberger: International Law, Vol. I, op. cit., 200-201.

87 The Youmans case (1926), Briggs: The Law of Nations, op. cit., 705-711.
88 The Janes case (1926); Schwarzenberger: International Law, Vol. I, op. cit., 201.

authorities to provide adequate protection to the foreigners who had needed it,[89] and upon the failure of the government of the State of residence to use due diligence to prevent injury to aliens.[90]

Although the overwhelming weight of authority of publicists sustained by the practice of States is in favour of granting aliens the national standard of treatment in respect of protection for their persons and property, diplomacy, international practice and arbitral decisions have established the rule that equality of treatment, while **prima facie** a fair defence, is not conclusive of international duty and responsibility. Thus, "bad faith, fraud, outrage resulting in injury cannot be defended on the ground that it is the custom of the country to which nationals must also submit", nor can it be maintained that the State concerned normally does not provide any protection whatever even for its own nationals.[91]

As regards the British State practice Lord Phillimore stated in Johnstone v Pedlar (1921) as follows:—"An alien **ami** (friend), once he is resident within the realm, is given the same rights for the protection of his person and property as a natural born or naturalized subject x x x. An alien **ami** complaining of a tort is in the position of an ordinary subject, and that no more against him than against any other subject can it be pleaded that the wrong complained of was, if a wrong done by command of the king or was a so called act of State. From the moment of his entry into the country the alien owes allegiance to the king till he departs

---

89 Chapman case (1930); Briggs: The Law of Nations, op. cit., 697-703.

90 Borchard: Diplomatic Protection of Citizens Abroad, op. cit., 213-228.

91 Although at the Hague Codification Conference of 1930, the Third Committee rejected by a vote of 23 to 17, a Chinese proposal intended to limit the international responsibility of State for the protection of aliens to the standard of treatment accorded by a State to its own nationals, it now appears that most of the newly independent States are in favour of placing the alien in respect of his right to life, liberty, personal property and protection and security therefor in conformity with the national laws and regulations, on a footing of equality with their nationals; League of Nations, Act of the Conference, Minutes of the Third Committee, 1930. V 17, 185-188. Borchard: "The Minimum Standard of the Treatment of Aliens", Proceedings of the American Society of International Law (1939). 54-57.

Oppenheim: International Law, Vol. I, op. cit., 687-688.

According to Survey of International Law, "the controversy, which was largely responsible for the negative result of The Hague Codification Conference, on a subject of whether a State can adduce the fact of non-discrimination as a reason for relieving it of its responsibility for the treatment of aliens has now been resolved so far as fundamental human rights and freedoms are concerned. The principle authoritatively asserted by arbitral tribunals that the plea of non-discrimination cannot be validly relied upon if the State does not measure up to a minimum standard of civilization has now found expression in the provisions of the Charter relating to human rights and fundamental freedoms. These must be deemed to be co-extensive with the minimum standard of civilization." United Nations Doc. A/CN.4/1, Nov. 5. 1948: Case Concerning Certain German Interests in Polish Upper Silesia (Merits) 1926. Rep. P.C.I.J. Series A. No. 7, 32-33.

from it, and allegiance, subject to a possible qualification . . . draws with it protection, just as protection draws allegiance."[92]

With regard to the practice of the United States, Mr. Butler, the Attorney General of the United States of America stated in 1857 that "Aliens coming within our territory are entitled to the same protection in their personal rights as our own citizens and no more";[93] and as to protection of property rights of foreign nationals, Mr. Adams, the Secretary of State of the United States of America stated that "there is no principle of the law of nations more firmly established than that which entitles the property of strangers within the jurisdiction of a country in friendship with their own to the protection of its sovereign by all the efforts in his power." He added that, that was the common rule of intercourse between all civilized nations.[94] Moreover, in **Matarazzo v Hustis** (1919) it was held that "an alien coming into the United States and residing here, even temporarily, is entitled to the protection of, and is subject to the provisions of, the Statutes of the United States and of treaties made with, while in force, are the supreme law of the land."[95]

Notwithstanding the claim of the leading Western nations that in accordance with the minimum standard of international customary law, every nation has certain minimum duties to perform with regard to alien's right to life, right to liberty and the right to own property, they too, like most other nations, have been entering into numerous treaties of amity and commerce; of friendship, commerce and consular rights or of friendship, commerce and navigation which promise and guarantee broad rights and privileges including most constant protection and security for the persons and property to the nationals concerned sojourning or resident within the territories of the contracting parties. By stipulating that the treatment of foreigners shall be in conformity with the applicable national laws and regulations, and also in conformity with the national and most favoured nation standards of treatment, these treaties have been aiming at prevention of injurious discriminations against aliens.[96] For instance,

92 (1921) 2. A.C. 262 (Great Britain, House of Lords);
   Briggs: The Law of Nations, op. cit., 554-555.
93 Moore: A Digest of International Law Vol. IV, 2.
94 Moore: A Digest of International Law, Vol. IV, 5.
95 Hackworth: Digest of International Law, Vol. III, 552.
96 Per Black J. in Hines v. Davidowitz et Al (1941), op. cit., Dispatch of Mr. Polk, Acting U.S. Secretary of State to Ambassador H.P. Fletcher, dated Dec. 13, 1918: Briggs: The Law of Nations, op. cit., 565; Report on Responsibility of States for Damage Done in their territories to the Person or Property of Foreigners (Guerrero Report), League of Nations Doc. 1926 V. 3. 20; American Journal of International Law, special supplement (1926), 176-180.

Clause I of Article II of the Treaty of Friendship, Commerce and Navigation concluded between the United States and Japan on April 2, 1953 provides as follows: "Nationals of either Party within the territories of the other Party shall be free from unlawful molestations of every kind, and shall receive the most constant protection and security, in no case less than that required by international law."[97]

Clause (1) of Article III of the Treaty of Friendship, Commerce and Navigation signed between the United States and Germany on October 29, 1954 provides as follows:—"Nationals of either Party within the territories of the other Party shall be free from molestations of every kind, and shall receive the most constant protection and security. They shall be accorded in like circumstances treatment no less favourable than that accorded to nationals of such other Party for the protection and security of their persons and their rights. The treatment accorded in this respect shall in no case be less favourable than that accorded to nationals of any third country or that required by international law."[98]

Since the middle of the nineteenth century, the Western nations appear to have been providing foreigners within their territories the freedom of access to their courts of law on a basis of equality with their nationals as a complementary right to the foreigners' right to protection and security for their persons and property. In the exercise of the freedom of access to the national courts of law, they have been enjoying the liberty to choose and employ legal practitioners of their choice. Hence some publicists take the view that the rights of access to courts of law and to judicial protection for the alien's person and property are some of the requirements of the minimum standard of international customary law which every nation should accord to aliens within its territory.[99] Closely related to these rights is the right to equal

---

97 United States Treaties and other International Agreements, Vol. 4, Part 2 (1953) (List No. 2863, 2067).

98 United States Treaties and other International Agreements, Vol. 7, Part 2 (1956), (List No. 3593), 1842. Article III of the Treaty between the United States and Italy of February 26. 1871: Article I of the Treaty between the United States and Japan of Feb. 21, 1911 and Article V of the Treaty of Friendship, Commerce and Navigation concluded between the United States and the Italian Republic on February 2, 1948 provide for the protection and security of aliens' persons and property in the host State; Hyde: International Law, Vol. 1, op. cit., 657.
Briggs: The Law of Nations, op. cit., 542

99 Schwavrzenberger: A Manual of International Law, Vol. I, op. cit., 99; Briggs: The Law of Nations, op. cit., 567.
Borchard: The Diplomatic Protection of Citizens Abroad, op. cit., 73.

protection of the laws. "Equal protection of the laws means sub-jection to equal laws applying to all in the same circumstan-ces."100 Several modern Constitutions specifically lay down that the State shall not deny to any person within its territories the equal protection of its laws. For instance, Article 3 of the Basic Law for the Federal Republic of Germany promulgated on May 23, 1949, provides as follows:—(1) All men shall be equal before the law; (2) Men and women shall have equal rights; (3) No one may be prejudiced or privileged because of his sex, descent, race, language, home land and origin, faith or his religious or political opinions. 101

As regards the alien's freedom of access to the national courts, the Supreme Court of the United States said in the course of its opinion in the case of **Barbier v Connolly** (1885) as follows: "The Fourteenth Amendment, in declaring that no State shall de-prive any person of life, liberty, or property without due process of law, nor deny to any person within its jurisdiction the equal protection of the laws," undoubtedly intended . . . that all persons should be equally entitled to pursue their happiness and acquire and enjoy property; that they should have like access to the courts of the country for the protection of their persons and property, the prevention and redress of wrongs, and the enforcement of con-tracts.102

In **Takahashi v Fish and Game Commission** Justice Black stated that the United States Congress has broadly provided: "All persons within the jurisdiction of the United States shall have the same right in every State and territory to make and enforce con-tracts, to sue, be parties, give evidence, and to the full and equal benefit of all laws and proceedings for the security of persons and property as is enjoyed by white citizens, and shall be subject to like punishments, pains, penalties, taxes, licences, and exactions of every kind, and to no other, 16, Stat. 140, 144, 8 U.S.C. s 41.

The protection of this section has been held to extend to aliens as well as to citizens. Consequently the section and the Fourteenth Amendment on which it rests in part protects all per-sons, "against State legislation bearing unequally upon them either because of alienage or colour. . . The Fourteenth Amendment and the laws adopted under its authority thus embody a general policy

---

100 Lindsley v. National Carbolic Co., (1910), 220 U.S. 61.
101 Peaslee: Constitutions of Nations, Vol. II, 30-31.
102 113 U.S. 27, 31 (1885);
 Hackworth: Digest of International Law, Vol. III, 564.

that all persons lawfully in this country shall abide "in any state" on an equality of legal privileges with all citizens under non-discriminatory laws."[103] By Section 156 of the Judicial Code of the United States, "the privilege of prosecuting claims against the United States in the Court of Claims, whereof such court, by reason of their subject matter, and character, might take jurisdiction" is accorded to "aliens who are citizens or subjects of any government which accords to citizens of the United States the right to prosecute claims against such government in its courts.[104]

Describing the British practice, Viscount Cave said in the case of **Johnstone v Pedlar** (1921) as follows: "Counsel for the appellant contended for the broad proposition that, where the personal property of an alien friend resident in this country is seized and detained by an officer of the Crown, and his act is adopted and ratified by the Crown as an act of State, the alien is without legal remedy. In my opinion this proposition cannot be sustained x x x an alien **ami** (friend) complaining of a tort is in the position of an ordinary subject, and that no more against him than against any other subject can it be pleaded that the wrong complained of was, if a wrong done by command of the king or was a so-called act of State. From the moment of his entry into the country the alien owes allegiance to the king till he departs from it, and allegiance . . . draws with it protection, just as protection draws allegiance."[105] In the case of **Massein v The King** (1934) Justice Maclean of the Canadian Exchequer Court said as follows: "My conclusion is that in England and here (Canada), an alien may maintain a petition of right. The friendly alien has access to our courts like any subject. . . This is far from saying that an action could not be maintained by a petition of right by any friendly alien against the Crown . . . I might point out that under the Customs Act an alien is subject to the same penalties and forfeitures and enjoys the same rights and remedies as a subject; no distinction is of course made between them. . . A friendly alien while in this country, as a matter of law, is in the allegiance of the Crown, and so long as he remains in this country, with the permission of the sovereign, express or implied, he is a subject to local allegiance, with a subject's rights and obligations. This principle was discussed at great length in the House of Lords in **Johnstone v Pedlar,**

103 334 U.S. 410, 68 S. Bt. 1138 (1948);
   Hurd v. Hodge, 334 U.S. 24; 68 S. Bt. 847;
   Katz & Brewster: The Law of International Transactions and Relations, op. cit., 125-135.
104 Hackworth: ibid., 565.
105 (1921) 2. A.C. 262;
   Briggs: The Law of Nations, op. cit., 552-555.

(1921) 2. A.C. 262, and I would refer to that authority".[106] Similarly, the right of action against the government of the State is accorded to foreigners in several other countries.[107] Further, about 64 per cent of the national Constitutions contain provisions relating to the right of making petitions to the State officials as one of the fundamental rights of the individual.[108] It appears that in several national Constitutions, this right of petition is available to aliens more or less on a footing of equality with the nationals.[109] Apart from the right of suit against the government, the aliens are accorded the right to sue private persons; the right to be parties to suits by private individuals; the right to give evidence; the right to summon witnesses in their defence; the right to choose and employ counsel for purposes of prosecuting and defending their rights and interests and also defending themselves if accused of crime and the right to the full and equal benefit of all the national laws and proceedings for the security of their persons and property on a footing of equality with the nationals.[110]

As observed above in the treaties of amity and commerce concluded between nations, mutual freedom of access to the local

---

106 Annual Digest and Reports of Public International Law Cases (1938-1940) case No. 124, 372-374.

107 Denmark, Dominican Republic, France, Honduras, Japan and Norway could be cited as instances in this regard.
Hackworth: ibid, 565-566.

108 Peaslee: Constitutions of Nations, Vol. I, op. cit., 7.

109 Article 26 of the Constitution of the Argentine Republic provides for the right of all individuals; nationals and aliens—to petition the authorities.

110 Suits against private individuals include nationals, aliens and nationals and aliens; Katalla Co. v. Rones, 186, Fed. 30, 108 C.C.A., 132; Barrow Steamship Co. v. Kane, 170 U.S. 100, 18 Sup Ct. 526; 42 L. Ed. 964. Compania Mineva y. Compradora de Metales Mexicaro, S.A.V. American Metal Co., Limited, et. al; 262 Fed. 183, 187.

In Cunard S.S. Co., Limited v. Smith (1918) 255 Fed. 846, 848, the Circuit Court of Appeals for the Second Circuit said that "the law is . . . well established that aliens who are sui juris, except alien enemies, may maintain actions to vindicate their rights and redress their wrongs when brought in the proper courts. It has been held in numerous cases that one alien may sue another alien in the State courts, even on contracts made abroad or for a tort committed in a foreign community."

In Martinez v. Fox Valley Bus Lines, Inc. (1936), Annual Digest 1935-1937 case No. 151, Mr. Holly, District Judge of Illinois took the view that since even an alien who is unlawfully in the country must live he must have the right to earn a living by following the ordinary occupations of life including the right to make the ordinary contracts incident to existence. Further, in his view so long as he is permitted by the Government of the United States to remain in the country, he is entitled to the protection of the laws in regard to his rights of person and property including the protection of the Fourteenth Amendment to the Constitution of the United States of America. But in Coules v. Pharris (1933) (Annual Digest, 1933-1934 case No. 123), the Supreme Course of Wisconsin held that an alien who has entered unlawfully cannot sue.

Oppenheim: International Law, Vol. I, op. cit., 688-689.

Hackworth: Digest of International Law, Vol. III, 567-568.

Katz & Brewster: Law of International Transactions and Relations, 129.

courts together with cognate rights and privileges on a basis of equality with nationals, are being assured to the nationals of each contracting party within the territories of the other contracting party. For instance, Article IV of the treaty concluded between the United States of America and Japan (1935) provides: "(1) Nationals and Companies of either Party shall be accorded national treatment and most-favoured-nation treatment with respect to access to the courts of justice and to administrative tribunals and agencies within the territories of the other Party, in all degrees of jurisdiction both in pursuit and in defence of their rights . . ."[111] Article VI of the Treaty of Friendship, Commerce and Navigation entered into between the United States of America and the Federal Republic of Germany in 1954 provides: (1) Nationals of either Party shall be accorded national treatment with respect to access to the courts of justice and to administrative tribunals and agencies within the territories of the other Party, in all degrees of jurisdiction, both in respect and in defence of their rights . . . "[112]

Principles embodied in certain Conventions

The Declaration of the International Rights of Man adopted by the Institute of International Law at its meeting in New York in 1929 provided in Article 1 as follows:

"It is the duty of every State to extend to every person an equal right to life, to liberty, and to property, and to accord to all persons within its treritory the full and complete protection of its law without distinction of sex, race, language, or of religion."[113]

The Inter-American Convention on the rights and duties of States (1933): Provides in clause (2) of Article 9 that:

"Nationals and foreigners are under the same protection of the law and the national authorities and the foreigners may not

---

111 United States Treaties and other International Agreements (1953), Vol. 4, Part 2, 2067.
112 United States Treaties and other International Agreements (1956), Vol. 7, Part 2, 1845.
Similar provisions are found in the treaty between the United States and Honduras concluded on Dec. 7, 1927 (Article 1) and that between the United States and the Italian Republic entered into on Feb. 2, 1948; Hackworth: Digest of International Law Vol. III, 562; Briggs: The Law of Nations, op cit., 530-531 & 542-547.
Clause (4) of Article V provides inter alia that "the nationals . . . of either Contracting Party . . . shall be at liberty to choose and employ lawyers and representatives in the prosecution and defence of their rights before such courts, tribunals and agencies . . . exercise all those rights and privileges, in conformity with the applicable laws upon terms no less favourable than the terms which are or may hereafter be accorded to the nationals . . . and no less favourable than are or may hereafter be accorded to the nationals . . . of any third country."
113 Hackworth: Digest of International Law, Vol. III, 641-642.

claim rights other or more extensive than those of the nationals."[114]

European Convention for the protection of Human Rights and Fundamental Freedoms (1950)

By the terms of the Convention, the Contracting Parties guarantee to all persons within their jurisdiction a number of rights and freedoms, including the right to life; the right to liberty and security of the person; freedom from torture, slavery and servitude; freedom from arbitrary arrest, detention, or exile; the right to fair and public hearing by an independent and impartial tribunal in questions of the determination of civil rights and obligations or of any criminal charge; freedom from arbitrary interference in private and family life, home, and correspondence; freedom of thought, conscience, and religion; freedom to join trade unions; the right to marry and found a family.[115] By the conclusion of a Protocol on March 22, 1952, three additional rights were added: the right to property, the right of parents to choose the education to be given to their children, and the right to free elections.[116]

Under Article 24 of the Convention any Member State may refer an alleged breach of the Convention by any other Party to the European Commission of Human Rights consisting of a number of members equal to that of the High Contracting Parties. Under Article 25, the Commission may receive petitions from "any person, non-governmental organization or group of individuals claiming to be the victim of a violation by one of the High Contracting Parties of the rights set forth in this Convention."[117]

---

114 Signed at Montevideo on Dec. 26, 1933;
Hackworth: Digest of International Law, Vol. III, 640.

115 Robertson: "The European Court of Human Rights," Vol. 9, 1, The American Jounal of Comparative Law (1960), 1-2. These rights and freedom were taken from the Universal Declaration of Human Rights adopted by the General Assembly on Dec. 10, 1948, though they are defined in greater detail. Unlike the latter which is only a solemn statement of intentions of considerable moral value but without legal effect, the former, i.e., European Convention contains precise legal obligations.

116 Robertson: "The European Convention on Human Rights—Recent Developments," British Year Book of International Law (1951) 359-365.

The European Convention entered into force on Sept. 3, 1953. All the 15 members of the Council of Europe are now Parties with the exception of France, i.e., Austria, Belgium, Federal Republic of Germany, Greece, Iceland, Ireland, Italy, Luxembourg, Netherlands, Norway, The Saar, Sweden, Turkey, the United Kingdom and Denmark. Robertson: The European Court of Human Rights, op. cit., 1.

117 This jurisdiction of the Commission is, however, subject to two conditions: that the Party against which the complaint is made has declared that it recognizes the right of the individual petition and that at least five other States have made similar declarations. It may be added that in fact, since nine out of the 15 members of the Council of Europe have recognized the competence of the Commission to receive individual petitions, this remedy is now available to about 90 million Europeans. More-

Benelux Economic Union (1958)

The Treaty establishing the Benelux Economic Union provides in its Article 2 that:

"2. They shall enjoy (the nationals of each High Contracting Party) the same treatment as national of that State as regards:

    (a) freedom of movement, sojourn and settlement; x x x

    (g) exercise of civil rights as well as legal and judicial protection of their person, individual rights and interests."[118]

Article 9

A State may prohibit or regulate professional or business activities or any other employment of aliens within its territory.

Note : The Delegation of Iraq was of the view that the words "shall be free to" should be inserted in place of the word "may". The Delegation of Pakistan wished to keep its position open.

Commentary

State's right to regulate alien's economic activities

This Article emphasizes the right of the host State to regulate or even to prohibit the professional, business or similar activities of the aliens on its territory. The practice followed by most of the States which is in accord with this Article shows that the State of residence has the right to limit or prohibit the right of aliens to participate in certain professions and industries.[119]

Opinions of Writers

Hyde expresses his views in the matter in these terms: "A State may exercise a large control over the pursuits, occupations and modes of living of the inhabitants of its domain. In so doing it may doubtless subject-resident aliens to discrimination without necessarily violating any principle of international law. x x x

A State may reasonably exercise a rigid control over the practice of learned professions within its territory. Thus, it may prescribe tests of the fitness of persons to be permitted to practise,

---

over, as a condition of its exercise is the previous exhaustion of local remedies, several applications have been turned down for reasons of non-compliance with the rule of exhaustion of local remedies; Robertson: The European Court of Human Rights, op. cit., 2.

118 Katz & Brewster: The Law of International Transactions and Relations, op. cit., 82.

119 Moore: Digest op. cit., Vol., 13.

and that regardless of their nationality. Unless restrained by treaty, it may not unlawfully discriminate against aliens nor is it under any obligation to accept as assurances of fitness the degrees issued by foreign institutions of learning . . . The territorial sovereign must be free to establish for itself the extent and mode of recognising the attainments of persons trained in foreign countries. x x x

The practice of a particular profession, such as that of the law, may be fairly deemed to entail a connection with and devotion to the State within whose territory that privilege is sought to be exercised that is incompatible with the retention of allegiance to a foreign country. x x x

In a word, it seems to be clear that a State is on strong ground when it lays down the conditions under which learned professions may be practised within its territorial domain, and when also, in the course of so doing it sees fit to confine the privilege of practice to individuals who are its own nationals."[120]

Practice of Member States of the Committee

The Member Countries of the Committee, like other nations, claim the right to prohibit or restrict the participation of aliens in professions and gainful employments within their territories. Generally speaking, Ceylon, India, and Japan do not normally exclude foreign nationals from engaging in commercial or professional activities within their borders. Burma, Indonesia and Iraq exclude aliens from participating in certain professions, trades and occupations. Foreigners in Burma and Iraq are normally permitted to seek only temporary employments. Japan is in favour of engaging foreign experts or specialists for periods of short duration. Foreigners too are permitted to enter government service in Ceylon, India and Indonesia. Since in Burma and Iraq permanent positions in the service of the State are generally reserved for the nationals, foreigners can only become temporary government employees. Broadly, all the Member States of the Committee do not subject resident aliens to discrimination in respect of their professional or other occupational activities. But according to the United Arab Republic, the State of residence must have absolute discretion in the matter.[121]

---

120 Hyde: International Law, Vol. I, 656, 661-662.
121 Report of the Asian African Legal Consultative Committee, (Colombo, 1960), 113-114.
As observed above, according to Hyde, the State of residence has the right to subject resident aliens to discrimination without necessarily contravening any principle of international law; Hyde: International Law, Vol. I, 656.

A State has the undoubted right to exclude foreign nationals from professions and industries within its borders. Such a right seems to be firmly established not only by the weight of the authority of writers, but also by the sustained practice of States. Broadly, communities and groups seem to manifest a tendency towards reserving profitable economic activities for their own members.[122] In almost all countries, the restrictions are now, in a period of economic nationalism, much more severe.[123] From the above, it necessarily follows that a State possesses the right to regulate the professional and occupational activities of aliens, if it decides to permit them to participate in the said economic activities on its domain: and that a State may subject resident aliens even to discriminations without necessarily infringing any principle or rule of international law.[124] It may be observed that from the speeches and statements made by the delegates at the International Conference on Treatment of Foreigners. one can discern the prevalence of variant employment policies among the States of the international community.[125] Moreover, experience has shown that in recent years a growing number of States have been imposing national prohibitions or extensive restrictions upon the participation of foreigners in professions, gainful employments or commercial transactions within their borders. In some countries aliens entering their territories for purposes of obtaining gainful employments are required to register with the appropriate authorities of the State of residence, within a certain period of time after their arrival. After the expiry of that period of time, if he wants to seek any permanent employment he is required to produce a permit. It may be added that the issuance of a certificate or a work permit referred to above. is dependent upon a number of factors which include **inter alia** the employment situation in a given profession. occupation or industry, the number of aliens already present in the country and the granting of reciprocal treatment to its own nationals by the alien's home State.[126] The Belgian Law of February 20, 1939. concerning the protection of the profession of architect makes a clear distinction between architects of Belgian nationality

---

122 Katz and Brewster: The Law of International Transactions and Relations, op. cit., 122.
123 Oppenheim: International Law, Vol. I, 690.
124 Hyde: International Law. Vol I, 656.
125 This Conference was convened under the asupices of the League of Nations. League of Nations Publications, C. 97. M. 23. 1930 II (1930 II.5) 122-152.
   Hyde: International Law, Vol. I, 656.
126 Hackworth: Digest, Vol. III, 625-626.

and those of foreign nationality. Article 7 gives persons of Belgian nationality who satisfy the conditions set out in that article the right to bear the title of architect and to exercise that profession. That article does not apply to aliens. Article 8, para (1) permits foreign architects to exercise their profession in Belgium to the extent their country of origin grants reciprocity. In **Van Bogart and the Royal Association of Architects of Antwerp v Belgian State (Minister of Education) (1952)** the **Conseil d'Etat** of Belgium took the view that in the absence of a reciprocity treaty with his home State, no authorization to a foreign architect to practise his profession in Belgium could be granted under para (1) of Article 8 of the Belgian Law of February 20, 1939. Further in its view, para 2 of Article 8 of the said Law makes it possible to authorize persons of foreign nationality to act as architects in Belgium. It added that "the terms of the provision referred to above, as well as the preparatory work relating thereto, show clearly that such an authorization is not unlimited, but may be granted only in respect of a specific undertaking or for enterprises requiring the aid of foreign specialists."[127] In **Delgrance v. Belgian State (Minister for Economic Affairs) (1953)**, a German national's application to the Belgian Minister for Economic Affairs for a permit to practise the profession of translator-interpreter in Belgium was rejected on the ground that in the opinion of the Aliens Department of the Ministry of Justice he did not comply with the required moral standards therefor.[128]

In the case of **In re Galetzky (1951)** the **Conseil d'Etat** of France took the view that an alien is prohibited from exercising an industrial or commercial profession in France without obtaining a special permit therefor.[129] In **Sebe v Case Altimir (1937),** the Court of Appeal of Montpellier, France held that an alien who had entered into a contract of employment in France without the necessary permit as required by a Law of August 11, 1926, could not entertain an action against his employer for damages suffered in connection with an accident in the course of his employment, as provided by Art. 1 of the Law of April 9, 1898. [130] The **Tribunal Correctionnel** of Domfront, in **Syndicat des pharmaciens de l'orne, Bellet and Morellet v Valenza (1938)** held that an Italian national who possessed the necessary French qualifications to prac-

127 International Law Reports (1953), 302-303.
128 Ibid., 303-304.
129 International Law Reports (1951), Case No. 85, 291.
130 Annual Digest and Reports of Public International Law Cases (1938-1940), Case No. 128, 377.

tise the profession of a chemist was nevertheless precluded from doing so in the absence of reciprocity on the part of Italy, as required by Art. 2(2) of the French Law of April 19, 1898. Art. 2(2) of the said law provided: "Aliens, although possessing the French chemist's diploma, are precluded from exercising the profession of a chemist in France unless, by way of reciprocity, French nationals possessing a chemist's diploma issued by the country to which the alien belongs, are allowed to act as chemists in that country."[131] Further, under the Decrees of June and November 1938, the French Government has been empowered to fix, for each category of industry or commerce, the percentage of aliens permitted to be employed therein, and an alien is prohibited from practising an industrial or commercial profession in France without obtaining a special permit. Furthermore, the Decree of February 2, 1939, sets forth certain cases in which aliens must be refused a permit to exercise a commercial profession.[132]

The right of a State to refuse permission to an alien to participate in the commercial activities of the State was discussed by the Administrative Court of Appeal of Munster, West Germany, in the **Residence of Alien Trader Case** in 1954. The Court **inter alia** said: "It is significant that Articles 11 and 12 of the Constitution confer the rights of unrestricted movement, choice of occupation and place of work only on all Germans, and not on foreign nationals. . . . The authorities are entitled to take into account the fact that a particular trade is overcrowded and that it is therefore undesirable for aliens to engage in it. . . . "[133]

With regard to alien's right to practise professional accountancy work in the Philippines, Section 12 of Act No. 3105 provides as follows: "Any person who has been engaged in professional accountancy work in the Philippine Islands for a period of five years or more prior to the date of his application, and who holds certificates as certified public accountant or as chartered account, or other similar certificates or degrees in the country of his nationality, shall be entitled to registration as certified public account and to receive a certificate of registration as such certified public accountant from the Board, provided such country or State does not restrict the right of Filipino certified public

---

131 Annual Digest, (1938-1940), Case No. 129, 377-378.
132 In re Galetzky (1951), International Law Reports (1951), 291.
133 International Law Reports (1954), 209-210.

accountants to practise therein or grants reciprocal rights to Filipinos. . . ."[134]

In the case **of In re Schirer** (1958), the Federal Tribunal of Switzerland dealt with the alien's right to engage in economic activities in Switzerland. The Court said: "An alien who enters the country for the purpose of gainful employment must register with the Aliens Department of the place where he is staying within eight days and in any case before taking up employment. During the time limited for registration, he may be gainfully employed without a permit, provided that he does not obtain regular employment. After that time, any gainful employment requires a permit. Only an alien who has been granted permission to settle in the country may be gainfully employed without police restriction. . . . Every alien who is present in Switzerland without authorization to settle there requires a permit if he enters employment or if, after eight days, he is otherwise gainfully employed . . . 'gainful employment' is 'entering regular employment or any other activity normally exercised with a view to gain' . . . Article 3, para 1 of the Law concerning Establishment of Aliens does not even require proof that the alien actually received money; it is sufficient to prove activities normally pursued with a view to gain, i.e., exercised, according to common experience, for the sake of gain . . ."[135] Moreover, immigration into Switzerland is ordinarily permitted only for one definite type of work, usually as the employee of a named employer. Such employees are needed mainly by Swiss firms having some connections with Switzerland. By the decree of the Swiss Federal Council of November 3, 1944 the book-publishing business in Switzerland has been reserved to Swiss citizens "in order to protect it from excessive foreign influence (UBERFREMDUNG)".[136]

Before the First World War, the English law appears to have treated the aliens resident in Great Britain on a footing of equality with the British subjects. This is no longer the case, as the Aliens Restriction (Amendment) Act of 1919 has introduced certain prohibitions or restrictions on the occupational privileges or freedom of foreign nationals in the United Kingdom. For example. under this Act no alien is permitted to hold a pilotage certificate for any pilotage district in the United Kingdom. He cannot act as master, chief officer or chief engineer of any British merchant ships

---

134 Sison v. The Board of Accountancy and Ferguson (1949)—International Law Reports (1951). Case No. 7, 14-16.
135 International Law Reports (1953), 303-304.
136 Nussbaum: American Swiss Private International Law, (New York) 1960, **15.**

registered in the United Kingdom. He is not allowed to act as skipper or second-hand of any British fishing-boat, nor is he permitted to receive an appointment to the Civil Service of the United Kingdom.[137]

The right of States to limit or prohibit the employment of aliens on public works has frequently been upheld by the Courts of the United States. In Heim v McCall (1915), the Supreme Court of the United States upheld the validity of Section 14 of the Labour Law of 1909 of the State of New York, which provided: "In the construction of public works by the State or a municipality, or by persons contracting with the State or such municipality, only citizens of the United States shall be employed; and in all cases where labourers are employed on any such public works, preference shall be given to citizens of the State of New York. In each contract for the construction of public works a provision shall be inserted, to the effect that, if the provisions of this section are not complied with, the contract shall be void."[138] The Supreme Court of Rhode Island held that an ordinance of the city of Providence providing that licenses for the operation of motor buses within the city should be issued only to citizens was not in conflict with the Fourteenth Amendment to the Constitution of the United States of America.[139] The Supreme Judicial Court of Massachusetts expressed the opinion that a statutory provision limiting the issuance of licenses for hawking and peddling to persons who were citizens or who had declared their intentions to become citizens of the United States was not in conflict with the Fourteenth Amendment to the Constitution of the United States of America.[140]

Numerous statutory provisions have been enacted in the various States of the United States excluding aliens from engaging in certain professions, trades, and occupations, such as accountancy, architecture, medicine, engineering, law, optometry, pharmacy, teaching, auctioneering, barbering, taxidermy, peddling, mining, etc. These enactments have generally been defended on the ground that they represent a justifiable and necessary exercise of the police power.[141] For instance, the Statutes of Ohio, California and of many other States have barred aliens from the right to hold licenses for the sale of spirituous liquors.[142] California excluded aliens

---

137 Oppenheim: International Law. Vol. I, 689-690.
138 239 U.S. 175, 188, 191, 193 (1915); Hackworth: Digest, Vol. III, 622.
139 Gizzarelli v. Presbrey et al., (1922) 44 R.I. 333.
140 Commonwealth v. Hana (1907), 195 Mass. 262; Hackworth; Ibid.. 619.
141 Hackworth: Digest, Vol. III, 618.
142 Bloomfield v. State (1912), 86 Ohio 8t. 253, 266; 99 N.E. 309, 312 (1912)—
   De Grazier v. Stevens (1907) 101 Tex. 194, 195; Hackworth: Ibid., 618
   footnote

by statute from fishing in her tidal waters and the right to hold licenses for the practice of pharmacy.[143] In the State of New York, the issuance of a certificate of certified public accountant requires that the applicant therefor be a citizen of the United States or a person who has declared his intention of becoming such citizen.[144] Admission to the legal profession of the several States of the United States or of the territorial possessions thereof is generally conditioned upon among other things the possession by the applicant of American nationality.[145] Similarly, there are statutory prohibitions upon the aliens' participation in certain professions and industries, especially those related to the merchant marine and public communications. For instance, all officers of ships of the United States who "shall have charge of a watch, including pilots" must in all cases be citizens of the United States. However, the President of the United States may "whenever in his discretion the needs of foreign commerce may require" suspend this requirement.[146] Contracts for the construction of aircraft for the military and naval forces of the United States may be awarded only to citizens of the United States and to corporations of which three-fourths or more of the stock is owned by American citizens, and the members of the board of such corporations also must be citizens of the United States.[147] The Civil Aeronautics Act of June 23, 1938 authorized the Civil Aeronautics Authority to issue "airman certificates" specifying "the capacity in which the holders thereof are authorized to serve as airmen in connection with aircraft", subject to the proviso "That the Authority may, in its discretion, prohibit or restrict the issuance of airman certificates to aliens, or may make such issuance dependent on the terms of reciprocal agreements entered into with foreign governments." Under Section 7 of the Civilian Pilot Training Act of June 27, 1939 "no alien shall receive training under the provisions of this Act."[148] Section 310 of the Act of June 19, 1934 provides that licenses required for the operation of radio stations may not be issued to aliens.[149]

The occupational freedom of the aliens seeking admission into the United States was restricted by the provisions of the Immigra-

---

143 Takahashi v. Fish and Game Commission (1948), 334 U.S. 410; 68 S.Ct. 1138 (1948).
144 Chap. 15, Education Law, s 1492, Cahill's Consolidated Laws of New York, Second ed., (Chicago, 1930). 786:
   Hyde: International Law, Vol. 1, 662 footnote.
145 Rules for Admission to the Bar in the Several States and Territories of the United States, in force as on March 1, 1941, Twenty eighth ed . (St. Paul, 1941). Hyde: International Law, Vol I, 662. It appears that some of the above restrictions have been held unconstitutional.
146 40 U.S.C. ss. 221, 236: Hackworth: Digest, Vol. III, 625.
147 20 U.S.C. ss. 310(i): Hackworth: Digest, Vol. III, 625 footnote.
148 52 Stat. 1008: 53 Stat. 856: Hackworth: Ibid., 625 footnote.
149 48 Stat. 1086: 47 U.S.C. ss. 312: Hackworth: Ibid., 625 footnote.

tion Act of May 26, 1924. The Department of Labour also appears to have been making effort to prevent the aliens from exercising privileges of local trade bereft of international character. Further, non-quota immigrant aliens, such as those permitted by the above Act to enter for purposes of study, are not permitted during their limited period of sojourn in American territory to engage in occupations for gain except for purposes of supplementing income insufficient to cover necessary expenses.[150] Furthermore, under the Immigration and Naturalization Act of 1952 a variety of restrictions have been imposed upon the employment of foreigners in the United States. For instance, Section 212 of the Act provides **inter alia** as follows: "(a) Except as otherwise provided in this chapter, the following classes of aliens shall be ineligible to receive visas and shall be excluded from admission into the United States . . .

"(14) Aliens seeking to enter the United States for the purpose of performing skilled or unskilled labour (will be denied entry) if the Secretary of Labour has determined and certified to the Secretary of State and to the Attorney-General that (a) a sufficient number of workers in the United States who are able, willing, and qualified are available at the time . . . and place . . . to perform such skilled or unskilled labour, or (b) the employment of such aliens will adversely affect the wages and working conditions of the workers in the United States similarly employed."[151]

Similarly, the United States too appears to have acknowledged the right of other States to regulate the professions and industries of all the inhabitants, nationals and non-nationals, residing on their respective territories. Like most other States, it has been taking the view that each territorial sovereign has the discretion to recognize or reject the attainments of individuals trained in other countries. It has acknowledged the propriety of the application of this principle with respect to Americans seeking to practise a learned profession in a foreign State, provided there has been no discrimination against its nationals therein. Thus, in 1933 it declared that it recognized the right of the several Mexican States to prescribe rules and regulations relating to the new admissions to the medical profession insofar as they did not discriminate against American nationals as such.[152]

Nations have been entering into commercial treaties for purposes of securing the occupational freedom for their nationals with-

---

150 Hyde: International Law, Vol. I, 659-660.
151 66 Stat. 166-281, 8 U.S.C.A. ss. 1101-1503 s. 1182; Katz & Brewster; The Law of International Transactions and Relations, 134.
152 Hyde: International Law, Vol. I, 661.

in the territories of the other contracting parties. Such individuals are permitted to engage in certain enumerated professional and commercial activities which are not forbidden by the local law; to own, erect or lease and occupy appropriate buildings; to employ agents of their choice and generally to do anything incidental to and necessary for the enjoyment of any of the foregoing privileges and rights on terms of equality with the nationals and in conformity with all local laws and regulations duly established. For instance, Article VII of the Treaty of Friendship, Commerce and Navigation concluded between the United States of America and Japan in 1953 provides that: "(1) Nationals and companies of either Party shall be accorded national treatment with respect to engaging in all types of commercial, industrial, financial and other business activities within the territories of the other Party, whether directly or by agent or through the medium of any form of lawful judicial entity. Accordingly, such nationals and companies shall be permitted within such territories: (a) to establish and maintain branches, agencies, offices, factories and other establishments appropriate to the conduct of their business; (b) to organize companies under the general company laws of such other Party, to acquire majority interests in companies of such other Party; and (c) to control and manage enterprises which they have established or acquired. Moreover, enterprises which they control, whether in the form of individual proprietorships, companies or otherwise, shall, in all that relates to the conduct of the activities thereof, be accorded treatment no less favourable than that accorded to like enterprises controlled by nationals and companies of such other Party." x x x . Paragraphs (2) and (3) of Article VIII provides : "(2) Nationals of either Party shall not be barred from practising the professions within the territories of the other Party merely by reason of their alienage; but they shall be permitted to engage in professional activities therein upon compliance with the requirements regarding qualifications, residence and competence that are applicable to nationals of such other Party." "(3) Nationals and companies of either Party shall be accorded national treatment and most favoured-nation treatment with respect to engaging in scientific, educational, religious and philanthropic activities within the territories of the other Party, and shall be accorded the right to form associations for that purpose under the laws of such other Party."[154]

---

153 Briggs: The Law of Nations, 530-531.
   Hyde: International Law, Vol. I, 659.
154 In its resolution consenting to the foregoing Treaty of Friendship, Commerce and Navigation between the United States and Japan the U.S. Senate provided: "Article VIII, paragraph (2) shall not extend to profes-

Principles embodied in certain Conventions

The Treaty Establishing the European Economic Community
(March 25, 1957)

Article 48

1. The free movement of workers shall be ensured within the Community . . .

2. This shall involve the abolition of any discrimination based on nationality between workers of the Member States as regards employment, remuneration, and other working conditions.

3. It shall include the right, subject to limitations justified by reasons of public order, public safety, and public health:

(a) To accept offers fo employment actually made;

(b) To move about freely for this purpose within the territory of Member States;

(c) To stay in any Member State in order to carry on an employment in conformity with the legislative and administrative provisions governing the employment of the workers of that State and;

(d) To live, on conditions which shall be the subject of implementing regulations to be laid down by the Commission, in the territory of a Member State after having been employed there.[155]

The Treaty Establishing the Benelux Economic Union
(February 3, 1958)

Article 2

x   x   x

(2) They (i.e., the nationals of each High Contracting Party) shall enjoy the same treatment as nationals of that State as regards:

---

sions which because they involve the performance of functions in a public capacity or in the interest of public health and safety, are State licensed and reserved by Statute or Constitution exclusively to the citizens of the country, and no most-favoured-nation clause in the said treaty shall apply to such professions."

99 Cong. Records 9339 (July 21, 1955) United States Treaties and other International Agreements (1953), Vol. 4, Part 2, 2069-2070. This Treaty was signed in Tokyo on April 2, 1953, Katz & Brewster: The Law of International Transactions and Relations, 169-170; Similar provisions have been incorporated in several other treaties also. For instance, Art. (1) of the Treaty of Friendship, Commerce and Navigation entered into between the United States of America and the Italian Republic in 1948; and Arts. VII, VIII and XI of the Treaty of Friendship, Commerce and Navigation concluded between the United States and Germany in 1954 provide for the right of the nationals of either Contracting Party, to engage in commercial, professional and cognate activities within the territories of the Contracting Party; Briggs: The Law of Nations: 530-531 & 542-547; United States Treaties and Other International Agreements (1956) Vol. 7, Part 2, 1839-1869.

(a) freedom of movement, sojourn and settlement;

(b) freedom to carry on a trade or occupation, including the rendering of services;

x   x   x [156]

Article 10

An alien shall not be entitled to any political rights, including the right of suffrage, nor shall he be entitled to engage himself in political activities, except as otherwise provided by local laws. regulations and orders.

Commentary

Alien's exclusion from political activities

It is a well-established principle of international law that an individual in a foreign State is subject to the territorial supremacy of that State and that he is responsible to the latter for all wrongful acts he commits on its territory. He owes allegiance, which continues during the period of his residence, to the government of that State. From the duty of obedience flows the duty to abstain from engaging in injurious political activities in the State in which he resides. If an alien attempts to foment sedition, insurrection or other disorders, he becomes liable for prosecution for treason in the same manner as the nationals of that State. Thus, this principle which has been firmly established not only by the weight of authority of publicists but also by the sustained practice of States, has been incorporated in this Article.

Alien's exclusion from the exercise of political rights

Under this Article an alien is not entitled to the enjoyment and exercise of political rights. The practice of States indicates that the alien as a rule is excluded from the exercise of political rights in the State in which he resides. The term 'political rights', as interpreted and applied by the practice of States normally includes the right of suffrage, the right to hold high public office and the right to act as a juror.

It may be added that the above rights and duties of aliens are subject to applicable local laws, regulations and orders of the State of residence. This means that although aliens are not normally admitted to the exercise of political rights, they   may   be

---

156 Katz and Brewster: The Law of International Transactions and Relations,
82.
The Guardian (Manchester), July 5, 1961; The Economist (London), June
17, 1961, 1203-1206.

permitted to occupy some public offices and may even be required to render jury service, if the constitutional or public laws as well as the regulations of the State within the territory of which he resides so require or permit.[157]

Opinions of Writers

Oppenheim says: With his entrance into a State, an alien, unless he belongs to the class of those who enjoy so-called exterritoriality, falls at once under the territorial supremacy of that State. . . . He is therefore under the jurisdiction of the State in which he stays. x x x It must be emphasized that an alien is responsible to the local State for any illegal acts which he commits while the territory concerned is during war temporarily occupied by the enemy x x x A State can exclude aliens from certain professions and trade . . . Before the First World War there was a tendency to treat admitted aliens more and more on the same footing as citizens—poltiical rights and duties, of course excepted.[158]

According to **Hackworth,** "aliens are not as a rule admitted to the exercise of political rights. They are generally excluded from holding office under the Government x x x The right of aliens to hold public office . . . is determined by (the) Constitutions and laws (of the States) x x x Citizenship is very generally prescribed as a prerequisite to jury service . . ."[159]

Cutler maintains that "It is a commonplace that the foreigner owes a temporary obedience to the State in which he resides. The measure of this obligation varies with the relative permanence of the sojourn, but all aliens are subject to the local civil and criminal law . . . In addition to the duty of obedience aliens may be required to abstain from political agitation, and in fact from all matters which may be said to concern citizens exclusively. The penalty of the alien's intrusion into politics may be expulsion, or even assimilation to the national's political liabilities. The limitation also extends as a rule to public office, to jury service, and expressly or by implication to the exercise of franchise although in exceptional cases aliens may occupy municipal and the ordinary administrative posts and may be allowed or even required to serve on juries. Also resident aliens or declarants when the law makes them State citizens are sometimes allowed to vote.[160]

---

157 Oppenheim: International Law, Vol. I, op. cit., 679-680.
158 Oppenheim: Ibid., 679, 682, 689.
159 Hackworth: Digest of International Law, Vol. III. op. cit., 559-561.
160 Cutler, J. W.: "The Treatment of Foreigners," American Journal of International Law, (1933) Vol. 27, 227-228.

Practice of Member States of the Committee

In the matter of alien's political rights and duties, the practice of the member States of the Committee appears to be similar to that of most States. Broadly, an alien is not admitted to the exercise of political rights including the right of franchise, nor shall he be entitled to engage himself in the political activities in the State of residence. However, in the view of these States, since each State has the unlimited discretion in the matter, it can decide for itself whether or not to allow aliens certain political rights. Similarly it can determine for itself the problem of alien's participation in its political activities. In a word, the extent of the alien's political rights and the admissibility and scope of his participation in the political affairs are dependent entirely upon the applicable local laws, regulations and orders. Further, as an alien domiciled or resident in a State owes to that government a local and temporary allegiance and also is subject to its territorial jurisdiction, he is obliged to submit to all local laws, regulations and orders duly established and for the violation of which he may be prosecuted and punished just as a national of that State.

The constitutional and public laws of these countries normally confine the right of suffrage to individuals who are their own nationals. For instance, under the Constitution of the Union of Burma only Burmese citizens have the right to vote at any election to the Parliament of Burma (Article 76(2)). [161] As regards the qualifications of an elector in Pakistan Article, 143(1) of the Constitution of the Islamic Republic of Pakistan lays down inter alia that he may be a citizen of Pakistan.[162]

Aliens are generally excluded from holding high public offices. For instance, under the Constitution of the Union of Burma, the President must be a citizen of the Union who was, or both of whose parents were, born in any of the territories included within the Union. (Article 49)."[163] Articles 58 and 66 of the Constitution of India declare that no person shall be eligible for election as President or as Vice-President unless he is a citizen of India.[164] Similarly clause (5) of Article 45 of the Constitution of Indonesia requires inter alia that the President and Vice-President of Indonesia must be Indonesian citizens.[165] Article 2 of the Constitution of Japan enacts that the "Imperial Throne shall be dynastic and

---

161 Peaslee: Constitutions of Nations, Vol. I, 285.
162 Brohi: Fundamental Law of Pakistan. (Karachi, 1958), 139, 886.
    Chowdhury: Constitutional Development in Pakistan (Lahore, 1959), 226.
163 Peaslee: Constitutions of Nations, Vol. I, 291.
164 Peaslee: Constitutions of Nations, Vol. II, 235, 237.
165 Peaslee: Ibid., 377.

succeeded to in accordance with the Imperial House Law passed by the Diet."[166]

Practice of States other than Member States of the Committee

The generality of State practice indicates that aliens have no political rights and duties. They are normally excluded from holding important public offices. But in some States minor administrative posts are open to foreign nationals also. Such exclusions and concessions must be attributed to the policy of the State rather than to any requirement of the law of nations.

The right to the exercise of franchise is generally determined by the constitutional provisions of each country. For instance, under Article 23 of the Constitution of the Federal People's Republic of Yugoslavia all citizens of the Republic of Yugoslavia who are over eighteen years of age have the right of suffrage in Yugoslavia i.e., they have the right to elect and be elected to all organs of State authority.[167] The right to the exercise of franchise in the United States is determined by the laws of the various component States, subject to the provisions of the 15th and 19th Amendments to the Constitution of the United States.[168] In a multitude of cases, the Courts of the United States held that the aliens are not qualified to vote.[169] Under Section 1460 of title 48 of the United States Code, it is provided that in any territory organized by Congress the qualifications of voters and of office holders "shall be such as may be prescribed by the legislative assembly of each territory" subject to the condition that—". . . The right of suffrage and of holding office shall be exercised only by citizens of the United States above the age of twenty-one years, and by those above that age who have declared on oath, before a competent court of record, their intention to become such and have taken an oath to support the Constitution and Government of the United States."[170]

Aliens are not normally required to render jury service. But in exceptional cases they may be allowed or even required to serve on juries.[171] In the United States, like most other States, citizen-

---

166 The Constitution of Japan and Criminals Statutes (Japan, 1958), 4; According to Articles 42 and 43 of the Constitution of Japan the Diet, which is the highest organ of State power and the sole-law-making organ of the State, shall consist of two Houses—the House of Representatives and the House of Councillors; The Constitution of Japan, ibid., 10.
167 Peaslee: Constitutions of Nations, Vol. III, 760.
168 Peaslee: Constitutions of Nations, Vol. III, 595.
169 Gardina v. Board of Registrars of Jefferson County, 160 Ala. 155, 48 So. 788 (1909).
   Campbell v. Ramsey, 150 Kans. 368., Hackworth: Digest, Vol. III, 560 footnote.
171 Cutler: The Treatment of Foreigners, op. cit., 227-228.

ship is very generally prescribed as a pre-requisite to jury service. According to Hackworth: "Forty-four jurisdictions have legislation pertaining to the subject of aliens as jurors. Thirty-two provide that a juror must be a citizen, or cannot be an alien or may be challenged for alienage . . . Twelve States have statutes requiring a juror to be a qualified voter; and since an alien cannot so qualify, he is excluded . . . Indiana also provides that either a grand juror or juror in a criminal trial, may be challenged for alienage."[172]

As observed above, in some countries aliens are permitted to hold public office in some branches of social welfare service. For instance, Article 29 of the Constitution of the Republic of Nicaragua (1950) lays down that aliens may hold public office in the branches of social welfare and artistic planning, or in those that require special technical knowledge provided such offices do not involve authority or jurisdiction. To take public office is one of the rights of citizens of Nicaragua (Art. 32). Under Article 33, the following are the obligations of the citizens: To register in the Electoral Registers; To vote in popular elections and to perform council offices unless lawfully excused.[173] Under Section 3 of Article VII of the Constitution of the Philippines, no person may be elected to the office of President or Vice-President unless he be a natural-born citizen of the Philippines. Section 4 of Article VI lays down that no person shall be a senator unless he be a natural born citizen of the Philippines. Under Section 6 of Article VIII, no person may be appointed as a member of the Supreme Court of the Philippine Islands unless he has been five years a citizen of the Philippines.[174] Under Articles 34 & 35 of the Constitution of the Union of Soviet Socialist Republics, the Soviet of the Union and the Soviet of Nationalities are elected by the citizens of the USSR.[175] In accordance with Section 1 of Article II of the Constitution of the United States of America, no person except a natural born citizen, or a citizen of the United States, shall be eligible to the office of President and neither shall any person be eligible to that office who shall not have been fourteen years a resident within the United States.[176]

Citizenship of the United States has been prescribed as a prerequisite to the holding of several kinds of public offices and to

172 Hackworth: Digest, Vol. III, 561.
173 Peaslee: Constitutions of Nations, Vol. III, 7.
174 Peaslee: Ibid., 168, 172-73, 175.
175 The Supreme Soviet of the U.S.S.R. under Art. 33 of the Constitution consists of two Chambers: The Soviet of the Union and the Soviet of Nationalities—Peaslee: Ibid., Vol. III, 489, 491.
176 Peaslee: Ibid., Vol. III, 587.

the holding of positions on public boards and agencies, such as: Federal Farm Loan Board; Board of Advisors; Federal Industrial Institution for Women; Federal Radio Commission; United States Tariff Commission, etc. Further under the American Foreign Service Regulations, candidates for examination for appointment as foreign service officers must have been citizens of the United States for 15 years.[177]

The right of aliens to be appointed in public offices is normally determined by the Constitution or public laws and regulations of each country.[178] According to Cutler, nineteen States of the United States including Alaska and Hawaii have prohibitive constitutional laws or statutory provisions excluding aliens from the right of holding public offices. Several countries also have similar provisions excluding aliens from public appointments. The practice of States reveals that every foreigner born and residing in a country owes to that country allegiance and obedience to its laws as long as he remains in it, as a duty imposed upon him by the mere fact of his residence and the temporary protection which he enjoys, and is as much bound to obey its laws as nationals.[179] As regards the policy of the United States, Mr. Blaine, the Secretary of State stated in 1881 that "Every person who voluntarily brings himself within the jurisdiction of the country, whether permanently or temporarily, is subject to the operation of its laws, whether he be a citizen or a mere resident, so long as in the case of the alien resident, no treaty stipulation or principle of international law is contravened."[180]

As a rule, States do not permit aliens to engage in political activities within their borders. The practice of States establish the principle that it is within the prerogative of each State to punish political offences committed by foreign nationals on its domain, whether such offences are seditious or violent acts or publications inciting thereto. Advising its nationals in Korea against their intermeddling in the local politics, the Government of the United States

---

177 Hackworth: Digest, 559-560—It may be noted that under the foreign service regulations of most of the countries a male member for the foreign service who proposes to marry an alien must obtain the prior permission of his Government who has the right to inform the officer concerned that, if he marries such an alien he will have to resign. And as a rule a woman member of the foreign service will be required to resign upon marriage with a foreigner. For instance, Regulation No. 2 of the Foreign Service Regulations of the United Kingdom, like those of several other countries, imposes such restrictions on the marriage of a member of Foreign Service with a foreign national; The Foreign Office List and Diplomatic and Consular Yearbook for 1961, 83.

178 Hackworth: Digest, op. cit., 560.

179 Report of Mr. Webster, U.S. Secretary of State, to the President of the United States, (December 3, 1851); Moore: Digest, Vol. IV, 11.

180 Moore: Ibid., 13.

stated by a circular in 1897 in these terms: "The repeatedly expressed view of the Government of the United States is that it behoves loyal citizens of the United States in any foreign country whatsoever, to observe the same scrupulous abstention from participating in the domestic concerns thereof, which is internationally incumbent upon his Government. They should strictly refrain from any expression of opinion or from giving advice concerning the internal management of the country, or from any intermeddling in its political questions. If they do so, it is at their own risk and peril. Neither the representative of this Government in the country of their sojourn nor the Government of the United States itself, can approve of any such action on their part, and should they disregard this advice it may perhaps not be found practicable to adequately protect them from their own consequences. Good American citizens quitting their own land and resorting to another, can best display their devotion to the country of their allegiance, and best justify a claim to its continued and efficient protection while in foreign parts, by confining themselves to their legitimate avocations whether missionary work or teaching in schools, or attending the sick, or other calling or business for which they resort to a foreign country."[181]

In the opinion of Wharton, an alien under indictment for a political offence which had been committed at the instance of his own government, cannot plead by way of defence that he did the alleged offence at the command of his own government. He adds that "a foreigner cannot say that he is not bound to obey the laws of the State where he is sojourning. But if the act for which he is convicted is one enjoined by his own sovereign, then that sovereign must be held responsible."[182] As early as 1858, Mr. Cass. U.S. Secretary of State, in his dispatch to Mr. Clay. U.S. Minister to Peru stated: "If an alien, on going into a country sees that the former Government has been expelled or overturned by revolution and a new one set up in its place, he must submit to the authority thus established . . . if he resists the authority of the party in possession on the ground that another has the right of possession, he departs from his neutrality, and so violates the duty he owes to both the belligerents as well as to the laws of his own country."[183] Upon being informed that some American nationals in Australia had been participating in certain anti-government political associations, on May 15, 1931 the American Consul-

---

181 Moore: Ibid., 15.
182 Moore: Ibid., 15.
183 Moore: Ibid., 12.

General at Sydney, Australia was advised that the Government of the United States "cannot countenance any attempt of American citizens to foment disorders in foreign territory and that it will not be disposed to intervene to prevent their just punishment by the appropriate authorities."[184] Further, in **United States v Chandler** (1947), the District Court for the District of Massachusetts, United States took the following view in the matter: "All strangers are under the protection of a sovereign State while they are within its territory, and owe a local temporary allegiance in return for that protection." The Court added that while domiciled in the foreign State, the alien owed a qualified allegiance to it, that he was obligated to obey its laws and that he was equally amenable with citizens of that country to the penalties prescribed for their infraction.[185]

The practice of other States, like that of the United States, also establishes the above principle that an alien resident, whether permanently or temporarily, in a foreign State owes to the government of that State a local and temporary allegiance as long as he remains in it; that he is bound to obey all the laws in force; and that if he violates a law in force therein, he becomes liable for arrest and punishment according to the practice obtaining in that country. Likewise, if he participates in anti-government political activities in violation of the law of the State of residence, he becomes liable for punishment by the appropriate authorities and also he becomes liable for prosecution for treason in the same manner as the nationals of the receiving State. Thus two British trade union leaders Tom Mann in Germany and Ben Tillet in Belgium were arrested and deported to Great Britain for their attempt to spread trade unionism in those countries. Britain did not dispute the right of the State of residence concerned to expel the foreigners who had been obnoxious to the government. The Canadian Government expelled two foreign nationals called Carranza and Dubose, both on general grounds and for reasons connected with the maintenance of British neutrality during the Spanish-American War. According to Finlay, one of the Law Officers of the United Kingdom Government, "every State has by international law the right to expel aliens whose presence is considered dangerous."[186]

The question of resident alien's liability for prosecution for treason was discussed by courts of several countries. In *in re*

---

184 Hackworth: Digest. Vol. III, 554.
185 Annual Digest, (1947), Case No. 60, 128-129.
186 McNair: International Law Opinions, Vol. II, 111-112.

Friedman (1947) the Belgian Court of Cassation said: "Article 118 bis of the Penal Code (of Belgium) applies both to Belgian nationals and to aliens, even if the latter have enemy nationality. If it is proved that an alien has resided in Belgium under the protection of a permit of residence, (this will impose) duties towards the receiving State on him." Thus, under the law of Belgium aliens resident in Belgium could be tried for crimes against the external safety of the State (Art. 118 bis of the Penal Code). Article 4 of the Law of July 10, 1934, authorizes prosecution in Belgium for such crimes even when they have been committed outside the territory of the Kingdom by an alien.[187]

In **Re Penati** (1946) the Italian Court of Cassation held "According to Article 3 of the (Italian) Penal Code (of 1930), Italian criminal law binds all those, who whether they are Italian nationals or aliens, reside in Italy subject to the exceptions provided by Italian public law or by international law. There is no rule of Italian public law or of international law which exempts from punishment an alien who commits an act in Italy which constitutes a crime against the existence of the State, against its military defence, and against the duty of loyalty of the citizens towards the State which he attempts to undermine. Not only does no rule of this kind exist, but it is legally inconceivable, for no State can allow aliens who enjoy its hospitality to carry out activities which are contrary to its vital interests in the military and political sphere."[188]

In **Public Prosecutor v Drechsler** (1946) the Supreme Court of Norway made aliens resident in Norway liable to punishment for treason under Article 86 of the Norwegian Criminal Code of 1902 which reads as follows:

"(1) Any one who illegally bears arms against Norway or during a war in which Norway is engaged or with such war in view assists the enemy in word or deed or weakens Norway's ability to fight or that of any State allied with Norway, shall be sentenced to detention for at least three years or to imprisonment for not less than three years up to imprisonment for life.

(2) A Norwegian citizen domiciled abroad shall not be punished for committing any act which he was bound to do in obedience to the law of the country of his domicil."[189]

---

187 Annual Digest: Ibid., (1947), 127-128.
188 Annual Digest, (1946), Case No. 30, 74-75.
189 Annual Digest, Ibid., 73-74.

In several other cases the Norwegian Supreme Court held that aliens resident in Norway were liable to be tried and convicted for treasonable activities under the Criminal Code of Norway.[190] In Johnstone v Pedlar (1921) the House of Lords of the United Kingdom said that from the moment of his entry into the country until his departure from it, the alien owed allegiance to the Crown and that by reason of the said temporary allegiance, he could be tried, convicted and executed for any act of high treason.[191] Further, in Joyce v Director of Public Prosecutions (1946) the House of Lords affirmed the conviction of an American citizen who while holding a British passport had adhered to the "King's enemies" i.e., the Germans during the Second World War, and helped the latter through his anti-British broadcasting activities. The House of Lords took the view that the said American citizen having resided for many years in England owed a temporary allegiance to the British Crown even as a resident alien, that his possession of a British passport conferring privileges on him implied necessarily his continued allegiance to the British Crown, and that by his adherence to "the King's enemies" he became subject to the charge of high treason in the same manner as any other subject of the United Kingdom.[192]

The practice of the United States of America, like that of the United Kingdom, affirms the principle that an alien resident in a foreign State becomes liable for prosecution for treason if he wages war against that State, renders comfort to its enemies or engages in conspiracies against that State to which he is deemed to owe allegiance for the duration of his residence.[193] Upon being informed that an American citizen of Greek parentage had been arrested in Greece by the Greek authorities and was being held for trial by court martial on a charge of having participated in revolutionary activities, the American Legation in Paris was instructed on March 10, 1935 by the Government of the United States as follows: "While it was desirous of having its representatives extend their good offices with a view to assuring proper treatment and just trial, it could not properly intervene with the Greek Government on behalf of American citizens who had contravened

---

190 Public Prosecutor v. Thompson and Another (1946)
Public Prosecutor v. Karlsson (1946)
Annual Digest, Ibid., 74 footnote.
191 (1921) 2 A.C. 262 (H.L.); Katz and Brewster: op. cit., 104-108.
Dejager v. The Attorney-General for Natal, (1907) 2 A.C. 326.
192 (1946) 2 A.C. 347 (H.L.); Briggs: The Law of Nations, 578-Judge Lauterpacht: "Allegiance, Diplomatic Protection and Criminal Jurisdiction over Aliens", 9 Cambridge Law Journal (1947), 330-348.
193 Opinion of Wharton; Moore: Digest, Vol. IV, 14.

Greek law in such a serious matter as rebellion unless there was strong reason to believe that otherwise a grave miscarriage of justice would result . . . that in extending good offices it should bear in mind that the Supreme Court of the United States had held that aliens domiciled in the United States owe to the Government a local and temporary allegiance which continues during the period of their residence and that they may become liable for prosecution for treason in the same manner as citizens of the United States."[194]

As observed above, States have been granting aliens within their territories certain essential personal and civil rights by means of bilateral treaties on the basis of reciprocity. Although there has been an increasing willingness on the part of States to yield extensive civil rights including occupational and residential privileges to foreign nationals by means of conventional arrangements, they are unwilling to admit aliens to the exercise of political rights. Most of the treaties[195] of friendship, commerce and navigation and other types of commercial treaties expressly prohibit aliens from participating in political affairs within the territories of the contracting parties. For instance, Clause (3) of Article VIII of the Treaty of Friendship, Commerce and Navigation entered into between the United States and Japan on April 2, 1953 provides: "Nationals and companies of either Party shall be accorded national treatment and most-favoured-nation treatment with respect to engaging in scientific, educational, religious and philanthropic activities within the territories of the other Party, and shall be accorded the right to form associations for that purpose under the laws of such other Party", and Clause (5) of Article XXI provides: "Nothing in the present Treaty shall be deemed to grant or imply any right to engage in political activities."[196] Clause (2) of Article VIII of the Treaty of Friendship, Commerce and Navigation* of October 29, 1954 provides: "Nationals and companies of either Party shall be accorded within the territories of the other Party, national treatment and most-favoured-nation treatment with respect to engaging in scientific, educational, religious and philanthropic activities and shall be accorded the right to form associations for that purpose under the laws of that country. Nothing in the present Treaty shall be deemed to grant or imply any right to engage in political activities."[197]

---

194 Hackworth: Digest, Vol. III, 554-555.
195 Hyde: International Law, Vol. I, 650.
196 United States Treaties and Other International Agreements (1953), Vol. 4, Part 2, 2070-2079.
  * Concluded between the United States of America and Germany.
197 Ibid., (1956), Vol. 7, Part 2, 1848-1849.

Principles embodied in certain Conventions

Project No. 16: Diplomatic Protection prepared by the American Institute of International Law, (1925), provides:

"The American Republic to which the diplomatic claim is presented may decline to receive this claim when the person in whose behalf it is made has interfered in internal or foreign political affairs against the government to which the claim is made. The Republic may also decline if the claimant has committed acts of hostility toward itself."[198]

Article 7 of the inter-American Convention on the Status of Aliens signed on February 20, 1928, provides:

"Foreigners must not mix in political activities, which are the exclusive province of citizens of the country in which they happen to be; in cases of such interference, they shall be liable to the penalties established by local law."[199]

Article 11

Subject to local laws, regulations, and orders and subject also to the conditions imposed for his admission into the State, an alien shall have the right to acquire, hold and dispose of property.

Note : The Delegation of Indonesia, whilst accepting the provisions of this Article, stated that according to the new laws of Indonesia aliens cannot acquire title to property though they can hold property.

Commentary

Property rights of aliens

Article 11 deals with the acquisition of property by aliens and the protection of their vested rights. According to publicists, minimum standard of international law in favour of foreigners requires a modicum of respect for the property of foreign nationals within the territories of a State.[200] Giving expression to the well established principle of international law, this Article lays down that a foreigner shall have the right to acquire, hold and dispose of property in the State of residence. However, since under international

---

198 Amador, F.V. Garcia: Report on International Responsibility, A/CN.4/96, February 20, 1956, Annex 7, 3.

199 Hackworth: Digest, Vol. III, 561. It may be added that at the First Meeting of the Ministers of Foreign Affairs held in October 1939 at Panama, the American Republics reaffirmed their adherence to the principle of exclusion of foreigners from the enjoyment and exercise of strictly political rights as a general rule of international public law to be incorporated in the Constitutions and laws of States; Supplement to the American Journal of International Law, Vol. 35 (1941), 10.

200 Schwarzenberger: Manual, op. cit., 99.

law a State possesses the undoubted right to regulate the private ownership and control of property of all individuals on its domain, the above property rights of aliens are subject to the overriding operation of the national laws of that State. In a word, the property rights of aliens in a State are subject to the power of the host State to control and use all its wealth and resources as it likes.[201]

Opinions of Writers

Vattel states that "Every State has the liberty of granting or refusing to foreigners the power of possessing lands or other immovable property within her territory. If she grants them that privilege all such property possessed by aliens remains subject to the jurisdiction and laws of the country, and to the same taxes as other property of the same kind. The authority of the sovereign extends over the whole territory; and it would be absurd to except some parts of it, on account of their being possessed by foreigners. If the sovereign does not permit aliens to possess immovable property, nobody has a right to complain of such prohibition; for he may have good reasons for acting in this manner; and, as foreigners cannot claim any right in his territories . . . they ought not to take it amiss that he makes use of his power and of his rights in the manner which he thinks most for the advantage of the State. And, as the sovereign may refuse to foreigners the privilege of possessing immovable property, he is doubtless at liberty to forbear granting it with certain conditions annexed."[202]

As regards the property rights of aliens, **Moore** quotes the views of Mr. Adam, Secretary of State of the United States, which read as follows:—"There is no principle of the law of nations more firmly established than that which entitled the property of strangers within the jurisdiction of a country in friendship with their own to the protection of its sovereign by all the efforts in his power. This (has been the) common rule of intercourse between all civilized nations."[203]

---

201 It must be added that although a State has the power to control and use all the wealth and resources within its territories, publicists take the view that in the exercise of this power, it is obligated to act in accordance with recognized principles of international law as well as international agreements if any and with due regard for existing legal rights or interests, with adequate, prompt and effective compensation as one remedy, if the exercise of the power impairs them: Hyde: "Permanent Sovereignty over National Wealth and Resources", American Journal of International Law, Vol. 50, (1956). 854.

202 Katz & Brewster: The Law of International Transactions & Relations 114.

203 Moore: Digest, Vol. IV, 5.

Hyde observes: "A State enjoys an exclusive right to regulate matters pertaining to the ownership of property of every kind which may be said to belong within its territory. Thus it may determine not only the processes by which title may be acquired, retained or transferred, but also what individuals are to be permitted to enjoy privileges of ownership."[204]

Practice of Member States of the Committee

The Constitutions of most States contain provisions respecting property rights of the inhabitants residing within their borders. For instance, Clause (1) of Article 23 of the Constitution of Burma guarantees the right of private property and of private initiative of all the inhabitants—nationals and aliens alike—in the economic sphere. However, under Clause (2) of the same Article no person shall be permitted to use the right of private property to the detriment of the general public.[205] Clause (1) of Article 31 of the Constitution of India enacts that no person shall be deprived of his property except by authority of law.[206] Several legislative enactments and decisions of the courts of law of Ceylon tend to safeguard the property rights of individuals in Ceylon.[207] Under Article 2 of the Provisional Constitution of the Republic of Indonesia, every one within the territories of Indonesia has the right to own property individually as well as in association with others; no one shall be arbitrarily deprived of his property.[208] The public law of the United Arab Republic lays down that private property and homes are inviolable in accordance with the law.[209] The law of Iraq safeguards the right of ownership. No person's goods or property shall be expropriated except for the public benefit, and in the circumstances and in the manner prescribed by law, and on condition that just compensation is paid.[210] Article 29 of the Constitution of Japan provides: "The right to own or to hold property is inviolable . . . Private property may be taken for public use upon just compensation therefor."[211] As regards the protection of property rights of individuals in Pakistan, Article 15 of the Constitution

---

204 Hyde: International Law, Vol. I, 650.
205 Peaslee: Constitutions of Nations, Vol. I, 7, 282.
206 It may be added that clause (1) of Article 31 while recognizing the superior right of the State to take the private property of an individual, requires the authority of law before the property of the individual can be expropriated. Such power of expropriation can be exercised only by authority of law and not by a mere executive fiat or order; Shukla: Commentaries on the Constitution of India. (Lucknow, 1960) 3rd ed., 111.
207 Peaslee: Constitutions of Nations, Vol. III, 816.
208 Peaslee: Ibid., Vol. II, 374.
209 Peaslee: Ibid., Vol. I, 813 and Vol. III, 363, 364.
210 Peaslee: Ibid., Vol. II, 416.
211 The Constitution of Japan and Criminal Statutes (Japan, 1958), 8.

of the Islamic Republic of Pakistan provides: "No person shall be deprived of his property save in accordance with law. No property shall be compulsorily acquired or taken possession of save for a public purpose, and save by the authority of law which provides for compensation therefor and either fixes the amount of compensation or specifies the principles on which and the manner in which compensation is to be determined and given."[212]

In Burma, Ceylon and India, aliens are permitted to hold and inherit real porperty. On the basis of reciprocity, Japan permits foreign ownership of real property in Japan. According to the new laws of Indonesia although aliens are permitted to hold property, they are prohibited from acquiring title to real property. Iraq imposes restrictions on alien ownership of agricultural land. In the United Arab Republic, under the Land Reform Law, no foreigner can own agricultural land more than 200 acres per head. This restriction does not apply to buildings and properties of like nature. Alien's right of succession to real property is permitted subject to the maximum limit of 200 acres per head as referred to above. In the Syrian Region of the U.A.R., no alien could be an owner of buildings unless he has obtained the necessary permission therefor from the authorities. Further, no foreigner is permitted to own agricultural lands. However, an alien's right of succession to agricultural land is permitted.

While under the laws of Burma, Japan and the U.A.R., aliens could not be the sole or part owners of ships which sail under their respective national flags: those of Ceylon, India and Indonesia, do not impose any such restrictions in this regard. On the basis of the standard of reciprocity certain aliens in Iraq are permitted to be sole or part owners of ships registered in Iraq.[213]

Practice of States other than Member States of the Committee

Practice of States reveals that aliens are generally permitted to acquire property, but such property rights of individuals are regulated by the national legal systems concerned. Since a State has the right to regulate matters pertaining to the acquisition and ownership of property of every kind within its territory, it enjoys

---

212 Brohi: Fundamental Law of Pakistan (Karachi, 1958), 805.
It may be added that Article 15 contains two essential parts, the one prohibiting the deprivation of property "except in accordance with law," and the other prescribing that a law which authorises compulsory acquisition of property or the taking of its possession must provide for compensation either by fixing amount or by specifying the principles on which and the manner in which compensation is to be determined and given. Brohi: Ibid., 402-404.
213 Report of the Asian African Legal Consultative Committee (Third Session, 1960), 123-24.

514

the competence to determine not only the process by which title can be acquired, retained or transferred, but also what individuals are to be permitted to enjoy privileges of ownership.214 Recognizing this principle of international law, Mr. Kellogg, United States Secretary of State, stated as follows: "Every sovereign State has the absolute right within its own jurisdiction to make laws governing the acquisition of property acquired in the future. This right cannot be questioned by any other State. If Mexico desires to prevent the future acquisition by aliens of property rights of any nature within its jurisdiction, this Government has no suggestion whatever to make."215 The term 'property' interpreted and applied by the national courts of several States includes not only personal property and real property but also intangible and incorporeal rights such as patents, copyrights, leases, accounts and choses in action. In short, every thing which can command an exchangeable value would be designated as property.216

States do not seem to be disposed to prevent the acquisition of or succession to movable property by foreign nationals. However, several States exclude aliens "from the acquisition of certain classes of movables such as airplanes and ships, as well as impose other restrictions having for their purpose the conservation of the country's vital economic resources."217 For instance, under the laws of the United Kingdom and the United States of America, an alien cannot be sole or part owner of ships.218 The Act of June 5, 1920 lays down that no rights under the mortgage of a vessel of the United States may be assigned to any person not a citizen of the United States without the approval of the United States Shipping Board.219 Further, a vessel of the United States may not be sold by order of a District Court of the United States in any suit **in rem** in admiralty to any person not a citizen of the United States.220 In a word, personal property may generally be held and inherited by foreign nationals, subject to certain limitations in the public interest. In the case of **Fergus et el v Tomalinson**, as

---

214 Hyde: International Law, Vol. I, 650.
215 However, he takes the view that when any Government seeks to divest aliens of property rights, which have already been legally acquired, their home State has the right to make representations and efforts to avoid such action.
   Hyde: International Law, Vol. I, 650 footnote.
216 Brohi: Fundamental Law of Pakistan, 408.
217 Freeman: The International Responsibility of States for Denial of Justice (1938), 512; Briggs: The Law of Nations, 568.
218 Oppenheim: International Law, Vol. I, 680.
   Hackworth: Digest, Vol. III, 624-625.
219 41 Stat. 1004; 46 U.S.C. ss 961 (d); Hackworth: Digest, Vol. III, 624.
220 41 Stat. 1004; 48 U.S.C. ss 961 (e); Hackworth: Ibid., 625.

Administrator (1928), the Supreme Court of Kansas said: "But alienage is not at common law any obstacle to the acquisition of title to personal property by next of kin . . . No reason is apparent, therefore, why the husband in the instant case, although a British subject, may not inherit his wife's personal estate. The question needs no further elucidation."[221] It may, however, be added that under an Oregon Statute, the right of aliens residing outside of the United States or its territories to take personal property or the proceeds thereof by descent or inheritance was made dependent upon the existence of a reciprocal right under the law of the alien's country. Thus in **In re Braun'a Estate,** the Supreme Court of Oregon held that it was incumbent upon the claimants, non-resident citizens of Germany, to prove that Germany granted such reciprocal right to American citizens.[222] But, in the case of **Emery et al v Cooley, Administrator et al,** it was held by another court that where real property is sold under the direction of the terms of a will it becomes personalty and non-resident aliens may take the proceeds despite statutory prohibitions against the inheritance of real property by aliens.[223]

Although aliens are normally permitted to hold and inherit personal property, States have been concluding commercial treaties which **inter alia** grant the nationals of the respective countries the right freely to dispose of and to succeed to personal property on an equal footing with the nationals of the country in which the property is situated. For instance, Article 14 of the Consular Convention concluded between the United States of America and Sweden in June 1910 provides: "The citizens of each of the Contracting Parties shall have power to dispose of their personal goods within the jurisdiction of the other, by sale, donation, testament, or otherwise, and their representatives, being citizens of the other Party, shall succeed to their personal goods, whether by treatment or **ab testamento,** and they may in accordance with and acting under the provisions of the laws of the jurisdiction in which the property is found take possession thereof, either by themselves or others acting for them, and dispose of the same at their will, paying such dues only as the inhabitants of the country wherein such goods are shall be subject to pay in like cases."[224]

Similar provisions have been included in bilateral treaties of friendship, commerce and navigation entered into between the

---

221 Hackworth: Ibid., 666; 126 Kans. 427, 268 Pac. 849, 850 (1928).
222 Hackworth: Ibid., 666-667 footnote.
223 Hackworth: Ibid., 667 footnote.
224 Hackworth: Ibid., 668.

United States and Italy in 1948, the United States and Japan in 1953, and the United States and Federal Republic of Germany in 1954. The ownership of immovable property by aliens is frequently limited. Several States appear to be unwilling to permit the succession to and retention of title to immovable property within their borders by individuals other than their own nationals or by aliens who are non-residents. International law does not impose upon any State the duty to permit aliens to acquire title to real property although as a matter of fact this right is granted in some States by virtue of its own municipal laws and bilateral treaties.[225] In several decisions, courts in the United States have held that rights in real property are governed by local law in the absence of applicable treaty provisions. In **Orr v Hodgson** one United States court took the following view: "It has become the settled law of this country that, in the absence of a treaty to the contrary, a State may lawfully prohibit aliens from owning or acquiring any lands or any interest therein, within its borders."[226] Further, courts in the United States seem to recognize that the right of succession to real property is a matter for the determination of the country or State in which the land is situated and that it is governed by the laws in force therein at the time of the owner's death. Thus, in **United States v Crosby** Mr. Justice Story stated: "the Court entertained no doubt on the subject; and are clearly of opinion, that the title to land can be acquired and lost only in the manner prescribed by the law of the place where such land is situate."[227]

The United States is not at the present time disposed to yield by treaty, for the benefit of the nationals of a foreign contracting State, the privilege of acquiring lands within the territories of the United States except where such acquisition is by way of succession to the rights or interests in such lands as are possessed by the nationals of such States. The law of the United States relating to alien ownership of land has been laid down in 4 U.S.C.A. ss 1501-1512. Under ss 1501 of that law, "no alien or person who is not a citizen of the United States, or who has not declared his intention to become a citizen of the United States in the manner provided by law shall acquire title to or own any land in any of the territories of the United States except as hereinafter provided. The prohibition of this section shall not apply to cases in which the right to hold or dispose lands in the United States is secured by

---

225 Hyde: International Law, Vol. I, 651
   Freeman: The International Responsibility of States for Denial of Justice (1938), 512.
226 4 Wheat 453; Hackworth: Digest, Vol. III, 671 footnote.
227 7 Cranch 114; Hackworth: Ibid., 672 footnote.

existing treaties to citizens or subjects of foreign countries, which rights, so far as they may exist by force of any such treaty, shall continue to exist so long as such treaties are in force and no longer."

Under ss 181 of the Act of February 25, 1920, Ch. 85, ss 1, 41 Stat. 437, "deposits of coal, phosphate, sodium, potassium, oil, oil-shale, or gas and lands containing such deposits owned by the United States including those in national forests, but excluding lands acquired under sections 513-519 of Title 16, and those in incorporated cities, towns and villages and in national parks and monuments, those acquired under other Acts subsequent to February 25, 1920, and lands within the naval petroleum and oil-shale resources, except as hereinafter provided, shall be subject to disposition in the form and manner provided by sections 181-184, 185-188, 189-194, 201, 202-209, 211-214, 223, 224-226, 226(d), 226(e), 227-229(a), 241, 251, 261-263 of this title to citizens of the United States, or to associations of such citizens, or to any corporations organized under the laws of the United States, or of any State, or territory thereof, or in the case of coal, oil, oil-shale or gas, to municipalities. Citizens of another country, the laws, customs, or regulations of which deny similar or like privileges to citizens or corporations of this country (United States) shall not by stock ownership, stock holding, or stock control, own any interest in any lease acquired under the provisions of the said section."[228]

Moreover, since the common law rules relating to succession to real property have been incorporated into the common law of the several States of the United States, an alien in those States can take real property by devise subject to forfeiture but he cannot be allowed to inherit it. At present all States have modified the common law rules either by Statute or Constitution. In twenty States aliens are permitted to acquire and hold real property by testate and intestate succession. Other States, however, accord equal treatment only to alien friends, aliens who are eligible to citizenship, resident aliens, or aliens who have declared their intention to become citizens. Aliens who do not come within these special classifications have either no rights or else their rights are limited.[229]

---

228 As amended by Act of Feb. 27, 1927, Ch. 66, ss. 5, 44 Stat. 1058; Act of Aug. 8, 1946, Ch. 916, ss. 1, 11; 60 Stat. 950, 30 U.S.C.A. ss. 181, Katz & Brewster: The Law of International Transactions and Relations, 182.

229 Boyd: "Treaties Governing the Succession to Royal Property by Aliens", 51, Mich. L. Review, 1005 (1953).

In **Veuve Proust** v. **Kaing** (1949) the Tribunal de Paix Nantes of France held that in the absence of reciprocity, a Chinese national was not entitled to the benefit even of the provisions of the French law of September 1, 1948 which gave tenants security of tenure. The court said that "since Article 4 of the Law of September 1, 1948, does not expressly grant alien tenants security of tenure, the general rules of law in the matter must be applied . . . Accordingly, an alien can enjoy that security only if his national law grants analogous privileges to French nationals; if a diplomatic convention exempts him from the condition of reciprocity, or if a general clause of diplomatic treaty provides directly or indirectly for the assimilation of the alien to the French nationals."[230] French citizens in the United States may acquire real estate by inheritance or otherwise except where State laws forbid aliens to hold real property.[231]

An alien may not hold real estate in Mexico within a hundred kilometres of the frontier, nor within fifty kilometres of the coast; nor may he be interested in a Mexican company owning land in these zones. Further, foreigners are not to own more than forty-nine percent of the stock of companies formed to exploit rural agricultural lands. Any interest greater than this may be retained until death, after which if the heir is not qualified to hold as a Mexican citizen, he is allowed five years for disposal.[232] Article 27 of the Constitution of Mexico of January 31, 1917 (as amended) provides that the "general capacity to acquire ownership of lands and waters of the nation shall be governed by the following provisions: "(1) Only Mexicans by birth or naturalization and Mexican corporations have the right to acquire ownership of lands, waters, and their appurtenances, or to obtain concessions for working mines or for the utilization of waters or mineral fuel in the Republic of Mexico. The nation may grant the same right to aliens, provided they agree . . . to consider themselves as Mexicans in respect to such porperty."[233] Article 14 of the Organic Law of 1925 sustains the title of those owners of the subsoil who had performed some positive act of ownership. The rights of others could be confirmed only as fifty year concessions since by the Constitution of 1917, "the 'direct ownership of certain enumerated mineral substances, including oil, gas and petroleum is vested in the nation and is inalienable and unprescriptible.[234]

---

230 Annual Digest (1949), 259-260.
231 Cutler: The Treatment of Foreigners, Vol. 27, A.J.I.L. (1933), 239-243.
232 Ibid., 241.
233 Peaslee: Constitutions of Nations, Vol. II, 667.
234 Cutler: Op. cit., 241-242.

The Constitution of Poland provides in Article 95, paragraph 2 that "aliens shall enjoy on condition of reciprocity equality of rights with citizens of the Polish State and are subject to duties equal to those of the latter, unless Polish citizenship is expressly required by Statute." Under Article 99, "Statutes will determine the right of the State compulsorily to buy up land and to regulate dealings in land and also that it is only by statute that it can be determined how far rights of citizens and of their legally recognized associations to use freely land, waters, minerals and other natural resources may be limited for public reasons."[235]

Since no rule of international law imposes on a State the duty of according to the nationals of another State the right to acquire and hold real property within its borders, States conclude mostly bilateral treaties for this purpose. Many of the treaties between the United States and other powers contain provisions relating to acquisition of real property by their nationals within the territories of the other party. For example, Article I of the Treaty of Friendship, Commerce, and Consular Rights between the United States and Honduras, signed on December 7, 1927, provides that the nationals of each country in the territory of the other shall be permitted "to own, erect or lease and occupy appropriate buildings and to lease lands for residential, scientific, religious, philanthropic, manufacturing, commercial and mortuary purposes." It also provides in Article IV: "Where, on the death of any person holding real or other immovable property or interests therein within the territories of one High Contracting Party, such property or interests therein would, by the laws of the country or by a testamentary disposition, descend or pass to a national of the other High Contracting Party, whether resident or non-resident, were he not disqualified by the laws of the country where such property or interests therein is or are situated, such national shall be allowed a term of three years in which to sell the same, this term to be reasonably prolonged if circumstances render it necessary, and withdraw the proceeds thereof, without restraint or interference, and exempt from any succession, probate or administrative duties or charges other than those which may be imposed in like cases upon the nationals of the country from which such proceeds may be drawn."[236] Similar provisions are to be found in a large number of treaties to which the United States is a party.[237]

---

235 Sazonow v. District Land (Reform) Board of Bailystok, Annual Digest, (1919-1922), 247.
236 Hackworth: Digest, Vol. III, 672.
237 Arts. VII and VIII of the Treaty of Friendship, Commerce and Navi-

Several States take the view that with the yielding to an alien of the privilege of acquiring and holding property of any kind within its territories, the territorial sovereign finds itself subjected to a corresponding obligation to make reasonable endeavour to protect the same, and to abstain itself through any of its agencies, from conduct injurious to it.[238] They argue that when a State has permitted an alien either to engage in business or otherwise lawfully to acquire property, it cannot thereafter arbitrarily or unreasonably curtail his rights or confiscate the property. The United States has expressed its position on this question in the following terms: "When a nation has invited intercourse with other nations, has established laws under which investments have been lawfully made, contracts entered into and property rights acquired by citizens of other jurisdictions, it is an essential condition of international intercourse that international obligations shall be met and that there shall be no resort to confiscation and repudiation. . ."[239] Although the law of nations demands respect for private property, it recognises the right of the State to derogate from this principle, when its superior interest so requires. Thus, it allows expropriation for reasons of public benefit in time of peace and requisition in time of war.[240] In the view of some States, if a country wishes to nationalize a foreign-owned property it must make payment to foreign owners of the property nationalized.[241] It may be added that many modern Constitutions contain provisions which provide inter alia that private property shall not be taken for public use, without payment of compensation therefor.[242]

Principles embodied in certain Conventions

European Convention on Establishment[243]

Chapter II

Exercise of Private Rights

Article 4

Nationals of any Contracting Party shall enjoy in the territory of any other Party treatment equal to that enjoyed by nationals of

gation concluded between the United States and the Italian Republic on February 2, 1948 could be cited as an example. Briggs: The Law of Nations, 544-545.
238 Hyde: International Law, Vol. I, 655.
239 Orfield & Re: Cases and Materials on International Law (1955), 532; Anderson: "Basis of the Law Against Confiscating Foreigner-owned Property", Vol. 21, A.J.I.L. (1927), 685-695.
240 Cheng: General Principles of Law (London, 1953), 37.
241 Wilson: "Property Protection Provisions in United States Commercial Treaties": Vol. 45, A.J.I.L. (1951), 83-87.
242 The Fifth Amendment to the Constitution of the U.S.A. contains such a provision.
243 Signed in Paris on December 13, 1955.

the latter Party in respect of the possession and exercise of private rights, whether personal rights or rights relating to property.

Article 5

Notwithstanding Article 4 of this Convention, any Contracting Party may, for reasons of national security or defence, reserve the acquisition, possession or use of any categories of property for its own nationals or subject nationals of other Parties to special conditions applicable to aliens in respect of such property.

Article 6

(1) Apart from cases relating to national security or defence,

(a) Any Contracting Party which has reserved for its nationals, or, in the case of aliens including those who are nationals of other Parties, made subject to regulations the acquisition, possession or use of certain categories of property, or has made the acquisition, possession or use of such property conditional upon reciprocity shall, at the time of the signature to this Convention, transmit a list of these restrictions to the Secretary-General of the Council of Europe indicating which provisions of its municipal law are the basis of such restrictions. The Secretary-General shall forward these lists to the other Signatories;

(b) After this Convention has entered into force in respect of any Contracting Party, that Contracting Party shall not introduce any further restrictions as to the acquisition, possession or use of any categories of property by nationals of the other Parties, unless it finds itself compelled to do so for imperative reasons of an economic or social character or in order to prevent monopolisation of the vital resources of the country. It shall in this event keep the Secretary-General fully informed of the measures taken, the relevant provisions of municipal law and the reasons for such measures. The Secretary-General shall communicate this information to the other Parties.

(2) Each Contracting Party shall endeavour to reduce its list of restrictions for the benefit of nationals of the other Parties. It shall notify the Secretary-General of any such changes and he shall communicate them to the other Parties.

Each Party shall also endeavour to grant to nationals of other Parties such exemptions from the general regulations concerning aliens as are provided for in its own legislation.[244]

---

[244] Unification of Law, Vol. I, International Institute for the Unification of Private Law (Rome, 1957), 165-167.

Article 12

(1) The State shall, however, have the right to acquire, expropriate or nationalise the property of an alien. Compensation shall be paid for such acquisition, expropriation or nationalisation in accordance with local laws, regulations and orders.

(2) The State shall also have the right to dispose of or otherwise lawfully deal with the property of an alien under orders of expulsion or deportation.

Note : (1) The Delegation of Japan did not accept the provisions of this Article. According to its view, "just compensation" should be paid for all acquisition, nationalisation or expropriation and not "compensation in accordance with the local laws, regulations and orders." The Delegation could not accept the provisions of Clause (2) as such a provision would be contrary to the laws of Japan.

(2) The Delegation of Indonesia reserved its position on Clause (2) of this Article.

(3) The Delegation of Pakistan stated that though it accepted the provisions of this Article, the view of the Delegation was that acquisition, nationalisation or expropriation should be in the national interest or for a public purpose.

Commentary

Right of expropriation of foreign-owned property

Clause (1) of Article 12 embodies the principle that where a State has permitted an alien to acquire lawfully property on its territory, it must not thereafter arbitrarily deprive him of his property. This is known as the doctrine of respect for acquired rights, and respect for acquired rights is one of the recognised principles of international law. However, respect for acquired rights is not an absolute right. The enjoyment of acquired rights is permissible only in conformity with the national legal system. Further, the law of nations does not deny to a State the right to launch upon social and economic measures designed to serve the common welfare of its people, nor does it prohibit a State from determining its own system of economic structure intended to achieve the general welfare of its people. Thus, although the law of nations demands respect for private property of aliens, it also recognises the right of a State to derogate from this principle if its superior interests so require. It allows requisition and expropriation for reasons of public utility in time of peace and in time of war.[245] As a matter of fact, private property rights of aliens as well as of nationals are continually being seriously restrained, modified or suppressed in the exercise of what is known as "police power" or "eminent domain". If expropriation is exercised by the competent organ of a State in conformity with the general national legislation, principles of good faith, juridical equality between aliens, absence of discrimination against aliens as such, and conditional upon payment of compensations, such expropriation would be in keeping with dictates of international law and practice of the civilized nations of the present day world.[246]

Clause (2) of this Article gives expression to the effect of a well recognized rule of international law and State practice according to which an alien is under the jurisdiction of the State in which he happens to be, and is responsible to it for acts he commits on its territory. The foreign State has the right to dispose of or otherwise deal with the property of an alien who has been under orders of expulsion or deportation. If the host State's action in this regard is not arbitrary or unreasonable, if exercised in accordance with its applicable laws, regulations and the principle of good faith and if there has been no denial or delay of justice, his home State's right of protection over its nationals abroad does not arise.

Opinions of Writers

Oppenheim says: "The rule is clearly established that a State is bound to respect the property of aliens. This rule is qualified, but not abolished, by two factors: the first is that the law of most States permits far-reaching interference with private property in connection with taxation, measures of police, public health, and the administration of public utilities. The second modification must be recognised in cases in which fundamental changes in the political system and economic structure of the State or far-reaching social reforms entail interference, on a large scale, with private property. In such cases neither the principle of absolute respect for alien private property nor rigid equality with the dispossessed nationals offer a satisfactory solution of the difficulty. It is probable that, consistent with legal principle, such solution must be sought in the granting of partial compensation."[247]

---

245 Portuguese-German Arbitration (1919) Award II (1930); 2. United Nations Reports of International Arbitral Awards, 1035-1039; Norwegian Shipping Claims case (1922).

246 Standard Oil Co. case (1926); League of Nations, Bases of Discussion, 1929, Vol. 3, 33-37.

247 Oppenheim: International Law, Vol. I, 352.

Hyde says: "A State has the power to control and use its natural wealth and resources. It may thus enter into binding agreements for development of its national wealth and resources. In the exercise of this power, it is obligated to act in accordance with recognised principles of international law as well as international agreements with due regard for existing legal rights or interests, with adequate, prompt and effective compensation as one remedy, if the exercise of the power impairs them.

Such a formulation is essential to a measure of understanding among States exporting and importing capital whether or not a majority of the (General Assembly of the United Nations) places an article on self-determination in the Draft Human Rights Covenants, applicable to the taking of private property, it is wise to insure this minimum certainty of measuring of its legal implications."[248]

Practice of Member States of the Committee

Expropriation of foreign owned property for public purposes is permissible only against compensation under the laws of the countries in the Committee. Clause (4) of Article 23 of the Constitution of the Union of Burma lays down: "Private property may be limited or expropriated if the public interest so requires but only in accordance with law which shall prescribe in which cases and to what extent the owner shall be compensated. And Clause (5) states that subject to the conditions set out in the last preceding clause, individual branches of national economy or single enterprises may be nationalized or acquired by the State by law if the public interest so requires.[249] Article 27 of the Provisional Constitution of the Republic of Indonesia provides: "(1) Expropriation of any property or right for the general benefit cannot take place, except with indemnification and in accordance with regulations as established by law. (2) If any property has to be destroyed by public authority or has to be rendered useless either permanently or temporarily for the general benefit, such actions can only be taken with indemnification and in accordance with regulations as established by law, unless this law determines to the contrary."[250] Article 10 of the Iraqi Constitution provides: No person's goods or property shall be expropriated except for the public benefit, and in the manner prescribed by law, and on condition that just compensation is paid. Another paragraph of this

---

248 Hyde: "Permanent Sovereignty over National Wealth & Resources", Vol 50, American Journal of International Law (1956), 854.
249 Peaslee: Constitutions of Nations, Vol. I, 282.
250 Peaslee: Ibid., Vol. II, 374.

Article adds that goods or property may not be seized and prohibited goods be not confiscated except in accordance with law and that the general confiscation of movable and immovable property are absolutely forbidden.[251] In Iraq any criminal's property, be he a national or an alien, could be confiscated without making any discrimination between nationals and aliens . . . Under Article 31(2) of the Constitution of India, "no property shall be compulsorily acquired or requisitioned save for a public purpose and save by authority of a law which provides for compensation for the property so acquired or requisitioned and either fixes the amount of the compensation or specifies the principles on which and the manner in which, the compensation is to be determined and given; and no such law shall be called in question in any court on the ground that the compensation provided by that law is not adequate." Thus, although the Constitution of India provides for the State's power of compulsory acquisition and requisitioning of private property of nationals and aliens alike against compensation, yet the determination of the quantum of the compensation payable for the property taken has been left to the legislature. Under the Constitution (Fourth Amendment) Act of 1955, it is no more open to the Indian courts to go into the question of appropriation of private property by the State and enquire whether the true value of the property appropriated has been ensured.[252] Under Clause (3) of Article 29 of the Constitution of Japan, private property may be taken by the State for public use upon just compensation therefor.[253] In **Anglo-Iranian Oil Co. v. Idemitsu Kosan Kabushiki Kaisha** (1953), the High Court of Tokyo (First Civil Affairs Section) said in part:

"(a) There is an established principle of international law that in the event of a violent social reform or revolution in a State, whether or not the property of the nationals of that State is confiscated, property belonging to foreign nationality can only be expropriated with compensation. Moreover, such compensation must be "adequate, efficient and immediate compensation." This has been confirmed by the practice of many States, by precedents, and by the writings of acknowledged authorities.

"(b) As to whether the courts of a third country must recog-

---

251 Peaslee: Ibid., 416.
252 Bela Banerji, 1954, S.C.R. 41. Prior to the Constitution (Fourth Amendment) Act, 1955, the Courts in India had the power to go into the question on the ground that the compensation provided for by the State was not adequate. According to the practice of the Indian courts "compensation" means "a just equivalent of what the owner has been deprived of taking into account all the elements which make up the true value of the property appropriated."
253 The Constitution of Japan and Criminal Statutes, 8.

nize the effect of a law which is, as the nationalization law was, properly enacted by another State, or whether it is permissible to examine the validity or invalidity of such a law and then possibly refuse to recognize it, the practice of the various States is still divided, and no universally accepted principle of international law that the effect of a foreign law may be adjudged invalid by the courts of a State has yet been established . . . This Nationalization Law was enacted in Iran's own interests and in accordance with the Resolution of the General Assembly of the United Nations relating to the exploitation of the natural resources of the various countries. Furthermore, as stated in the conclusions, in view of the fact that the Nationalization Law is not a completely confiscatory law, contrary to the rights and interests of foreign nationals, but a law of expropriation subject to payment of compensation the courts feel bound to hold that it cannot try the validity or invalidity of such a law by examining the compensation and securing whether or not it is "adequate, effective and immediate". If, however, we take the view that we cannot pass on the validity or invalidity of such a law, we do in effect thereby actually recognize the validity of the law."[254]

Clause (1) of Article 15 of the Constitution of the Islamic Republic of Pakistan lays down that no person shall be deprived of his property save in accordance with law; and under Clause (2), no property shall be compulsorily acquired or taken possession of save for a public purpose, and save by the authority of law which provides for compensation therefor and either fixes the amount of compensation or specifies the principles on which and the manner in which compensation is to be determined and given. Clause (4) of the article provides that "property" in Clause (2) of the article shall mean immovable property, or any commercial or industrial undertaking, or any interest in any such undertaking.[255] Commenting on the scope of Article 15, Brohi observes as follows: "This Article has two essential parts, the one prohibiting the deprivation of property except in accordance with law, and the other prescribing that a law which authorises compulsory acquisition of property or the taking of its possession must provide for compensation either by fixing the amount or by specifying the principles on which and the manner in which compensation is to be determined and given. Broadly considered, the first part corresponds to the power which in American jurisprudence is called the

---

254 International Law Reports (1953), 305-313; Katz & Brewster: The Law of International Transactions & Relations, 830.
255 Brohi: Fundamental Law of Pakistan, 805.

"police power" of the State and the second, the power of "eminent domain."[256]

In the case of **Mira Khan and others v Meharban Husain and others** (1951) it has been held that the term "acquisition" is a wide concept, meaning procuring or taking property permanently or temporarily and it does not necessarily mean acquisition of legal title by the State in the property taken possession of. The court declined to impose upon the term "acquisition" a narrow meaning on the ground that such a construction would introduce a technicality which would unnecessarily curtail the meaning of the expression, with the result that a law enacted to deal with requisition would be valid even if it did not make provision for payment of any compensation. In the words of Mr. Rahman C. J. : "In the context of immovable property, acquisition may be accepted as transference of the ownership rights to the acquiring authority, as contrasted with requisition which would vest a temporary right of use of the property in that authority. The right of possession is but part of the full right of ownership. **Omne majus continct in se minus**—the greater contains the less, is a well-known maxin of the law."[257]

Practice of States other than Member States of the Committee

Some States take the view that when a State has permitted an alien either to engage in business or otherwise lawfully to acquire property, it cannot thereafter arbitrarily or unreasonably curtail his rights or confiscate the property.[258] The Secretary of State Huges has expressed the position of the United States on this question in the following terms: "When a nation has invited intercourse with other nations, has established laws under which investments have been lawfully made, contracts entered into and property rights acquired by citizens of other jurisdictions, it is an essential condition of international intercourse that international obligations shall be met and that there shall be no resort to confiscation and repudiation."[259] Although the law of nations demands respect for private property, it recognizes the right of the

---

256 Brohi: Ibid., 404: The American courts have evolved the doctrine of "police power", "eminent domain" and "taxation power" as limiting the application of "due process" clause. Police power, eminent domain and taxation power are those powers, the exercise of which whether by the Government of the Federation or the States is not held to be in conflict with the due maintenance of the protection of the "due process of law" which is given to the individual by the Constitution of the United States in its 5th and 14th Amendments: Brohi: Ibid., 365-366.

257 Pakistan Legal Decisions (1956), Karachi 338; Brohi: op. cit., 411.

258 Stowell: International Law (1931), 171.

259 Orfield and Re: Cases and Materials on International Law (London, 1956), 532.

State to derogate from this principle, when its superior interest so requires. Thus, it allows expropriation for reasons of public utility in time of peace and requisition in time of war.[260] Expropriation of private property, whether national or foreign for reasons of public benefit was recognized by the Permanent Court of Arbitration in the **Norwegian Shipping Claims case (1922)** [261] and the Permanent Court of International Justice in the **German Interests Case (Merits) (1962)**.[262] The right was described by the Permanent Court of Arbitration in these terms: "The power of a sovereign State to expropriate, take or authorise the taking of any property within its jurisdiction which may be required for the public good or for the general welfare (has the status of a legal right)."[263] Thus, a government may take foreign-owned property for its own use making that property its own. If a country wishes to nationalize any foreign-owned property it must pay compensation to the foreign owner of the property nationalized. This rule seems to have been established not only by the overwhleming weight of opinions of publicists, but also by the sustained practice of Western nations and of international judicial tribunals. The Soviet Union too accepted in a series of treaties the rights of new investors in that country. According to the Secretary of State Hull of the United States, "the taking of property without compensation is not expropriation. It is confiscation." While admitting that all sovereign nations have the right to expropriate private property within its territories, he added that the universally recognised principles of the law of nations require that such expropriation be accompanied by provision on the part of a State for adequate, effective and prompt payment of compensation for the properties seized.[264]

As regards the right of a State to nationalize foreign owned property within its territory, it appears that the United Kingdom, like the United States, normally does not question the general right of a government to expropriate in the public interest and on payment of adequate compensation, but in its view this right does not justify expropriations essentially arbitrary in character. While confiscation is theoretically prohibited in modern times, the doctrine of just compensation for property taken has been embodied in the Constitutions of most countries of the world.[265] Clause (xxi) of

---

260 Portugo-German Arbitration (1919), Award II (1930), Vol. 2 U.N. Reports of International Arbitral Awards, 1035-1039; Cheng: General Principles of Law. 37-38.
261 Orfield and Re: Cases and Materials on International Law, 502-505.
262 Rep. of P.C.I.J. 1926, Ser. A, No. 7, 22.
263 Cheng: General Principles of Law. 38.
264 Hyde: International Law, Vol. I, 710-711.
265 Cutler: The Treatment of Aliens. op. cit., 240; Hyde: International Law, Vol. I, 714.

the Commonwealth of Australia Constitution Act of 1900 confers on the Commonwealth Parliament the power of—"acquisition of property on just terms from any State or person for any purpose in respect of which Parliament has power to make laws."[266] Sub-Clause (2) (vi) of Article 44 of the Constitution of Ireland provides: "The property of any religious denomination or any educational institution shall not be divested save for necessary works of public utility and on payment of compensation." Under Clause (3) Article 14 of the West German Constitution (1948), "Expropriation shall be admissible only for the well-being of the general public. It may be effected only by legislation or on a basis of law which shall regulate the nature or extent of compensation. Compensation shall be determined after just consideration of the interests of the general public and participants. Regarding the extent of compensation an appeal may be made to ordinary courts in case of dispute." And Article 15 provides, "Land and landed property, natural resources, and means of production may for the purpose of socialization be transferred to public ownership or other forms of public controlled economy by law which shall regulate the nature and extent of compensation. . ."[267] The doctrine of just compensation for property taken has been embodied in the Constitutions of every republic of the American continent.[268] For instance, Article 63 of the Constitution of the Republic of Nicaragua lays down that no one may be deprived of his property except by judicial judgment, a general tax, or for public use or social interest according to law and upon prior payment in cash of just compensation.[269]

As regards the law of England, Blackstone observes: "So great is the regard of the law for private property, that it will not authorize the least violation of it . . . the Legislature alone can and indeed frequently does, interpose and compel the individual to acquiesce. But how does it interpose and compel? Not by absolutely stripping the subject of his property in an arbitrary manner; but by giving him a full indemnification and equivalent for the injury thereby sustained.[270] Thus property in England can be compulsorily acquired for public purposes only if a Statute authorises the executive organ of the State to do so. It is an established rule of construction of instruments that express words must exist in such a Statute

---

266 Basu: Commentary on the Constitution of India (Calcutta, 1955), Vol. I, 343.
267 Basu: Ibid., 343-344.
268 Hyde: International Law, Vol. I, 714.
269 Peaslee: Constitutions of Nations, Vol. III, 10.
270 Blackstone's Commentaries, Book I, 139; Basu: Commentary on the Constitution of India, 342-343.

before the intention to authorize the taking of property without compensation could be given effect to. In the case of **De Keysers' Royal Hotel Ltd., v. The King** (1920) the House of Lords stated **inter alia:** "When powers covered by this Statute (i.e., Defence of Realm Regulations) are exercised by the Crown it must be presumed that they are so exercised under the statute, and therefore subject to the equitable provision for compensation which is to be found in it . . . if the commandeering of the buildings in this case had not been expressly done under statutory powers . . the Crown must be presumed to have acted under these statutory powers and thus given to the subject the statutory right to compensation,"[217] **Prima facie** the subject or national of a State at peace with the United Kingdom is, while resident in that country, entitled to the protection of the Crown accorded to British subjects.[272] This rule applies also to foreign owned property in the United Kingdom.

The law of the United States relating to the taking of property is regulated by the Fifth and Fourteenth Amendments to the Constitution of the United States of America. The provision in the Fifth Amendment to the Constitution of the United States that private property shall not "be taken for public use, without just compensation" is unconditional in scope and extends to aliens as well as to citizens. Likewise, aliens are protected by the provision in the Fourteenth Amendment prohibiting the States from depriving "any person of life, liberty, or property, without due process of law."[273] The American law permits the Government to take property of an alien for public benefit with just compensation. Under the American law, such a taking would normally be in the form of an assertion of the power of eminent domain.[274] **In Berman v Parker** (1954), an act authorizing the establishment of a District Columbia Redevelopment Land Agency and the adoption of a comprehensive land use plan was held valid under the "Due Process Clause." The particular taking of plaintiff's commercial property in the execution of such a land use plan was held a proper exercise of the power of "eminent domain" for a public purpose, though the plan contemplated redevelopment of the property taken under the management of a private agency and the possible uses under the plan included commercial purposes.[275] In the **United States v. Kansas City Life Insurance Co.,** (1950), the claimant was held entitled to just compensation for

271 (1920) A.C. 508: Brohi: Fundamental Law of Pakistan, 414-415.
272 Johnstone v. Pedlar (1921), A.C. 262; Katz & Brewster: The Law of International Relations and Transactions, 104-108.
273 Hackworth: Digest, Vol. III, 653.
274 Katz & Brewster: Op. cit., 779.
275 348 U.S. 26; 75 S.Ct. 98 (1954).

destruction of agricultural value of his land by government's maintenance of Mississippi river in that vicinity continuously at high water level in the interest of navigation.[276]

According to the practice of States and the law of nations the taking of foreign owned property with compensation is known as "expropriation". There are frequent instances in the past where in time of peace, the expropriation or destruction of the immovable property of foreign nationals has been deemed to require the payment of full compensation.[277] In **Anglo-Iranian Oil Co., Ltd., v. Jaffrate** (The Rose Mary) (1953) the Supreme Court of Aden held that the Iranian Law of 1951 was confiscatory in that it failed to provide "any compensation", and was therefore in violation of international law which was part of the common law of Aden.[278] In **Anglo-Iranian Oil Co. Ltd. v. Societa S.U.P.O.R.** (1954) the Civil Tribunal of Rome (Italy) said in part: "In the Italian legal system as shown by several decisions, there is a recognized power of expropriation even in relation to immovables which the administration had undertaken by contract not to expropriate. The exercise of such power, therefore, could not be regarded as contrary to Italian public order. In Italy, furthermore, the right to extract minerals is a personal right the expropriation of which is not subject to compensation. But a right to indemnity is recognized by the Iranian law of 1951 which indicates that it is subject to a preliminary administrative procedure and ultimately to judicial control. This law is not contrary to the Iranian Constitution which provides for equitable compensation, and in the proceedings before the International Court of Justice Iran recognized not only the right to indemnity, but also the possibility of its enforcement through ordinary Iranian courts under Iranian law, such recognition binds the Iranian State towards plaintiff. However, neither by Italian law nor by generally recognized norms of international law is it required that the quantum of the idemnity be effectively adequate to the value of the object taken. It is enough that there is compensation. There was, furthermore, a public economic interest in the nationalisation, and therefore the law cannot be held "political" and denied effect in Italy. This also showed that the law was not discriminatory, while its alleged confiscatory character was disproved by the motivation (protection of Iranian public interest) and the recognition of the right to compen-

---

276 339 U.S. 779; 70 S.Ct. 885 (1950); Katz & Brewster: Op. cit., 780.
277 The Sicilian Sulphur Monopoly case (1838); The Finlay case; The Reverened Jonas King case (1853); Orfield and Re: Cases and Materials on International Law, 533-534; Moore: Digest, Vol. VI, 262-264.
278 1 Weekly Law Reports 246; International Law Reports (1953), 316.

sation. The text of the law shows no intention to persecute, and there is no room for research into the underlying subject motives of the legislatures not revealed by the text."[279]

Nationalization of foreign-owned property in modern times

Under customary international law, every sovereign State has the right to nationalize all property, whether owned by nationals or foreigners, situated on its domain. In the case of foreign owned property, such nationalization must be done in good faith, it must be for purposes of promotion of general welfare of the masses, the State must pay just compensation to the foreign owners of the property nationalized and there must be no discrimination against foreign owners as such. Such nationalization or expropriation of foreign-owned property is not unlawful.[280]

In modern times nationalization of foreign-owened property has become more and more widespread. The practice of expropriating foreign property by nationalization has spread from Soviet Russia to other countries in Europe, Latin America, Asia and Africa. In the view of some writers the Mexican expropriations and the Soviet nationalizations could be regarded as the forerunners of many incidents of nationalization of private property and that the Iranian nationalization of the property of the Anglo-Iranian Oil Company, a corporation whose majority stock is owned by the British Government will not be the last governmental nationalization of foreign-owned private property. Further, in their view, it would seem that no part of the world may be immune from this rapidly growing phenomenon. It may be added that even industrially advanced countries like France and the United Kingdom, have themselves entered upon the nationalization of certain of their own industries, some of whose stock was owned by aliens. [281]

Requirements of compensation in modern times

Although several nations claim that customary international law requires that once a foreigner has been permitted to acquire property or property interests in a country in full compliance with its municipal law, and it cannot thereafter take or destroy such existing or vested property rights with adequate compensation yet the realities of the modern world would make it impossible in many cases to adhere to the principle of full compensation. The principle of just compensation has to give way to considerations of debtor's

---

279 Katz & Brewster: The Law of International Transactions and Relations, 828.
280 Cheng: General Principles of Law, 49-50.
281 Kuhn: Nationalization of Foreign-Owned Property and its Impact on International Law, Vol. 45, A.J.I.L. (1951), 709-712.

political and economic instability or its capacity to pay. Immediately after the Second World War, the industrially advanced nations began to appreciate that the actual attainment of compensation for their nationals in cases of the nationalization of their property must be dependent upon a variety of factors, such as the economic and political instability as well as the ability to pay off the debtor country. This consideration was instrumental for settling the claims of the United States nationals against the Federal People's Republic of Yugoslavia by the agreement of July 19, 1948, under which the United States accepted a lump sum payment of seventeen million dollars in full settlement of the claims of American property owners whose property in Yugoslavia had been nationalized, although the actual market value of that property was much greater. Further, this new settlement is known as **en bloc** method of settlement, whereby one settlement is made on behalf of all interested nationals instead of an individual protection being offered to each property owner resulting in individual awards. Several important changes result from this type of an overall compensation agreement: (a) the property owner now looks to his own government for compensation; (b) although provision is made for part-payment of an award, complete payment cannot be made until all claims have been filed and adjudicated, since until that time the amount of ademption to which all claimants must submit will be unknown. This results from the fact that the **en bloc** settlement is likely to be less than the full market value of the property nationalized.

Under the International Claims Settlement Act of 1950, the Government of the United States has set up an International Claims Commission with power "to examine, adjudicate, and render final decisions, with respect to claims of the Government of the United States and of its nationals, not only under the terms of the agreement between the United States and Yugoslavia, but also under the terms of any agreement thereafter concluded with other Governments (excepting those at war with the United States in World War II) arising out of the nationalization or other taking of property, where the Government of the United States has agreed to accept from that Government a sum in **en bloc** settlement thereof." The Act expressly provides that in the decisions of claims, in addition to the provisions of the particular agreement, the Commission is to apply "the applicable principles of international law, justice and equity."[282]

---

[282] Orfield and Re: Cases and Materials on International Law. 534-535; Minnesota Law Review, Vol. 36 (1952) Kuhn: "Nationalisation of Foreign-Owned Property and its Impact on International Law, op. cit., 710.

The post-war (War II) nationalization agreements concluded between the Government of the United Kingdom and the Latin American countries provide for the payment of just and equtable compensation for the expropriation of British owned properties in that part of the world. The actual compensation paid as a result of the Anglo-Mexican Agreement concerning the expropriation of British owned oil properties in Mexico appears to have amounted only to about one-third of the real value of the oil properties taken. In the Anglo-Argentinian and the Anglo-Uruguayan Purchase Agreements the compensation agreed upon appears to represent about 60 per cent of the capital value involved. In the agreement between the United Kingdom and Poland, and in the agreement concluded between the United Kingdom and Czechoslovakia (1949) the compensation stipulated is understood to be one-third of the value of the British investments nationalized by Poland and Czechoslovakia. In the agreement between the United Kingdom and Yugoslavia (1949) the settlement appears to represent 50 per cent of the value of the British investments in Yugoslavia. By and large, it is said that the United Kingdom agreed to insist merely on the principle of compensation in case of expropriation ranging from one to two-thirds of the value of British investments in the countries concerned, but not on the latter of its contractual rights. It has been content to waive portions of British claims, taking into account equitable considerations such as the general post war difficulties and the scarcity of foreign exchanges in such under-developed countries.

It may be added that in the agreements between France and Belgium, France and Canada, France and Switzerland, and France and the United Kingdom regarding the French nationalized gas and electricity industries, the compensation appears to have amounted to 70 per cent of the value of the holdings of these contracting parties in these nationalized properties. Further, it was agreed that the aliens were to be treated in respect of payment of compensation on the same footing as the French nationals. Furthermore, it was agreed that in the event of France subsequently granting more favourable treatment to creditors of any other country a most favoured reservation comes into operation.[283]

Views taken by International Judicial Tribunals

Earlier judicial pronouncements emphasized the principle of just compensation. In the Norwegian Shipping Claims Case (1922)

---

[283] Orfield and Re: Cases and Materials on International Law, 534-535. Schwarzenberger: "The Protection of British Property Abroad" Vol. 5, Current Legal Problems (1952), 295.

(United States of America v. Norway), the Permanent Court of Arbitration held that just compensation must be paid to the alien claimants, both under the municipal law of the United States and the law of nations. In **Spanish Zones of Morocco Claims (1924)** (Great Britain v. Spain) the Special Arbitral Tribunal held that under international law an alien could not be deprived of his property without just compensation. The same view was taken by the Special Arbitral Tribunal in the case of **Goldenberg & Sons v. Germany (1928)** (Rumania v. Germany). [284] In the **Chorzow Factory** case (1928), the Permanent Court of International Justice adopting the above view held that expropriation was lawful under international law only if fair compensation had been paid. It said that "reparation must, as far as possible, wipe out all the consequences of the illegal act and re-establish the situation which would, in all probability, have existed if that act had not been committed. Restitution in kind, or, if this is not possible, payment of a sum corresponding to the value which a restitution in kind would bear; the award, if need be, of damages for loss sustained which would not be covered by restitution in kind or payment in place of it—such are the principles which should serve to determine the amount of compensation due for an act contrary to international law."[285]

Principles embodied in certain Conventions
European Convention on Establishment (1955)

Chapter VI

.... Nationalization

Article 23

Without prejudice to the provisions of Article I of the Protocol to the Convention on the Protection of Human Rights and Fundamental Freedoms, nationals of any Contracting Party shall be entitled, in the event of expropriation or nationalisation of their property by any other Party, to be treated at least as favourably as nationals of the latter Party.[286]

---

284 17 A.J.I.L. 362 & 368; Annual Digest (1923-24) No. 85, 157-163.
285 The doctrine of just compensation has been challenged, however, by a number of governments and some writers. Some reject not only the principle of "full" or "just" compensation but also the theory of "some compensation" or "compensation". Some argue that the requirement of compensation applies only in the case of expropriation which involves discrimination against aliens or against particular aliens. Others lay emphasis upon the freedom of States to expropriate property in the course of a general programme of economic or social reform without payment of "compensation" or at least without payment of "full" or "prompt" compensation.
    Katz & Brewster: The Law of International Transactions & Relations, 833; Friedman: Expropriation in International Law (1953); Wortley: Expropriation in Public International Law (1959); Rep. P.C.I.J. Ser. A No. 17; Schwarzenberger: International Law, Vol. I (1957), 3rd ed., 654.
286 Unification of Law, International Institute for the Unification of Private Law, (Rome, 1957), Vol. I, 177.

Article 13

(1) An alien shall be liable to payment of taxes and duties in accordance with the laws and regulations of the State.

(2) An alien shall not be subjected to forced loans which are unjust or discriminatory.

Note : 1. Clause (1) of this Article was accepted by all Delegations except that of Japan. The Delegation of Japan wished a proviso to that clause to be inserted to read as follows:

"provided that the State shall not discriminate between aliens and nationals in levying the taxes and duties."

2. Clause (2) was accepted by the Delegations of Burma, India, Indonesia and Iraq. The Delegate of Ceylon wished the clause to be drafted as "An alien shall not be subjected to forced loans." The Delegate of Pakistan suggested the following draft: "An alien shall not be subjected to loans in violation of the laws, regulations and orders applicable to him." The Delegate of the United Arab Republic was of the view that the draft should be as follows: "An alien shall not be subjected to unjust forced loans."

Commentary

Liability of aliens to payment of taxes

Article 13 gives expression to a general rule of State practice relating to the alien's liability for taxation and other cognate payments in the State of residence. Under international law, not only the State has the power to tax all persons within its border, but also it may even impose discriminatory taxes. However, a discrimination against or between aliens would be regarded as an unfriendly act towards the home State of the aliens affected and would no doubt give rise to protest and reprisal. Therefore, the privilege of discriminatory taxation is not resorted to in the modern times. Forced loans or confiscatory levies have been regarded as unreasonable in time of peace or in the absence of an exceptional emergency. Under Article 13 an alien shall be liable to payment of all taxes and duties established by law. In this regard their liability is as much as that of the nationals of the State of residence. Similarly under Clause (2) of this Article, an alien must not be subjected to forced loans which are unjust and discriminatory in character. In a word, for tax purposes, alien individuals are to be treated on a footing of equality with the nationals of the State of residence.

Opinions of Writers

Oppenheim says: "A State has wider powers over aliens of the latter kind (i.e., individuals who take up their residence in another State or for some length of time), it can make them pay rates and taxes. . . ."[287]

Hackworth observes: "In general, States have authority as an incident of sovereignty, to tax aliens resident within their territory and their property there situated. In theory, States are presumed to limit the taxation of non-resident aliens to their property situated within the jurisdiction of the taxing State and the income derived from sources therein."[288]

Hyde states: "In levying taxes to defray the expenses of government, no duty is imposed upon a State to leave unburdened either property owned by aliens, or persons who may themselves be aliens. Nor does any principle of international law forbid the territorial sovereign to impose, in some instances, a heavier burden upon the interests of such individuals than is placed upon those of its own nationals. The existing practice in so far as it is manifested by conventional arrangements tends, however, to place aliens generally upon an equal footing with nationals. Save in cases indicating a marked abuse of power, or a disregard of the terms of a treaty, the United States does not appear to find in the taxation of its nationals or of their property abroad reasons for diplomatic remonstrance or interposition. An abuse of power is seen when the laws of the taxing State are violated, or when a tax is fairly to be deemed confiscatroy in character or when the imposition of a tax marks the duplication of a previous collection by a governmental entity in **de facto** control of the area to which such tax appertains." . . . In general, all immovable property within the territory of a State, regardless of the residence or nationality of the owner, is, with a few notable exceptions which are explainable on precise grounds, subject to taxation; likewise, all movable property therein, provided it may be fairly regarded as incorporated in the mass of property there belonging. Difficulties may arise in ascertaining whether a particular chattel falls within such a category, and is to be so regarded. Normally the problem is oftentimes one of fact rather than law. . . . Personal taxes levied upon individuals subject thereto may assume a variety of forms. When they are levied upon aliens, the law of nations appears to offer few restrictions beyond the possible requirement that the tax be in a broad

287 Oppenheim: International Law. Vol. I, 680.
288 Hackworth: Digest, Vol. III, 575.

sense uniform and general in its operation. Such individuals may be subjected, for example, to the payment of a poll tax, or of an income-tax; and in the latter case, in the treatment of the resident alien, the tax may doubtless be assessed according to the amount of income from whatsoever source derived, and whether or not from assets outside of the taxing State. It may be doubted, moreover, whether any rule of international law forbids discrimination on grounds of alienage."[289]

Practice of Member States of the Committee

In all the Member Countries of the Committee except in Japan aliens are expected to pay taxes, rates and duties in accordance with the laws and regulations of the State. According to Japan aliens shall be liable to payment of taxes and duties in accordance with the municipal laws and regulations of the State concerned and that the State should not discriminate against aliens in this regard. Burma, India, Indonesia and Iraq take the view that aliens shall not be subjected to forced loans which are unjust or discriminatory. While according to Ceylon an alien shall not be subjected to forced loans which are unjust, in the view of Japan, aliens shall not be subjected to forced loans. Pakistan takes the view that an alien shall not be subjected to loans in violation of the laws, regulations and orders applicable to him. According to the United Arab Republic, he shall not be subjected to unjust forced loans.

Practice of States other than Member States of the Committee

Practice of most States confirms the rule that a State has the power to impose taxes upon all immovable and movable property within its jurisdiction regardless of the residence or nationality of the owner. This power is inherent in the sovereignty of the State of residence the exercise of which unless abused cannot in general be made the subject of diplomatic remonstrance. Generally the State has wider powers over resident aliens than those aliens who are merely travelling about the country or stay only temporarily on the territory in regard to the payment of rates and taxes.[290] The view of the United States of America in this regard was clearly expressed by Mr. Hamilton Fish, the United States Secretary of State, in 1876 in the following terms: "Foreigners who have chosen to take up their residence, to purchase property, or to carry on business in a foreign country, thereby place themselves under the jurisdiction of the laws of that country, and may fairly be called upon to bear their fair share of the general public burdens, when

---

289 Hyde: International Law, Vol. I, 663-664, 666, 671-672.
290 Oppenheim: International Law, Vol. I, 680.

539

property imposed upon them and other members of the community alike. As a general proposition, the right to tax includes the power to determine the amount which must be levied, and the objects for which that amount shall be expended. These powers are incident to sovereignty, the exercise of which, unless abused, cannot in general be made the subject of diplomatic remonstrance."[291] The United States Acting Secretary of State, Mr. Porter, stated in 1885 as follows: "Taxation may no doubt be imposed in conformity with the law of nations, by a sovereign on the property within his jurisdiction of a person who is domiciled in and owes allegiance to a foreign country. It is otherwise, however, as to a tax imposed not on such property, but on the person of the party taxed when elsewhere domiciled and elsewhere on a citizen. Such a decree is internationally void, and an attempt to execute it by penalties on the relatives of the party taxed gives the person so taxed a right to appeal for diplomatic intervention to the government to which he owes allegiance. To sustain such a claim it is not necessary that the penalties should have been imposed originally and expressly on the person so excepted from jurisdiction. It is enough if it appears that the tax was levied in such a way as to reach him through relatives."[292] Mr. Nielsen, the Solicitor for the Department of the State of the United States, took the following view in 1921: As a general rule, it may be stated that nations possess the exclusive right of imposing taxes upon property situated within their territories and of determining the purpose to which the revenues derived from such taxes shall be devoted. If, therefore, the taxes are general and uniform in their operation, and make no discrimination against the property of the citizens of a particular country, it would not ordinarily be within the province of the government of that country to make any representations in regard thereto."[293]

Practice of most States indicates that all movable and immovable property situated within the territory of a State, regardless of the nationality or residence of the owner are normally subject to taxation.[294] In the case of movable property, according to the practice of the United States, if that movable property may fairly be regarded as incorporated in the mass of property situated in the United States, then that property becomes liable to payment of taxes.

---

291 Mr. Fish's dispatch to Mr. Cushing, Minister to Spain, dated January 12, 1873; Moore: Digest, Vol. IV, 21.
292 Moore: Digest, Ibid., 22.
293 Hackworth: Digest, Vol. III, 576.
294 Burnet v. Brooks, 288 U.S. 378; Winans v. Attorney-General, (1904) A.C. 287, 290.

540

According to the law of the United States, real estate and tangible personal property are situated in the United States if they are physically situated therein. Certificates of stock, bonds, bills, notes and other written evidence of intangible property which are treated as being the property itself are property situated in the United States physically situated therein.295 Further, it has been held that a vessel having no permanent location within another State of the Union, possesses an artificial situs for purposes of taxation at the domicile of the owner.296 The courts of the United States held that moneys, notes and evidences of credit may be taxed in the State where they are employed and found, irrespective of the legal home of the owner.297

Personal taxes levied upon individuals subject thereto may assume a number of forms. When they are levied upon aliens, the law of nations appears to offer few restrictions beyond the possible requirement that the tax be in a broad sense uniform and general in its operation. Such individuals may be subjected for example, to the payment of a poll-tax, or of an income-tax; and in the latter case, in the treatment of the resident alien, the tax may undoubtedly be assessed according to the amount of income from whatever source derived, and whether or not from assets outside of the taxing State.298 As a general rule, the question of the liability of a foreign national to payment of income tax depends upon residence rather than citizenship.299 In the matter of internal charges or taxes, resident aliens are generally accorded treatment on a footing of equality with the nationals. For instance, under the International Revenue Code of 1939, resident aliens are liable equally with citizens of the United States to the payment of income tax on their entire income. This is true even though the alien's income is derived wholly from sources without the United States. However, such aliens are allowed a credit for "the amount of any such taxes paid or accrued during the taxable year to any foreign country, if the foreign country of which such alien resident is a citizen or subject, in imposing such taxes, allows a similar credit to citizens of the United States residing in such country."300 When a tax is levied upon the income of a non-resident alien, it is obviously in the nature of a tax upon his

---

295 Hackworth: Digest, Vol. III, 590.
296 Southern Pacific Co. v. Kentucky, 222, U.S. 63; Hyde: International Law Vol. I, 666 footnote.
297 New Orleans v. Stempel, 175 U.S. 309; Metropolitan Life Ins. Co. v. New Orleans, 205 U.S. 395; Burke v. Wells, 208 U.S., 14; Hyde: International Law, Vol. I, 666-667 footnote.
298 Hyde: International Law, Vol. I, 671-672.
299 Hackworth: Digest, Vol. III, 575 footnote.
300 53 Stat. 556; 26 U.S.C. ss 11, 12, 131(a) (3); Treasury Regulations 103 (Income tax 1940), Secs. 19. 11-2. 211-1; Hackworth: Digest, Vol. III, 579.

property within the control of the territorial sovereign rather than a personal tax.

In the United States for federal tax purposes, alien individuals are divided into resident aliens, non-resident aliens engaged in business in the United States, and non-resident aliens not engaged in business in the United States. The latter are further divided into non-resident aliens having gross United States income of not more than $15,400 and those having in excess of $15,400 of such income. Resident alien individuals are generally taxable the same as United States citizens upon income from all sources, whether within or without the United States. Non-resident aliens engaged in United States business at any time during the year are taxable at regular rates on income, including capital gains, from sources within the United States, less foreign taxes paid and other allowable deductions. Non-resident aliens not engaged in trade or business in the United States pay tax at a flat 10 per cent rate on their "fixed or determinable annual or periodical income" (including certain capital gains) if such income does not exceed $15,400 during the taxable year. If it does, the regular tax rates apply, but the aggregate tax may not be less than the tax computed at the 10 per cent rate.[301] A property tax may be uniformly applied to aliens in inter-State and foreign commerce as well as citizens in inter-State commerce. Under the commerce clause of the United States Constitution a franchise tax may not be imposed upon aliens engaged solely in foreign commerce. A direct income-tax such as California's, which applies to

---

[301] Non resident alien individuals are covered by the United States Internal Revenue Code of 1954, ss. 871-874.

It may be added that no comprehensive definition of the term "engaged in trade or business within the United States" is provided by the Internal Revenue Code of 1954 or the decided cases. The decided cases serve only as examples of what the courts have accepted or rejected as constituting United States business. Thompson, Smith: "Foreign Business Operating in the United States", Legal Problems of International Trade, Edited by Paul O. Proehl, (Illinois, 1959), 282-310.

The meaning of the term "resident alien" under the income tax laws of the United States (Internal Revenue Code of 1939) is stated as follows in section 19.211-2 of Treasury Regulations 103 (Income Tax, 1940): "An alien actually present in the United States who is not a mere transient or sojourner is a resident of the United States for purposes of the income tax. Whether he is a transient is determined by his intentions with regard to the length and nature of his stay. A mere floating intention, indefinite as to time, to return to another country is not sufficient to constitute him a transient. If he lives in the United States and has no definite intention as to his stay, he is a resident. One who comes to the United States for a definite purpose which in its nature may be promptly accomplished is a transient; but if his purpose is of such a nature that an extended stay may be necessary for its accomplishment, and to that end the alien makes his home temporarily in the United States, he becomes a resident, though it may be his intention at all times to return to his domicile abroad when the purpose for which he came has been consummated or abandoned. An alien whose stay in the United States is limited to a definite period by the immigration laws is not a resident of the United States within the meaning of this section, in the absence of exceptional circumstances; Hackworth: Digest, Vol. III, 580.

local profits of tax-payers engaged solely in foreign commerce will be upheld.[302] It may be added that "the net estate of a resident alien dying in the United States is subject to the same tax as that imposed upon the estate of a citizen."[303]

Although in the matter of internal charges or taxes, resident aliens in most States are generally accorded treatment on a footing of equality with the nationals, the commercial treaties and treaties of friendship, commerce and navigation concluded between nations also contain provisions relating to the liability of the nationals of either contracting party within the territories of the other, to taxation and other charges. These provisions seek to grant national standard of treatment in the matter of taxation. Further, these treaties contain most-favoured-nation clauses providing that each signatory will give the other's nationals any advantage in taxation which it grants to the nationals of any third country. Friendship and non-discrimination are the essence of the provisions, and they provide the foundation for equal treatment in all possible respects by each country of the nationals of the other. Article 1 of the treaty of December 8, 1923 concluded between the United States of America and Germany provides: "The nationals of either High Contracting Party within the territories of the other shall not be subjected to the payment of any internal charges or taxes other or higher than those that are exacted of and paid by its nationals."[304] Article IX (1) of the Treaty of Friendship, Commerce, and Navigation entered into between the United States of America and the Italian Republic on February 2, 1948 provides: "Nationals, corporations and associations of either High Contracting Party shall not be subjected to the payment of internal taxes, fees and charges imposed upon or applied to income, capital, transactions, activities or any other object, or to requirements with respect to the levy and collection thereof, within the territories of the other High Contracting Party:

> (a) more burdensome than those borne by nationals, residents and corporations and associations of any third country;

---

302 Thompson: Foreign Business in the United States. op. cit., 303.

303 Hackworth: Digest, Vol. III, 589; Hyde: International Law, Vol. I, 673.

304 44 Stat. 2132; Hackworth: Digest, Vol. III, 577. Interpreting the term 'within' in Art. 1 of the Treaty of 1929, the State Department of the United States observed as follows: "Except in isolated cases a German national resident without the United States but temporarily in the United States for business or pleasure, can hardly be said to be within the United States within the meaning of the above provision" of the Treaty of December 8, 1923; Hackworth: Ibid., 577 footnote.

(b) more burdensome than those borne by nationals, corporations and associations of such other High Contracting Party, in the case of persons resident or engaged in business within the territories of such other High Contracting Party, and in the case of corporations and associations engaged in business therein, or organised and operated exclusively for scientific, educational, religious, or philanthropic purposes. . . ."[305]

Similarly several bilateral treaties also provide that no higher or other duties, charges or taxes of any kind shall be levied within the territories of either party, upon any personal property, money or effects of their respective nationals, on the removal of the same from their territories reciprocally, either upon the inheritance of such property, money or effects, or otherwise, than are or shall be payable in each State upon the same, when removed by a national of such State, respectively.[306]

It may be added that the Economic Committee of the League of Nations pointed out that tax discriminations against aliens may amount to their eviction even aside from the special difficulties arising from double taxation. It recommended the granting of national treatment in the matter of all taxes, duties (except on imports and exports) and other fiscal charges, no matter by what authority levied. This is to apply to charges on the person or property, on all rights and interests, including commerce, industry and occupations.[307]

During the nineteenth century foreigners domiciled in a country were not exempted from any contribution that was considered as necessary for the protection of the country. The home States of the individuals affected emphasized in particular upon the principle of equality of treatment of aliens and nationals. Thus, Mr. Dodson of the British Foreign Office advised on January 8, 1851 that British subjects in foreign countries are not exempt from forced loans in respect of their real or personal property "provided such loans are enforced as a general measure throughout (the Lombardo-Venetian Kingdom) applicable alike to Natives and Foreigners". Similarly Phillimore advised on December 24, 1866 that "subjects

---

305 Briggs: The Law of Nations, 545.
306 Article VII of the Convention of April 26, 1826 concluded between the U.S.A. & Denmark, 8 Stat. 342; Hackworth: Digest, Vol. 3, 669.
307 Report of Government Experts, League of Nations Doc. C.562.M.178, 1928 II; Cutler: "The Treatment of Aliens", op. cit., 236-237.

domiciled and resident in a belligerent State, which they do not choose to leave in time of war, should bear their share in the expense of defending the country in which they reside from the attack of an enemy and are liable to pay a 'war tax'." Collier, Coleridge and Twiss advised on August 26, 1870, "that British subjects having property in France are not entitled to any special protection for their property or to exemption from military contributions, to which they will be liable in common with the inhabitants of the place in which they reside or in which their property may be situated. This applies whether they are resident in France or not."[308] However, practice of most States in recent times clearly indicates that aliens must not be subjected to payment of forced loans or confiscatory charges in peace time or in the absence of exceptional emergency. Broadly, such impositions on aliens would be regarded as unreasonable in the modern times. As a matter of fact, even exorbitance of amount, unfairness and looseness of amount and gross misapplication of taxes have been made the grounds of diplomatic protest, despite the internal nature of these taxes.[309]

Principles emobodied in certain Conventions

European Convention on Establishment (1955)

CHAPTER VI

Taxation . . .

Article 21

1. Subject to the provisions concerning double taxation contained in agreements already concluded or to be concluded, nationals of any Contracting Party shall not be liable in the territory of any other Party to duties, charges, taxes or contributions, of any description whatsoever, other, higher or more burdensome than those imposed on nationals of the latter Party in similar circumstances; in particular, they shall be entitled to deductions or exemptions from taxes or charges and to all allowances, including allowances for dependents.

2. A Contracting Party shall not impose on nationals of any other Party any residence charge not required of its own nationals. This provision shall not prevent the imposition in appropriate cases .

---

308 McNair: International Law Opinions, (Cambridge, 1956), Vol. II, 136-137.
309 Cutler: Ibid., 236.

of charges connected with administrative formalities such as the issue of permits and authorisations which aliens are required to have, provided that the amount levied is not more than the expenditure incurred by such formalities.[310]

Article 14

(1) Aliens may be required to perform police, fire-brigade or militia duty for the protection of life and property in cases of emergency or imminent need.

(2) Aliens shall not be compelled to enlist themselves in the armed forces of the State.

(3) Aliens may, however, voluntarily enlist themselves in the armed forces of the State with the express consent of their home State which may be withdrawn at any time.

(4) Aliens may voluntarily enlist themselves in the police or fire-brigade service on the same conditions as nationals.

Note : The Delegation of Indonesia reserved its position on the whole Article. The Delegation of Iraq reserved its position on clause (3) of this Article. The Delegation of Japan wished clause (3) of this Article to be deleted.

Commentary

Liability of aliens to be compelled to serve in auxiliary forces, national and civic

Article 14 establishes the right of the State of residence to compel resident aliens to serve in auxiliary forces such as militia parties, national and civil guards to maintain social order during emergency. But they shall not be compelled to enlist themselves in the military service of the State. It is a well-established principle of international law that citizens or subjects of the country residing in another, though bound by their temporary allegiance to many common duties, must not be compelled to serve in the regular armed forces of that country. There is no principle more distinctly and clearly settled in the law of nations than the rule that resident aliens not naturalized are not liable to perform military service. Such a rule is firmly established not only by the overwhelming weight of authority of outstanding writers on international law, but also by

---

310 International Institute for the Unification of Private Law, Unification of Law, Vol. I, (Rome, 1857), 177.

the sustained practice of States.[311] However, they can, if permitted, voluntarily join the regular armed forces of the host State. When they are enlisted to serve in the military, police, fire-brigade and other services of similar character, whether voluntarily or not, they shall be entitled to similar conditions of service as the nationals.

Opinions of Writers

Hall says: "The broad rule has . . . been mentioned that as an alien has not the privileges, so on the other hand he has not the responsibilities attached to membership of the foreign political society in the territory of which he may happen to be. In return, however, for the protection which he receives and opportunities of profit or pleasure which he enjoys, he is liable to a certain extent, at any rate in moments of emergency, to contribute by his personal service to the maintenance of order in the State from which he is deriving advantage, and in some circumstances, it may even be permissible to require him to help in protecting it against external dangers."[312]

Moore says: "The voluntary enlistment of an alien in the military service raises in itself no international question. The modern tendency, however, is to exclude aliens from such service, and this seems to be in harmony with sound principles."[313]

Oppenheim says: "A State has wider powers over aliens of the latter kind; it can make them pay rates and taxes, and can even compel them in case of need, and under the same conditions as citizens, to serve in the local police and the local fire brigade for the purpose of maintaining public order and safety. On the other hand, an alien does not fall under the personal supremacy of the local State; therefore he cannot, unless his own State consents, be made to serve in its army or navy, and cannot, like a citizen, be treated according to discretion."[314]

Hackworth states: "The right of admission to service in the military forces of the United States is generally limited to citizens or to persons who have declared their intention to become citizens."[315]

---

311 Moore: Digest, Vol. IV, 52-53.
312 Hall, William Edward: A Treatise on International Law, (1895) 4th Ed., 215.
313 Moore: Digest, Vol. IV, 50.
314 Oppenheim: International Law, Vol. I, 680-682.
315 Hackworth: Digest, Vol. III, 598.

Fenwick observes: "International law recognizes a distinction between the status of those aliens who are merely transient visitors in a foreign country and those who have established a permanent residence there with apparent intention of remaining indefinitely. Not only must domiciled aliens obey the local laws and pay the normal taxes, whether upon person or upon property imposed by the State, but should the necessity arise they may be called upon by the State to perform such public duties as police and militia service, as distinct from military service, as well as to submit to special measures, such as quarantine regulations, restricting their personal liberty and the enjoyment of their property in the interest of the public welfare. Domicile thus creates a sort of qualified or temporary allegiance. A delicate question is presented when the State in which the alien is domiciled goes to war with the State of which he is a citizen. In such a case, while the alien may not be drafted into military service, he is at the same time bound not to contribute by an overt act to the success of the State of his nationality; and he may be punished for high treason and may be subjected to other penalties imposed by State law upon such offences."[316]

Practice of Member States of the Committee

In most of the Participating Countries of the Committee, resident foreign nationals may be required to serve in police, fire-brigade and other auxiliary forces of similar character for purposes of protection of the place of residence as well as property from depredation in times of national catastrophies or danger. According to Burma, Ceylon, and the United Arab Republic, aliens may with the express consent of their home State voluntarily enlist themselves in the military service of the State of residence, but such consent can be withdrawn at any time.

Practice of States other than Member States of the Committee

Practice of most States reveals that aliens can lawfully be compelled to serve in auxiliary forces such as militia, patrols, national and civic guards. Thus Herbert Jenner, the Law Officer, gave the following opinion on February 21, 1831 to the British Government: ". . . I have the honour to report that individuals who are permanently resident in a foreign country, cannot upon general principles, claim to be exempted from assisting in the defence of the State, in which they may have established themselves. The principal if not the only ground upon which such a claim can be

---

316 Fenwick: International Law, (New York, 1948), 3rd Ed., 271.

548

maintained. is that which is founded upon treaty; and in many cases similar to the present, His Majesty's Government have declined to interfere where no such privilege or exemption had been conceded by treaty. I am therefore humble of opinion, that neither the situation of the British residents in Antwerp, nor the service which they are called upon to perform are such as to justify an extraordinary interference in their behalf for the purposes suggested by them."[317] Similarly, Mr. Dodson, another Law Officer of the British Government reported on May 9, 1836 as follows: ". . . I am of opinion there is nothing repugnant to the Law of Nations on the requisition of the Belgian Government that British subjects should serve in the Civic Guard in common with the native inhabitants of Belgium. Every State unless bound by treaty to the contrary has a right to call upon foreigners living under its protection, and enjoying the benefits of its Laws, to assist in providing for the maintenance of order in the country."[318] Upon the liability of aliens residing in Leghorn to be compelled by the Austrian Government to serve in the local national guard, Mr. Harding, the British Law Officer, gave the following opinion on December 6, 1860: "In the absence of any treaty stipulations, I see nothing contrary to the law or practice of nations in the compelling of foreign residents to serve in common with natives, under ordinary and reasonable limitations, in the militia or national guard; more especially in time of peace."[319] The same view was taken by the United States of America also. For instance, Mr. Davis, the United States Assistant Secretary of State, stated on February 17, 1870 in his dispatch to the American Consul at Curacao as follows: "When complaint was made during our late rebellion that British subjects were compelled to serve in the Virginia and Missouri militia, Lord Lyons was instructed by his Government "that there is no rule or principle of international law which prohibits the Government of any country from requiring aliens resident within its territories, to serve in the militia or police of the country, or to contribute to the support of such establishment. This appears to be the kind of service required of American citizens, in common with all others, in the island of Curacao. The commutation for such service—eight dollars per annum—appears to be moderate and reasonable. It is therefore not deemed advisable at present to raise any question upon this subject."[320] Mr. Fish, the Secretary of State of the United States, gave the following

317 McNair: International Law Opinions, Vol. II, 115.
318 McNair: Ibid., 115 footnote.
319 McNair: Ibid. 115-116.
320 Moore: Digest. Vol. IV, 57-58.

instructions to the American Minister on April 6, 1871: "I must decline to enter into the question to what extent and under what circumstances do our citizens, native or naturalized (in the absence of treaty stipulations), owe military service to a foreign government in whose dominions they are domiciled for commercial or other purposes. They certainly do not stand on the same footing as mere travellers or temporary sojourners. I do not perceive any good reason why a government (in the absence of treaty stipulations) may not require from domiciled foreigners the discharge of such civic duties as service upon juries, in the ordinary municipal arrangements for the prevention and extinguishment of fires, and other duties of like character."[321] As regards the liability of aliens to be compelled to serve in the regular armed forces of the country in which they happen to be, Lord McNair observes as follows: "the problem was comparatively new in 1822, and that no general principles had been established."[322] Mr. Robinson, the British Law Officer, gave the following opinion on September 18, 1822: "I have the honour to report that the claim of exemption from the military defence of the country in which individuals are domiciled is not to be maintained on general and absolute principles, as a privilege belonging to foreigners so domiciled, because the condition of their establishment there must depend on the laws and customs of the country; and the principal if not the only grounds of exemption are those that may be founded on treaty, or custom, or the transient purposes of occasional residence, which are protected by the general courtesy of States. The practice of different governments differs materially as to the manner of forming the military service, and although the nature of such service in this country may not afford instances of foreigners being constrained to serve in person, I think the result of former references on this subject would not warrant one to advise that there are any general principles of exemption so recognized as to furnish a certain and safe basis for the claim of such privileges on behalf of British subjects domiciled abroad. In the present case, much may depend on the terms on which British merchants may have been allowed to reside in the Netherlands in times of amity between the two governments; and the correspondence which has passed on this subject will probably elucidate the specific grounds on which this exemption has been claimed. On the information which I at present possess I feel a great difficulty in suggesting any observations that can be opposed with effect to the demand of the Netherlands Government."[323] However,

---

321 Moore: Ibid., 58.
322 McNair: International Law Opinions, Vol. II, 113.
323 McNair: Ibid., 113-114.

550

in his opinion on the subject of a law passed by the Government of the Canton de Vaud, compelling all foreigners of whatever country to perform military service, or to pay a tax in lieu thereof. Mr. Dodson, the British Law Officer stated as follows: "I am of opinion that Her Majesty's Government would be justified in claiming exemption from general military service as contradistinguished from the civic-service of the country, for British subjects who may be temporarily resident in the Canton de Vaud. But with respect to the particular case of Mr. Freeman who appears to be permanently settled in the Canton, having married a native of the country, and purchased a large landed property there, it appears to me that Her Majesty's Government cannot, in the absence of any treaty, claim for him an exemption from the tax referred to. The question as to how far the government of a State is entitled to require the military services of foreigners resident within its dominions is at all times one of great delicacy: but the above is the best opinion I am able to form as applicable to the circumstances of the present case."[324]

Respecting the question of the liability of British subjects to perform military service in the United States, the British Law Officers, Harding, Atherton and Palmer, delivered on September 30, 1861, their joint opinion in these terms: "Whilst Her Majesty's Government might well be content to leave British subjects, voluntarily domiciled in a foreign country, liable to all the obligations ordinarily incident to such foreign domicile (including, where imposed by the municipal law of such country, service in the Militia, or National Guard, or Local Police, for the maintenance of internal peace and order, or even to a limited extent, for the defence of the territory from foreign invasion), it is not reasonable to expect that Her Majesty's Government should remain entirely passive under the treatment to which we understand British subjects are actually exposed in various States of the former Union; such, for instance, as being embodied and compelled to serve in regiments, perhaps nominally of 'Militia', but really exposed not only to the ordinary accidents and chances of war, but to be treated as rebels or traitors in a civil war, involving many questions in which they, as aliens, cannot, simply by reason of their domicile, be supposed to take interest; as to which they may be incompetent to form an opinion; and in the determination of which they are precluded from freedom of choice and action. No State can justly frame laws to compel aliens, resident within its territories, to serve, against their will, in armies

---

324 McNair: Ibid., 114-115.

ranged against each other in a civil war. A fortiori, in the absence of any such law, they cannot justly enforce the service."[325]

Mr. Seward, Secretary of State of the United States, in his dispatch to Mr. Gamble stated in 1862 that he could hardly suppose that there existed anywhere in the world, the erroneous belief that aliens were liable to military duty in the United States. Halleck in his 'International Law' describes the Anglo-American practice as follows: "In 1861, during the American Civil War, the British Government declared that if enforced enlistments of British subjects for the war were persisted in, the Government would be obliged to concert with other neutral powers for the protection of their respective subjects; but neither in the Northern or Southern States was the discharge of any British subject enlisted against his will refused on proper representation. There is no rule of international law prohibiting the government of any country from requiring aliens to serve in the militia or police, yet at the above-mentioned date the British Government intimated that, if the United States permitted no alternative of providing subsitutes, the position of British subjects to be embodied in that militia would "call for every exertion being made in their favour on the part of Her Majesty's Government." The British Government in 1862 informed Mr. Stuart that as a general principle of international law neutral aliens ought not to be compelled to perform any military service (i.e., working in trenches), but that allowance might be made for the conduct of authorities in cities under martial law and in daily peril of the enemy, and in 1864 the British Government saw no reason to interfere in the case of neutral foreigners directed to be enrolled as a local police for New Orleans. By the United States Act, April 14, 1802, naturalized aliens are entitled to nearly the same rights and are charged with the same duties as the native inhabitants; and aliens not naturalized, if they have at any time assumed the right of voting at a State election or held office, are, according to the opinion of Mr. Attorney-General Bates, liable to the acts for enrolling in the national forces. (See also, Act 3rd March 1863, and Act 24th February 1864; Proclamation of President May 8, 1863). This was acted on during the American Civil War, and tacitly acquiesced in by the British Government."[326]

Although the right to serve in the military forces of a country is generally limited to nationals or to individuals who have declared

---

325 McNair: Ibid., 125.
326 Wheaton: A Digest of International Law (Washington, 1836), Vol. II, 502-503.
Moore: Digest, Vol. IV. 54-55.

their intention to become nationals, in several commercial treaties concluded between nations, the compulsory enrolment of foreign nationals in the forces of the host State likely to be used for purposes other than police duties has been expressly guarded against. Provisions have been incorporated in a number of treaties between the United States of America and other countries granting exemption from compulsory military service to the nationals of the respective countries in the armed forces of the other. It may be added that certain treaties also contain provisions granting exemption with respect to forced loans, requisitions and military exactions. In this regard, the Acting Secretary of State of the United States, stated on August 9, 1918 as follows: "It may be argued that the number of treaties providing for the exemption of citizens or subjects of the contracting parties from military service abroad is evidence of a practice among nations to draft aliens into their forces. I cannot, however, concur in this argument, as it seems to me that these treaties may as well be regarded as evidence that nations might, in the exigency of war, be inclined to break the law and practice of nations under which aliens are exempted from compulsory military service abroad in an international war. A review of the diplomatic history of the United States in respect to compulsory military service discloses that, so far as the history of the United States is concerned, most countries whose subjects or ctiizens have been affected by military service in the United States have strongly protested against such service, as has the United States when the case was reversed. It will be observed that the military service against which the strongest protest is made is that of service in an international war or in a great war like the Civil War, which partook of the nature of an international war, rather than service in the militia in peace time, or in the police force for the preservation of order, or in the exigency of a besieged city under military law. It should be borne in mind, however, that the legislation of the United States while, of course, binding upon persons within its territory, and the announcements of Secretaries of State of the United States are not sufficient upon which to base a conclusion as to the rule of international law on this subject. . . From this convenient summary it will be observed that it is not the practice of nations to compel aliens to serve in their armies."[327]

However, a number of more recent treaties concluded by the United States contain provisions similar to those in Article VI of the Treaty of December 8, 1923 with Germany which provides: "In

---

[327] Hackworth: Digest, Vol. III, 599 footnote.

the event of war between either High Contracting Party and a third State, such Party may draft for compulsory military service nationals of the other having a permanent residence within its territories and who have formally according to its laws declared an intention to adopt its nationality by naturalization, unless such individuals depart from the territories of said belligerent Party within sixty days after a declaration of war."[328]

In **Polites v. The Commonwealth and Another** and **Kandiliotes v. The Commonwealth and Another** (1945), the High Court of Australia had occasion to review the extent of the liability of resident aliens for compulsory military service in time of war. Mr. Justice Starke summed up the practice of States in this regard in these terms: "(1) It is not permissible to enrol aliens, except with their own consent, in a force to be used for ordinary national or political objects. (2) Aliens may be compelled to help to maintain social order, provided that the action required of them does not overstep the limits of police, as distinguished from political action. (3) They may be compelled to defend the country against an external enemy when the existence of social order or of the population itself is threatened, when, in other words, a State or part of it is threatened by an invasion or savages or uncivilized nations."[329]

The Australian practice has been set out also by Mr. Justice Williams in **Polites v. The Commonwealth and Another**, and **Kandiliotes v. The Commonwealth and Another** (1945) wherein he stated that "It is submitted that there is an accepted rule of public international conduct, evidenced by international treaties and conventions, authoritative textbooks and practice, having the general hallmarks of assent and reciprocity (per Lord Macmillan in **Compania Naviera Vascogado v. S.S. Cristina**, (1938) A.C. 485 at p. 497) that any nation, when at war, will not compel the nationals of another State who are within its jurisdiction to enlist and serve in its armed forces. As at present advised, it appears to me that the treaties and conventions, authoritative textbooks and practice are sufficient to establish the rule of conduct in question."[330]

---

328 Hackworth: Ibid., 601.
Nevertheless, the former United States practice of granting general exemption from military, as shown by pre-war treaties, seems to be giving place to a policy of agreeing to the drafting of declarants who remain in the country during the war. This appears to be a product of World War and the treaties which allowed the drafting by the Allies of the another's resident nationals.

329 Annual Digest and Reports of Public International Law Cases (1943-45), 216.

330 Annual Digest and Reports of Public International Law Cases (1943-45), 217.

It is a universally accepted rule of international law that an individual may voluntarily enter the military service of a foreign government. Such a rule is firmly established also by the sustained practice of States. For instance, the United States Department of State replied on December 13, 1922, to a communication from the Turkish Government requesting that all Ottoman subjects in the military service of the United States be discharged, with the privilege of re-enlistment, as follows: "As pointed out in the Secretary's note to you, dated May 3, 1922, any Ottoman subjects who may now be in the Army of the United States are in it at their own request and not as the result of compulsion. I am aware of no such rules as that suggested by the Ottoman Department of Foreign Affairs, forbidding one country to employ in its military service subjects or citizens of a foreign country who freely offer themselves for such service. Under the laws of the United States an Ottoman subject who has declared his intention of becoming an American citizen may freely enter into a contract of enlistment in the United States Army, and such a contract is not believed by this Government to be in any way affected by a subsequent withdrawal of the declaration of intention."[331]

The practice of most other States also indicates that an alien may waive his alienage and voluntarily enlist in a foreign army, if permitted to do so by the laws of that country. Moreover, in the view of the United States, as those of most States, under the law of nations a person voluntarily enlisting himself in the armed forces of a foreign government owes that government temporary allegiance and must look to it for protection. Having accepted services in the armed forces of a foreign State, he cannot look for protection to his own government against the legitimate consequences of his conduct.[332]

Principles embodied in Certain Conventions

The Inter-American Convention concerning the Status of Aliens (1928)

Article 3

Foreigners may not be obliged to perform military service; but those foreigners who are domiciled, unless they prefer to leave the country, may be compelled, under the same conditions as nationals, to perform police, fire-protection, or militia duty for the

---

331 Hackworth: Digest, Vol. III, 601.
332 Hackworth: Ibid., 601 footnote.

protection of the place of their domicile against natural catastrophies or dangers not resulting for war.[333]

European Convention on Establishment (1955)

CHAPTER VI

. . . Compulsory Civilian Services . . .

Article 22

Nationals of a Contracting Party may in no case be obliged to perform in the territory of another Party any civilian services, whether of a personal nature or relating to property, other or more burdensome than those required of nationals of the latter Party.[334]

Article 15

(1) A State shall have the right in accordance with its local laws, regulations and orders to impose such restrictions as it may deem necessary on an alien leaving its territory.

(2) Such restrictions on an alien leaving the State may include any exit visa or tax clearance certificate to be procured by the alien from the authorities concerned.

(3) Subject to the local laws, regulations and orders, a State shall permit an alien leaving its territory to take his personal effects with him.

Note : The Delegate of Pakistan reserved his position on Clause (3). The Delegates of Ceylon and United Arab Republic wished the following clause to be retained in this Article:

> "An alien who has fulfilled all his local obligations in the State of residence, shall not be prevented from departing from the State of residence."

Commentary

Alien's departure from the host State

Article 15 embodies the principle that a State shall not prevent an alien from leaving its territory, provided he has fulfilled all his local obligations such as payment of rates, taxes, fines, private

---

333 This Convention was signed at Havana on February 20, 1928; The United States excepted this Article from its ratification of the Convention; 46 Stat. 2754; Hackworth: Digest, Vol. III, 600 footnote. It may be added that the European tendency seems to be towards total exemption from military charges, as well as from training and service. Cutler: "The Treatment of Foreigners" op. cit., 232-233.

334 Unification of Law, op. cit., 177.

debts and the like. Freedom of departure of aliens from the State of residence is one of the well recognized principles of international law.[335]

As a State holds only territorial and not personal supremacy over aliens within its boundaries, arbitrary refusal to permit aliens to depart from a country is regarded as a violation of the elementary principles of international law and practice. Further, this Article affirms the right of an alien subject to the local laws and regulations to take his personal effects away with him when he leaves the State of residence. In a word, grossly unfair restrictions on the departure of aliens and outright arbitrary impositions on his right to take his personal property away with him may be regarded as violative of human rights and fundamental freedoms.

Opinion of Writers

Oppenheim states: "Since a State holds only territorial and not personal supremacy over an alien within its boundaries, it can never, in any circumstances, prevent him from leaving its territory, provided he has fulfilled his local obligations, such as payment of rates and taxes, of fines, of private debts, and the like. An alien leaving a State can take his property away with him on the same conditions as a national, and a tax for leaving the country, or tax upon the property he takes away with him, cannot be levied."[336]

Practice of Member States of the Committee

Requirement of exit visa or tax clearance certificate

The Participating States of the Committee take the view that a State has the right to impose such restrictions as it sees fit on an alien leaving its territory. Such restrictions or requirements may include an exit visa or a tax clearance certificate from the alien before leaving the State. Under the laws of Burma and Indonesia, an alien must obtain a permit before leaving the country, whereas in Ceylon and India, it is not necessary. In Japan, although this is not necessary, he may be required to produce an 'Exit Visa'. In Iraq such permit may sometimes be required. Normally Ceylon and the

---

335 From the rule that an enemy alien possesses the freedom of departure from the belligerent State even in time of war, it necessarily follows that an alien has this right in time of peace. Thus Vattel writing in 1758, stated that it was a point of good faith on the part of a belligerent not to detain enemy subjects who had entered the State under an implied promise of being able to return in freedom and safety and he found it a general practice among nations to allow merchants full time to wind up their affairs and withdraw from the country: Vattel: Droit des gens, Book III, s. 63; Fenwick, International Law, 601.

336 Oppenheim: International Law, Vol. I, 690.

United Arab Republic do not require the alien to produce an exit visa before leaving the State, but under exceptional circumstances, this may be considered necessary from nationals as well as foreigners leaving these States. Burma favours the view that restrictions and prohibitions may be imposed upon the departure of criminals, who wish to escape from the country. The Immigration Control Order of Japan does not contain anything concering the prohibition of the departure of foreign nationals from Japan, but an alien who is alleged to have committed a crime may not be permitted to leave the country. Restrictions on the departure of an alien from Ceylon and the United Arab Republic are not imposed except when the individual concerned is required in connection with a crime he is alleged to have perpetrated, but they take the view that an alien who has fulfilled all his local obligations in the State of residence, shall not be prevented from departing from the State of residence.

Practice of States other than Member States of the Committee

The policy of the United States was clearly stated by its Official Representative in Geneva in 1955 in these terms: "The United States recognizes that Chinese in the United States who desire to return to the People's Republic of China are entitled to do so and declares that it has adopted and will further adopt appropriate measures so that they can expeditiously exercise their right to return." The practice of several State's shows that generally a foreign national leaving a State is allowed to take his property away with him on the same conditions as the citizens or subjects of the country. However, before he is allowed to take his personal property, money or effects, he is expected to have fulfilled all his local obligations. For instance, in the **Umbreit** (1908) case, the Wisconsin Supreme Court said it was the duty of the State to protect its citizens by preventing the removal of the assets of his debtor found within the State in order that he might be able to satisfy his claim in the State of his domicile.337 It may be added that bilateral commercial treaties concluded between nations generally provide inter alia for the freedom of removal of property by the nationals of each contracting party from the territory of the other. For instance, Article VII of the Convention of April 26, 1826 concluded between the United States of America and Denmark provides: "The United States and His Danish Majesty mutually agree that no higher or other duties, charges or taxes of any kind shall be levied in the territories or dominions of either party, upon any personal pro-

---

337 Discotogesellschaft v. Umbreit, 208 U.S. 570, 578-580, 581-582. Hackworth: Digest. Vol. III, 666.

perty, money or effects of their respective citizens or subjects, on the removal of the same from their territories or dominions reciprocally, either upon the inheritance of such property, money or effects, or otherwise, than are or shall be payable in each State upon the same, when removed by a citizen or subject of such State, respectively."[338]

Principles embodied in certain Conventions

European Convention on Establishment (1955)

CHAPTER II

Exercise of Private Rights

Article 4

Nationals of any Contracting Party shall enjoy in the territory of any other Party treatment equal to that enjoyed by nationals of the latter Party in respect of the possession and exercise of private rights, whether personal rights or rights relating to property.[339]

In 1957, the United Kingdom concluded conventions with Sweden, Germany, Israel, and Belgium. One of the principles incorporated in these conventions is that the persons who go from the territory of one party to that of the other should keep that which they have acquired under the legislation of the former party or enjoy corresponding rights under the legislation of the latter.

Article 16

(1) A State shall have the right to order expulsion or deportation of an undesirable alien in accordance with its local laws, regulations and orders.

(2) The State shall, unless the circumstances warrant otherwise, allow an alien under orders of expulsion or deportation reasonable time to wind up his personal and other affairs.

(3) If an alien under orders of expulsion or deportation fails to leave the State within the time allowed, or, after leaving the State, returns to the State without its permission, he may be expelled or deported by force, besides being subjected to arrest, de-

---

338 Hackworth: Digest. Vol. III, 669; Arts. I and V(2) of the Treaty of Friendship, Commerce and Navigation concluded between the United States of America and the Italian Republic in 1948 also provides for this right i.e., freedom of removal of property by aliens; Briggs: The Law of Nations, 530-531, 542-543; State practice points to the fact that a tax for leaving the country or a special tax upon the property that are taken away by an alien is not normally levied.

339 Unification of Law, op. cit., 165.

tention and punishment in accordance with local laws, regulations and orders.

Commentary

The expulsion or deportation of aliens

Clause (1) of Article 16 deals with the undoubted right of a State to expel aliens from its territories for reasons bearing upon the public welfare of the State. The right to expel aliens rests upon the same foundations as the right to exclude aliens. According to Borchard, the right of expulsion is not limited by treaties which guarantee to the citizens of the contracting parties the right of residence and travel, or of trade, and other rights.[340] A State may decide for itself whether the continued presence within its territory of a particular alien is so adverse to the national interests that the country needs to rid itself of him. A conclusion in the affirmative gives rise to the privilege of expulsion.[341] It may be added that the right of a State to expel aliens from its territory naturally includes stateless persons also.[342] In the exercise of this right there must be, as in the case of admission of aliens, no discrimination against the citizens of a particular foreign State as such.

Expulsion must be effected in a reasonable manner

Under Clause (2) of this Article, expulsion or deportation must, for humanitarian reasons, be effected in a reasonable manner and without unnecessary injury to the alien affected. Although a State may exercise its right of expulsion according to its discretion, it must not abuse its right by proceeding in an arbitrary manner. In the case of expulsion or deportation of an alien who has been residing within the State for some length of time and has established some business or professional connections there, this Article provides that he must be given some reasonable time to wind up his interests. Further, it is implied that an alien under an expulsion order should not normally be exposed to unnecessary indignity prior to expulsion. In the view of McNair, although a State has the right to expel aliens from its territory, it is accountable to other States for any hardship or loss thus inflicted beyond what is inevitable in the fact of expulsion.[343] According to Article XXX of the regulations of the Institute of International Law (1892): "The

---

340 Borchard: The Diplomatic Protection of Citizens Abroad, (1915), 48-49. Briggs: The Law of Nations, 536.
341 Hyde: International Law, Vol. I, 230.
342 McNair: International Law Opinions, Vol. II, 109.
343 McNair: International Law Opinions, Vol. II, 109.

act of decreeing expulsion shall be notified to the expelled individual. The reasons on which it is based must be stated in fact and in law."[344] Thus, it appears that as the alien's home government has the right to inquire into the reason for and the manner of expulsion of its national, where the procedure applied in the course of expulsion has manifested a harsh treatment against the national of a foreign State, his home government could be justified in making diplomatic representation and protest against such capricious or unreasonable exercise of the power of expulsion.

Forcible expulsion of aliens

Although expulsion must be effected in a reasonable and humane manner and without unnecessary injury and indignity to the alien affected, under Clause (3) of this Article, the State has the right to waive the above requirements in certain cases of expulsion. Where an alien under expulsion order refuses to leave the State or is likely to evade the authorities, or after having left, returns without authorization, force may be used for the purpose of his expulsion. Thus if necessary, he may be, in accordance with the applicable laws, regulations and orders, arrested, detained, punished and forcibly deported.

Opinions of Writers

Bonfils writes: "A State has the right to expel from its territory aliens, individually or collectively, unless treaty provisions stand in the way. . . . In ancient times, collective expulsion was much practised. In modern times it has been resorted to only in case of war. Some writers have essayed to enumerate the legitimate causes of expulsion. The effort is useless. The reasons may be summed up and condensed in a single word: **The public interest of the State.** Bluntschli wished to deny to States the right of expulsion, but he was obliged to acknowledge that aliens might be expelled by a simple administrative measure. (French law of Dec. 3, 1849, Arts 7 & 8—Law of Oct. 19, 1797, Art. 7) An arbitrary expulsion may nevertheless give rise to a diplomatic claim."[345]

Hall says: "If a country decides that certain classes of foreigners are dangerous to its tranquillity, or are inconvenient to it socially or economically or morally, and if it passes general laws forbidding the access of such persons, its conduct affords no ground for complaint. Its fears may be idle; its legislation may be harsh; but its action is equal. The matter is different where for identical

---

344 Hyde: International Law, Vol. I, op. cit., 232.
345 Manual du Droit Int. Public, s. 442; Moore: Digest, Vol. IV, 68.

561

reasons individual foreigners, or whole class of foreigners who have already been admitted into the country, or who are resident there, are subjected to expulsion. In such cases the propriety of the conduct of the expelling government must be judged with reference to the circumstances of the moment."[346]

Taylor states: "Every independent State possesses, certainly in theory, the right to grant or refuse hospitality. Undoubtedly such a State possesses the power to close the door to all foreigners whom for social, political or economic reasons it deems it expedient to exclude; and for like reasons it may subject a resident foreigner or a group of them to expulsion, subject of course to such retaliatory measures as an abuse of the excluding or expelling powers may provoke. At the very beginning of our national life the government of the United States recognized the fact that "every society possesses the undoubted right to determine who shall compose its members, and it is exercised by all nations in peace or war. A memorable example of the exercise of this power in time of peace was the passage of the Alien Law of the United States in the year 1798. . . . It may always be questionable whether a resort to this power is warranted by the circumstances, or what department of the government is empowered to exert it; but there can be no doubt that it is possessed by all nations, and that each may decide for itself when the occasion arises demanding its exercise."[347]

"Darut in his monograph on the expulsion of aliens, states that the right of the State to order a foreigner immediately to leave its territory, as it was established in France by the law of Dec. 3, 1849, and as it generally is found in the legislation of countries with the exception of England and Greece, has been the subject of protests by some writers, who regard it either as an infraction of the so-called right of asylum, or as an invasion of the imprescriptible rights of the individual man. Darut, however, maintains that the right of expulsion is an incident of sovereignty, and is essential to the preservation of the ends for which the State exists."[348]

Practice of Member States of the Committee

The laws of Burma and India relating to expulsion of foreigners have provided their executive authorities with ample discretion

---

346 Hall, William Edward: A Treatise on International Law, 4th Ed., (Oxford, 1895), 223-224.
347 Taylor, Hannis: A Treatise on International Public Law, (Chicago, 1901), 231-232.
   Moore: Digest, Vol. IV, 68.
348 Darut: De 1, Expulsion des Etrangers, Aix, 1902.

in the matter. Expulsion or deportation from Ceylon is regulated
by Sections 28 and 31 of the laws of Ceylon. Undesirable persons
can be deported from Indonesia. Article 10 of the Residents Act
of 1938, sets out the grounds on which aliens could be deported
from Iraq. and in Iraq's view for reasons of national interest and
security the State of residence possesses the undoubted right to
expel or deport aliens from its territory. There are provisions in the
laws of Japan for the deportation of aliens. In the view of Japan, a
State has the right to order expulsion or deportation of an undesirable alien for reasons of security or public order, but it must be in
accordance with its applicable laws and regulations. However, aliens
permanently settled in Japan cannot be deported unless a special
permission for the purpose has been obtained from the Ministry of
Justice. Though, there are no specific grounds which could justify
deportation of foreigners from the United Arab Republic, yet under
certain general principles expulsion is permissible. For instance,
when aliens endanger the security, public order. or morality of the
country. and when they are unable to look after themselves, they
could be deported. Although in the United Arab Republic deportation was originally used only as a punishment. now a foreigner
committing certain crimes renders himself liable for deportation.

According to Burma. an alien in transit through a State without the necessary travel documents could be expelled. In such matters. Ceylon. India and Indonesia do not make any distinction between aliens and nationals. In Iraq and Japan foreigners in transit
are treated just as aliens. In the matter of deportation the laws of
the United Arab Republic make no distinction between a resident
alien and the one in transit. Theoretically speaking. a political refugee could be deported from Burma to a country where he might
be persecuted. but in practice. she refrains from doing so. A political refugee could be deported from Ceylon to a country where he
might be exposed to persecution. Such cases in Indonesia will normally receive sympathetic consideration. According to India and
Iraq. if the political refugee's conduct deserves or justifies such a
course of action, he could be deported to that country. Japan states
that he could be sent to a country of his choice. Just as in the case
of extradition. deportation of a political refugee to such a country
is not permissible under the laws of the United Arab Republic.

According to the general practice of Burma, Ceylon, India, and
Indonesia, if no State could be found to receive an expelled alien,
he would be sent to the State to which he belongs, but if he is a
stateless person he could be detained in the country concerned. In

Iraq and Japan they are liable for detention. Under the laws of the United Arab Republic, according to the discretion of the Ministry of Justice, such an alien could be put under surveillance or house arrest, until he could be deported, and the deportation order remains valid until its cancellation by the very authority that issued it.

The law of Burma contains provisions to deal with the question of unauthorized return of an expelled alien. The Constitution of Ceylon provides for safeguards against such occurrences. Under Section 11-2 (a) of the relevant law of India entry of the expelled person will not be permitted. If an expelled alien returns unauthorizedly to Indonesia, he becomes liable for deportation. As no alien could enter Iraq without a valid visa, the expelled alien seeking unauthorized entry will become liable for prosecution. Once an alien is deported from Japan he cannot enter again. In the United Arab Republic, during the pendency of a deportation order, if that alien returns unauthorizedly, he renders himself liable for punishment. However, the Ministry of the Interior has the right to decide upon the re-admission of an expelled alien.

No safeguards are provided for in the Constitution of India against arbitrary, harsh and unjustified expulsion of aliens from India. In Indonesia though there are no explicit safeguards against such expulsion, they could appeal to the Ministry of Justice, and in Iraq they could approach the executive authorities or recourses could be had even to the courts of Iraq in this regard. Aliens subjected to such arbitrary expulsion have the right of appeal to the courts of law in Japan. A foreigner who is aggrieved by an arbitrary, harsh and unjustified expulsion order may prefer an appeal to the Council of State for the cancellation of the harsh or illegal order.

Burma, India, Indonesia, Iraq and Japan are of the view that the government of the State of residence has discretion in regard to expulsion or deportation of foreign nationals from its domain. Ceylon takes the line that for reasons of public security, an alien may be expelled from a State. The United Arab Republic thinks that deportation is to be viewed purely as an exceptional security measure designed for the public welfare, and that it is not meant to be a penalty or wholesale measure or screen for the furtherance of private interests. All States in the Committee except Pakistan agree that the home State of an expelled alien must not refuse to receive him back into its territory.[349]

---

[349] Report of the Asian African Legal Consultative Committee, Third Session (Colombo 1960), 148-150.

Practice of States other than Member States of the Committee

The right of States to expel aliens from their territories for reasons of public welfare as well as peace, tranquillity and safety is generally recognized. States enjoy a wide discretion as to the grounds for expulsion, for instance, Belgium expelled in 1896 Mr. Ben Tillet, a British subject for organizing a strike in Belgium. The British Law Officers took the view that the right of the Belgian Government to expel Mr. Ben Tillet was undoubted.[350] Similarly, Tom Mann was expelled in 1896 from Germany for advocating the spread of Trade Unionism in Germany.[351] Mr. Jaurès, the French Socialistic leader was expelled from Germany for advancing the socialist opposition to the Government's foreign policy.[352]

In 1901, George Kennan, an American citizen was expelled by the Russian Government for his criticisms of the Russian Government in a book which he had published some years ago in relation to the penal institutions of Siberia.[353]   According to Chapter 313 of Volume II of the Russian law, foreigners who have come into Russia can be expelled only upon the decision of a court of law or by order of the higher police authorities. Further, foreigners whose behaviour is suspicious and they who are not desirable as residents within Russia may be expelled by order of the Minister of the Interior.[354]   The Canadian Government expelled two persons called Carranza and Dubose, both on general grounds and for reasons connected with the maintenance of British neutrality during the Spanish-American war.[355] The British and American practice also establishes the right of a State to expel from its territory aliens unless there are treaty provisions to the contrary. Some States which value individual liberty and abhor arbitrary powers of the State organs and officials, do not readily expel aliens. The Government of the United Kingdom had, until December 1919, no power to expel even the most dangerous alien without the recommendation of a court of law, or without an Act of Parliament making provision for such expulsion, except during war, occasions of imminent national danger or great emergency. American practice was emphasized by Secretary of State Mr. Gresham in 1894, in these words: "This Government does not propose to controvert the principle of international law, which authorises every independent State to expel

350 McNair: International Law Opinions, Vol. II, 111-112
351 Ibid., 111-112.
352 Moore: Digest. Vol. IV, 69-70.
353 Moore: Ibid., 94-95.
354 Moore· Ibid., 95
355 McNair: International Law Opinions, Vol. II, 112.

objectionable foreigners or classes of foreigners from its territory. The right of expulsion or exclusion of foreigners is one which the United States, as well as many other countries, has upon occasion exercised when deemed necessary in the interest of the Government or its citizens."[356]

Although it is generally recognized that States possess the power to expel, deport or reconduct aliens, expulsion or reconduction must normally be effected in a reasonable manner and without unnecessary hardship to the individual affected. The reasonable exercise of the privilege of expulsion would appear to demand some respect for the consequences of the connection between the alien and his habitat. Thus, the procedure that may not be inequitably applied to a transient visitor, may on the other hand, work grave hardship to one who through protracted residence within the territory of the expelling State, has dug his roots deep into its commercial or economic life as a participant therein. While this circumstance should not, and does not, deprive the territorial sovereign of its privilege as such, it justifies the challenging of the methods and manner that ignore the injury necessarily entailed when a permanent resident is compelled on short notice to depart from the country.[357] In cases of arbitrary and unreasonable expulsions of resident aliens, the home States of the expelled individuals have made diplomatic representations to the States concerned and asked for the reasons for the expulsions. Thus, Mr. Root, Secretary of State of the United States, stated in 1907 that: "The right of government to protect its citizens in foreign parts against a harsh and unjustified expulsion must be regarded as a settled and fundamental principle of international law. It is no less settled and fundamental that a government may demand satisfaction and indemnity for an expulsion in violation of the requirements of international law."[358]

Arbitrariness in the methods applied in the particular case, rather than in the choice of the individual concerned or in the determination to expel him, usually constituted the main cause of foreign protests and it has been subjected to sharpest criticism.[359] In several such cases, the home States of the aliens exacted indemni-

---

356 Hyde: International Law: Vol. I, 230.
357 Lauterpacht: The Function of Law in the International Community (1933), 289.
    Oppenheim: International Law, Vol. I, 691-92; In re Manoel de Campes Moledo: Annual Digest & Reports of Public International Law Cases (1929-1930), Case No. 164.
358 Communication to the Minister in Caracas, Feb. 28, 1907, For Rel. 1908, 774, 776; Hackworth: Digest, Vol. II, 690.
359 Hyde: International Law, Vol. I, 231.

ties from the States concerned for the arbitrary and unreasonable expulsion of their subjects. Great Britain obtained from Nicaragua in 1895 an indemnity for the expulsion of twelve British subjects who had been arrested and expelled for alleged participation in the Mosquite rebellion.[360] In Ben Tillett case (1896), the British Law Officer took the following view: "The right of the Belgian Government to expel Mr. Ben Tillet is undoubted. But the arrest and detention and the various circumstances of hardship with which they were accompanied are, in our opinion, altogether in excess of anything which could be justified as incidental to the right of expulsion . . . In cases of urgency, arrest as a preliminary to expulsion, may possibly be justified as a measure of precaution. In this case it seems to have been quite unnecessary. . . The arrest was followed by a detention quite unnecessary in its duration . . . we suggest that the Belgian Government ought to express regret for what has occurred, and make some compensation to Mr. Tillett."[361] In the Maal Case (1903), Umpire Plumley of the Netherlands-Venezuaelan Mixed Claims Commission held that, although every government has the right to exclude or expel foreigners from its territory if they are obnoxious and prejudicial to the public order or the welfare of the State, nevertheless this must be accomplished with due regard to the convenience and the personal and property interests of the person expelled. In this case, the foreigner while under arrest, had been "subjected to the indignity of being stripped of all his clothing and made the subject of much mirth and laughter on the part of the bystanders." Observing that the State had failed to regard the person of another as something to be held scared," the Umpire awarded $500 to the Netherlands Government "solely because of these indignities" perpetrated against its national in Venezuela. In Boffolo case (1903) between Italy and Venezuela, the arbitrator summed up the general right of expulsion and the mode of its exercise in these words: "(1) A State possesses the general right of expulsion; but (2) Expulsion should only be resorted to in extreme instances, and must be accomplished in the manner least injurious to the person affected; (3) The country exercising the power must, when occasion demands, state the reasons of such expulsion before an international tribunal, and an inefficient (insufficient) reason or none being advanced, accepts the consequences."[362]

---

360 Fenwick: International Law, 269.

361 McNair: International Law Opinions, Vol. II, 112.

362 Briggs: The Law of Nations, 535. It may be added that the **Institut de Droit International**, while recognizing the right of expulsion to the full extent, has adopted a project designed to temper its practical application; Taylor: A Treatise on International Public Law, 233.

The deportation, as distinct from expulsion, of an alien who has entered or attempted to enter the territory of a State in violation of its immigration or exclusion laws is regarded as merely incidental to their enforcement. Within such a category may be placed the cases of aliens who, after having failed to comply with conditions upon which their admission was permitted, as by having overstayed a brief period of permitted sojourn, or by having failed to maintain the status on which their entrance was permitted, are in due course, obliged to leave the country. According to the existing statutory law of the United States, the deportation of an alien is made the consequence not merely of an unlawful entrance into its territory, but also of the commission of certain classes of offences within a specified period after entrance, and of others, at any time thereafter.[363] Further, the penalty for the alien's intrusion into local politics may also be deportation. In some States destitute aliens, vagabonds, suspicious aliens without papers of legitimation, foreign criminals who have served their term of imprisonment, and individuals of similar character, are without any formalities, arrested by the police and reconveyed to the frontier for the purpose of banishment. It appears that the home State of such aliens has the duty to receive them, since a State cannot refuse to receive such of its nationals[364] as are expelled from other States. The legislation and judicial practice of many countries show that an alien may not be deported to a country or territory where his person or freedom might be threatened on account of his race, religion, nationality or political views.[365]

Principles Embodied in certain Conventions

Lausanne Convention respecting Conditions of Residence, signed by Turkey, the British Empire, France, Italy, Greece, Rumania and Yugoslavia (1923).

Article 7. (ii) Turkey reserves the right to expel, in individual cases, nationals of the other Contracting Powers, either under the order of a Court or in accordance with the laws and regulations relating to public morality, public health or pauperism, or for reasons affecting the internal or external safety of the State. . . . .

The expulsion shall be carried out in conditions complying with the requirements of health and humanity.[366]

---

363 Hyde: International Law, Vol. I, 235.
364 Oppenheim: International Law Vol. I, 694-95; Hackworth: Digest, Vol. III, ss. 293-302.
365 Article 33 of the Geneva Convention on the Status of Refugees (1951), United States ex rel. Weinberg v. Schlotfeld (1938), 26 F. Suppl. 283.
366 Signed at Lausanne on July 23, 1923, 28 League of Nations Treaty Series, 159; Briggs: The Law of Nations, 537.

Inter-American Convention on the Status of Aliens (1928)

Article: "For reasons of public order or safety, States may expel foreigners domiciled, resident, or merely in transit through their territory. . . ."[367]

European Convention on Establishment (1955)

CHAPTER I

. . . Expulsion

Article 3

1. Nationals of any Contracting Party lawfully residing in the territory of another Party may be expelled only if they endanger national security or offend against ordre public or morality.

2. Except where imperative considerations of national security otherwise require, a national of any Contracting Party who has been so lawfully residing for more than two years in the territory of any other Party shall not be expelled without first being allowed to submit for the purpose before a competent authority or a person specially designated by the competent authority.

3. Nationals of any Contracting Party who have been lawfully residing for more than ten years in the territory of any other Party may only be expelled for reasons of national security or if the other reasons mentioned in paragraph 1 of this Article are of a particularly serious nature.

Supplementary Protocol*

Section 1

(a) Each Contracting Party shall have the right to judge by national criteria;

(3) the circumstances which constitute a threat to national security or an offence against ordre public or morality;

(b) Each Contracting Party shall determine whether the reasons for expulsion are of a "particularly serious nature". In this connection account shall be taken of the behaviour of the individual concerned during his whole period of residence.

---

367 Adopted at Havana on February 20, 1928.
    Hudson: International Legislation, Vol. IV, 2374.
* Under Art. 32 of this Convention, the supplementary protocol attached to this Convention shall form an integral part of it.

Section III

(a) The concept of "ordre public" is to be understood in the wide sense generally accepted in continental countries. A Contracting Party may, for instance, exclude a national of another Party for political reasons. . . .

(b) The Contracting Parties undertake, in the exercise of their established rights, to pay due regard to family ties.

(c) The right of expulsion may be exercised only in individual cases.

The Contracting Parties shall, in exercising their right of expulsion, act with consideration, having regard to the particular relations which exist between the Members of the Council of Europe. They shall in particular take due account of family ties and the period of residence in their territories of the persons concerned."[368]

Article 17

A State shall not refuse to receive its nationals expelled or deported from the territory of another State.

Note : The Delegate of Pakistan suggested the addition of the word "normally" before the word "refuse".

Commentary

Deported alien must be readmitted into his home State

Giving expression to a well-established principle of customary international law and State practice, this Article makes it obligatory on the part of every State to receive back on its territory its nationals expelled or deported from another State.

Opinions of Writers

Oppenheim says: The home State of an individual has the duty "of receiving on its territory such of its citizens as are not allowed to remain on the territory of other States. Since no State is obliged by the Law of Nations to allow foreigners to remain within its boundaries, it may, for many reasons, happen that certain individuals are expelled from all foreign countries. The home State of expelled persons is bound to receive them on the home territory."[369]

---

368 Katz & Brewster: The Law of International Transactions and Relations, 80-81; Unification of Law, op. cit., 165, 187-189.
369 Oppenheim: International Law, Vol. I. op. cit., 646, 695.

570

Hyde observes: "The effective expulsion of an alien normally calls for co-operative acquiescence by the State of which he is a national. Thus it is generally deemed to be its duty to receive him if he seeks access to its territory. Nor can it well refuse to receive him if during his absence from its domain he has lost its nationality without having acquired that of another State."[370]

Practice of Member States of the Committee

All the Member States of the Committee except Pakistan take the view that the home State of the expelled or deported alien shall not refuse to readmit him if he wants to return to his country. According to Pakistan a State must not normally forbid the entrance of its expelled nationals. Thus it may be possible for the State to deny him admission in case of necessity.

Practice of States other than Member States of the Committee

Practice of most States establishes the rule that the alien's home State must not refuse to take back its own national who is expelled from abroad. Deportation takes place normally to the individual's country of origin. Some States do not resort to deportation of an alien who is able to establish that no foreign State will receive him on its domain. In **United States ex rel. Hudak v. Uhl.**, the court took the view that the petitioner, a national of Poland was not entitled to insist to be deported to Canada.[371] During the Second World War the Courts in the United States in some cases ordered the handing over of the deported individuals belonging to countries under enemy occupation, to the appropriate authorities of their governments-in-exile.[372] In **Staniszewski v. Watkins** (1948) a District court in the United States held that since the alien who was detained as an undesirable alien was a stateless person and that no State could be found to receive him, he ought not to be deported.[373]

Principles embodied in certain Conventions

I.   The **Lausanne Convention** respecting Conditions of Residence concluded by Turkey, the British Empire, France, Greece, Italy, Japan, Rumania and Yugoslavia (1923).

Article 7: ". . . The other Contracting Powers agree to receive the persons thus expelled, and their families at any time. . ."[374]

---

370 Hyde: International Law, Vol. I, 231.
371 Annual Digest (1935-37), Case No. 161, 342-344.
372 Moraitis v. Delany, Annual Digest (1941-42), Case No. 96, 318-326; Hackworth: Digest, Vol. III, ss, 293-302.
373 Annual Digest, 1948, Case No. 80, 265-268.
374 Signed at Lausanne on July 23, 1923, 28 League of Nations Treaty Series, 159.

571

II. Inter-American Convention on the Status of Aliens (1928)

Article 6: ". . . States are required to   receive their nationals expelled from foreign soil who seek to enter their territory."[375]

Article 18

Where the provisions of a treaty or convention between any of the signatory States conflict with the principles set forth   herein, the provisions of such treaty or convention shall prevail   as between those States.

Commentary

The principles embodied in the Report of the Committee contain recommendations concerning the status and treatment of aliens and the various Articles of this Report set out what the Committee considers to be the appropriate   mode   of treatment under the general principles of international law in the light of the practice of the States. This Article recognises the position that States may by bilateral or multilateral arrangements vary their rights and obligations under the general principles of law. Article 18 provides that where there are such treaties and conventions the provisions of them will override the general principles embodied in these Articles.

---

[375] Adopted at Havana on Feb. 20. 1928; Hudson: International Legislation, Vol. IV, 2374; Briggs: The Law of Nations, 530; Harvard Law School: Research in International Law; Nationality, Responsibility of States, Territorial Waters (1929), 233.

(8) DRAFT CONVENTION TO GRANT MUTUAL LEGAL AID, 1961

Adopted in Tokyo on February, 1961, at the Fourth Session of the Asian-African Legal Consultative Committee.

Text from ASIAN-AFRICAN LEGAL CONSULTATIVE COMMITTEE, Report of the Fourth Session, pp. 199-232, 375.

LEGAL AID

Introductory Note

The subject of Free Legal Aid was referred to the Committee by the Government of Ceylon under the provisions of Article 3 (c) of the Statutes of the Committee as being a matter of common concern on which exchange of views and information was desirable between the Participating Countries. At the First Session held in New Delhi the Commitee appointed the Member for Ceylon as Rapporteur on the subject. At the Second Session held in Cairo the Committee decided that the Delegation of Ceylon should continue to act as Rapporteur on the subject and requested all other Delegations to furnish the Rapporteur with statements of the laws and practice prevalent in their respective countries on the subject. The Governments of Burma, India, Indonesia, Japan, Pakistan, and the United Arab Republic submitted memoranda on the subject, and at the Third Session held in Colombo the Rapporteur presented his Report on Free Legal Aid. The Committee considered the Rapporteur's Report and directed the Secretariat to circulate the same amongst the Governments of the Participating Countries. The Committee decided that any specific questions which may be raised by the Governments of the Participating Countries on this Report should be placed before the Committee for consideration at its Fourth Session. The Committee considered the subject at its Fourth Session held in Tokyo, and on the recommendations of a Sub-Committee, decided to publish the Report of the Rapporteur together with all other materials contained in the Brief of Documents and to present the same to the Governments of the Participating Countries.

RAPPORTEUR'S REPORT ON LEGAL AID

(By Mr. Justice H. W. Thambiah, Q.C. Rapporteur)

The Rapporteur called for information through the Secretariat to acquaint himself with the legal aid organisations obtaining in the Member Countries. The Secretariat has furnished reports from the following Member Countries: BURMA, INDIA, INDONESIA, JAPAN, PAKISTAN and the UNITED ARAB REPUBLIC. The system of legal aid obtaining in Ceylon is prepared by the Rapporteur and is annexed to Appendix.

The Rapporteur submits his Report and thanks the Committee for the honour conferred upon him by appointing him as Rapporteur on this subject.

The recommendations in the Report do not represent the views of the country of the Rapporteur.

The recommendations are purely tentative for the consideration of the Committee.

H. W. THAMBIAH

1. The very existence of free government depends upon making the machinery of justice so effective that the citizens of the democracy shall believe in its impartiality and fairness. Where society constitutes both rich and poor, legal aid for the needy should be provided so as to ensure that belief.

2. Many Constitutions of the world enshrine the principle of equality before the law. Jennings, in his work on the Law of the Constitution (3rd Ed., page 49) says :

> "In England, the right to sue and be sued, to prosecute and be prosecuted, for the same kind of action should be same for all citizens of full age and understanding, and without distinction of race, religion, wealth, social status, or political influence."

3. In spite of the benevolence of the judges to help the underprivileged in cases that come up before them, still those who cannot afford to engage the services of a competent lawyer, cannot expect to have equal justice in a court of law. Individual efforts by charitable minded lawyers to help the poor cannot meet the needs of the poor.

4. The Magna Carta, the Englishmen's Charter of Justice, states that :

> "To none will we sell, to none will we deny, to none will we delay right or justice."

The VIth Amendment to Article 7 of the American Constitution declares that :

"In all criminal prosecutions, the accused shall enjoy the right to a speedy and public trial by an impartial Jury of the State and district wherein the crime shall have been committed, which district shall have been previously ascertained by law, and to be informed of the nature and cause of accusation; to be confronted with the witnesses against him; to have compulsory process for obtaining witnesses in his favour, and to have the assistance of counsel for his defence."

Article II of the Soviet Constitution reads as follows :

"In all Courts of the U.S.S.R. cases are heard in public, unless otherwise provided for by law, and the accused is guaranteed the right to defence."

5. The Preamble to the Charter of the United Nations states that one of the avowed objects of the United Nations is to re-affirm faith in fundamental human rights, in the dignity and worth of the human person, in the equal rights of men and women and all nations, large or small.

6. The intricacies of the law, the tangled growth of precedent and legislation, the recondite mysteries of the writings of the jurists, the customary usages, often conflicting and uncertain, make the administration of the law, one of the most difficult tasks in modern times.

7. Mr. Justice Sutherland summed up the need of the layman for counsel in these trenchant words :

"Even the intelligent and educated layman has small and sometimes no skill in the science of law. If charged with crime, he is incapable generally, of determining for himself whether the indictment is good or bad. He is unfamiliar with the rules of evidence. Left without the aid of counsel, he may be put on trial without a proper charge, and convicted upon incompetent evidence, or evidence irrelevant to the issue or otherwise inadmissible. He lacks both the skill and knowledge adequately to prepare his defence, even though he may have a perfect one. He requires the guiding hand of counsel at every step in the proceedings against him. Without it, though he may not be guilty, he faces the danger of conviction because he does not know how to establish his innocence. If that be true of men of intelligence, how much more true is it of the ignorant and illiterate, or those of feeble intellect."

8. The matter becomes more complicated when a layman is pitched against a trained lawyer. A layman is usually no match for a skilled prosecutor whom he confronts in the court room. He needs the aid of counsel, lest he be the victim of over-zealous prosecutors, of the law's complexity, or of his own ignorance, or bewilderment. These are some of the reasons why the right to be represented by counsel in a court of law is a fundamental right. If the right to sue or be sued in a court of law is to be treated in the

tribunals as a fundamental right, the auxiliary right to be represented, is also an auxiliary fundamental right without which the earlier right will be just a mockery.

9. The granting of legal aid is essential in any democracy or any form of government that believes in equal justice to all. The world is gradually becoming aware that the grant of legal aid is essential, if there is going to be equality before the law. In some ancient systems of law, legal battles were fought by means of sinews hired by the combatants. This in turn gave way to the present legal system by which eminent lawyers were engaged by men who have long purses. Is justice to be denied to the poor merely because they are unable to find the fees to pay a competent lawyer or even a lawyer of moderate competence? From whatever angle one considers this question, it is an inescapable conclusion, that legal aid should be granted to poor litigants who are unable to provide the means to prosecute or to defend their suits.

10. In this Report some of the fundamental issues involved in formulating a scheme for legal aid are discussed. An organisation which will facilitate the grant of legal aid to foreigners who seek such aid in the countries who are Members of this Committee is also adumbrated. Further work is necessary to finalise this scheme.

Legal aid defined

11. Legal Aid is essentially an organised effort on the part of the Bar and the Society to provide the service of lawyers free or for a token charge, to persons who cannot afford to pay the lawyer's fees. Such services may consist not only of granting professional consultation but also may include assistance in negotiation, the preparation of legal documents and representation in court.

12. The poor are handicapped not only in engaging the services of a lawyer but also in defraying the necessary expenses for the conduct of the litigation. In the course of litigation, it may be necessary to make investigations, preparatory to litigation, which may involve expenditure of money. It may be necessary to find the means to summon witnesses who will be called upon to give evidence in a court of law. Under certain systems of law, a deposit of money in court for the maintenance of such witnesses is necessary. When witnesses come to give evidence, they have to be maintained in a place where the court is situated till the case ends. It may also be necessary under certain systems of law, to provide security for costs before a person brings an action against another. In criminal cases, it may be necessary to find money to provide bail. These are all expenses which a litigant has to incur in litigation. Therefore, the mere granting of assistance of counsel will not be sufficient, unless some provision is made to meet most of the expenses which have been set out.

Legal aid as it exists in certain countries

13. In the twentieth century, it has dawned upon many nations to provide some type of legal aid service to those citizens

576

who are unable to provide the money for such purposes. In some countries, legal aid is in an embryonic stage whereas in other countries it has reached different stages of maturity.

14. In Appendix I, the legal aid as it exists in Western Democracies is given in bare outline.

15. In Appendix II, the legal aid as it exists in the Member-Countries of the Asian-African Legal Consultative Committee is set out.

16. The Rapporteur takes this opportunity to thank the Member Countries who sent a resume of the legal aid systems in those countries.

17. A survey of the legal aid systems obtaining in the Member Countries of the Asian-African Legal Consulative Committee reveals that legal aid is still in its infant stage in these countries. A concerted effort should be made by the Member Countries to provide legal aid not only to their citizens but also to those non-citizens whose country affords their citizens reciprocal treatment by granting legal aid.

18. In Appendix III, a draft convention to be entered into by the Member States of this Committee to grant legal aid to one another's nationals is appended.

19. In this Report the essentials of legal aid are discussed in broad outline. The type of legal aid which a country can provide for a citizen will depend on its legal system, the organisation of its Bar, the amount of money which the country can afford to spend on legal aid, the form of government, and various other factors. Hence, the form of legal aid obtaining in one country may not be suitable to another. But in broad outline, there are certain essentials of legal aid. Hence, the Rapporteur has endeavoured to discuss some of the essentials of legal aid in this Report so that each Member-State may devise the form of legal aid service which is most suited to it. At the end of this Report, a working scheme to grant legal aid to foreign nationals of the Member State of this Committee who seek such assistance in another Member State is adumbrated.

Persons to whom legal aid should be given ·

20. Since the expenses to grant free legal aid should either come from the coffers of the State or from the community chest, or through the funds provided by charitable organisations, an eclectic attitude should be adopted in granting legal aid to persons. In the first place, legal aid should not be made available to those who due to their penurious circumstances are unable to provide the necessary expenses to conduct their litigation. Hence, in many countries, the means test is applied. In considering this test, the disposable income of a person who seeks legal aid and the disposable capital, are matters that are taken into account.

21. By disposable income is meant the income that the applicant gets after deducting the necessary expenses from his gross income. If the members of his family are also earning and are sharing a common hearth and roof, the question will arise as to whether in computing the disposable income of an applicant, account should not be taken of the income earned by the other members. This is particularly applicable to countries where the common joint family system exists either **de jure** or **de facto**. If such a system should exist, and if the members of the family share the same hearth, and bring into hotchpot their earnings, it is nothing but reasonable that the disposable income of the applicant, should be considered by adding the disposable incomes of each earning member and dividing the aggregate sum by the number of individuals who provide such income. Such tests have been applied in certain countries.

22. What is meant by necessary expenses which have to be deducted from the gross income to arrive at the disposable income will naturally vary according to the locality of the place, and from State to State. In countries where there is a scheme of compulsory insurance, usually the amount contributed towards such a scheme is deducted from the gross income in order to compute the disposable income. Since a parent is under a legal obligation to provide maintenance for his wife, certain sums, although they may not be quite commensurate with the amounts he spends on his wife and children, are deducted from his gross income in order to arrive at the disposable income.

23. The income tax payable, and interest paid on loans which are secured, which could easily be proved, such as loans obtained on pawns or mortgages, are also deducted in arriving at the disposable income. In this matter the practice of each country will naturally vary, and each country has to determine what items should be deducted from the gross income to arrive at the disposable income.

24. A person may not have a sufficient disposable income but still may have enough disposable capital to proceed with his case. There is no reason why in such a case, legal aid should be given to such persons. Therefore, as stated earlier, not only the disposable income test is applied but also the disposable capital test is resorted to before a person is granted legal aid. In computing the disposable capital, the residing house, provided it does not exceed a certain value is often deducted. The following items are also deducted, such as :

    (a) the necessary wearing apparel,
    (b) essential implements of trade or agriculture,
    (c) the subject matter of the action,
    (d) debts created by mortgage bonds and crown debts.

Also certain articles which have a religious significance, such as the "thali" worn in South India or in Ceylon or the engagement or wedding ring among those people who are in the habit of exchanging such rings, are not taken into computation in arriving at the disposable capital.

25. In considering the disposable capital, it would not be just to take into account any capital which is owned by the children in their own right. Further, in certain countries, in computing the disposable capital, the question as to whether the capital is in an available state is taken into account. A person may have landed property but he may not be in a position either to raise the money or to sell the property in view of the restrictions placed upon the grant. Such properties are also excluded from the computation of disposable capital. In computing the disposable capital, the capital of the husband and wife often are aggregated together if they are not legally separated.

26. The quantum of the disposable income or the disposable capital which a person should have, to enable him to ask for legal aid, is a matter that has to be fixed by the legislature of each country. This again may vary from place to place in each country, as the income in a village would not be the same as the income in a metropolitan area. Since a certain amount of flexibility should be allowed in such a matter in any legislation that is passed, it is best to allow this matter to be regulated by regulations which may be altered from time to time.

Partial legal aid

27. Should legal aid be extended to persons whose means are above the limit set out for poor persons who obtain free legal aid but whose income is not sufficient for them to proceed with litigation without selling all that they have or reducing themselves to a state of penury? Broadly speaking, in any Welfare State which could afford to grant legal aid to such persons, such aid should be given. But a Welfare State may have other pressing problems, and the grant of legal aid to this class of persons, may enlarge the scope of the legal aid, and may cause a heavy strain on the coffers of the State. In countries where legal aid has not been developed, this step is not recommended, since the State should feel its way and find out how far it could give legal aid first to those who cannot afford any money at all to proceed with their litigation. It is only when that class is served the matter has to be considered as to whether the class envisaged earlier should be given legal aid.

28. When such legal aid is given, it is often called partial legal aid because the applicant is asked to contribute part of the expenses. The amount, that a person who receives partial aid, has to contribute has to be fixed on a sliding scale according to the income or capital of that person. This, again will vary from place to place and from State to State and is a matter that has to be regulated by some regulation which could easily be changed.

29. If the disposable income or disposable capital is above a particular ceiling limit, then no legal aid should be given to that

579

person. But legal aid in serious criminal cases should be given to all citizens who cannot afford the services of a lawyer.

Prima facie case test

30. It is not sufficient for a person to establish that his means are such, that he should be given free legal aid. In a civil case, he should further show that he has a **prima facie** case, either to prosecute or to defend an action. A State, a charitable institution or lawyers cannot be expected to give free legal aid or partial legal aid **to** persons who are engaged in vexatious litigation and whose chances of success are remote. Hence, in addition to the means test, the **prima facie** test is to be applied in all civil cases. When it is stated that a person should have a **prima facie** case, it is not meant that there should be certainty of success or even a high probability of winning the case. But a circumspect lawyer who examines the evidence, both documentary and oral available in a case, has to form a fair estimate as to whether a person has got a **prima facie** case either to defend or to proceed with an action. If such a case is established, then a person should get legal aid, provided of course, he satisfies the other tests.

31. The **prima facie** test case cannot be applied with strictness in criminal cases. In criminal cases when a person is prosecuted, it may not be possible to predict the result of the case or to formulate a defence. Further, in considering the grave consequences that would accrue to the person who is facing a grave criminal charge, the State should often provide legal aid in all cases where a person is charged with serious offences.

32. Where a person is charged with a statutory offence or a minor offence, it is not necessary that free legal aid should be given, unless some complexity of the law or fact makes a judicial officer to take the view that legal assistance is necessary in the interests of justice. In such cases, if a judicial officer who hears the case asks for assistance, a poor person should not be placed in a less advantageous position than a person who could afford to defend himself and the necessary assistance should be given.

Test of reasonableness

33. A further test is also applied in granting legal aid. There may be cases where the means and merits of the case are such that an applicant is entitled to legal aid, but the amount involved may be so trivial or obtaining a decree may be a sheer wastage of time as his opponent may not have the means to satisfy the decree. It may be that, although a person is entitled to legal aid, still the litigation may be so protracted that very heavy expenses will be involved which will not be commensurate with the fruits of the litigation, even if successful. In such cases, it must be left to a certifying authority to refuse legal aid. Provision is found in many systems of legal aid obtaining in various countries that it must be reasonable in all the circumstances of the case to grant legal aid. In crimi-

nal cases, naturally, this test will have little significance because in those types of serious criminal cases, in which legal aid is given, it will be in the interest of justice to grant such legal aid. This test is therefore chiefly applied to civil matters. In criminal matters also this test is applied. If the nature of the crime is such that a person will lose his life or liberty in the event of a conviction, the test of reasonableness is easily satisfied.

Legal aid to juristic persons in countries which follow the Anglo-American system of jurisprudence

34. In Anglo-American jurisprudence and systems based on it, juristic persons are either corporations aggregate or corporations sole. By corporations sole is meant certain public offices which are personified. Corporations aggregate consist of companies and other incorporated societies. In such systems the question as to whether legal aid should be given to juristic persons does not loom large. No question arises as to whether legal aid should be given to corporations sole. In dealing with corporations aggregate, their resources are such that normally no legal aid need be given. But in countries which follow the civil law system, certain foundations, charitable institutions are personified. In such cases, the question arises as to whether legal aid should be given to charitable institutions, scholarship foundations, hospitals, poor relief and parish authorities, etc. In the Netherlands, Luxemburg and Venezuela, legal aid has been granted to such institutions. In Argentina, anybody who wants to apply for the help of the court in charitable matters generally is given legal aid. The question as to whether legal aid should be given to juristic persons has been a disputed one among continental jurists and this dispute has found its echo in the various legislations of the world. A number of States, such as Brazil expressly state that juristic persons are not capable of receiving legal aid.

35. The Polish States have refused to give legal aid to juristic persons. Dr. Cohn submits that in this respect the Polish States have obviously followed the opinion prevailing among the German processualist theoreticians, who have long unsuccessfully opposed the view of the German courts according to which juristic persons are excluded from the benefits of legal aid.

36. In England, the United States of America, Scotland and the Dominions, legal aid in favour of juristic persons have never been and perhaps probably for a long time, will not be considered seriously. It is submitted that this approach is a salutary one.

Are both parties entitled to legal aid?

37. The question as to whether legal aid should be granted to both parties, if each party satisfies the conditions under which such aid is given, is a vexed one.

38. Under the Italian Law, legal aid is never granted to both parties to an action. (See Italy, Royal Decree Concerning Free Legal Aid to the Poor of December 20th, 1923: No. 3282. Article 15, Sub-section 2—L. 174). A few countries, however, grant legal aid to the defendant if it has already been granted to the plaintiff in the same action, provided he satisfies the conditions under which it is given. In such cases, a less exacting inquiry is held so far as the defendant is concerned. Thus, in Luxemburg and in Brazil the defendant is not required to show that his case is a **causa probablis**. In countries where legal aid is given only to one person, one proceeds on the assumption that both parties to an issue could not have a **causa probablis**. Dr. Cohn states that this is an erroneous view. He states as follows: (59 Law Quarterly Review p. 364) :

"It is quite possible that both parties do, indeed, have a good cause. As long as witnesses have not been heard and their doubtful points of law have not been decided or a difficult clause in the contract being authoritatively interpreted, it is quite possible that both parties have indeed a **causa probablis**. Every day cases are brought before courts which counsel on each side must have believed that his client had a good cause. Equally unfounded is the restriction of legal aid to plaintiff only, which is distinctly found in a number of North American States. The poor defendants deserve protection nor less urgently than the poor plaintiffs."

39. While agreeing with Dr. Cohn on the desirability of granting legal aid to both parties, if they satisfy the requirements and conditions of such aid, in practice, this question seldom arises. The certifying authority has to make up his mind one way or the other as to whether legal aid should be given to a person. But there may be cases where both parties deserve legal aid. In such cases, there should be a requirement that in dealing with the merits of the case, the same certifying authority should look into the cases of both parties.

40. A number of countries provide that before a decision about the application of the grant of legal aid is made, both parties should be heard and an attempt should be made to elicit the true facts as far as possible on their statements and documents. Usually the certifying authority tries to bring about a settlement after hearing both parties. But should there be a requirement that in every case both parties should be heard before a certifying authority decides that legal aid should be given to one party or the other or both, the grant of legal aid becomes dilatory and cumbersome. In English and Scottish law the opponent of both parties has to be informed of the grant of legal aid. This is done in the expectation that this will often prove a strong motive in favour of an amicable settlement of the dispute between the parties. But a majority of States require neither a hearing of both parties, nor a notification and allow the application on an **ex parte** hearing.

41. In some countries a nominal fee is charged in all cases in which a poor litigant applicant wishes to submit a case for consideration. Although the sum may be small, it may be an incentive for a person not to bring frivolous claims in a court of law and ask for legal aid. The imposition of a small fee may deter a person from bringing actions in the lower courts after picking up small quarrels and molesting people.

Legal aid to non-citizens and Stateless persons

42. In a country there will be not only citizens and the persons who belong to other States, but also the so-called "stateless" persons. Among the foreigners who belong to other countries, some of them may be resident and others may be non-resident. The question arises whether legal aid should be granted to foreigners and stateless persons.

43. The class that has often been described as "Stateless" persons may be found in many countries. The treatment meted out to some of these stateless persons has ranged from equality to sub-human treatment and has led to international conflicts and disagreements in the world. The United Nations drew up a Convention containing a Charter of the Stateless Persons in New York on February 28, 1954 [See U.N. Document A/CONF. 2/108/Art. 16(ii)]. These documents provide that each contracting country in which a stateless person or a refugee is habitually resident, as the case may be, shall treat such persons as "a national in matters pertaining to access to courts, including legal assistance". Further, any State that claims to be one of the civilized nations, should not deny legal aid to its stateless persons. It is submitted that legal aid should be granted to all stateless persons.

44. In dealing with foreigners, many countries have entered into conventions to grant reciprocal legal aid. Thus, England by April, 1953 had entered into some 20 legal aid conventions with foreign countries (See 97 Solicitors' Journal, p. 336). So far as the Asian countries are concerned, it is desirable that conventions should be entered into between the Member States to provide reciprocal legal aid. A draft convention on this matter is set out in the Appendix to this report to be adopted by the Member Countries.

45. Among foreign nationals, a distinction has to be made between resident and non-resident nationals. In many countries, there are organisations which look after the interests of non-resident foreign nationals. A few of the organisations which cater for this class are: Aegious, organised by the Italian Red Cross; B'Rith Church World Service; Family Welfare Associations; Hebrew Immigrant Society; International Catholic Migration Commission; International Red Cross; International Social Services; Lutheran Refugee Service; St. Raphael's and some others.

46. Many non-governmental organisations have considered this matter. In 1954, the Committee on Legal Aid of the Inter-

national Bar Association conducted a survey of legal aid facilities throughout the world. The results of this survey were published in a small booklet called "Littlewood Report" which was submitted at the Monaco Conference. This Report disclosed that little or no difference was made in the service provided to citizens and non-citizens in the countries that provide legal aid, although in certain countries reciprocity of legal aid has been insisted upon.

47. Mr. Orison S. Marden submitted a Paper to the International Bar Association at Oslo in 1956 on the "Ways and Means of Improving Legal Aid Facilities for Foreign Nationals, Whether Resident or Non-Resident". After referring to the "Littlewood Report" in this paper he said :—

> "Where any difference exists, it should be remedied as expeditiously as possible in the interests of international harmony and goodwill."

48. In 1950, Dr. Raphael Agababien of Iran submitted a Paper on "International Legal Assistance". He strongly urged that legal assistance should be given to aliens through the offices of the Red Cross. This matter was further discussed at the Fourth International Conference of the International Bar Association held at Madrid in 1952. At this Conference, it was resolved that "all member associations be urged to assist the Committee of the International Red Cross in the attempt to see that legal aid and advice is provided to foreigners and stateless persons, such assistance to be provided through existing organisations."

49. In England, legal aid has been made available not only to those resident in England and Wales irrespective of nationality but also to non-residents who require aid in the English courts. In the Case of **Ammar v. Ammar** (1954) (2 All England Reporter, p. 365) legal aid was granted to a husband who lived in Cyprus to sue for divorce in the Scottish courts. The English Legal Aid Act of 1949 places the foreign litigant on the same footing as the resident litigant in the matter of receiving legal aid. Hence, there should be no distinction between resident or non-resident foreign nationals in this matter.

50. There may be difficulties which a certifying authority may encounter in granting legal aid to foreign nationals. Under many systems of law, when a person is not resident in a country, he may have to give security of costs. A foreign national who asks for legal aid may not have the necessary funds to grant security for costs. If the other party has to give security for costs, he should be relieved from such an obligation on grounds of equity and justice.

51. Another difficulty that would arise is to find out the means of a foreign national. Information on this matter could be obtained through the various diplomatic channels.

52. A set up of an International Legal Aid Association has

been envisaged. A Committee has been appointed by the International Bar Association to furnish a Report on this matter. It will be of great interest to those who are interested in legal aid to read this Report when it is submitted. It may be that the Asian and African countries may not be in a position to launch expensive schemes in granting legal aid to foreign nationals in view of the other pressing social problems in their countries. It is submitted that so far as these countries are concerned, conventions should be entered into on the basis of reciprocity. A draft convention on this matter is annexed as Appendix III.

Scheme to grant legal aid to nationals of Member States

53. It is submitted that a step in the right direction will be taken if the Member Countries after entering into bilateral conventions to grant mutual legal aid to non-nationals set out a working scheme. A scheme is suggested at the end of this Report.

The cases in which legal aid should be given

54. As legal aid cannot be rationed, in strict theory, in all cases, where a person satisfies the requirements of legal aid, such aid should be made available. But on grounds of economy, such a step would be detrimental to countries which have to spend large sums on other welfare schemes. Hence, those countries who do not have large sums of money to devote for legal aid purposes, should confine themselves in granting legal aid only to a limited class of cases. A distinction should be made between civil and criminal cases. Under the term civil cases are included not only civil litigation in courts but also those civil suits tried in statutory tribunals and criminal courts.

55. In civil matters legal aid should be given only to those types of cases where the poor and needy habitually figure, such as maintenance cases, divorce cases, cases involving the custody of infants, workmen's compensation cases, action to obtain damages arising out of the wilful or negligent act of a person, action to recover wages, etc. For a start, legal aid may be given in these cases before a State launches on a more ambitious scheme.

56. In many countries, legal aid is refused in certain types of cases which are fought out merely for the purpose of prestige or purification of public life than to obtain relief by way of actual compensation. Such cases are defamation, slander, election petitions, cases where a member of the public files an action against a public officer for holding office without authority. These and other similar actions, although desirable, are still not of such urgency and importance as to deserve legal aid. Hence, many countries have refused legal aid in these types of cases. After excluding these cases where legal aid will not be granted, every country that starts a scheme of legal aid, is well advised to include in a schedule, which may be altered from time to time, the types of cases

in which legal aid should be given in civil matters.

57. In criminal matters, since the liberty of the subject is involved, a more generous approach should be made. But there are certain types of criminal cases where a person is charged with a statutory offence which does not involve any term of imprisonment if the person is found guilty. In such cases, legal aid is not necessary. In cases, which will end in incarceration, if the person charged is convicted, legal aid should be granted. Here again, a country that starts legal aid for the first time, should be careful to grant it only in serious types of criminal cases as the grant of legal aid in all types of criminal cases may be cumbersome and expensive.

58. The question arises whether in criminal cases legal aid should be given at the earliest opportunity or only in the trial court where the matter would be heard. Since it is of utmost importance that a person should have legal aid at the earliest opportunity, and since timely intervention by a legal expert may bring about the discharge of a prisoner at an early stage, legal aid should be given at the very inception. Hence, many countries have provided that as soon as a person is arrested for an offence, he is entitled to legal aid.

59. In considering the types of cases in which legal aid should be granted, a State may vary its policy from time to time and it is advisable that in any legislation inaugurating a legal aid scheme, it should empower the State to pass regulations from time to time setting out the types of cases in which legal aid will be granted. Once the scheme starts working, it may be possible to enlarge the types of cases in which legal aid should be granted.

Who should recommend the grant of legal aid?

60. One of the important matters in any legal scheme is the question as to who should constitute the authority to recommend the grant of legal aid. This question has been answered differently in different countries. Three systems may be recognized :

(a) The older system which is still in force in a large number of countries places the responsibility in the hands of professional body of lawyers. The organisations of the lawyers on this matter are different in various countries. In some countries, such as England, Scotland and Rumania, the Advocates' Association or a Committee consisting of lawyers has full power to decide about the grant of legal aid. In other countries such as Brazil, Belgium, France and Italy and in the Swiss Cantons, there is a special bureau with power to decide on the applications for the grant of free legal aid. In these bureaus, members of the legal profession have a few seats. These bureaus are in most cases arranged hierarchically. There are bureaus attached to the inferior and superior courts, the trial court and to the Court of Appeal, and so on. An appeal lies from a division of a bureau attached to an inferior court to the bureau attached to the superior court. These bureaus are, in fact, tribunals. In Belgium and France the bureaus consist exclusively of advocates.

(b) In England, there are two bodies that function. In considering the means of a person, a special committee determines this fact. On this committee, there are laymen who are interested in social service and who function along with lawyers. Further, the question as to whether a person has any merits to deserve legal aid is considered exclusively by professional bodies of lawyers.

In certain countries, lawyers and government officials function in such bureaus. In Italy, for example, the commission consists of a judge, an official of the Department of Public Prosecutions and a member of the Bar. In certain countries, the body consists only of lawyers. The advocates who are members of this commission are in all cases chosen by their professional bodies.

(c) In certain countries the decision for the grant of legal aid lies with an administrative authority. Thus, in Denmark the President of the Police, in Iceland and in Norway the Minister of Justice decides whether free legal aid is to be granted or not. This system has also been adopted in a number of Swiss Cantons.

61. In certain countries a curious mixture between the first and the third system is in force. Thus in Haity, a decision to grant or refuse legal aid lies with the Minister of Justice. Before giving a decision the Minister has to be advised by a consultative committee consisting of no less than 5 members, composed of the Government Commissioner, a Justice of the Peace of the Capital, and three advocates, who are appointed by the Minister. The Commissioner on his part has to hear Procurator-General so that the apparatus dealing with the applications of poor persons for legal aid is made complicated than that dealing with the claims itself.

62. But a large number of countries has adopted a third system in which the court itself decides the question whether or not legal aid should be granted. In an overwhelming majority of cases, the court which decides whether legal aid should be given or not is the same court which ultimately decides the claim itself. The decisions of the court in most cases are subject to an appeal. This system has been adopted not only in a number of Continental States such as the Netherlands, Germany, Austria, Czechoslovakia, Poland, most of the Swiss Cantons, Spain, Greece but also in a number of American States. This system has many disadvantages, in that it is a judge who has to do the extra work. If in addition to his onerous duties he has also to decide whether legal aid should be granted or not, undue strain is placed on his working capacity. Further, it is not quite desirable that the court that finally hears

the case should also consider the question whether legal aid should be granted to a deserving litigant. In considering this issue the court has to go into the merits of the case. It is true no doubt that with the legal training a judge has, he will not be consciously influenced by whatever decisions he has arrived at at an **ex parte** hearing when he is asked to decide the matter **inter partes** at the final hearing. But in such cases it is difficult on psychological grounds to shed whatever views a judge has formed at the **ex parte** hearing. Therefore, in the interests of justice, a person who considers whether a person has sufficient merits in his case to grant legal aid should not be the judge.

63. It has been suggested by many jurists who are interested in legal aid, that there should only be one body who should decide both the question of means as well as the question whether a person who asks for legal aid has sufficient merits in his case. This is a very desirable suggestion that should be taken up seriously. If there are two bodies functioning independently on these two matters, legal aid will not only be delayed but it becomes expensive to the State. It is also submitted that if there is only one body that decides both these matters, in such a body the majority of members should be lawyers as the body has to decide the question whether there are sufficient merits in the case to warrant the grant of free legal aid. It is desirable that lay people should also find a place in it.

The organisation to recommend the grant of legal aid

64. The form of organisation to grant legal aid may vary in different countries. Without going into the details of the organisation, four main types could be recognised.

65. In certain countries, legal aid is granted only by private organisations who do not depend on government subsidies for help. Thus, there are many organisations in the United States of America which grant legal aid without getting any help from the Government. It may be difficult to find such organisations in other countries of the world whose financial resources are meagre and do not compare favourably with those of the United States of America. Legal aid cannot be allowed to depend on private organisations.

66. There are organisations started by lawyers throughout the various parts of the world. The burden of granting the services to help the poor falls heavily on the lawyers. The legal profession is not merely a mercenary calling. During the early Roman period, the service of the legal profession was given gratuitously. Later, though fees were charged by lawyers, the legal profession was still considered a vocation serving society. Many lawyers have recognised this obligation and founded many societies which grant legal aid to poor persons.

Who should grant legal aid?

67. Should the legal profession alone carry the burden of giving legal advice to those who need it? The answer to this question should be in the negative. Dr. Cohn says:

"Poverty is a social state which—apart from those cases where it is due to the fault or to the special circumstances of an individual—is the result of social conditions in whose creation and maintenance the whole of society partakes. Society itself acting through its self constituted agent, the State, should therefore find the means to alleviate it as far as possible. Legal aid is one of the means to alleviate the consequences of poverty. For this reason it should be a burden on the entire community, not on one individual group only. In the same way as municipal schools are opened for those who cannot afford to send their children to schools where school fees have to be paid, in the same way as Public Health Offices, Fire Precaution Services, Police Forces, etc., are available to supplement the efforts which every individual necessarily makes to preserve itself and property against illness, fire and fees, in the same way the State should supplement the efforts of the individual to stand up for his rights, the rights which the same State has granted to them."[1]

Gratuitous services by the legal profession

68. In many countries where the legal profession performs the duty of granting legal aid, free of charge, legal aid services have not been a success. Thus, in spite of the best efforts of the legal profession in England before the Rushcliffe Commission Report was implemented, and in spite of the earnest efforts on the part of the Indian lawyers, to grant legal aid free of charge, the system was a failure in both these places. The Report of the Rushcliffe Commission sets out the reasons why such a venture cannot be a success. Members of the legal profession are not all in affluent circumstances to grant legal aid, and spend their time in the granting of free legal aid, thus depriving themselves of earning a livelihood from other sources. The most members of the legal profession could do is to give their services free, but legal aid does not consist merely of the grant of free services. As stated earlier, unless financial aid is given to a litigant to find the means to prepare a case and also court fees are waived, legal aid cannot be a success. The members of the legal profession after sacrificing their time and energy cannot be expected also to contribute towards these expenses.

69. In some countries the municipalities have taken upon themselves the obligation to grant legal aid to those who live within their limits. Thus, in Germany, Poland, Finland and some

---

1 59, Law Quarterly Review, p. 370.

American towns, legal aid is organised and administered by municipalities. On the question as to whether municipal corporations should be entrusted with the organisation of legal aid services, it would be apposite to quote a passage from the memorandum of the Association of Municipal Corporations submitted to the Rushcliffe Commission. This memorandum stated as follows:

> "We take the view that it is not the proper function of a local authority to supervise and act on behalf of individual rate-payers in private matters where the other rate-payers (who also contribute to the salaries of local authority) are concerned. In our opinion, the objections apply to State services as administered by officers directly paid and employed by the State."

> "We consider that it would be disadvantageous if the close, confidential and privileged relationship which exists between solicitor and client should be replaced by the relationship of a member of the public towards the State or a municipal officer. Moreover, there is a considerable body of law in which the State and the local authorities are concerned on the other side."

70. It is submitted further, that legal aid should be kept away from party politics in municipalities. It is submitted that any legal aid scheme should not be entrusted to municipalities or local bodies.

State Subsidized Service by Lawyers

71. In some countries the administration and machinery of the legal aid is given over to a body of lawyers but the State gives an annual grant to this body in order that they may run the scheme. Such is the scheme in England and Scotland. The Bhagwati Commission recommended a similar scheme to be worked in Bombay. This scheme no doubt will work very well if the members of the legal profession organise themselves and consider legal aid as a service to the people. This system has many advantages over other systems if the person who asks for legal aid is given a choice of lawyers from a panel, and the members of the legal profession realise their duties and responsibilities and enrol themselves in this panel in large numbers. If this is done, legal aid will be a reality to the poor litigant.

72. In such an organisation the lawyers cannot be expected to receive the normal fees which they could charge, if they were retained by private clients. They often receive something nominal and this would enable the State to provide legal aid to a large number of its citizens. The State, however, should relieve a poor litigant of court expenses and also should grant the necessary expenses for him to prepare his case such as expenses involved in summoning of witnesses, typing of briefs, preparing of plans, etc.

Public Defenders

73. In certain countries, legal aid in criminal cases is taken over by the State and the scheme is run by officials who are employed by the State. The persons who are appointed by the State to grant the aid, are known as 'Public Defenders'. Three methods of supplying counsel to indigent prisoners are in use today. These are by assignment to private counsel, by assignment or reference to voluntary defenders or to Public Defenders. A method that is mostly used is to assign in court individual lawyers who are entrusted with a particular case to defend indigent prisoners at the trial. This system obtains in many Asian and European countries. Lawyers of experience do not ask or are not prepared to take assignments. Assignments are taken by lawyers who are juniors in the profession and who wish to obtain some experience in courts. The question arises whether inexperienced lawyers should be foisted on the public and entrusted with legal aid work. The appointment of an experienced lawyer, as a permanent official in each jurisdiction to grant legal aid to poor litigants, has been considered an improvement on the assignment system. The Committee that was appointed to evaluate the legal aid systems in the United States of America, recommended that the appointment of a Public Defender would not be economical but would be desirable in cities where the population is large.[2]

74. The assigned counsel system does not operate satisfactorily because, apart from the inexperience of the lawyers who are prepared to give such services, the volume of cases may be too great for them to tackle them. A relatively small group of lawyers practises in criminal courts, and it is not possible for those lawyers to take up the defence on a large scale of prisoners who are unable to provide means for their defence. The fee that is payable may not be adequate and this may not attract the lawyers of experience. On the other hand, if the fees are increased, it may prove prohibitive to the State.

75. With the advancement of knowledge in detection and investigation of crime, the prosecuting counsel has become such a specialist that the average practioner is no match for him. Hence, it is necessray to train somebody who himself would specialise in the defence of criminals. Usually an assignment is made only at the trial and it is too late for the assigned counsel to get instructions in order to defend the prisoner who has been entrusted to him. In cases where the assigned counsel are not paid, they may not have the necessary incentive to work for their clients and do their best. On reviewing the position in America, the Committee that was appointed to consider the legal aid organisations in America, came to the view that public defenders are best suited to cities with large populations.

---

2 Equal Justice for the Poor, p. 80.

591

76. The Public Defender System, however, has been subject to severe criticism. Dr. Cohn states, as follows:

"In a few countries, most strangely enough all belonging to the Anglo-American group, the advocate assisting the poor persons is a public official. This solution has not received the approval of the majority of countries, and rightly so. It is essential that the advocate should be a member of a free profession. This would guarantee its independence."

"The prisoner who obtains legal aid, and is assisted by a Public Defender, may have a feeling that the Public Defender is also appointed by the State who is the other party to the litigation. He may feel that just as the Crown Advocate walks out of one room, another representative of the State is walking out of another room to help him. He may, therefore, not have the confidence which he would have in a member of the free legal profession."[3]

Hence, there is much to be said against the Public Defender System but where the finances of the State would not permit the running of a legal aid scheme through the lawyers then there is no aternative but to appoint a public defender.

77. The public defender should be selected in such a way as to secure his tenure of office, otherwise he may be liable to be influenced by others. In America, public defenders are selected by the civil service or appointed by judges or in a few cases, selected by the people. The voluntary defenders are selected by a Board of Directors of private organisations with which they are associated. Most opposition to the Public Defender System is based on the fear that public defenders will not be independent, since the salaries are paid by the government as in the case of prosecutor. But in actual practice, in America, most public defenders are as vigorous in defending their clients as are private counsel. The method of selecting the public defenders may have an important bearing on the quality of the professional independence of the defence.

78. An important compromise is being tested in one large city in America, where the cost of the existing legal aid societies for the litigant defender service, is being covered by the payment of the County Treasury. The defender himself is subject to the supervision by a Board of Directors of the Bar. The effectiveness of this system has to be evaluated after this system has worked for a number of years.

79. The advantages of the Public Defender System are as follows:

---

3 59, Law Quarterly Review, p. 368.

(1) Such a system is more efficient and economical, especially for larger cities.

(2) Adequate service can be provided for all indigent prisoners.

(3) The prisoner can be furnished counsel with expert knowledge in the criminal law and practice. This is not always the case, if the appointment is made from the Bar generally.

(4) Certain procedural delays can be eliminated by the availability of the public defender, and it is easier for him to prepare the case.

80. Taking the pros and cons of the Public Defender System in criminal cases, it is both cheaper and less expensive for a State to appoint public defenders in large cities. Here again, this cannot be a universal rule that can be applied in all cases. If the members of the Bar of any particular country are prepared to grant legal aid, then they may be able to appoint special public defenders from their panel of lawyers who will be specialists in criminal law and procedure.

Machinery for legal aid

81. In order that legal aid may be granted effectively, it is necessary that a country should be divided into areas and each area should be administered by a special body of persons. In England, the country is divided into twelve areas, each area is administered by an Area Committee consisting of 16 members—12 practising solicitors and 4 practising barristers. In each area, there are a number of Local Committees. Each Area Committee has a secretarial staff at Headquarters. The Area Committee is responsible for the administration of the scheme within its own area, and in particular, it is required to hear and determine appeals from the refusals to grant certificates on legal grounds by Local Committees within its area and to consider applications for certificates, to conduct proceedings in the Appellate Courts, to prepare and maintain panels of Barristers and solicitors who are prepared to work under the scheme, and to deal with all questions as regards payment to barristers and solicitors for such work.

82. The duties of the Local Committee, on the other hand, are limited to the consideration of applications for legal aid other than the applications for legal aid in Appellate Courts and the issue of Civil Aid Certificates.

83. The Law Society co-ordinates the whole system, acting through the Legal Aid Committee consisting of solicitors and barristers who are elected. This body considers matters of major policy, gives advice and assistance to the Area Committee in connection with numerous problems that arise and secure uniformity of practice. It also provides the staff and premises for the adminis-

tration of the scheme and maintains under its control the central accounting machinery.

84. In England, the responsibility of working the legal aid scheme is given to the Law Society which receives an annual grant from the State. But in countries where the burden of granting legal aid is taken upon by the State itself, a different set-up has to be envisaged. Still the country has to be divided into a number of areas for the purposes of granting legal aid in an efficient manner. In such cases, it is suggested that Legal Aid Bureaus should be established by the State in each area. It is preferable if these bureaus are situated within the court premises itself or close to it. It would not cost the State very much to erect a room or two by the side of the court buildings within the court premises. This would involve very little expense when compared with the other overhead charges that the State will have to bear if private organisations are financed to do this work. These offices should be opened at regular hours during the day time and should be in charge of some official who should be prepared to receive legal aid applications, interview the applicants, and to forward the papers to the determining authority responsible for recommending legal aid.

85. Legal aid in many countries have failed, because legal aid bureaus with regular hours of office work were not established. The establishment of such legal aid bureaus is a pre-requisite to the running of an efficient scheme of legal aid. Such bureaus must be within the easy reach of every litigant and should be situated in such a way that considering the means of communications available in a country, a litigant should be in a position to reach this office with expedition and the least expense. It is also suggested that those who man the Legal Aid Bureaus should be specialists and there should be a special grade of officers known as Legal Aid Officers who will be selected according to their qualifications and efficiency. These officers, by passage of time, will obtain the necessary experience and efficiency to run legal aid centres. These officers should also maintain a record of the decisions of the determining authority, carry out all correspondence and maintain accounts It is suggested that where legal aid is granted by the Government with the aid of the Bar, the lawyers should assist the State by actually appearing in cases or by giving advice. Payment has to be made to them for such services. They should apply to the Legal Aid Bureau for payment and the payment should be made on presentation of proper vouchers from the Legal Aid Fund.

Legal Aid Fund

86. It is also suggested that a separate fund known as the 'Legal Aid Fund' should be created by statute, and such fund should be under the control of a responsible officer, preferably the Minister of Justice who will be responsible to the Parliament of

his country. The funds should be constituted of contributions from the Central Government, donations from Local Bodies, charitable institutions, individuals, associations, costs recovered in aided cases, etc. In order to encourage donations, it is suggested that such donations should be declared free of income tax. Further sources to augment this fund should be investigated, and if money could come from such sources, every effort should be given to fill the coffers of the Legal Aid Fund.

Publicity

87. In many countries where legal aid organisations have been set up, they have proved failure because of the lack of adequate publicity. It is futile to establish Legal Aid Bureaus, when the public do not know of their existence and the services they provide. Hence, in countries where legal aid has been a success, adequate publicity has been given to the fact that Legal Aid

Bureaus exist in the near vicinity. In America, the existence of Legal Aid Bureaus are publicised not only through periodicals, papers and the radio but also by pamphlets which are distributed to the public. In the United States even dramatic productions are based on the actual cases before the legal aid organisations and are sometimes nationally televised. These programmes are arranged by the National Legal Aid Association with the object of acquainting the public with the legal aid services available to persons of very limited means.[5]

88. The least requirement for giving publicity to a Legal Aid Bureau is to affix a name board to the office. It is suggested that there should be advertisements in the Press at regular intervals apprising the people of the various centres where Legal Aid Bureaus are situated. It would also be helpful if the names and addresses of such bureaus are displayed outside every legal aid office. Leaflets containing information as to the services available and the wisdom of taking advice in time before one goes to court, should be freely made available at such centres and other public places such as post offices, police stations, court houses, kacheries and the remand prisons. It is also suggested that in every summons, warrant or other process that are issued from the court, there must be appended a statement in the language of the country, the location of the nearest Legal Aid Bureau.

Legal Aid Certificates

89. When an applicant satisfies the test that would enable him to obtain legal aid, he should be given a legal aid certificate issued by the Bureau duly signed by the officer in charge. Once the certifying authority has approved an application for legal aid, the applicant must be notified of the decision by a form which offers him the certificate and gives him the information necessary to enable him to decide whether or not he wishes to proceed on the

---

5 American Bar Association Journal, May, 1954.

terms and conditions offered to him by the determining authority. The applicant must be given a certain length of time in order that he may make up his mind, whether to accept or not the terms and conditions set out in the legal aid certificates. If the applicant notifies his acceptance, the officer in charge of the Legal Aid Bureau would get in touch with the organisation that is responsible for the appointment of a lawyer to aid him in his litigation.

90.   In some countries, from the decision of the determining authority granting or refusing legal aid, an appeal is given to a higher authority.   Indeed it would be a desirable thing if such an organisation could be set up, but often the setting up of such organisations would prove to be not only expensive but its effect would be dilatory and may defeat the ends of justice.   Each country will have to consider whether an appeal should be granted from the decision of the certifying committee to a higher authority or not.

Amendments to Certificates

91.   After legal aid is granted, there may be cases where the financial circumstances of the assisted person may improve to such an extent that he should not be entitled to free legal aid any more. It should, therefore, be open to his opponent or to any other person to show that the applicant's circumstances have improved since the grant of the certificate.   If the determining authority is satisfied that the applicant's means have improved to such an extent that he would not be entitled to legal aid, an order should be made declaring the certificate inoperative as from that date.   The certificate will also be amended to show the changed circumstances. Further, it may be amended to show that there has been an extension or limitation of its duration according to the circumstances of the case.   A certificate should be operative only for a short period of time in the first instance and power should be given to the determining authority to extend the period from time to time.

92.   In many countries the following grounds have been considered to be sufficient for the withdrawal of facilities:

(a) where the assisted person so requests;

(b) where the disposable income or the disposable capital increases above a ceiling limit;

(c) where the assisted person's solicitor or counsel has given up the case and the determining authority is satisfied that counsel was justified in so doing by reason either of his being required to conduct the case in a manner which may be unreasonable or likely to lead to unjustifiable expense;

(d) where there is wilful failure on the part of the assisted person to supply information;

(e) where false statements are knowingly made by the assisted person in regard to the case;

(f) where there is any act of commission or omission on the part of the assisted person which in the opinion of the determining authority disentitles the person to any further aid;

(g) where it subsequently transpires that a person has applied for and obtained the certificate on grounds which he knows were false.

Effect of Discharge or Revocation of Certificates

93. The effect of the discharge of a certificate will depend on the grounds on which such discharge takes place. If a certificate is discharged because a false statement has been made in obtaining the grant of such a certificate, then all costs incurred up to that time will have to be recovered as a fine, since one cannot place a premium on fraud. But if the discharge took place on the ground that the financial means have improved or that counsel had to give up the case as a result of an unreasonable request on the part of a legally-aided person to conduct a case in such a manner so as to incur needless expenditure, then any costs recovered up to that date should not be claimed. Where a certificate has been revoked on the ground that the assisted person obtained it by wilful suppression of facts or wilful mis-statements, he should be treated as a person who was not entitled to legal aid **ab initio.** Hence. in such a case, in addition to any penalty which may be imposed. such an applicant should be made liable to pay the full amount of the costs incurred on his behalf.

Emergency Certificates

94. Sometimes it may be necessary for an emergency certificate to be granted to a person who applies for legal aid. The grant of a regular certificate for legal aid involves time. but there may be cases of urgency where if legal aid is not given in time, the ends of justice will be defeated. Such will be the case where, for example, an injunction is asked for or against a party on frivolous grounds, and the party is too poor to employ a lawyer and asks for legal aid to resist such an application. Hence, the grant of emergency certificates may become necessary in certain types of cases. In such cases, the question arises as to whether these certificates should be recommended by the same determining authority or whether it should be left to the court that hears the action to grant an emergency certificate which will remain in operation till a permanent certificate replaces it. There should also be provision in an emergency certificate that in the event of a discovery of any fact which necessitates the refusal of a legal aid certificate. the emergency certificate should cease to have any effect on the determining authority's finding.

95. In criminal cases the grant of legal aid certificates may prove not only dilatory but also may defeat the ends of justice.

Hence. it is suggested that in serious types of cases, such as murder etc.. where the magistrate proceeds to the spot and holds a preliminary inquiry, the suspect who is in custody should be informed that he has a right to employ a lawyer and all cross-examination of the witnesses who are examined should not be proceeded with till the prisoner is in a position to find a lawyer under the legal aid scheme.

Obligations of the Legal Aid Profession in Legally Aided Cases

96. Apart from the legal obligation that arises between the client and the solicitor, there may be special obligations which a lawyer owes to the legally aided person as well as to the panel that appoints him in legally aided cases. It is not necessary to discuss the relationship between the lawyer and client as this is well known in legal systems. The lawyer is under a duty to maintain strict confidence. Under many systems of law, communications issued to lawyers by clients are privileged. It is also the duty of the lawyer to follow the cannons of conduct set up by the professional body to which he belongs. Apart from these duties, a counsel who undertakes the duty of appearing for a legally aided person, should have the following duties:

(a) make such reports as may be required by the relevant committee on the progress and disposal of the case;

(b) set out the reasons for giving up, or refusing to take up a case assigned to him;

(c) draft a petition of appeal and sending of a report to the determining authority as to whether there is or is not an arguable case;

(d) not decline to appear in a case, except for good reasons.

97. The interests of the legally aided litigant should be sufficiently safeguarded so that his proctor or advocate should not abandon the case without good reason. It should not be permissible for a proctor or advocate to accept an assignment and then abandon the case entrusted to him in favour of the other retainers. There are cases, however, where a counsel who appears in a legally aided case, may not be in a position to appear in the case. In such cases he should, at the earliest available opportunity, hand over the brief to the officer in charge of the Legal Aid Bureau so that other alternative arrangements could be made. It should also be permissible for a counsel who has appeared in a legally aided case to withdraw from the case if the litigant is unreasonable in his demands regarding the conduct of the case. Since such an applicant has the unlimited resources of the State or some charitable organisation to conduct his case, he may become unreasonable and bring pressure on the lawyer to protract the proceedings of the case unduly or to incur unnecessary expenditure. In such cases, it is the duty of the lawyer towards the State as well as towards his profession, to refuse to go on with the case. It is also most undesir-

able that a lawyer who has been assigned legal aid work, should try to either obtain payment or presents from the legally aided person. This would lead to abuses which would render not only the grant of legal aid nugatory but also encourage corrupt practices. Hence, there should be a provision that any lawyer who is given legal aid work under the Legal Aid Scheme, should only be paid out of legal aid funds by the proper authorities. Further, he should be prohibited from receiving any monetary or other gifts for his services.

Resignation from Panel

98. A member of a panel may at any time think it fit to resign from the panel. In such a case, he should send a written application to the authority that maintains the panel. However, the lawyer who resigns should continue to act in those cases which have already been assigned to him, otherwise it may be possible for any lawyer to give up a case entrusted to him under a legal aid scheme and appear in a more lucrative case. There should be nothing to prevent a lawyer from reconsidering his decision resigning from the panel and applying to rejoin the panel.

Exclusion from the Panel

99. In many countries, there are provisions which set out grounds or reasons which would enable an authority to exclude persons from the panel of lawyers who could be assigned legal aid work. It is necessary that there should be a 'Panel Complaints Tribunal'. This tribunal should have jurisdiction to inquire into the omissions and commissions alleged against a lawyer who has been assigned a job of work by the legal aid authorities. Such panels exist in England and other places. If, after hearing evidence, the panel is satisfied that a lawyer who has been assigned legal aid work, has either neglected his work or is guilty of any misconduct, then it should be at liberty to expunge the name of the lawyer from the panel. If he is guilty of misconduct involving professional integrity, the Panel Complaints Tribunal should be in a position to report the matter to the proper authority.

Measures to render justice inexpensive

100. If definite measures are taken in a country to render justice less expensive, it will facilitate the grant of legal aid. This may be done by the simplification of the procedure both in civil and criminal cases which will enable the courts to grant speedy and efficient justice. This could also be achieved by the appointment of Conciliation Boards which will have jurisdiction to settle minor and trivial disputes between parties. It is a matter of common experience, that trivial disputes often lead to serious crimes or may lead to expensive civil litigation. Hence, if these matters are settled in a reasonable way by an independent body consisting of

persons who are appointed for their integrity and ability as members of the Conciliation Board, it may be possible to settle the differences between the parties, and the parties may not thereafter go to courts. Such Conciliation Boards have been working satisfactorily in various parts of the world. But in considering the constitution of these Conciliation Boards, very great care must be taken that proper people are appointed as members of this board. Often people with political propensities or corrupt people, may creep into such boards and there may be maladministration by the board, and the ends of justice will not be served. Such boards, if properly constituted may act as a sieve to hold up unnecessary litigation and thus enable the courts to deal only with serious civil disputes and offences.

101. In certain countries the law Is uncertain. Many continental countries have partially solved this problem by the codification of their laws, but codification alone will not solve the uncertainty of the law. In many countries, therefore, a scheme has been devised that there should be a revision of the code after a passage of years. It is of the utmost importance for the speedy administration of justice that the law must not only be certain but should be known. Hence the codification of the law is a right step that would help the poor litigant to obtain justice in courts.

Legal advice

102. The question as to whether legal advice should precede legal aid or vice versa is a controversial one. In England, the Rushcliffe Commission recommended a scheme to provide legal advice at a nominal cost, but the State has deferred this matter for some time. The Law Society of England, however, has inaugurated a legal advice scheme in 1949 but in view of the high cost involved, it is engaged in preparing a new legal advice scheme somewhat different to that planned in 1949.

103. If a person knows beforehand his rights and duties, he may be reasonable enough not to launch on expensive litigation or even to defend a just claim which has been brought against him. Hence, it is of the utmost importance that he should obtain proper and competent legal advice on any matter in which he is involved at the earliest opportunity.

104. Law is a specialised subject, and it is essential that poor litigants should obtain legal advice on legal matters. In many countries, the legal advice is granted voluntarily by the Bar Association. This is a commendable step, but a State cannot complacently look on and say that there are others who are prepared to give legal advice and thus shirk the primary responsibility which is cast on it to grant legal advice to those who require it. The laws are created by the State and the poor litigant is not responsible for the complexities and uncertainties of the law. If a State passes a law, it is also the bounden duty to explain the intricacies of the law to its citizens. It is suggested that a properly constituted legal

600

advice scheme financed by the State should be made available to all poor litigants. Experience has shown that if a legal advice scheme is properly inaugurated and worked, the number of institutions of cases will be greatly diminished. This may prevent even serious crimes being committed. It is suggested that a legal advice scheme should precede a legal aid scheme.

105. In many countries, the applicant is asked to pay nominal sum in order that he may obtain legal advice. This is a very salutary provision because it may prevent a person from rushing to a legal aid bureau and asking for advice on trivial matters. Sometimes legal advice may not be sufficient and it may be necessary to draft correspondence or to draft pleadings. etc. It is suggested that the drafting of legal correspondence should be part and parcel of the work of the Legal Advice Committee but in dealing with the drafting of pleadings, as this forms part of the court work, it can only be entrusted to a lawyer who can appear in courts and if a legal aid service is not provided for in a country, it may not be possible to perform this service to an applicant.

A scheme to grant legal aid to nationals of the Member States in another Member State

Without resorting to the expediency of establishing an International Legal Aid Organisation a simple machinery could be devised by which one Member State of this Committee can give legal aid to the nationals of another State in deserving cases.

This scheme could be worked through the Ministry of Justice of each country. The Ministry of each country could entertain applications for legal aid from a person who is the national of another Member State. On receipt of such application, the Ministry will send the application to the Ministry of the State of which the applicant is a national and the latter will make the necessary inquiries as to the applicant's means, and whether the applicant has exhausted any remedy in his country, etc.

The Ministry of Justice of the country to which the applicant belongs shall then forward the necessary information to the Ministry of Justice of the country in which the application is made, and the latter shall refer the matter to the legal aid organisation. if any, who will take up the matter at that stage. If there is no legal aid organisation in the country, its government should appoint a lawyer who will inquire into the merits of the case and recommend whether legal aid should be given or not. If it is recommended that legal aid should be given either by any legal aid organisation or lawyer to whom the matter has been referred to, then legal aid should be given.

The scheme set out is only meant to apply to civil matters and is not suitable for criminal cases. In serious crimes, legal aid should be given to any foreign national without any investigation as to his means or the merits of the case if such a person is not in a position to defend himself. A foreign national may be totally ignorant of the language and the laws of the country in which he is charged with the offence and it is one of the fundamental rights of such a person that he should be given legal aid in such cases if conviction will end in incarceration.

In civil matters, if there is a provision of law that a person should deposit security either to bring or defend an action, such a requirement should be waived if a determining authority decides that the merits of the case and the means of the applicant are such, that he should be given legal aid. The same privilege should be extended to nationals of the State when they bring or defend an action against a foreign national who is given legal aid.

If an applicant is successful in his litigation all expenses incurred by the State granting legal aid should be recovered out of the costs awarded to him or the fruits of the litigation. To ensure such recovery the expenses incurred in the litigation should be made a first charge on the costs and fruits of litigation.

In order to work this scheme, it is necessary to establish in each of the Member States of this Committee, some form of legal aid service. The necessity of establishing such a service has already been stressed.

For this scheme to work satisfactorily the mode in which a non-national who wishes to seek legal aid should be duly published and all Embassies in that country should be furnished with the necessary information.

It is submitted that should the Member States enter into a covenant to give legal aid to the nationals of one another, then a sub-committee should be appointed to draw up the details of the scheme.

DRAFT CONVENTION
TO GRANT MUTUAL LEGAL AID
TO THE NATIONALS OF THE MEMBER STATES
OF
THE ASIAN-AFRICAN LEGAL CONSULTATIVE COMMITTEE

WHEREAS it has become expedient that legal aid should be given to deserving nationals of one of the Member States of the Asian-African Legal Consultative Committee who seek such aid in another Member State of this Committee, it is mutually agreed between the Governments of the Countries who are signatories of this Covenant as follows:

(a) The Signatories to this Covenant agree to grant legal aid in their country to the nationals of the other Signatories as they grant to their own nationals, and subject to the rules and nationals governing the grant of legal aid to foreign nationals in their country, if any.

(b) The Signatories to this Covenant agree to grant legal aid in their respective countries to the nationals of other Member States who cannot afford to retain lawyers to defend themselves in all criminal cases which are punishable with imprisonment without an option of a fine.

(c) The Signatories to this Covenant agree to give all assistance and help by furnishing information incidental to the granting of legal aid in cases where such help or information is required by another Member State which is a party to this Covenant.

(9) DRAFT CONVENTIONS RELATING TO RECOGNITION AND ENFORCEMENT OF FOREIGN DECREES IN MATRIMONIAL MATTERS, 1961

Adopted in Tokyo on February, 1961, at the Fourth Session of the Asian-African Legal Consultative Committee.

Text from ASIAN-AFRICAN LEGAL CONSULTATIVE COMMITTEE, Report of the Fourth Session, pp. 376-392, 406-415, 426-428.

Introductory Note

The subject of Recognition of Foreign Decrees in Matrimonial Matters was referred to the Committee by the Government of Ceylon under the provisions of Article 3(c) of the Statutes of the Committee as being a matter on which exchange of views and information between the Patricipating Countries was desirable. At the First Session held in New Delhi, the Committee appointed the Member for Ceylon as Rapporteur to prepare and present a Report on the subject. At the Second Session held in Cairo the Rapporteur presented his Report on the subject but the delegations present at the Session were of the opinion that the Report needed further consideration before the Committee would be in a position to discuss the subject fully. The Delegation of the United Arab Republic also presented a Draft Convention on the subject. At the Third Session held in Colombo in January 1960 the Committee did not have adequate time to consider the subject in detail and it was decided that the subject should be placed on the Agenda of the Fourth Session. The Committee decided to request the Governments of the Participating Countries to express their views on the provisions of the Draft Convention as suggested by the Rapporteur in his Report and the Draft Convention presented by the Delegation of the United Arab Republic. The Committee considered the subject at its Fourth Session held in Tokyo and, on the recommendations of a Sub-Committee, decided to publish the Report of the Rapporteur together with all other materials contained in the Brief of Documents and to present the same to the Governments of the Participating Countries.

RAPPORTEUR'S REPORT ON THE RECOGNITION AND ENFORCEMENT OF FOREIGN DECREES IN MATRIMONIAL MATTERS
By Mr. Justice H. W. Thambiah, (Rapporteur)

At the last Session of the Asian Legal Consultative Committee I was asked to send a report on the above subject. I have the honour to submit my report.

This subject involves three distinct but connected topics. Firstly, the question has to be considered as to how the courts of a particular country are prepared to recognise declaratory decrees such as divorce, nullity of marriage and separation a **mensa et thoro** entered into by the courts of another country. Secondly, the question arises as to how far the courts are prepared to enforce the mandatory parts of such decrees. Both matters can be settled by legislation of any country. The third question is whether States cannot come to any agreement to give matrimonial reliefs to one spouse who is in one country when the other spouse is within the jurisdiction of another country by the enforcement of mandatory orders. It is the last aspect that has to be considered at an international assembly.

An attempt is made to give a historical account of the efforts made by governmental and non-governmental bodies to solve this question and certain tentative proposals are made on all three questions referred to.

In Appendix I, a short resume of the law on the subject in the Asian countries is given. I am indebted to the contributions made by various members of the Assembly. In Appendix II the English Law and the laws in certain Dominions are discussed. In Appendix III is given the draft convention prepared by the Committee of Legal Experts, knwon as Annex. 1. Appendix IV contains a draft convention discussed at the 47th Conference of the International Law Association held at Dubrovnik (1958), on the custody of infants.

DIVORCE JURISDICTION: Spouses who wish to bring matrimonial actions or who wish to obtain maintenance orders, in cases where the other spouse is resident in another country, are forced with several problems. In view of the insistence of the laws of many countries that only the court where the husband is domiciled is competent to hear matrimonial actions, a wife who has been deserted by her husband is confronted with many difficulties if she wishes to bring an action for a decree dissolving the marriage or declaring it a nullity. If she wishes to enforce any order for alimony, either for herself or her children, if the husband's domicile happens to be a foreign country, she has to embark upon an expedition to his country in order to obtain any relief. In her penurious condition, she may not be able to find the assistance to go to a foreign country and initiate litigation. Even if she succeeds in obtaining such a decree, when she comes back to her own country she will encounter various difficulties in enforcing the order. Procedural difficulties as well as the exchange control regulations would make it almost impossible for her to obtain the fruits of her litigation. Many international institutions have taken up this question with a view to securing an early solution, as the various problems that have been created by deserted wives and children during the period after the cessation of World War I and more and more governmental and voluntary bodies studied these problems and made renewed efforts to solve them as the problem of deserted wives and children became serious after World War I, and it became a world problem by the end of World War II. During the period of the War, military personnel stationed in foreign countries contracted matrimonial alliance in these countries and on the cessation of hostilities returned to their countries, leaving the wives and children behind. The numbers of such cases assumed such proportions that not only international institutions and bodies but also governments of various countries have appointed commissions to go into this matter. Further, there is no uniformity in the recognition of foreign divorce decrees. Under the existing systems of law, divorce valid in one country may not be valid in another country.

Even in the countries which recognise decrees entered by a foreign court, there is no uniformity on the question whether the mandatory part of a decree ordering maintenance could be enforced. An attempt is made to place before the Committee various efforts made to tackle these problems.

Earlier efforts made in other countries

Attempts were made by a number of governments to ensure reciprocity of matrimonial decrees by the Hague Convention of June 1902, but this has been almost a dead letter. The Bustamante Code of 1928 which dealt with this matter was ratified by most of the South and Central American States. In Europe, except for the Scandinavian Convention of 1931 and two or three bilateral Agreements on this topic between two or three central European States, the conflicting situation still remains. Mr. Jaffe, sometime the Secretary-General of the International Law Association failed to move the International Law Commission of the United Nations to consider this Convention.

The Draft Convention of the International Law Association

A draft convention for the mutual recognition of judgments in divorce and nullity of marriage was adopted by the International Law Association at the Conference at Prague in 1947. This project was intended to mitigate the rigours and hardships which involved a number of people who were free from the legal tie of marriage in one State but were legally bound in marriage according to the law of the State to which they belonged. Such marriages have been called "limping marriages", a term of art adopted by the Royal Commission on Marriage and Divorce of Britain. The purpose was that this Draft Convention should form the basis of a treaty or convention between one State and another. The scheme received the blessing of the American branch. It was drafted by a Committee of Experts on which one of the leading English authorities on the law of divorce, Mr. William Latey, Q.C. was a member. Its terms were first adopted at the Oxford Conference in 1932. It was later amended at the Cambridge Conference in 1946, and was finally put into the shape in which it was received at the International Law Association in 1947. The plan, however, received no support from any of the governments in Europe. It is an attempt to get rid, as far as it is practicable of the anomaly by which a person divorced in one country may yet remain lawfully married in another country. It was the result of work of experts on the principal systems of law for a period of over 20 years. The Draft Convention got round the conflicts of jurisdiction by providing for alternative bases of jurisdiction i.e. (1) domicile (2) nationality (3) eighteen months continuous residence. The main features of the plan adopted at Prague may be outlined as follows:

(1) By an International convention, each contracting State will legislate that any final decree of divorce, a vinculo matrimonii pronounced by a competent court in such State, shall at the request of either party to the suit, be recorded in the competent court of any other contracting State, which shall hold such decree valid.

(2) Such decree must be a final one, pronounced by a competent court of the State (a) in which the spouse is domiciled when the suit is instituted; or (b) of which, according to the lex fori, either party is a national when the suit is commenced; or (c) in which either party has resided for at least a year of the eighteen months immediately preceding the institution of the suit.

(3) When the lex fori so requires but not otherwise, the domicile of a married woman shall be the same as that of the husband.

The lack of uniformity in regard to jurisdiction in divorce arises from different principles applied in different States. Some States adopt domicile as the basis of divorce jurisdiction as in the British courts (subject to some amendments) and Ceylon courts. Others accept nationality as the basis (as in certain European States). Still other States adopt residence as in certain European countries and in the United States of America.

The Prague Draft Convention proposed certain safeguards against the abuse of the system by any State setting up a sort of divorce where a divorce may be had for the asking, whatever the merits of the matrimonial difference. The safeguards include (a) a minimum period of actual residence, and (b) a provision by which mutually contracting States will specify which courts are competent courts.

The views of the Royal Commission on marriage divorce in England

The British Royal Commission on Marriage and Divorce has been considering the whole problem of the conflicts of divorce jurisdiction including the Prague Convention of 1947, and its main recommendations, summarised by William Latey, Q.C. appeared in an article entitled "Jurisdiction in Divorce and Nullity", (see the International and Comparative Law (Quarterly) October, 1956, p. 1 et seq) The Commission's proposals may be set out briefly as follows:

So far as jurisdiction in divorce suits is concerned, (1) the Court shall have jurisdiction if at the commencement of the suit (a) the petitioner is domiciled in England; (b) the petitioner is in England and the last joint matrimonial residence was in the same place; and (c) the parties to the marriage are both resident in England. Provided that no decree will be granted under (b) and (c) unless the personal law or laws of both parties recognise a ground sufficient for a divorce or nullity—a ground substantially similar to that on which a divorce is sought in England. (2) Personal law or laws of both parties would in the circumstances of the case permit the petitioner to obtain a divorce on some other grounds. In this context, the word "England" must also include Scotland.

In addition to the jurisdiction referred to, courts in England and Scotland may also hear cases of divorce if the petitioner is a citizen of the United Kingdom and Colonies within the meaning of the British Nationality Act, 1948 and is domiciled in a country the law of which requires questions of personal status to be determined by the law of the country of which the petitioner is a national and not on the basis of the petitioner's domicile or residence. In such cases the issues are to be determined by the domestic laws of England and Scotland as if the petitioner was domiciled in these countries when the suit is commenced.

The recommendation, if accepted, will enable the courts in England and Scotland to hear a suit for presumption of death coupled with the dissolution of marriage if, when the suit is commenced, the petitioner is domiciled or resident in these countries.

The Commission also dealt with the vexed question of wives being allowed, under the laws of the United Kingdom, a separate domicile. It decided that the wife's separate domicile should be recognised only for the single purpose of divorce jurisdiction. Thus, the right of the wife to bring an action for divorce on the ground of residence was recognised. The Commission, however, generally refused to recognise the separate domicile of the wife for other purposes as such a course would be inconsistent with the pirnciple of life-long partnership.

THE VIEWS OF THE ROYAL COMMISSION ON FOREIGN DECREES

The Commission also went into the question of foreign decrees. It recommended that the courts in England and Scotland should recognise the validity of a divorce decree obtained by judicial process or otherwise:

(a) According to the law of (i) the domicile of both spouses or (ii) the domicile of either spouse or

(b) If it is such that it would be recognised by the law of the country of the either spouse; (Armitage v. A.G. (1906) p. 135). (In such cases the European conception of domicile as approximating to habitual residence would be accepted).

(c) According to the law of the country of which one spouse was a national or both were nationals or would be recognised by the law of such a country.

(d) In circumstances substantially similar to those in which the courts in England exercise divorce jurisdiction in respect of persons not domiciled in either England or Scotland.

(e) Before the coming into operation of any statute altering the basis of divorce jurisdiction in England or Scotland, in circumstances substantially similar to those in which the courts in those countries exercise jurisdiction on the date of the divorce; or

(f) In any other Commonwealth country within a period of three years after the coming into operation of any statute altering the basis of divorce jurisdiction as obtained in England and Scotland in circumstances substantially similar to those in which the courts in England and Scotland exercise divorce jurisdiction before the alteration of the jurisdiction took place; or

(g) Any country designated in the Order-in-Council.

The Commission also considered the question of religious divorce. Many European women of the Christian faith were married to men who belonged to other religions. In such cases the question that arises is whether the husband could obtain a valid divorce if it is one recognised by his religious law. The Commission took the view that in some cases the spouses would be subjected to personal laws—one imposed on them by their religion and the other by their domicile or their nationality, and took the view that the latter should prevail without creating hardships for English or Scot women who so marry.

Under the head the "nullity of marriage" the Commission reviewed the anomalous state of the law governing jurisdiction in England arising out of decisions which seem largely to have ignored the principles and procedure of the old ecclesiastical codes that have been perpetuated by statutes. In these courts jurisdiction and nullity were based on the residence of the applicant in any particular diocese. The domicile did not enter into such a matter. Under the common law, unaltered in that respect, there was no distinction between void and voidable marriages. The Commission, however, distinguished between void and voidable marriages and recommended it as the basis of jurisdiction and recognised this distinction when they discussed the basis of jurisdiction. In the case of void marriages, they proposed that either putative spouse may apply for a declaration of status if he or she was domiciled in England or Scotland when the suit is commenced. If the marriage is alleged to be void on any ground other than the lack of formalities, the issue will be determined according to the personal law of one or other or both the parties. But if the marriage is celebrated outside England or Scotland, it will not be declared void if valid according to the law of the country in which the parties intended to make their matrimonial home. The Commission also considered the problem of marriages which were declared null and void as a result of colour bar in certain States such as the Union of South Africa and some States of the United States of America. Such cases were not, however, regarded by the Royal Commission as raising a valid objection to their proposal inasmuch as the court decree is merely declaratory of the position under the personal laws of the party. In the case of voidable marriages, they recommended that the court in England and Scotland be deemed to have jurisdiction if at the commencement of the suit (a) the petitioner is domiciled in these countries (b) the petitioner is resident in these countries, provided the place where the parties last resided was in these countries and (c) the spouses are resident in these countries when the place where the parties last resided was in these countries and (d) the spouses resided in England. There is also the important proviso that the courts will not grant a decree unless the personal law of one or other or both at the time of the marriage recognises as sufficient a ground for nullity of marriage substantially similar to one on which annulment is sought for in England or in Scotland. The Commission also considered the question of foreign decrees of nullity and the proposed basis of jurisdiction in nullity suits in the draft code which is substantially the same as that of divorce. To facilitate the proofs of foreign law, they proposed that in any matrimonial proceedings, the certificate in writing of an accredited embassy or legation official, duly authenticated by seal, shall be admissible as evidence of the law of that country and the fact that a ceremony of marriage has taken place in another country may be proved by evidence of one of the parties to the marriage by a local marriage certificate.

A HISTORY OF THE DRAFT CONVENTION ON THE RECOGNITION AN DENFORCEMENT ABROAD OF MAINTENANCE OBLIGATIONS

By its resolution 390 H (XIII), the Economic and Social Council requested the Secretary General to convene a Committee of Experts in order to frame the text of a model convention or model reciprocal law, or both, on the enforcement abroad of maintenance obligations. The resolutions of this Committee were to be submitted to this Council not later than at its sixteenth session for its consideration and recommendations to governments.

It was also agreed that members of each branch should urge upon their respective governments to give instructions to their delegates at the United Nations to press their adaption.

The draft convention was approved by the United Nations on 20th June, 1955 in New York by 41 States and actually signed by 17 including the Scandinavian countries and other countries in Europe (See speech of Mr. Latey, Q.C. at the Dubrovnik Conference—1956 p. 386).

The Secretary General appointed a committee of seven members consisting of:

1. Mrs. Marcelle Kraemer-Bach, Member of the Bar Paris, France.

2. Professor Kurt Lipstein, Trinity College, Cambridge, United Kingdom, replacing Professor Harold Cooke Gutteridge, University of Cambridge, United Kingdom, who was unable to attend.

3. Mr. Maris Matteucci, Secretary General of the International Institute for the Unification of Private Law, Rome.

4. Mr. Anis Aaleh, Director General at the Ministry of Justicem Beirut, Lebanon.

5. Professor Edward Marrits Meijers, Leyden, Netherlands.

6. Professor Francisco Clementino de Santiago Dantas, Member of the Bar, Rio de Janeiro, Brazil.

7. Professor Hessel Edward Yntema, University of Michigan, Ann Arbor, Michigan, United States of America.

The Committee met at Geneva from the 18th to the 28th August 1952, and prepared a report (E/AC. 39/1) which contains very valuable information regarding the background of the Committee's work, its composition and organisation and the result of its deliberations. Two draft conventions were drawn up by the Committee, namely:

(1) draft convention on the recovery abroad on the claims for maintenance;

(2) draft of a model convention on enforcement abroad of maintenance orders.

These draft conventions were intended to ameliorate the conditions of women and children deserted without means of subsistence by those who were responsible for their support and who have gone to another country. Before the 2nd World War, the largest group of this category consisted of the wives and children of immigrants who established themselves in a new country and failed to support their dependents. After the war, the number of abandoned women and children has greatly increased in view

611

of the mass displacement of military personnel who returned to their homeland and who were married while they were stationed outside their home country. A claimant who seeks to enforce her right against a man who lives in another country is faced with considerable legal difficulties and expense. On the initiative of various benevolent societies, several attempts were made in the past two and half decades to find legal means which would alleviate their sufferings and make it easier for them to obtain support from the defaulter abroad. The preparatory work on this subject before the War was done by the Internaitonal Institute for the Unification of Private Law under the auspices of the League of Nations. But this commendable effort was interrupted by the War. After the War it was taken up by the United Nations.

At the instance of the Social Commission, the Institute prepared a draft convention which was submitted by the Secretary General to States for their comments. This draft was considered at the th Session of the Council in August 1951. More States, such as Argentina, Belgium, Italy and the Philippines have indicated their general approval of the Institute's draft (E/CN. 5/236). Other governments such as the United States (E/CN-5/236, p. 33) and the United Kingdom (E/CN.236), struck a dissentient note and stated that the Institute's draft cannot be used as a working basis for an international convention because it was not considered suitable to the legal system of their countries. Subsequently the Council by resolution 390 (XIII) requested the Secretary General to prepare one or two working drafts and to convene a Committee of Experts, using the Secretary's draft as the basis when reporting the text of one or more model conventions to be submitted to the Council. A Committee of Experts from seven countries met in Geneva in August 1952 and considered the two draft conventions submitted to them by the Secretary General.

The Committee also had before it a number of documents which had been prepared when the Special Commission and the Economic and Social Council had considered the question on enforcement abroad of maintenance obligations in 1952. Among these documents were Secretary General's report, the draft convention and explanatory report of the International Institute for the Unification of Private Law and the comments of the Governments of Argentina, Belgium, Burma, Canada, Chile, Denmark, Egypt, India, the Netherlands, Norway, Pakistan, the Philippines, Sweden, the Union of South Africa, the United Kingdom of Great Britain and Northern Ireland, and the United States of America, the comments of specialised agencies, namely, the International Labour Organisation and the International Refugee Organisation, the comments of the Parliamentary Non-Governmental Organisation, the International Committee of Red Cross, the International Federation of Free Trade Unions, the Canadian Welfare Council, the Family Welfare Association, the International Law Association, the Catholic Union for Special Services, the Inter-Parliamentary Union of the United States for New Americans.

The Committee also had before it a resolution adopted by the 2nd Conference of non-governmental organisations interested in immigration and the documents of some of the records of relevant discussions held in the Economic and Social Council. It also had a resolution adopted by the 3rd conference of non-governmental organisations interested in immigration, a communication from the International Union for Child Welfare relating to illegitimate children whose fathers belong or belonged to troops stationed outside their home countries and a note from the International Labour Office in connection with the transfer of funds.

After a careful and exhaustive study of the two preliminary drafts sent by the Secretary General, the Committee took the view that a new solution to the problem could not be effected by trying to achieve any degree of uniformity in the laws of different countries as regards the enforcement of foreign judgments. For these reasons, the Committee thought it advisable to develop the system contained in the Secretary General's 2nd draft which envisaged the establishment of judicial and administrative co-operation between States and provide for effective legal assistance to claimants for maintenance. It was thought that many States would enter into the convention on the basis of this system. It also suggested that States should examine the possibility of making further progress by concluding bilateral or multilateral treaties or by adopting a uniform set of laws aimed at achieving uniformity in the procedure on enforcement of foreign maintenance orders.

Therefore it decided to try separately the question of the enforcement of orders of foreign courts from the distinct question of assistance to claimants for maintenance and to deal with the latter under what they call the draft multilateral convention.

In drafting the multilateral convention, the Committee departed from the system of the United States Uniformity Laws in not adopting the procedure whereby an action commenced in one court should continue in another. It also made an effort to reduce to the absolute minimum the provisions involving change in the procedure of the various countries. States were free to make their own choice of establishing agencies responsible for carrying out the functions provided in the convention and to employ methods of judicial co-operation already in vogue in international practice such as letters and requests. The procedure adumbrated by the draft multilateral convention (Annexure 1) prepared by the Committee may be succinctly stated as follows:

(a) a preliminary and summary hearing in the country where the claimant resides, the findings of which could be used by the court where the action is commenced;

(b) immediate and direct transmission of documents and

conveyance to the agency in another country so as to avoid loss of time which is inevitable when the usual red-tapism is followed by sending the papers through the usual diplomatic or consular channels;

(c) the prosecution by the receiving agency of maintenance actions on behalf of the claimants and in the courts of the respondent's country;

(d) all possible facilities with regard to legal aid and, if funds are realised, as a result of the enforcement of the decree, for the sending of the funds to the claimants by relaxing the Exchange Control Regulations.

The draft convention prepared by the Committee is set out in Appendix III of this report.

The Draft on the Enforcement Aabroad of Maintenance obligations

In preparing the draft on the enforcement abroad of maintenance obligations, the Committee substantially followed the text prepared by the Secretary General, which was based on the draft of the International Institute for the Unification of Private Law. Having stated that this draft was not appropriate for use as a model for a multilateral convention the Committee recommended to the Governments that this draft may be used as a model bilateral treaty or uniform law.

ADOPTION OF THE DRAFT CONVENTION
OF THE COMMITTEE OF LEGAL EXPERTS

At the 1954 Edinburgh Conference of the International Law Association the proposals contained in the Draft Convention known as Annex 1 of the report of the Committee of Legal Experts, appointed under the United Nations for recovery and enforcement of maintenance orders, were adopted but emphasis was laid on the necessity for introducing therein a specific article whereby a maintenance order would be mutually enforceable as between the contracting States, notwithstanding the fact that such order may be subject to variation by the court that makes it. The Conference further recommended that Article 9 of the Convention (Annex 1) should be amended to read as follows:

"The provisions of this Convention apply to maintenance orders as originally made or as made from time to time."

The members of the Association through the intermediary of each branch were requested to urge upon their respective governments to give instruction to their delegates at the United Nations to press for the adoption of this Convention (Annex 1) without delay (See Report of the 46th Conference of the Intrenational Law Association, 1954, p. 357).

Mr. J. H. C. Morris in his article "The Recognition of American

614

Divorces in England" (See the British Year Book of International Law (1952)) has ably shown that, if one adopts the draft Convention of the Committee of Legal Experts, the special defences available in England for attacking a decree of divorce such as that it is against public policy or that it is defective as a result of procedural errors or fraud has been practised to obtain the decree or that there has been want of notice or that the foreign court lacked internal competence, or that, in practice such a court is ineffective in dealing with foreign decrees, will not be available.

Recommendations

It is suggested that the Committee should adopt the Annexure 1 set out in the report of the International Legal Experts which is set out in Schedule III as a basis on which legislation could be introduced in the countries of the Asian Legal Consultative Committee as it is the best solution so far offered on a difficult subject. It is also recommended that bilateral agreements be entered into between States on the lines suggested by th Royal Commission on foreign decrees subject to necessary changes or to adopt the draft conventions for the mutual recognition of judgments on divorce and nullity of marriage adopted at the Prague Conference in 1944.

The difficulties of the Draft Convention of Internal Experts

At the Sessions of the International Law Association, held on the 12th August 1954, Mr. W. Percy Grieve of the United Kingdom summarised the proposals of the draft convention prepared by the Committee of Experts of the United Nations and also set out the difficulties of administering this scheme. He said (See the Report of the 46th Conference held at Edinburgh in 1954, p. 350)—"The proposal of the draft convention, if I have properly understood it, appears to be as follows:

A wife deserted by her husband may go to an organisation in her own country, which if it is satisfied that she is married to the man in question and that she has a prima facie case, would then transmit the dossier to country of the husband. There the husband could be summoned before a court or a judge and asked if he admitted deserting his wife. No difficulty of a practical kind would arise if he did admit it. On the other hand, it is plain that his answer might raise issues of a very complex kind. He might, for instance, say that far from having deserted his wife, she had turned him out or that she was living in adultery and for that reason he had left her. Such issues would have to be tried before the husband could be compelled to maintain his wife. Madame Kraemar Bach suggested that the draft Convention provides for the evidence of the husband in such a case to be taken by means of a Commission Regatoire. That would mean, I presume, that the husband (and his witnesses) would have to testify before a judge or court or magistrate and have their depositions taken. In the same way, presumably, the evidence of the complaining wife would have been taken (or would be taken) in her own country. This method of hearing the parties would appear to give rise to the following difficulties:

"(a) How is the evidence of the respective parties to be tested? Unless it were tested by cross-examination or, at any rate, by a close interrogation by the presiding magistrate (a method which is alien to English law) such testimony would be of little value. Clearly, therefore, the draft Convention is defective to that extent, if no provision is made for the parties to be represented by counsel or advocate.

(b) If such provision is made it will entail, as well indeed the whole scheme, very considerable expense. Has attention been drawn to this matter, and is it thought that the governments of the respective countries concerned will be prepared to bear the expenses involved? In the United Kingdom, such expenses might be provided for under the Legal Aid Scheme, but not all countries have such a scheme.

(c) In which country is the final decision on the merits of the issues between the parties to be decided: in that of the husband or in that of the wife? Justice would seem to require that the final decision of establishing her case must clearly be on the wife.

(d) Has attention been paid to the dangers which will arise if the final decision on the issues between the parties is to be given by a judge who has been one of the parties (and his or her witnesses) in person and has not seen the other, but only his or her deposition? There would seem to be at least some likelihood of such a judge being sympathetic towards the party whom he has seen, if that party is a good witness." Hence Mr. Grieve tentatively suggested for the consideration of the meeting that justice might better be done if the final decision between the parties were given by a third judge who has seen neither of them. after the study of the depositions.

At the Edinburgh Conference (1954) the International Law Association approved the draft Convention known as Annex 1 of the Committee of Experts appointed under the United Nations for the recovery and enforcement of maintenance orders, but emphasised the necessity of introducing therein a specific article whereby a maintenance order should be mutually enforceable as between the contracting States, notwithstanding the fact that such order may be subject to variation by the Council which makes it. The Conference recommended that the Article 9 of Annex 1 shall be amended to read as follows: "The provisions of this Convention apply to maintenance orders originally made or. arranged from time to time".

Guardianship and Custody of Infants

Closely connected with decrees for divorce is the subject of guardianship and custody of infants. A distinction should be drawn between guardianship and custody. A distinction is drawn between guardianship and custody both made in English common law and systems based on the civil law. Custody concerns the

616

rights of parents or one of the parents to determine the upbringing of the child. The rights and actual care and control and of access form the totality of rights covered by custody. Guardianship connotes the care and control of children who are alone in the world. either because these parents are dead or cannot be traced or because they are unable to look after these children.

International Conventions

International conventions deal only with the broader aspect of guardianship. Reference may be made to the following treaties and conventions on this matter:

The Hague Convention Concerning Guardianship of Infants of 12th June, 1902, Treaties of Montevideo of 12th February 1889, Second Montevideo Treaty on International Civil Law of 19th March 1940, Bustamante Code of 13th March 1928. These conventions combine provisions regarding jurisdiction to appoint guardians and to frame rules governing choice of law. The Hague Convention emphasises the pre-eminent jurisdiction of the courts of the country whose nationality the prospective ward possesses (Art. 2) but also recognises the supplementary jurisdiction of the courts of the prospective ward's residence (Art. 2). It allows even a cumulation of guardians (Art. 4). The lex patriae is to apply uniformity (Arts. 1 to 5) and the guardian who is so appointed is to be recognised by all contracting States except where the lex situs of property exclude it (Art. 6). The local authorities here also could act in accordance with these laws. (See Makarov Quellendes Internationalen Privatrechts (1929) p. 352, Martens Recueil 2nd Ser. XXXI. p. 724). The Treaties of Montevideo of 12th February 1889 combine in principle jurisdiction and choice of law by concentrating the proceedings in the courts of the residence of the prospective wards (Arts. 19-20). (See Treaties of Montevideo of 12th February, 1889, Makarov, p. 269, Martens Recueil 2nd Ser. XVIII—pp. 443-53).

The second Treaty of Montevideo of 19th March 1940 follows in practice the previous convention. Jurisdiction to appoint a guardian is concentrated in the courts of the domicile of the prospective ward (Art. 26). The law of the ward's domicile determines the rights and duties of the guardian (Art. 27). There is a proviso that where the ward has property abroad, the law of domicile of the ward is to be applied in conjunction with the lex sitae (Art. 28). (For the text the Second Montevideo Treaty on International Civil law of 19th March 1940 vide 1943, 37 American Journal of International Law. Supplement 141). The Bustamante code of 13th February 1928, (See Makarov, p. 397) lays emphasis upon the regulation of the Choice of law (Arts. 84, 86, 87, 88, 93 and 94). The right of authorities to intervene is governed by the lex fori (Art. 91). Thus the courts of the prospective ward's national State or domicile do not enjoy a pre-eminent jurisdiction.

Custody of Infants

Custody of infants presents a more complex problem. Questions of custody often arise between husband and wife who live separately and is often embodied in decrees for divorce.

Several jurisdictions may be concerned especially if one of the parents has taken the child abroad. Further custody orders are variable and may require revision. The problem of choice of law may be complex as to nationality, domicile or residence of the respecitve parents and possibly of the child differ from each other.

In English private international law, the distinction between guardianship of infants proper on the one hand and the custody (including access) of infants on the other hand, is not clear. At common law the father is the guardian and the proper remedy when the child was kept away is the writ of **Habeas Corpus.** When the Court of Chancery developed a concurrent remedy its effect was to make the infant a ward of the Court of England. Hence the **lex fori,** the English law determined not only the exceptional power of the court to assume jursidiction but also the nature and extent of its exercise. Since the court represents the Sovereign, who is **parens patriae** the view was taken that courts in England had jurisdiction in matters of custody over British infants abroad. [See Hope v. Hope (1854), 4 De. G.M. & G. 328, Dwason v. Jav (1854) 3 De G.M. & G. 764, Re Willoughby (1885) 30 Ch.D. 324.] The jurisdiction of English courts in matters of custody of infants abroad who are British subjects is restricted to those who are citizens of the United Kingdom and Colonies and are domiciled in England. The jurisdiction of the English Court also extends if the infant is abroad and is a national and if the personal law is English Law (See Phillips v. Phillips (1944) W.N. 141; 60 T.L.R. 395—Re Luck (1940) Ch. 865 (908). However, the English courts only exercise this jurisdiction sparingly. [R. V. Sandback (1951) 1 K.B. 61; Harris v. Harris (1949) 2 A.E.R. 318, 322; Wakeham v. Wakeham (1954) 1 W.L.R. 366; Delp v. Deep—The Times—26-5-55.]

The Scottish law is the same. The court of the infants domicile has jurisdiction over him even when he is abroad. But in Scotland questions of political allegiance and protection are disregarded. [Hamilton v. Hamilton (1955) S.L.T. 16.]

The same appears to be the position in Canada and Australia (See Report of the International Conference, 1956, p. 414). Cer-r tain rules have been developed by the English courts governing custody of foreign nationals.

If no foreign custody order exists English courts will **assume** jurisdiction if the child is in England and make **temporary orders.** The English law is applied in such cases.

This subject was discussed at the 47th Conference of the International Law Association. The draft convention for custodianship was considered and is reproduced as Appendix IV.

It is suggested that this draft convention be adopted mutatis mutandis.

It is also suggested that the respective governments be advised to frame legislation in conformity with the views expressed by the Prague Convention of the International Law Association in 1947 for the mutual recognition of judgments in divorce and nullity of marriage subject to any variation.

1. DRAFT CONVENTION ON THE RECOVERY ABROAD OF CLAIMS FOR MAINTENANCE

Preamble

Considering that the situation of dependents left without means of support by persons in another country constitutes a pressing humanitarian problem: and

Considering that the prosecution or enforcement abroad of claims for maintenance gives rise to serious legal and practical difficulties; and

Considering that it is therefore necessary to facilitate the prosecution of claims and the enforcement of judgments for maintenance, in cases where the claimant resides or is present within the territory of one Contracting Party and the respondent is present within the jurisdiction of another Contracting Party,

Wherefore the Contracting Parties have agreed as follows:

Article 1

Definition

In this Convention:

(a) "Claimant" means the person who claims to be entitled to maintenance by an ascendant. descendant, or spouse. The terms "ascendant" and "descendant" mean all persons related in direct line either by blood or by operation of law;

(b) "Respondent" means the person from whom maintenance is claimed;

(c) "Transmitting agency" means the agency appointed to assist claimants within its territory and to expedite the transmission abroad of papers in order to facilitate the prosecution of maintenance claims;

(d) "Receiving agency" means the agency designated by each Contracting Party to receive from transmitting agencies papers relating to claims for maintenance and to assist claimants in the territories of other Contracting Parties in the prosecution of such claims.

Article 2

Designation of Agencies

1. Each of the Contracting Parties may designate one or more agencies which shall act in its territory as the transmitting

agency. Such transmitting agency may be a judicial or administrative agency in accordance with the law of each Contracting Party.

2. The different functions of the transmitting agency in the preparation of the papers in the case and their transmission to the receiving agency may be entrusted to separate authorities.

3. In the event that one of the Contracting Parties has not designated a transmitting agency, any authority having the power to render maintenance orders may act as a transmitting agency.

4. Each of the Contracting Parties shall, at the time when the instrument of ratification or accession is deposited, designate a receiving agency, public or private; such receiving agency may be designated a transmitting agency within the meaning of paragraph 1.

5. Each Contracting Party undertakes to communicate without delay to the other Contracting Parties any designation of the transmitting agency and any change which may occur in the designation of the receiving or transmitting agency.

6. The agencies contemplated in the preceding paragraphs are authorized to communicate directly with corresponding agencies in the territories of the other Contracting Parties.

Article 3

Presentation of Claims

1. If a claimant resides or is present within the territory of one Contracting Party and the respondent is present within the jurisdiction of another Contracting Party, the claimant may make application to the transmitting agency of the State in which such claimant resides or is present, requesting such agency to transmit the necessary papers relating to his claim to the receiving agency of the State where such respondent is present.

2. A hearing may be held, on the motion of the transmitting agency or at the request of the claimant, providing the law of the State of such agency so allows.

Article 4

Application

1. The application shall state:

(1) The name, nationality, profession, age and address of the claimant;

(b) the name, nationality, profession, age and address of the respondent, in so far as known to the claimant;

(c) the relief sought, indicating the amount and the manner of the payment;

(d) the grounds upon which the claim is based and any other pertinent information, in particular as regards the financial and the family circumstances of the claimant and of the respondent;

620

(e) the names and addresses of witnesses, if a hearing is requested by the claimant.

2. The application shall be accompanied by all pertinent documents, and by a statement of the places where supplementary documents may be found.

Article 5

Transmission of Claims for Maintenance

1. The transmitting agency shall summarily determine whether the application, the accompanying documents and the evidence presented at any hearing which may have been held, make out a case for transmission to the receiving agency. If the agency so determines, the reasons for such determination and, where appropriate, evidence of the claimant's need of free legal aid and exemption from costs shall be added to the papers in the case.

2. Such papers, duly certified and listed in an inventory, together with the transcript of any hearing which may have been held, shall be transmitted directly and without delay by the transmitting agency to the receiving agency designated by the State in which the respondent is present, unless such papers are withdrawn by the claimant for direct transmission to a counsel chosen by him.

Article 6

Transmission of Claims Reduced to Judgment

A claimant who has recovered a judgment for maintenance may make application to have the record of the judgment transmitted under the provisions of Articles 3 and 5 as evidence of the claim. In such case, the record may substitute for the documents prescribed in Article 4, and the proceedings contemplated in Article 7 may include, in accordance with the law of the tribunal in which such proceedings are instituted, proceedings by exeauatur or by a new action based upon the initial judgment.

Article 7

Proceedings in the Competent Tribunal

1. In the absence of a duly legalised declaration to the contrary by the claimant, the receiving agency, upon receipt of the papers in the case, shall be authorised to cause proceedings to be instituted and prosecuted in a competent tribunal, as well as to procure the execution of such judgment as may be rendered, and shall do so without delay.

2. The law of the tribunal shall govern such proceedings.

3. If, under the law of the tribunal, the papers submitted do not constitute evidence, the tribunal may, nevertheless, after examining the papers, make an interim order for the payment of maintenance while the proceedings are pending.

Article 8

Letters of Request

If provision is made for letters of request in the laws of the two Contracting Parties concerned, the following rules shall apply in the proceedings contemplated in Article 7:

(a) If the tribunal deems it necessary to obtain further evidence, and, in particular, to have the facts ascertained by a hearing in another country, it may address letters of request either to the competent tribunal of the State where the evidence is to be taken or to any other authority or institution designated by the State where the request is to be executed.

(b) In order that the parties may attend or be represented, the requested authority shall give notice of the date on which and the place at which the proceedings requested are to take place, to the receiving agency of the State wherein the respondent is present and to the transmitting agency of the State wherein the claimant resides or is present, or, in case a transmitting agency has not been designated, directly to the claimant.

(c) Letters of request shall be drawn up either in the language of the requested authority or in a language agreed upon between the two interested States, or it shall be accompanied by a translation into one of such languages, certified by a sworn translator of the requesting or of the requested State.

(d) Letters of request must be executed within a period of four months, dating from the receipt of the letters by the requested authority.

(e) The execution of letters of request shall not give rise to reimbursement of fees or costs of any kind whatsoever. Nevertheless, in the absence of agreement to the contrary, the requested State shall be entitled to demand of the requesting State reimbursement of payments made to witnesses or to experts, and of costs which may have been incurred by the failure of one or more witnesses to appear voluntarily.

(f) Execution of letters of request may only be refused;

(1) If the authenticity of the letters is not established;

(2) If the State in the territory of which the letters are to be executed deems that its sovereignty or safety would be compromised thereby.

Article 9

Variations of Maintenance Orders

The provisions of this Convention apply also to applications for variation of maintenance orders.

Article 10

Exemptions and Facilities

Exemptions and Facilities

1. Claimants residing or present in the territory of another Contracting Party shall be given equal treatment, and shall be granted the same exemptions in the payment of the costs and charges incurred in any proceedings under this Convention, as residents of the State where such proceedings occur.

2. If the law of the tribunal requires any bond or other security of persons residing or present abroad, claimants residing or present in the territory of another Contracting Party shall be exempt therefrom in all proceedings under this Convention unless, in the case of a Federal State, such exemption would discriminate as against claimants residing or present in other member States or sub-divisions of such federal State.

3. No fees shall be chargeable for certification and legalization of documents in any proceeding under this Convention.

Article 11

Transfer of Funds

1. In order to ensure and expedite the free transfer to the territories of other Contracting Parties of funds payable on account of maintenance obligations judicially established in the courts of a Contracting Party in the cases contemplated in this Convention, each such Party undertakes, in case of exchange restrictions, to accord to such transfers the highest priority provided for capital services.

2. Each Contracting Party reserves the right:

   (a) To take the necessary measures to prevent transfers of funds pursuant to paragraph 1 for purposes other than the bona fide payment of existing maintenance obligations;

   (b) To limit the amounts transferable pursuant to paragraph 1, to amounts necessary for subsistence.

Article 12

Supplementary Arrangements

In order to facilitate compliance with the provisions of the present Convention, the Contracting Parties may, by domestic legislation, or by bilateral or multilateral conventions, provide for any matters not regulated, or insufficiently regulated, in the present Convention.

Article 13

Remedies outside the Convention

The remedies provided in this Convention are in addition to, and not in substitution for, any other remedies.

Article 14

Federal State Clause

No provision of this Convention shall be deemed to affect, or to impose any obligation in respect of, any matter not within the constitutional competence of a federal State, a Party to this Convention.

Article 15

Ratification and Accession

1. This Convention shall be open for ratification or accession on behalf of any Member of the United Nations, any non-Member State which is Party to the Statute of the International Court of Justice, or member of a specialized agency, and also any other non-Member State to which an invitation has been addressed by the Economic and Social Council. Ratification or accession shall be effected by the deposit of a formal instrument with the Secretary-General of the United Nations.

2. The word "State" as used in the preceding paragraph shall be understood to include the territories for which each Contracting Party bears international responsibility, unless the State concerned, on ratifying or acceding to the Convention, has stipulated that the Convention shall not apply to certain of its territories. Any State making such a stipulation may, at any time thereafter, by notification to the Secretary-General extend the application of the Convention to any or all of such territories.

Article 16

Entry into Force

1. This Convention shall come into force on the thirtieth day folloiwng the date of deposit of the second instrument of ratification or accession in accordance with Article 15.

2. For each State ratifying or acceding to the Convention after the deposit of the second instrument of ratification or accession, the Convention shall enter into force on the thirtieth day following the date of the deposit by such State of this instrument.

Article 17

Denunciation

Any Contracting Party may denounce this Convention by written notification to the Secretary-General of the United Nations. Denunciation shall take effect one year after the date of receipt of the notification by the Secretary-General.

Article 18

Settlement of Disputes

Any dispute which may arise between any two or more Contracting Parties concerning the interpretation or application of this Convention which is not settled by negotiation shall at the request of any one of the parties to the dispute be referred to the International Court of Justice, or, in case the latter should not have jurisdiction, to an arbitrator appointed by the President of the International Court of Justice for decision, unless they agree to another mode of settlement.

Article 19

Reservations

In the event that any State submits a reservation to any of the articles of this Convention at the time of ratification or accession, the Secretary-General shall inform of the reservation to all States which are Parties to this Convention and to the other States referred to in Article 15. Any Contracting Party which objects to the reservation may, within a period of ninety days from the date of the communication, notify the Secretary-General that it does not accept it. Any State thereafter acceding may make such notification at the time of its accession. In such case the Convention shall not enter into force as between the objecting State and the State making the reservation.

Article 20

Deposit of Convention and Languages

The original of this Convention, of which the Chinese, English, French, Russian and Spanish texts are equally authentic, shall be deposited with the Secretary-General of the United Nations, who shall transmit certified true copies thereof to all States referred to in Article 15.

2. DRAFT CONVENTION FOR CUSTODIANSHIP

Article 1

Primary Jurisdiction

The courts listed in the attached Schedule shall have jurisdiction to make orders for the custody of infants.

Article 2

Subsidiary Jurisdiction

Where jurisdiction under Article 1 has not been exercised the courts of the country in which the infant is resident at the time of the commencement of the proceedings shall have jurisdiction to make an order for the custody of the infant.

Article 3

Concurrent Jurisdiction

(i) Where separate proceedings have been commenced

contemporaneously under Articles 1 and 2 respectively, the proceedings by virtue of Article 2 shall, on application to that court, be stayed, pending the determination by the competent court under Article 1.

(ii) Notwithstanding the power to stay any such proceedings the court seized with the dispute under Article 2 may, if it thinks fit, for the reasons set out in Article 5, proceed to determine the issue.

Article 4

Recognition and Enforcement

Where an order under Article 1 has been made, such order shall be both recognised and enforced in the countries who are parties to this Convention.

Article 5

Jurisdiction to Vary

Notwithstanding an order under Article 4 a court of any country in which the infant is resident during the period of any proceedings under any article of this Convention, may, if it thinks fit, vary any order made under Article 1 having regard to events which have occurred since the order under Article 1 was made.

Provided that, when the infant has been removed in pursuance of an attempt to seek a change of custody in disobedience to an order under Article I no such variation under this Article shall be permissible.

Article 6

Access

Any order for custody under the provisions of this Convention may, but need not, be accompanied by an order allowing any party whom the court making the order regards as a poorer party access to the infant on such terms as the court thinks fit.

Article 7

Variations of Access Order

Notwithstanding any order of access made under Article 6, a court of any country in which the infant is present may, if it thinks fit, vary or rescind any order made under Article 6.

Article 8

General Principles

In any proceedings before any court particular attention shall be paid to the best interests of the infant.

Article 9

Definitions

In this Convention.

"Access" means the right to have the care and control of the infant for such period or periods or at such times as the court making the order decrees.

"Custody" means the legal right to determine the upbringing of the infant and shall include the care and control of such infant.

"Infant" means any person who by the law of the court seized with the issue has not reached the age of majority.

Schedule

Under Article 1 of this Convention the following courts shall have jurisdiction:

1. (a) The courts of the country of which the infant is national.

   (b) The courts of the country of which the infant is national do not administer a uniform system of laws, those courts of that country shall have jurisdiction which are competent according to the jurisdictional rules of the law of that country.

2. The courts of the country exercising jurisdiction in divorce, nullity, judicial separation and other such matrimonial proceedings, provided that such jurisdiction in general and the order made thereunder in particular are recognised by the laws of the courts exercising jurisdiction by virtue of Articles 1-3 inclusive.

DRAFT AGREEMENT ON THE RECOGNITION AND ENFORCEMENT OF FOREIGN JUDGMENTS IN MATRIMONIAL MATTERS

Article 1

Definitions

In applying this Agreement, the following definitions shall be taken into consideration:

(a) A foreign judgment means any decision issued by a judicial authority in any of the contracting States.

(b) A final judgment means an enforceable judgment which is irrefutable by any of the ordinary procedures of refuting judgments.

627

(c) The force of execution of the judgment means its capability of being compulsorily executed.

Article 2

A foreign judgment issued in matters of nullity of marriage, dissolution, divorce, maintenance of spouses and custody shall enjoy the res judicata, stipulated in the State where it was issued within the scope of the res judicata of the judgments issued by courts of the State in whose territory its effects are required to be maintained, without need for taking any procedure relative to it.

This judgment shall have the force of execution, enjoyed in the State where it was issued, within the scope of the force of execution of judgments issued by the courts of the State requested to execute it in its territory, after undertaking the procedure stipulated by the law of this State.

Article 3

The foreign judgment shall not have the effects stated in the afore-mentioned articles, unless the following conditions have been verified.

1. That the judgment is final and issued by a judicial authority, internationally competent, according to its law.

2. That it was issued according to regular procedures which enabled the defendant to submit his defence.

3. That it shall not contradict any judgment issued by the courts of the State in whose territory its effects are required to be maintained, and that there is no other action between the same parties on the same subject matter already standing before these courts and had been commenced before filing the suit at the foreign court which issued the judgment whose effects are required to be maintained.

4. That the judgment does not involve anything of a nature to violate the public policy of the State in whose territory its effects are required to be maintained.

5. That the court issuing the judgment has applied the applicable law, according to the rules on conflict of laws stated by its law.

Article 4

The law of every contracting State shall determine the competent judicial authority to which the request for the execution of the judgment may be submitted. the procedures to be followed in its adjudication and the means of refuting the judgment relative to it.

Article 5

The competent judicial authority, requested to maintain the **res judicata** of the judgment, or issue a decision for its enforcement, shall not be allowed to investigate the subject matter settled by the judgment.

Article 6

When there are two foreign judgments or more, the effects stated in article 2, shall pertain to the judgment which was issued by a competent court, according to a rule set by its law, in closer agreement with the rules of international competence stipulated by the law of the State in whose territory the effects are required to be maintained.

Article 7

Requests for execution should be supported by the following documents:

(1) A certified true copy of the judgment desired to be executed, duly authenticated by the competent authorities and attested as being executory.

(2) The original summons of service of the text of the judgment desired to be executed, or an official certificate to the effect that the text of the judgment had been served.

(3) A certificate from the competent authority to the effect that the judgment desired to be executed, is final and executory.

(4) A certificate that the parties were duly summoned to appear before the competent authority, in case the judgment, desired to be executed, was in default.

(10) FINAL REPORT OF THE COMMITTEE ON DUAL NATIONALITY, 1964

Adopted in Cairo on February-March, 1964, at the Sixth Session of the Asian-African Legal Consultative Committee.

Text from ASIAN-AFRICAN LEGAL CONSULTATIVE COMMITTEE, Report of the Sixth Session, Part I, pp. 31-36.

INTRODUCTORY NOTE

The subject of Dual Nationality was referred to the Committee by the Government of the Union of Burma under the provisions of Article 3(b) of the Statutes of the Committee. The Governments of Burma, Japan and the United Arab Republic submitted memoranda on the subject and the United Arab Republic also presented a Draft Agreement for consideration of the Committee.

During the First Session held in New Delhi, the Delegations of Burma, Indonesia and Japan made brief statements on the problem of dual nationality but the Committee decided to postpone further consideration of the subject as the Delegations of India, Ceylon, Iraq and Syria had reserved their position on this subject.

During the Second Session held in Cairo, the views of the Delegations were ascertained on the basis of a questionnaire prepared by the Secretariat. The main topics discussed during the Second Session were: (1) the acquisition of dual nationality; (2) the position of a resident citizen who is simultaneously a citizen of another State and the rights of such a citizen; (3) the position of a non-resident citizen possessing dual nationality; and (4) the position of an alien possessing dual nationality. The Delegations were of the opinion that it would be desirable to reduce the number of cases of persons possessing dual nationality by means of enacting suitable national legislation or by concluding international conventions. It was, however, felt that unless there was uniformity in nationality laws and unanimity on the fundamental principles of nationality, it would be very difficult to achieve the desired objective by means of a multilateral convention. The Committee decided that the Secretariat should prepare a report on the subject on the basis of the discussions held during the session and that this report together with the draft agreement submitted by the United Arab Republic should be taken up for consideration during the Third Session.

At the Third Session held in Colombo, the Committee had a general discussion on the subject, and the unanimous view of the Delegations was that some preparatory work should be done by the governments of the participating countries on the basis of the report of the Secretariat before the Committee could finally make its recommendations on the subject. The Committee therefore decided to request the governments of the participating countries to study the report of the Secretariat and the Draft Agreement submitted by the Delegation of the United Arab Republic and to communicate their views to the Secretariat in the form of memoranda indicating particular problems which have arisen in this regard and suggesting specific points which they desire the Committee to take up for particular study and consideration.

At the Fourth Session held in Tokyo, the Committee gave further consideration to the subject and decided to request the Delegation of the United Arab Republic to prepare a revised draft of a convention in the light of the comments received from the governments of the participating countries for consideration at the Fifth Session of the Committee. The Committee also directed the Secretariat to request the governments which had not given their comments to do so as early as possible and thereafter to forward the comments on to the Delegation of the United Arab Republic.

At the Fifth Session held in Rangoon in January 1962, the subject was fully considered by the Committee on the basis of a draft of an Agreement submitted by the Delegation of the United Arab Republic. The Committee also had before it written memoranda on the subject submitted by the Governments of Burma, Ceylon, Indonesia, Iraq and Japan. After a detailed discussion on the various aspects of the subject the Committee adopted a preliminary report containing the draft Articles embodying principles relating to the elimination or reduction of dual or multiple nationality.

At the Sixth Session of the Committee held in Cairo in 1964, the subject was finally discussed on the basis of the preliminary report adopted at the Fifth Session and the comments received thereon from the Delegates. The Committee drew up and adopted its Final Report containing Model Rules embodying principles relating to elimination or reduction of dual or multiple nationality. It was decided to submit the Final Report to the Government of Burma and the Governments of the other countries.

FINAL REPORT OF THE COMMITTEE ADOPTED AT THE SESSION

Model articles embodying principles relating to elimination or reduction of dual or multiple nationality

GENERAL PROVISIONS*

ARTICLE 1

It is for each State to determine under its own law who are its nationals. This law itself shall be recognised by other States in so far as it is consistent with international conventions, international customs, and the principles of law generally recognised with regard to nationality.

Note: The Delegate of Thailand stated that with the exception of the principle of compulsory recognition he accepted the other principles incorporated in this Article.

ARTICLE 2

Questions as to whether a person possesses the nationality of a particular State shall be determined in accordance with the law of that State.

Note: The Delegate of India reserved his position on this Article.

ARTICLE 3

Alternative (A)

For the purpose of these Model Articles the age of majority of a person shall be determined according to the law of the State the nationality of which is to be acquired, retained, or renounced.

Alternative (B)

The age of majority shall be determined according to the laws of the State, the nationality of which is relevant for the matter under consideration, provided that for the purposes of Articles 5 and of Article 7, the majority age (in the event of any conflict of

---

*As regards Dual Nationality, the Delegation of Pakistan stated that the Government of Pakistan recognises no second nationality in a citizen except that in the United Kingdom; a citizen of Pakistan has all the rights of a citizen of the United Kingdom including the right of vote. The Delegation of Ghana reserved the position of his Government on these Articles.

State laws) shall be the majority age under the law of the State which prescribes a higher age.

Nationality of Married Women

ARTICLE . 4

(1) If a woman who is a national of one State marries a national of another State, or if a husband acquires a nationality other than that he had on the date of marriage, the nationality of the wife shall not be affected.

(2) Nevertheless if she, in either of such cases, voluntarily acquires the nationality of her husband, she loses *ipso facto* the other nationality.

Nationality of Children

ARTICLE 5

(1) A minor follows ordinarily his father's nationality. If the minor is born out of wedlock, or if the nationality of his father is unknown or if his father has no nationality, he follows his mother's nationality.

(2) Nevertheless, if a minor born to a national of one State in another State is deemed in accordance with the laws of each of the two States to be its national, he should opt for one of these two nationalities within one year from the date of attaining his majority age in accordance with the provisions of Article 7.

but expressed the view that the principle of nationality of the State of birth instead of the principle of mother's nationality should be adopted. The Delegates of Burma and Thailand accepted the provisions of clause (2) of this Article. The Delegates of Ceylon, India and the United Arab Republic were in agreement that clause (2) of this Article was not necessary. The Delegate of Indonesia reserved his position on clause (2) of this Article. The Delegate of Japan reserved his position on paragraph (2) of Article 5 of the draft.

Adoption

ARTICLE 6

In case of valid adoption, the adopted minor shall follow his adopter's nationality.

Note: The Delegates of Burma, Indonesia and the United Arab Republic accepted this Article. The Delegates of Indonesia and the United Arab Republic took the view that the minor should have an option after he attains majority to choose between his original nationality and the nationality of his adopter. The Delegate of Thailand stated that the words "be entitled to" should be inserted between the word "shall" and the word "follow". This Article was not accepted by the Delegates of Ceylon, India and Japan.

Option

ARTICLE 7

A person who knows that he possesses two nationalities acquired without any voluntary act on his part should renounce one of them in accordance with the law of the State whose nationality he desires to renounce, within twelve months of his knowing that fact or within twelve months of attaining his majority age, whichever is the latter.

Note: The Delegates of Burma, Ceylon, India Thailand and the United Arab Republic accepted this Article. The Delegate of Indonesia reserved his position on this Article although he expressed the view that the option available to the individual must be of obligatory character and that States should by means of agreement provide for dealing with cases where the individual does not exercise the option. The Delegate of Japan was not in favour of imposing any obligation on an indivdual to exercise the option.

Active Nationality

ARTICLE 8

A person having more than one nationality shall be treated as having only one nationality in a third State. A third State should, however, recognise exclusively the nationality of the State in which he is habitually and principally resident or the nationality of the State with which in the circumstances he appears to be in fact most closely connected.

ARTICLE 9

A person possessing two or more nationalities of the contracting States, who has his habitual and principal residence within the territory of one of these States with which he is in fact most closely connected, shall be exempt from all military obligations in the other State or States.

Note: The Delegate of Iraq reserved his position on this Article.

ARTICLE 10

Without prejudice to the provisions of Article 9, if a person possesses the nationality of two or more States, and under the law of any one of such States has the right, on attaining his majority age, to renounce or decline the nationality of that State, he shall be exempt from military service in such State during his minority.

Note: The Delegates of Indonesia and Iraq reserved their position on this Article.

Explanatory Note: These Articles are intended to serve only as model rules as embodying certain Principles relating to elimination or reduction of Dual or Multiple Nationality. The provisions of each of the above Articles are independent of each other.

---

(11) FINAL REPORT OF THE COMMITTEE ON THE LEGALITY OF NUCLEAR TESTS, 1964

Adopted in Cairo on February-March, 1964, at the Sixth Session of the Asian-African Legal Consultative Committee.

Text from ASIAN-AFRICAN LEGAL CONSULTATIVE COMMITTEE, Report of the Sixth Session, Part I, pp. 40-42.

The Asian-African Legal Consultative Committee at its Third Session held in Colombo in January 1960 decided to take up for consideration the question of Legality of Nuclear Tests, a subject which had been suggested by the Government of India under Article 3(c) of the Statutes of the Committee, being a legal matter of common concern to all the States participating in the Committee.

At its Fourth Session held in Tokyo in February 1961, the Secretariat of the Committee presented before it the relevant material both from the scientific and legal points of view, which formed the basis of discussion at that session. After a general discussion the Committee decided to study the matter further and to take up the question for fuller consideration at its Fifth Session. The Committee decided that it would not concern itself with the question regarding the use of nuclear weapons in time of war, but that it would confine itself to an examination of the problem of the legality of nuclear tests in time of peace.

In accordance with the decision taken by the Committee at its Tokyo Session, the Secretariat prepared a report which was placed before the Committee at its Fifth Session held in Rangoon in January 1962, on the basis of which the matter was further considered.

The Committee heard the views and expressions of opinion on the various topics arising on this subject from the Members for Burma, Ceylon, India, Indonesia, Japan, Pakistan, Thailand, and the United Arab Republic. Thereafter further comments were submitted by member governments.

At the Sixth Session of the Committee held in Cairo in February-March 1964, the Committee considered the report prepared by the Secretariat and the comments received from Governments. The Committee took into account the various United Nations resolutions and international agreements relevant to the subject and the scientific data placed before the Committee. It also noted

636

with satisfaction the conclusion of the Treaty of 5th August 1963 prohibiting nuclear tests, which has had a considerable effect upon the ultimate outcome of the Committee's deliberation.

The Committee has formulated the following conclusions, stating that they apply equally to test explosions of nuclear weapons carried out by anyone for whose action the State is responsible in international law;

CONCLUSIONS

1. As sufficient evidence regarding the harmful effects of the underground test explosions of nuclear weapons is not at present available to the Committee, the Committee is unable at this stage to express any opinion on the legality or otherwise of such test explosions. The conclusions hereinafter set out are therefore referable to all test explosions of nuclear weapons other than underground test explosions.

2. Scientific evidence examined by the Committee shows that every test explosion of nuclear weapons results in widespread damage, immediate or delayed, or is capable of resulting in such damage; the present state of scientific knowledge does not indicate that the harmful effects of such test explosions can reasonably be eliminated. Such test explosions not only cause direct damage, but pollute the atmosphere and cause fall-out of radioactive material and also increase atomic radiation, which are detrimental to the well-being of man and also affect future generations.

3. Having regard to its harmful effects, as shown by scientific data, a test explosion of nuclear weapons constitutes an international wrong. Even if such tests are carried out within the territory of the testing State, they are liable to be regarded as an abuse of rights (*abus de droit*).

4. The principle of absolute liability for harbouring dangerous substances or carrying on dangerous activities is recognised in international law. A State carrying out test exlosions of nuclear weapons is therefore absolutely liable for the damage caused by such test explosions.

5. Test explosions of nuclear weapons are also contrary to the principles contained in the United Nations Charter and the Declaration of Human Rights.

6. Test explosions of nuclear weapons carried out in the high seas and in the airspace there above also violate the principle of

the freedom of the seas and the freedom of flying above the high seas, as such test explosions interfere with the freedom of navigation and of flying above the high seas and result in pollution of the water and destruction of the living and other resources of the sea.

7. Test explosions of nuclear weapons carried out in trust territories and non-self governing territories also violate Articles 73 and 74 of the United Nations Charter.

———

(12) FINAL REPORT OF THE COMMITTEE ON RECIPROCAL ENFORCE-MENT OF JUDGMENTS, SERVICE OF PROCESS AND RECORDING OF EVIDENCE IN CIVIL AND CRIMINAL CASES, 1965

Adopted in Baghdad on April 1, 1965, at the Seventh Session of the Asian-African Legal Consultative Committee.

Text from ASIAN-AFRICAN LEGAL CONSULTATIVE COMMITTEE, Report of the Seventh Session, Part 2, pp. 107-115.

The questions relating to "Reciprocal Enforcement of Judgments, Service of Process, and Recording of Evidence among States both in Civil and Criminal Cases"have been referred to this Committee under Article 3 (b) of its Statutes by the Government of Ceylon with a view to formulate a uniform set of rules to ensure reciprocal recognition and enforcement of foreign judgments and to facilitate the service of process and recording of evidence in foreign countries.

At the Sixth Session of the Committee held in Cairo in 1964, the subject was considered by a Sub-Committee appointed for the purpose, consisting of the Representatives of Ceylon, India, Iraq and the United Arab Republic on the basis of a study prepared by the Secretariat and certain memoranda submitted by the Delegations of Ceylon and the United Arab Republic. The Sub-Committee placed before the Committee a report containing two draft agreements, one on the subject of "Recognition and Enforcement of Judgments", and the other on the subject of "Service of Process and Recording of Evidence."

The Committee at the present Session took up for consideration the Report of the Sub-Committee appointed at the Cairo Session. It was agreed in the Committee to give detailed consideration to the provisions of the two drafts prepared by the Sub-Committee on the basis that those provisions, if adopted, would be recommended as model rules on the subject for consideration of the Governments. The Committee, after a careful consideration of the Report of the Sub-Committee, is agreed on the adoption of the model rules on the subject, which are set out in Annexures I and II to this Report.

The Committee decides to submit this Report to the Government of Ceylon and the Governments of other participating countries in the Committee as the Final Report of the Committee on the subject.

MODEL RULES ON THE RECOGNITION AND ENFORCEMENT OF FOREIGN JUDGMENTS IN CIVIL CASES

Article 1

In these model rules:

(a) A *foreign judgment* means a decision made by a judicial authority whose jurisdiction does not extend to the State in which its enforcement is sought.

(b) A *final judgment* means a judgment which is enforceable in the State in which it was delivered.

(c) *recognized* means being given effect to as a *res judicata* according to the law of the State in which its effects are sought to be maintained.

(d) *enforceable* means capable of being compulsorily executed.

Article 2

These rules shall apply to foreign judgments in civil cases, including commercial cases, whereby a definite sum of money is made payable. It shall not apply to judgments whereby a sum of money is payable in respect of a tax, fine or penalty.

Note:—The Delegations of India and Pakistan desired express provision excluding (1) arbitration award, even if such an award is enforceable as money decree or judgment, (2) order for the payment of money arising out of matrimonial proceedings.

Article 3

A foreign judgment shall be recognized as conclusive and be enforceable between the parties thereto as if it had been issued by a court of the State in which its enforcement is sought.

Article 4

A foreign judgment shall not be recognized or enforced unless the following facts are verified:

(a) that it is final and conclusive.

(b) that it is issued by a court which is internationally competent.

(c) that it is issued according to a procedure which would enable the defendant to submit his defence.

(d) that it does not violate the public policy or morality of the State in which enforcement is sought.

(e) that it is not obtained by fraud.

(f) that it does not conflict with any judgment, delivered by any court of the State in which enforcement is sought, between the same parties on the same subject matter in an action instituted earlier.

(g) that there is no action, instituted earlier, pending between the same parties on the same subject matter in the State in which enforcement is sought.

Note:—(I) Regarding Clause (b) of the Article.

The Delegations of India and Ceylon desired that the expression "a court which is internationally competent" should be defined to mean a court having jurisdiction which satisfies the following requirements:

(1) (a) the judgment debtor has voluntarily appeared in the proceedings for the purpose of contesting the merits and not solely for the purpose of:

(i) contesting the jurisdiction of the said court, or

(ii) protecting his property from seizure or obtaining the release of seized property; or

(iii) protecting his property on the ground that in the future it may be placed in jeopardy of seizure on the strength of the judgments; or

(b) the judgment debtor has submitted to the jurisdiction of the said court by an express agreement; or

(c) the judgment debtor at the time of the institution of the proceeding ordinarily resides in the State of the said court; or

(d) the judgment debtor instituted the proceeding as plaintiff or counterclaimed in the State of the said court; or

(e) the judgment debtor, being a corporate body, was incorporated or has its seat (*siege*) in the State of the said court, or at the time of the institution of the proceedings had its place of central administration or principal place of business in that State; or

(f) the judgment debtor, at the time of the institution of the proceeding, has either a commercial establishment or a branch office in the State of the said court and the proceeding is based upon a cause of action arising out of the business carried on there; or

(g) in an action based on contract, the parties to the contract ordinarily reside in different States and all, or substantially all, of the performance by the judgment debtor was to take place in the State of the said court; or

(h) in an action in tort (*delict* or *quasi delict*) either the place where the defendant did the act which caused the injury or the place where the last event necessary to make the defendant liable for the alleged tort (*delict* or *quasi delict*) occurred in the State of the said court.

(2) Notwithstanding anything in clause (1), the court which issued the judgment shall not have jurisdiction:

(a) in the cases stated in sub Clauses (c), (e), (f) and (g), if the bringing of proceedings in the said court was contrary to an express agreement between the parties under which the dispute in question was to be settled otherwise than by a proceeding in that court

(b) if by the law of the country in which enforcement is sought exclusive jurisdiction over the subject matter of the action is assigned to another court;

The bases of jurisdiction recognized in the foregoing clauses are, however, not exclusive and the court in which enforcement is sought may accept additional bases.

The Delegations of Ghana and Pakistan desired that Clause (b) of Article 4 be altered as follows: "that it had been issued by a court of competent jurisdiction".

Note:—(II) Regarding Clause (c) of this Article,

· The Delegations of India and Pakistan suggested that the following be substituted:

"that it had been issued according to a procedure which gives the defendant reasonable notice of the proceeding and reasonable opportunity of submitting his defence and follows the principles of natural justice".

Note:—(III) Regarding Clause (f) of this Article.

The Delegations of the United Arab Republic desired that the clause should be as follows:

"that it does not contradict any judgment delivered by a court of the State in which enforcement is sought".

Note:—(IV)—Regarding Clause (d) of this Article

The Delegations of India and Pakistan desired that the following clauses should be added to the Article as clauses (h) and (i):

(h) that it is not founded on a refusal to recognize the law of the State in which enforcement is sought in cases where such law is applicable.

(i) that it does not sustain a claim founded on a breach of any law in force in the State in which enforcement is sought.

Article 5

A foreign judgment shall not be recognized or be enforceable except by a formal decision made by the appropriate court in accordance with the procedural requirements of the State in which enforcement is sought.

Note:—The Delegation of India and Pakistan desired an additional provision to the following effect:

"Proceedings for enforcement shall be stayed on proof of

appeal being filed or other steps being taken to have the judgment set aside".

Article 6

The appropriate judicial authority required to recognize or direct the enforcement of a foreign judgment shall not investigate the merits of that judgment.

Article 7

Requests for recognition or enforcement should be supported by the following documents:

(a) A certified true copy of the judgment sought to be executed duly authenticated by the appropriate authorities.

(b) A certificate from the appropriate authority to the effect that the judgment sought to be enforced is final and executory.

(c) A certificate that the parties were duly summoned to appear before the appropriate authority in cases where the judgment was obtained in default of appearance of either party.

MODEL RULES FOR THE SERVICE OF JUDICIAL PROCESS AND RECORDING OF EVIDENCE IN CIVIL & CRIMINAL CASES

PART ONE—General Provisions

Article 1

In these model rules:

(a) *Judicial Process* means every type of document, which is required to be served on a party or witness in civil or criminal proceedings.

(b) *Recipient* means the person on whom such process is intended to be served.

(c) *Requesting State* in *Part Two* means the State which requests the service of judicial process in the territory of another State and in *Part Three* means the State from which a request·to record evidence emanates.

(d) *Competent Authority* in *Part Two* means the authority which is empowered to record evidence in terms of these Rules.

PART TWO—Service of Process

Article 2

(a) Judicial process shall be served in accordance with the law of the State in which such service is to be effected. Provided that if the requesting State desires such process to be served in accordance with its own law, the request shall be complied with unless it conflicts with the law of the State where the service is to be effected.

(b) If the recipient is a national of the requesting State, the process may be served by a Consular Officer of the requesting State provided that the State in which it is to be served shall bear no responsibility.

Note:—The Delegation of Ghana desired the omission of the proviso to Clause (a).

Article 3

Subject to the provisions of Article 2, a request for the service of judicial process shall be made as follows:

(a) The Letter of Request shall be addressed by a Diplomatic or Consular Officer of the requesting State to the competent authority of the State where such process is to be served.

(b) It shall state the full name, address and such other information as is necessary to identify the recipient.

(c) Two copies of the process to be served shall be annexed to the Letter of Request and where the process is not drawn up in the language of the State in which it is to be served, it shall be accompanied by a translation in duplicate.

Article 4

(a) A request for service of process made in accordance with the preceding provisions shall be complied with unless:

(1) the authenticity of the request for service is not established; or

(2) the State to which the request is made considers it to be contrary to its public policy.

644

(b) The competent authority by whom the request is executed shall furnish a certificate in proof of such service or
explain the reasons which have prevented such service.

PART THREE—Recording of Evidence

Article 5

When evidence is required to be recorded in a civil or criminal
proceeding by a court of one State in the territory of another State,
such evidence shall be taken in accordance with the following
provisions.

Article 6

A request to record evidence shall be executed by the competent
authority in accordance with the law in force in that State, provided
that if the requesting State desires it to be executed in some other
way, such request shall be complied with unless it conflicts with
the law of the State in which such evidence is to be recorded.

Article 7

(a) The Letter of Request shall be addressed by a Diplomatic or Consular Officer of the requesting State to
the competent authority of the State where such evidence
is to be recorded.

(b) The Letter of Request shall be drawn up in the language
of the State where the evidence is to be taken or be
accompanied by a translation in such language. The
Letter of Request shall state the nature of the proceeding for which the evidence is required and the full
name and address of the witnesses whose evidence is
to be recorded.

(c) The Letter of Request shall either be accompanied by
a list of interrogatories and documents, if any, to be
put to the witness or it shall request the competent
authority to allow such questions to be asked *viva voce*
as the parties or their representatives shall desire to ask.

Article 8

A request for the recording of evidence made in accordance
with the aforesaid provisions shall be complied with unless:

(1) The authenticity of the Letter of Request is not established;
or

(2) The State to whom the request is made considers it
to be contrary to its public policy.

(13) FINAL REPORT OF THE COMMITTEE ON THE RIGHTS OF REFUGEES, 1966

Adopted in Bangkok on August 8-17, 1966, at the Eighth Session of the Asian-African Legal Consultative Committee.

Text from ASIAN-AFRICAN LEGAL CONSULTATIVE COMMITTEE, Report of the Eighth Session, Part 2, pp. 207-219.

The Government of the United Arab Republic by a reference made under Article 3(b) of the Statutes requested this Committee to consider the subject of "The Rights of Refugees" in general and in particular the following issues :

1. Definition of refugees and their classifications.

2. The relation between the problem of refugees and the preservation of peace and justice in the world.

3. Principles guiding the solution of refugee problem :

   (a) The right of asylum.

   (b) The right of repatriation and resettlement.

   (c) The right of indemnification.

4. Rights of refugees in the country of residence :

   (a) The right to life and liberty.

   (b) The right to fair trial.

   (c) The right to speech, conscience and religion.

   (d) The right of employment.

   (e) The right to social security.

   (f) The right to education.

5. International assistance to refugees :

   (a) Travel documents-visas.

   (b) Financial assistance.

   (c) Technical assistance.

   (d) International co-operation in the field of refugees : International agreements and International Agencies.

2. The subject was placed on the Agenda of the Sixth Session of the Committee for consideration. At that Session the Committee generally discussed the subject on the basis of a note prepared by the Secretariat and a memorandum submitted by the Office of the United Nations High Commissioner for Refugees. The Committee after a general discussion on the subject decided to direct the Secretariat to collect further material, particularly on the issues relating to compensation, the minimum standard of treatment of a refugee in the State of asylum and the possibility of constitution of international tribunals for determination of compensation which could be claimed by a refugee. The Secretariat, in accordance with the directions of the Committee, submitted a comprehensive note on the subject including certain Draft Articles on the Rights of Refugees to serve as a basis of discussion in the Committee. The Secretariat with the assistance of the United Nations High Commissioner for Refugees had collected considerable material on the subject, which was placed before the Committee.

3. The Committee gave detailed consideration to this subject at its Seventh Session held in Baghdad in March 1965 and adopted an Interim Report containing provisional formulation of certain principles concerning the status and treatment of refugees. The Committee had, however, decided to postpone consideration of the question relating to implementation of the right of a refugee to return to his homeland and the right to compensation, which rights were recognised and embodied in the Draft Principles provisionally adopted by the Committee at its Baghdad Session. The Committee also postponed consideration of the provisions of the United Nations Refugee Convention of 1951.

4. The Interim Report drawn up by the Committee at its Baghdad Session was transmitted to the Governments of the participating countries as also to the United Nations High Commissioner for Refugees for their comments. Detailed comments were received on the Interim Report which have been placed before the Committee for consideration.

5. The Committee, having regard to the importance of the subject to the participating States and the urgency of the problem, decided to take up this subject as the first item on the agenda of this Session, and gave detailed consideration to it at its second, third, fourth, fifth, sixth, seventh, eighth and ninth meetings. The Committee was greatly assisted in its task by the Legal adviser to the United Nations High Commissioner for Refugees who attended as observer at the invitation of the Committee and participated in the discussions. The Committee

also had the benefit of hearing the views of the representative of the League of Arab States who attended the Session and took part in the deliberations.

6. The Committee, on a careful consideration of the various aspects of the subject, came to the conclusion that having regard to the fact that the Committee's functions under its Statute were of an advisory character, the appropriate manner in which it could deal with the subject of refugees was to define the term "refugee" and formulate the principles regarding the right of asylum, the rights and obligations of refugees, and the minimum standard of treatment in the state of asylum. The Committee considered that it would be up to the Government of each participating State to decide as to how it would give effect to the Committee's recommendations whether by entering into multilateral or bilateral arrangements or by recognising the principles formulated by the Committee in their own municipal laws. In this view of the matter the Committee has formulated the general principles on the subject which are set out in the *Annexure* to this Report.

7. The Committee considered the question as to whether any provision should be made for the implementation of the right of a refugee to return to the State or Country of his nationality as also his right to receive compensation which have been provided for in the Articles containing the principles concerning treatment of refugees as adopted by the Committee at this Session. The Delegate of Ceylon expressed the view that it was neither possible nor necessary to make any provision for implementation of these rights. The Delegate of Japan was of the view that the circumstances were not ripe for making any recommendation on this question, and the Delegate of Pakistan was of the opinion that it was not practicable at present to make any provision in this respect. The Delegates of Ghana, India, Indonesia and Thailand were of the view that this question should be kept pending and might be examined by the Committee at a suitable time, and it was so decided.

8. The Committee also came to the conclusion that it was not necessary to examine in detail the provisions of the 1951 U.N. Convention on Refugees as the same had been taken note of by the Committee in formulating the principles on the subject.

9. The Committee records its deep appreciation of the assistance rendered to the Committee by the Office of the United Nations High Commissioner for Refugees in the matter of collection of material as also of assistance given to the

Committee in the deliberations on this subject at the Sixth, Seventh and Eighth Sessions.

Sd/- SANYA DHARMASAKTI
PRESIDENT

ANNEXURE

PRINCIPLES CONCERNING TREATMENT OF REFUGEES

Article I

Definition of the term "Refugee"

A Refugee is a person who, owing to persecution or well-founded fear of persecution for reasons of race, colour, religion, political belief or membership of a particular social group:

(a) leaves the State of which he is a national, or the Country of his nationality, or, if he has no nationality, the State or Country of which he is a habitual resident; or,

(b) being outside such State or Country, is unable or unwilling to return to it or to avail himself of its protection.

Exceptions :

(1) A person having more than one nationality shall not be a refugee if he is in a position to avail himself of the protection of any State or Country of which he is a national.

(2) A person who prior to his admission into the Country of refuge, has committed a crime against peace, a war crime, or a crime against humanity or a serious non-political crime or has committed acts contrary to the purposes and principles of the United Nations shall not be a refugee.

Explanation : The dependents of a refugee shall be deemed to be refugees.

Explanation : The expression "leaves" includes voluntary as well as involuntary leaving.

NOTES

(i)   The Delegation of Ghana reserved its position on this Article.

(ii) The Delegations of Iraq, Pakistan and the United Arab Republic expressed the view that, in their opinion, the definition of the term "Refugee" includes a person who is obliged to leave the State of which he is a national under the pressure of an illegal act or as a result of invasion of such State, wholly or partially, by an alien with a view to occupying the State.

(iii) The Delegations of Ceylon and Japan expressed the view that in their opinion the expression "persecution" means something more than discrimination or unfair treatment but includes such conduct as shocks the conscience of civilised nations.

(iv) The Delegations of Japan and Thailand expressed the view that the word "and" should be substituted for the word "or" in the last line of paragraph (a).

(v)   In Exception (2) the words "prior to his admission into the Country of refuge" were inserted by way of amendment to the original text of the Draft Articles on the proposal of the Delegation of Ceylon and accepted by the Delegations of India, Indonesia, Japan and Pakistan. The Delegations of Iraq and Thailand did not accept the amendment.

(vi) The Delegation of Japan proposed insertion of the following additional paragraph in the Article in relation to proposal under note (iv) :

"A person who was outside of the State of which he is a national or the Country of his nationality, or if he has no nationality, the State or the Country of which he is a habitual resident, at the time of the events which caused him to have a well-founded fear of above-mentioned persecution and is unable or unwilling to return to it or to avail himself of its protection shall be considered refugee".

The Delegations of Ceylon, India, Indonesia, Iraq and Pakistan were of the view that this additional paragraph was unnecessary. The Delegation of Thailand reserved its position on this paragraph.

Article II

Loss of status as refugee

1. A refugee shall lose his status as refugee if—

(i) he voluntarily returns permanently to the State of which he was a national or the Country of his nationality or if he has no nationality to the State or the Country of which he was a habitual resident ; or

(ii) he has voluntarily re-availed himself of the protection of the State or Country of his nationality ; or

(iii) he voluntarily acquires the nationality of another State or Country and is entitled to the protection of that State or Country.

2. A refugee shall lose his status as a refugee if he does not return to the State of which he is a national, or to the country of his nationality, or, if he has no nationality, to the State or Country of which he was a habitual resident, or if he fails to avail himself of the protection of such State or Country after the circumstances in which he became a refugee have ceased to exist.

Explanation :

It would be for the State of asylum of the refugee to decide whether the circumstances in which he became a refugee have ceased to exist.

NOTES

(i) The Delegations of Iraq and the United Arab Republic reserved their position on paragraph 1 (iii).

(ii) The Delegation of Thailand wished it to be recorded that the loss of status as a refugee under paragraph 1 (ii) will take place only when the refugee has successfully re-availed himself of the protection of the State of his nationality because the right of protection was that of his country and not that of the individual. ·

Article III

Asylum to a refugee

1. A State has the sovereign right to grant or refuse asylum in its territory to a refugee.

2. The exercise of the right to grant such asylum to a refugee shall be respected by all other States and shall not be regarded as an unfriendly act.

3. No one seeking asylum in accordance with these Principles should, except for overriding reasons of national security or safeguarding the populations, be subjected to measures such as rejection at the frontier, return or expulsion which would result in compelling him to return to or remain in a territory if there is a well-founded fear of persecution endangering his life, physical integrity or liberty in that territory.

4. In cases where a State decides to apply any of the abovementioned measures to a person seeking asylum, it should grant provisional asylum under such conditions as it may deem appropriate, to enable the person thus endangered to seek asylum in another country.

Article IV

Right of return

A refugee shall have the right to return if he so chooses to the State of which he is a national or to the country of his nationality and in this event it shall be the duty of such State or Country to receive him.

Article V

Right to compensation

1. A refugee shall have the right to receive compensation from the State or the Country which he left or to which he was unable to return.

2. The compensation referred to in paragraph 1 shall be for such loss as bodily injury, deprivation of personal liberty in denial of human rights, death of dependants of the refugee or of the person whose dependant the refugee was,

and destruction of or damage to property and assets, caused by the authorities of the State or Country, public officials or mob violence.

NOTES

(i) The Delegations of Pakistan and the United Arab Republic were of the view that the word "also" should be inserted before the words "such loss" in paragraph 2.

(ii) The Delegations of India and Japan expressed the view that the words "deprivation of personal liberty in denial of human rights" should be omitted.

(iii) The Delegations of Ceylon, Japan and Thailand suggested that the words "in the circumstances in which the State would incur state responsibility for such treatment to aliens under international law" should be added at the end of paragraph 2.

(iv) The Delegations of Ceylon, Japan, Pakistan and Thailand expressed the view that compensation should be payable also in respect of the denial of the refugee's right to return to the State of which he is a national.

(v) The Delegation of Ceylon was opposed to the inclusion of the words "or country" in this Article.

(vi) The Delegations of Ceylon, Ghana, India and Indonesia were of the view that in order to clarify the position the words "arising out of events which gave rise to the refugee leaving such State or Country" should be added to paragraph 2 of this Article after the words "mob violence".

Article VI

Minimum standard of treatment

1. A State shall accord to refugees treatment in no way less fovourable than that generally accorded to aliens in similar circumstances.

2. The standard of treatment referred to in the preceding clause shall include the rights relating to aliens contained in the Final Report of the Committee on the Status of Aliens, appen-

ded to these principles, to the extent that they are applicable to refugees.

3. A refugee shall not be denied any rights on the ground that he does not fulfil requirements which by their nature a refugee is incapable of fulfilling.

4. A refugee shall not be denied any rights on the ground that there is no reciprocity in regard to the grant of such rights between the receiving State or Country of nationality of the refugee or, if he is stateless, the State or Country of his former habitual residence.

NOTES

(i) The Delegations of Iraq and Pakistan were of the view that a refugee should generally be granted the standard of treatment applicable to the nationals of the country of asylum.

(ii) The Delegation of Indonesia reserved its position on paragraph 3 of the Article.

(iii) The Delegations of Indonesia and Thailand reserved their position on paragraph 4 of the Article.

Article VII

Obligations

A refugee shall not engage in subversive activities endangering the national security of the country of refuge, or in activities inconsistent with or against the principles and purposes of the United Nations.

NOTES

(i) The Delegations of India, Japan and Thailand were of the view that the words "or any other country" should be added after the words "the country of refuge" in this Article. The other Delegations were of the view that such addition was not necessary.

(ii) The Delegation of Iraq was of the view that the inclusion of the words "or in activities inconsistent with or against the principles and purposes of the United Nations" was inappropriate as in this Article what was being dealt with was the right and obligation of the refugee and not that of the State.

Article VIII

Expulsion and deportation

1. Save in the national or public interest or on the ground of violation of the conditions of asylum, the State shall not expel a refugee.

2. Before expelling a refugee, the State shall allow him a reasonable period within which to seek admission into another State. The State shall, however, have the right to apply during the period such internal measures as it may deem necessary.

3. A refugee shall not be deported or returned to a State or Country where his life or liberty would be threatened for reasons of race, colour, religion, political belief or membership of a particular social group.

NOTES

(i) The Delegations of Ceylon, Ghana · and Japan did not accept the text of paragraph 1. In the view of these Delegations the text of this paragraph should read as follows :

A State shall not expel or deport a refugee save on grounds of national security or public order, or a violation of any of the vital or fundamental conditions of asylum".

(ii) The Delegations of Ceylon and Ghana were of the view that in paragraph 2 the words "as generally applicable to aliens under such circumstances" should be added at the end of the paragraph after the word "necessary".

Article IX

Nothing in these articles shall be deemed to impair any higher rights and benefits granted or which may hereafter be granted by a State to refugees.

(14) FINAL REPORT OF THE COMMITTEE ON RELIEF AGAINST DOUBLE OR MULTIPLE TAXATION, 1967

Adopted in New Delhi on December, 1967, at the Ninth Session of the Asian-African Legal Consultative Committee.

Text from ASIAN-AFRICAN LEGAL CONSULTATIVE COMMITTEE, Report of the Ninth Session, Part 3, pp. 98-107.

The subject of Relief Against Double or Multiple Taxation was referred to the Committee by the Government of India under the provisions of Article 3 (c) of the Statutes of the Committee for exchange of views and information between the participating countries.

2. The Committee took up the subject for preliminary discussion during its Fourth Session held in Tokyo in 1961. A Sub-Committee was appointed at that Session to examine in what manner the Committee should treat the problem of avoidance of double or multiple taxation and fiscal evasion. The Committee at that Session on the recommendations of the Sub-Committee decided that the Secretariat should request the Governments of the participating States to forward to the Secretariat the texts of agreements on avoidance of double taxation concluded by them and the texts of the provisions of their municipal laws concerning the subject. The Committee also directed its Secretariat to draw up a questionnaire and the topics for discussion and send the same to the Governments of the participating countries.

3. In accordance with the directions of the Committee the Secretariat invited the Governments of the participating States to send answers to the quetionnaire and their views on the topics for discussion. The Secretariat also prepared a brief dealing with the topics mentioned in the questionnaire on the basis of the information supplied by the Governments of the participating countries as also on the general State practice as gathered from different sources, such as international agreements, municipal legislations of different countries and studies done by governmental and private organisations.

4. At the Sixth Session of the Committee held in Cairo in 1964 a Sub-Committee was appointed to examine the question

on the basis of the information collected by the Secretariat. The Sub-Committee after a preliminary exchange of views recommended that though bilateral double taxation agreements provided a practical solution to the financial problems which arose from the economic intercourse of nations, it was desirable to have an exchange of views on the techniques employed by the participating States, their experiences and practices with a view to drawing up of a model multilateral convention. The matter was again considered by a Sub-Committee appointed at the Seventh Session held in Baghdad in 1965. That Sub-Committee reported that the conflicting interests of the countries, the varied patterns of their taxing laws, different tax structures and absence of a universally acceptable system of tax distribution among various countries would make the task of proposing any model agreement on this subject to be extremely difficult. Nevertheless, having regard to the vital importance of the subject to developing countries for economic co-operation, expansion of trade and business, exchange of technical knowledge and cultural activities, flow of capital and business enterprises, the Sub-Committee thought that certain broad principles should be formulated for consideration of the Governments of the participating States. 'The Sub-Committee therefore drew up certain general principles but excluded from the scope of its report the questions relating to tax on trade, business, industry and other related topics. The subject was further considered by another Sub-Committee appointed at the Eighth Session. That Sub-Committee was able to formulate certain general principles on the topics left over from the Seventh Session.

5. The Reports submitted by the Sub-Committees appointed at the Seventh and the Eighth Sessions were placed before this Committee for consideration at this Session. The Committee after general discussion of the reports of the two Sub-Committees have found the principles formulated by the Sub-Committees generally acceptable. Having regard to the fact that the Committee's functions under its Statutes are of an advisory character, the Committee considers that the appropriate manner in which it could deal with this subject is to formulate the principles for avoidance of double or multiple taxation and it would be upto the Government of each participating State to decide as to how it would give effect to the Committee's recommendations whether by entering into multilateral or bilateral arrangements or by incorporating the principles formulated by the Committee in their own municipal laws. In this view of the matter the Committee has formulated the general principles on the

subject which are set out in the *Annexure* to this Report.

Sd.- (C. K. Daphtary)
President. ·

ANNEXURE

General principles recommended for adoption in international agreements for avoidance of double or multiple taxation of income

PART I

GENERAL

1. Relief against double taxation of the same income by two or more countries is given either unilaterally or by the countries concerned entering into bilateral or multilateral agreements providing for such relief.

2. Bilateral agreements which take care of the special relations between the two countries afford the most practical method for providing relief against double taxation.

3. The laws of the Contracting States should contain provisions empowering their Governments to grant relief against double or multiple taxation unilaterally and also to enter into bilateral or multilateral treaties or agreements setting forth the principles for granting such relief on a reciprocal or non-reciprocal basis and to implement them.

4. The laws in force in each of the contracting States will govern the assessment and taxation of income in that State except where express provision to the contrary is made in the agreement.

5. The agreements should cover the taxes on income and capital gains imposed under the law of each of the Contracing States.

6. The agreements should provide that they will also apply to any other taxes of a substantially similar character imposed in each of the Contracting States subsequent to the date of the agreements.

7. The Contracting States shall not impose upon the nationals of other countries more burdensome taxes than they impose upon their own nationals.

658

PART II

DEFINITIONS

8. The agreements should contain definitions of important terms used therein, such for example as "person", "company", "enterprise of a Contracting State", "resident of a Contracting State", "permanent establishment" etc.

9. The term "person" includes natural persons, companies and all other entities which are treated as taxable units under the tax laws of the respective Contracting States.

10. "Company" will mean any body corporate or entity which is treated as a body corporate for tax purposes under the tax laws of the respective Contracting States.

11. "Enterprise of a Contracting State" will mean an industrial or commercial enterprise or undertaking carried on in that Contracting State by a resident of that State.

12. The expression "resident of a Contracting State" will mean any person who under the law of that State is a resident of that State for the purpose of taxation in that State and not a resident of the other Contracting State for the purpose of taxation in that other State.

13. A "company" will be deemed to be a resident of the Contracting State in which its business is wholly managed and controlled.

14. (i) The term "permanent establishment" will mean a fixed place of business in which the business of the enterprise is wholly or partly carried on and will include a place of management, a branch, an office, a factory, a workshop, a warehouse, a mine, a quarry or other place of extraction of natural resources and a permanent sales·exhibition.

(ii) An enterprise of one of the Contracting States should be deemed to have a permanent establishment in the other Contracting State if it carries on in that other State a construction, installation or assembly project or the like.

(iii) The use of mere storage facilities will not constitute the place a permanent establishment.

OR

The use of mere storage facilities or the maintenance of a place of business exclusively for the purchase of goods or merchandise and not for the purpose of display or for any processing of such goods or merchandise in the territory of purchase will not constitute a permanent establishment.

(iv) A person acting in one of the Contracting States for or on behalf of an enterprise of the other Contracting State will be deemed to be a permanent establishment of that enterprise in the first mentioned State if—

    (a) he has and habitually exercises in the first mentioned State a general authority to negotiate and enter into contracts for or on behalf of that enterprise, or

    (b) he habitually maintains in the first mentioned State a stock of goods or merchandise belonging to that enterprise from which he regularly delivers goods or merchandise for or on behalf of the enterprise, or

    (c) he habitually secures orders in the first mentioned enterprise wholly or almost wholly for the enterprise itself or for the enterprise and other enterprises which are controlled by it or have a controlling interest in it.

v) A broker of a genuinely independent status who merely acts as an intermediary between an enterprise of one of the Contracting States and at prospective customer in the other Contracting State will not be deemed to be a permanent establishment of the enterprise.

(vi) The fact that a company is a resident of a Contracting State and has a subsidiary company which is resident of the other Contracting State or which carries on trade or business in that other State (whether through a permanent establishment or otherwise) shall not of itself constitute that subsidiary company a permanen establishment of its parent company or shall not constitute either company a permanent establishment of the other.

660

PART III

ALLOCATION OF TAX JURISDICTION

15. Income from immovable property may be taxed by the State in which such property is situated.

16. Royalties and profits from operation of mines, quarries and of extraction and exploitation of other natural resources may be taxed by the State in which such mining or quarrying operations are carried on.

17. Profits derived by a resident of one of the Contracting States from operations of international shipping or flights may be taxed by the State in which the enterprise is registered or where its business is wholly managed or controlled unless the vessel or aircraft is operated wholly or mainly between places in the other Contracting State. In the alternative, if this allocation is considered disadvantageous to participating countries, this source may be allocated exclusively to the taxing jurisdiction of the State in which the profits are earned.

18. Industrial and commercial profits of an enterprise of one of the Contracting States should be taxed in the other Contracting State only if that enterprise carries on trade or business in that other Contracting State through a permanent establishment situated therein. Such taxes should be levied only on such profits of that enterprise as are attributable to the permanent establishment situated in the taxing State.

19. Income from movable capital, such as, dividends paid by a company, interests on bonds, loans, securities or debentures issued by Governments, local authorities, companies or other corporate bodies should be taxed in the country where the investment is made and not in the country of residence of the recipient of such income.

20. Capital gains derived from the sale, exchange or transfer of a capital asset, whether movable or immovable, should be taxed only in the State in which the capital asset is situated at the time of such sale, exchange or transfer. For this purpose the *situs* of the shares of a company should be deemed to be the country in which the company is incorporated. (Capital assets would not include movable property in the form of personal effects like wearing apparel, jwellery and furniture held for personal use by the tax payer or any member of his family dependent on him).

21. Remuneration including pensions and gratuities paid in one of the Contracting States for services rendered therein,

out of Government funds or funds belonging to a local authority, in the other Contracting State should not be taxed in the first mentioned Contracting State.

22. Profits or remuneration for professional services (including services as a director) derived by an individual who is a resident of one of the Contracting States may be taxed in the other Contracting State only if such services are rendered in the territory of that other State.

23. A professor or a teacher from one of the Contracting States who receives remuneration for teaching during a period of temporary residence not exceeding two years at a University, college, school or other educational institution in the other Contracting State should not be taxed in that other State in respect of such remuneration.

24. An individual from one of the Contracting States who is temporarily present in the other Contracting State solely as—

    (a)   a student at a University, college or school, or

    (b)   as a business apprentice, or

    (c)   as a recipient of a grant, scholarship or other allowance or award for the primary purpose of study or research, from religious, charitable, scientific or educational organisations—

should not be taxed in that other Contracting State in respect of remittances from abroad for the purposes of his maintenance, education or training, in respect of a scholarship and in respect of any amount representing remuneration from an employment which he exercises in that other territory for the purpose of practical training.

25. An individual from one of the Contracting States who is present in the other Contracting State solely as a student at a University, college or school in that other State, or as a business apprentice, should not be taxed in that other State for a period not exceeding three consecutive years in respect of remuneration from employment in such other State if the remuneration (a) constitutes earnings necessary for his maintenance and education and (b) does not exceed a certain sum to be settled by agreement between the Contracting States.

26. Royalties and profits earned as a consideration for the use of, or the right to use any copyright, patents, trademarks, trade-names, designs etc. will be taxable in the State in which such property is used.

PART IV

MISCELLANEOUS

27. As a means of giving relief against double taxation of the same income the Contracting States may as far as possible adopt the method of exemption in preference to the tax credit method. Alternately, they may use a combination of both the methods.

28. If the tax credit method is used in preference to the exemption method, the agreements should provide that special tax concessions which are given by way of incentive measures designed to promote economic development, such as, tax holidays or development rebates, should not be taken into consideration in granting relief against double taxation and full credit should be given for the tax which would normally have been payable, but for such concessions.

29. The Contracting States should exchange such information as is necessary for carrying out the provisions of the agreements. The information so exchanged should be treated as secret and should not be disclosed to any persons other than hose concerned with the assessment and collection of taxes which are the subject of the agreement. No information should be exchanged which would disclose any trade, business, industrial or professional secret or any trade process.

30. If the action of the taxing authorities of one of the Contracting States results in double taxation contrary to the provisions of the agreement, any tax-payer may make representations to the competent authority of the Contracting State of which the tax-payer is a resident and that authority should be given the right to present his case to the appropriate authorities of the taxing State. Every effort should be made to come to an agreement with a view to avoiding double taxation and ensuring fair implementation of the agreement between the two States.

(i) *In regard to paragraph 19 :*

The Delegation of Japan stated that the principal taxing authority should be vested in the country of residence of the recipient of income and, therefore, the tax to be charged in the country where the investment is made should be restricted to certain limits.

(ii)   *In regard to paragraph 20* :

The Delegation of Japan stated that capital gains in regard to movable property other than those pertaining to a permanent establishment or to a fixed base may be taxed in the country of residence of the alienator.

(iii)   *In regard to paragraph 28* :

The Delegation of U.A.R. pointed out that the U.A.R. tax laws grant certain exemptions on tax on profits of an industrial or commercial establishment in Free Zones and also on wages and salaries paid by such establishments in Free Zones to foreigners in their employment. The U.A.R. Delegation is of the view that such concessions also should not be taken into account in granting relief against double taxation.

D. DOCUMENTS OF THE AFRO-ASIAN RURAL RECONSTRUCTION ORGANIZATION

A. BASIC DOCUMENTS

(15) CONSTITUTION, 1962

Adopted in Cairo on March 19-31, 1962, at the 2nd
Afro-Asian Rural Reconstruction Conference. Amended
at the 10th Session of the Executive Committee and
ratified by the 4th General Session of the Conference
in Accra, October, 1971.

PREAMBLE

Whereas the Governments in various countries of the continents of Africa and Asia and the national farmers' organizations, in those countries, accepting this Constitution :

Being determined to launch concerted and, wherever possible, coordinated action to reconstruct the economy of their rural people and revitalise their social and cultural life ;

Being convinced that, in the developing countries of Africa and Asia, where very similar problems confront the task of rural reconstruction, such a concerted action could be possible through a joint, planned and coordinated efforts of the Governments and the people ;

Agree hereby to establish the Afro-Asian Rural Reconstruction Organization, hereinafter referred to as the "Organization", which may afford an opportunity to the representatives of the Governments and the rural people ;

To jointly discuss their problems and exchange views, ideas, information and experiences ;

To formulate plans, devise means and take necessary action for the achievement of the above objectives.

Article I

FUNCTIONS

The functions of the Organization shall be :

1. To develop understanding among members for better appreciation of each others'

problems and to explore, collectively, opportunities for coordination of efforts for promoting welfare and eradication of hunger and poverty amongst rural people in Africa and Asia ;

2. To assist the member countries in obtaining financial and technical assistance for their Rural Development Programmes, from the financial and Specialised Agencies like the International Bank for Reconstruction and Development (World Bank), the Asian Development Bank, the African Development Bank, various organs of the United Nations including its specialised Agencies, the national and governmental or non-official agencies in the developed and developing countries etc. ;

3. To collaborate with the appropriate international and regional organizations and agencies, national level governmental or non-governmental agencies in the developed and developing countries for the purpose of taking such action as may accelerate the pace of Rural Development in the member countries ;

4. To lay the views of the Organization before any Committee, Commission or Organization—international, regional, national etc ;

5. To assist in the formation and development of non-governmental, non-political and non-sectarian organizations of farmers and the establishment of healthy relationship between them and the governmental agencies responsible for agricultural development and rural reconstruction ;

6. To promote principles of cooperation and cooperative activities in the various phases of the life of the rural people ;

7. To promote exchange of farmers and experts from one country to the other ;

8. To organise international and regional meetings, seminars, conferences, exhibitions and fairs and produce literature and undertake publicity ;

9. To initiate studies on subjects of common interests and collect, analyse, interpret and disseminate data, statistics and information useful to members ;

10. To consider the possibilities of and assisting, in if necessary, the disposal or exchange of surplus agricultural commodities among members and others ;

11. To raise funds by contributions and donations and hold property, movable or immovable, in any member country or outside ;

12. To do all things incidental to and take all actions calculated to achieve the objects of the Organization.

Article II

MEMBERSHIP

1. The membership of AARRO shall be open to :

    (a) All countries invited to the First or Second Afro-Asian Rural Reconstruction Conference held in New Delhi and Cairo during 1961 and 1962 respectively. List of countries at Annexure I,

    (b) Any other country in Africa and Asia, not represented at the above two Conferences, provided it is a full or associate member of the United Nations or any of its Specialised Agencies and is included in the regional set up as at present prescribed for the African and Asian regions by the Food and Agricultural Organization (African Region, Near East Region and Asia and Far East Region) as per the Statement at Annexure II,

2. Any other country geographically situated within the Australasian Region such as Australia and New Zealand, may apply for Associate Membership of the Organization. The Associate Members will enjoy all the rights and will be subject to all the obligations, except that they will not have the right to vote ;

3. The membership of AARRO, Full or Associate, can be held by the Government of a country, or, with the approval of the Government concerned, by a governmental or non-governmental apex level organization of farmers and rural people interested in Rural Development ;

4. Application for membership under the above clauses shall be made by the government or by the interested body through the Government, on the prescribed form (Specimen at Annexure II) and shall be presented to the Secretariat of AARRO ;

5. The countries covered under Clause 1 and 2 will automatically become members of the Organization as soon as the formal Notice of Acceptance is received in the Secretariat ;

    (a) The applications received from the countries or the organizations covered under Clause 1 (b) above will be circulated by the Secretariat among the full members of the Organization for admission as a full member of AARRO. In case no objection is received within 90 days of the issuance of the circular, the Secretary General would admit the country concerned as a member of the Organization ;

    (b) In case of any objection, the matter shall be referred by the Secretary General to the General Session of the AARRO Conference for its final decision ;

6. All the new members admitted during the interval between the two General Sessions of the AARRO Conference shall be reported to the General Session of the AARRO Conference for formal ratification.

Article III

ORGANS OF THE ORGANIZATION

The Organs of the Organization shall be (1) the Conference, (2) the Executive Committee and (3) the Secretariat.

Article IV

CONFERENCE

1. There shall be a Conference of the Organization in which each member country will be represented by a delegation. The Conference shall be known as the Conference of the Afro-Asian Rural Reconstruction Organization or the AARRO Conference.

2. The supreme authority regarding all matters relating to the Organization shall vest in the AARRO Conference whose decision shall be final and binding on all concerned.

3. No delegation shall represent more than one member country.

4. Each member country shall be entitled, through its delegation, to vote at any session of the Conference, provided that no delegation shall have more than one vote.

5. The Conference may extend invitation to any international or regional organization, governmental or non-governmental, to be represented at its session on conditions laid down by the Conference, but no delegate representing such organizations shall have the right to vote.

6. The Conference shall adopt its own rules of procedure.

7. The Conference shall determine the policies and approve the budget of the Organization.

8. The Conference shall exercise full control over the finances of the Organization including the holding of movable and immovable assets, if any, and make rules for the administration of the same by the Executive Committee.

9. (a) The Conference shall formally ratify the admission of new members admitted into the Organization during the interval between its two General Sessions ; and

   (b) The Conference shall also take decision, by a three-fourths majority vote of the members present and voting, on pending cases, if any, for the membership of the Organization.

Article V

SESSIONS OF THE CONFERENCE

1. The Conference shall, at each general session, decide the venue of the next General Session of the Conference, and the date thereof, if possible.

2. The Conference shall meet in a General Session atleast once within the period of thirty-six months from the date of conclusion of the past Conference.

3. A Special Session of the Conference shall be convened by the Secretary General on the receipt of a requisition from two-thirds of the members of the Organization.

Article VI

PRESIDENT AND VICE-PRESIDENTS

1. The AARRO Conference shall elect one President at each of its regular General Sessions. It shall also elect, at the same time, two Vice-Presidents, one each from the African and Asian Regions.

2. The President shall be the formal head of the Organization. He shall preside over the General Sessions of the AARRO Conference, the meetings of the Executive Committee and any other meetings of the AARRO.

3. The President shall enjoy a casting vote in case of a tie.

4. The President shall exercise, during the interval between the two Sessions of the Executive Committee, all the powers of the Executive Committee of AARRO. All decisions of the President shall, however, be placed before the next meeting of the Executive Commitee for confirmation.

5. The President may delegate to one of Vice-Presidents the authority to his exercise and powers functions.

Article VII

EXECUTIVE COMMITTEE

1. The Conference shall, at each session, elect nine members, who, with the President and the Vice-Presidents, shall constitute the Executive Committee of the Organization. This Executive Committee shall hold office until the new election is held. All office bearers and members of the Executive Committee may be eligible for re-election.

2. The out-going President of the Organization shall be an ex-officio member of the Executive Committee.

3. Five members of the Executive Committee shall form the quorum.

4. Any vacancy occuring on the Executive Committee on any account whatsoever shall be filled by the Executive Committee by appointing another member. The Secretary General shall make suitable proposals to the Executive Committee in this behalf. Any member so appointed will hold office till the current term of the Executive Committee.

5. The Executive Committee shall adopt its own rules of procedure.

6. The Executive Committee shall meet atleast three times in between the two General sessions of the AARRO Conference. Of these, atleast one Session shall be during the non-Conference years.

7. The meeting of the Executive Committee shall also be convened by the Secretary General, if two-thirds members of the Executive Committee request him to do so.

8. The Executive Committee shall deal with all matters which are entrusted to it by the Conference and shall take all steps to implement the decisions and policies of the Conference.

9. The Executive Committee shall enjoy, during the interval between two general sessions of the AARRO Conference, all the powers of the Conference.

10. The Executive Committee may establish any committee which may be required in the interest of the Organization.

Article VIII

SECRETARY GENERAL AND STAFF

1. The Secretary General shall be appointed by the Conference on such terms and conditions as it may lay down from time to time.

2. The Secretary General shall carry out the policies and programmes of the Organization.

3. The Secretary General shall prepare all documents and papers for the consideration of the Executive Committee and the Conference. He shall supervise and direct the work of the Secretariat.

4. The staff of the Organization shall be appointed by the Secretary General in accordance with the terms and conditions laid down by the Conference and the Executive Committee, from time to time.

5. The Secretary General shall participate in the meetings of the Executive Committee and the Conference without the right to vote.

6. The Secretary General shall be competant to receive contributions from members and other sources. He shall prepare the budget of the Organization in accordance with the directives of the Conference and the Executive Committee. The Secretary General would also have the accounts of the Organization audited and present these to the Executive Committee for approval and submission to the Conference.

Article IX

MEMBERSHIP CONTRIBUTIONS

1. The membership contribution payable by each member, Full or Associate, shall be determined by the Conference from time to time.

2. The membership contribution for the current year shall be paid by each member within sixty days of the conclusion of the previous financial year.

3. The financial year of the Organization shall be the Gregorian Calendar year, i.e. from January 1st to December 31st of each year.

Article X

FUNDS AND ASSETS

The Executive Committee shall determine the procedure to raise, hold, invest and administer the funds and assets, movale and immovable, of the Organization.

Article XI

HEADQUARTERS AND REGIONAL OFFICES

1. The Headquarters of the Organization shall be at New Delhi, India as has been decided by the Conference.

2. The Conference may establish Regional and other Offices of the Organization and assign to them such functions as may be required.

Article XII

LANGUAGES

The working languages of the Organization shall be English and French.

Article XIII

AMENDMENT OF THE CONSTITUTION

1. The Constitution may be amended by the Conference by a two-thirds majority of the total members of the Organization provided that :

(a) At least one hundred and twenty days' notice of such amendment has been received by the Secretariat before the date of the commencement of the next

Conference ; and

(b) It has been communicated to the members by the Secretariat at least sixty days before the date of commencement of the next Conference.

2. Amendments to the Constitution may also be proposed by the President, Vice-Presidents or the Secretary General and shall be governed by the procedures laid down above.

Article XIV

WITHDRAWAL FROM MEMBERSHIP

1. Any member may withdraw from the Organization by submitting a written notification to the Secretariat.

2. The member country fulfilling the above provision shall be permitted to withdraw after the expiry of a period of one year from the date of the receipt of such notification by the Secretariat. However, it shall be liable to discharge all obligations of membership untill the period of one year is over.

Article XV

DISSOLUTION

1. The Organization may be dissolved, at any time, by a decision of the Conference arrived at by a three-fourths majority of the total members of the Organization.

2. The above decision shall provide for the discharge of all liabilities and the disposal of all funds or assets of the Organization.

Article XVI

The Constitution of AARRO as adopted by the Second Afro-Asian Rural Reconstruction Conference held at Cairo from March 19 to 31, 1962, and as amended thereafter from time to time, shall be binding on all members of the Organization.

List of Countries invited to the First and Second

Afro-Asian Rural Reconstruction Conference in 1961 and 1962

ASIAN COUNTRIES

1. Afghanistan
2. Burma
3. Ceylon
4. Cambodia
5. Malaysia
6. Indonesia
7. Iran
8. Iraq
9. Japan
10. Jordan
11. Laos
12. Lebanon
13. Nepal
14. Pakistan
15. Philippines
16. Saudi Arabia
17. Thailand
18. Turkey
19. Yeman
20. Vietnam (South)
21. India
22. Korea
23. Syria

AFRICAN COUNTRIES

1. Cameroun
2. Ethiopia
3. Ghana
4. Liberia
5. Morocco
6. Sudan
7. Tunisia
8. UAR
9. Libya
10. Togo
11. Guinea
12. Somalia
13. Nigeria
14. Federation of Rhodesia & Nyasaland
15. Republic of Chad
16. Madagascar
17. Republic of Gabon
18. Republic of Senegal
19. Republic of Ivory Coast
20. Tanganyika
21. Central African Republic
22. Upper Volta
23. Mauritania
24. Mali
25. Niger
26. Zanzibar

ASIAN AND FAR EAST REGION

1. Burma
2. Cambodia
3. Indonesia
4. Japan
5. Korea
6. Laos
7. Malaysia

8. Pakistan
9. Philippines
10. Thailand
11. Viet-Nam (South)
12. Ceylon
13. India
14. Nepal

NEAR EAST REGION

1. Afghanistan
2. Baheren
3. Iran
4. Iraq
5. Jordan
6. Kuwait
7. Lebanon
8. Libya

9. Pakistan
10. Qatar
11. Saudi Arabia
12. Somali Republic
13. Syrian Arab Republic
14. United Arab Republic
15. Yemen
16. Cyprus

AFRICA REGION

1. Algeria
2. Cameroun
3. Central African Republic
4. Chad
5. Congo (Brazzaville)
6. Republic of Congo
7. Dahomey

8. Gabon
9. Gambia
10. Ghana
11. Guinea

12. Ivory Coast
13. Liberia
14. Mali
15. Mauritania
16. Morocco
17. Nigeria
18. Niger
19. Senegal
20. Sierra Leone
21. Togo
22. Tunisia
23. Upper Volta

EAST AFRICAN REGION

1. Botswana
2. Ethiopia
3. Kenya
4. Lesotho
5. Madagascar
6. Malawi
7. Ruwanda
8. Sudan
9. Tanzania
10. Uganda
11. Zambia

(15) RULES OF PROCEDURE OF THE ORGANIZATION, 1962

Adopted in Cairo on March 19-31, 1962, at the 2nd
Afro-Asian Rural Reconstruction Conference. Amended
at the 10th Session of the Executive Committee and
ratified by the 4th General Session of the Conference
in Accra, October, 1971.

A. THE CONFERENCE

I. SESSIONS OF THE CONFERENCE

1. General Session :

   (a) Venue and Dates :

Rule : 1.   The Conference shall meet in a General Session at least once during the period of thirty six months. It shall, at each Session, decide the date and place at which the next General Session will be held.

Rule : 2.   The General Session should be held alternately in the continents of Africa and Asia. Any Member Country may extend an invitation to the Conference to hold the next General Session in its country. This invitation will, as a rule, be communicated to the Secretary General by the the Member country before opening of the preceding General Session of the Conference.

Rule : 3.   The opening date and the period of the General Session shall be decided by the Secretary General in consultation with the host country, atleast 180 days before the commencement of the Conference.

   (b) Change of Venue and Dates :

Rule : 4.   An occasion may arise when, in the opinion of the Secretary General, it may not be feasible or advisable to hold the General Session of the Conference, in the country whose invitation has been accepted by the Conference. The Secretary General would, in that case, apprise the President of the facts as also might suggest alternate venue. The President might take an appropriate decision and direct the Secretary General to hold the General Session at an other place on the same dates or other dates.

2. Special Session :

Rule : 5.   A special session of the Conference shall be convened by the Secretary if a request is received from atleast two-thirds of the Member Countries of the Organization. This Session shall be ordinarily convened at the Headquarters of the Organization within ninety days of the receipt of the request.

3. *Notices of Sessions* :

le : 6. The Secretary General shall, in the case of a General Session convey notices regarding the venue and the dates of the Session, to Member Countries at least forty-five days in advance.

II. AGENDA

1. *General Session*

(a) Provisional Agenda :

le : 7. The Provisional agenda of the General Session shall be prepared by the Secretary General and communicated to the Member Countries not less than sixty days before the opening of the Session. The contents of the Provisional Agenda shall be :

  (i) Election of President and two Vice-Presidents of the Organization ;

  (ii) Report by the Secretary General since the last General Session of the Conference ;

  (iii) Establishment of Conference Commissions and Committees and election of their office bearers ;

  (iv) Items, proposed by any Member Country, whose inclusion has been agreed to by the Executive Committee in consultation with the Secretary General ;

  (v) Reports of the Executive Committee :—Consideration & Adoption ;

  (vi) Draft Programme of Work and Budget Proposals ;

  (vii) State membership and membership contribution ;

  (viii) Scale of proposed membership contribution ;

  (ix) Amendments to the Constitution, if any ;

  (x) Election of the Executive Committee ;

  (xi) Decision of the venue and dates of the next General Session of the Conference.

  (xii) Any other item with the permission of the Chair.

2. *Special Session*

le : 8. The provisional Agenda for a Special Session of the Conference shall be prepared by the Secretary General and communicated to Member Countries not less than thirty days before the opening of the Session. The contents of the Provisional Agenda shall be :

(i) Any items proposed for consideration in the request received by the Secretary General in accordance with Rule 5 ;

(ii) Any other item approved by the Executive Committee for inclusion in th Agenda.

3. *Supplementary Items* :

Rule : 9.   Any Member Country may, at least fourty-five days before the opening of the Genera Session, request the inclusion of supplementary items on the Agenda. Suc supplementary items shall appear on a Supplementary List which shall be circulate by the Secretary General to the countries at least twenty days before the opening o the Session and shall be presented to the Steering Committee for its consideratio and recommendation to the Conference.

Rule : 10.   The Steering Committee shall recommend, on the basis of the Provisional Agenda, an the Supplementary List if any, the final agenda which will be presented by th President of the Conference for adoption, as soon as possible, after the opening o the Conference.

Rule : 11.   During a Session of Conference, items may be amended or deleted from the fina Agenda by a two-thirds majority of the votes of the members present. New items o importance and urgent character may also be added to the Agenda by the approva of the two-thirds majority of the members present and voting. But no such item shall be considered in the absence of a report on it by the Secretary General, unles the Conference shall otherwise decide in a case of urgency.

Rule : 12.   Annotated agenda notes will be sent along with the Provisional Agenda. Th documents and reports required for consideration of the various items on th provisional Agenda will however, be furnished to the Members as early as possibl before the opening of the Session. The draft programme and budget estimate proposed by the Executive Committee will be furnished to the Members at least thirt days before the opening of the Session. Notes on any emergency items introduce in the Agenda will be furnished at least fourty-eight hours before the consideratio of the item.

III. DELEGATIONS

1. *Composition* :

Rule : 13.   The delegation of each Member Country shall be composed of not more tha ten delegates.

Rule : 14.   Each deligation may also include not more than ten alternate delegates and as man advisers and experts from each country as it may deem necessary. The head of deligation may designate any alternate to act as representative and notify the President of the Conference accordingly.

Rule : 15. The names of these delegates and alternate delegates, experts and advisers shall be communicated to the Secretary General by members not less than thirty days before the opening of the Session of the Conference.

2. *Provisional Admission* :

Rule : 16. Any delegation or representative, to whose admission a member country has made objection, shall be provisionally seated with the same rights as other delegation or representatives, until the Steering Committee has reported and the Conference has given its decision.

IV. ORGANIZATION OF THE CONFERENCE

1. *Opening of the Session* :

Rule : 17. At the opening of each Session of the Conference, the head of the delegation from the country of the past President shall preside until the Conference has elected the new President.

2. *President and Vice-President* :

Rule : 19. Immediately after the inauguration of the Conference and of the address the past President, the Conference shall elect the President of the Conference. The Conference shall also elect two Vice-Presidents, one to represent each of the two continents of Africa and Asia.

Rule : 20. The President, and in his absence, one of the Vice-Presidents named by him shall preside over the Plenary Sessions of the Conference and the meetings of the Steering Committee. He will declare the opening and closing of the Plenary Sessions and discussions, proposed limitation of time on speeches, observance of rules, accord right to speak, put questions to vote and announce decisions. He shall rule on points of order and, subject to the present rules, shall control the proceedings and the maintenance of order.

Rule : 21. The President or the Vice-President acting temporarily as President shall not vote but may designate a member of his delegation to vote for his country.

V. COMMISSIONS & COMMITTEES

1. Commissions :

Rule : 22.   The Conference shall establish, at each General or Special Session, such Commission: Committees and Subsidiary Bodies as deemed necessary for the transaction of the business of the Session. Each Commission, Committee or Subsidiary Body establishe by the Conference may appoint such Drafting Committees as it may need and the: shall elect their own officers.

Rule : 23.   Any Commission or Committee established by the Conference shall consist of on representative of each delegation present at the Session, assisted by such othe members of their delegation as he may require. The Composition of subsidiar Bodies shall be determined in the resolution by which such bodies are established.

Rule : 24.   Each Commission or Committee set up by the Conference, in which all membe countries are represented shall have a Chairman, two Vice-Chairmen and, if necessar a Rapporteur who will be elected by the Conference.

Rule : 25.   The Chairman of each Commission or Committee shall have, in relation to meeting of his Commission or Committee, the same powers and duties as the President of th Conference in relation to the Plenary Sessions. In the absence of the Chairmar one of the Vice-Chairmen will preside.

Rule : 26.   Any other Sub-Committee, or Subsidiary Body set up by the Commission or th Committee, in which only a limited number of members are represented, shall elec a Chairman, and if necessary, a Vice-Chairman and also Rapporteur.

2. Steering Committee :

Rule : 27.   The Conference shall also elect a Steering Committee consisting of its heads of participating delegations or their nominees.

Rule : 28.   The functions of the Steering Committee shall be :

(a)   to fix the hour, date and the order of business of Plenary Session of th Conference ;

(b)   to coordinate the work of the Conference, its Commissions, Committees an Subsidiary Bodies ;

(c)   to consider requests for new items to be put on the Agenda and make a Repor on the subject to the General Conference ;

(d)   to assist the President in directing the general work of the sessions.

Rule : 29. The President of the Conference shall preside at the meetings of the Steering Committee. The Secretary General or, if he is unable to attend, his representative shall serve as the Secretary of the Committee.

VI. SECRETARIAT

Rule : 30. The Secretary General shall act as the Secretary at all Sessions of the Conference including the meeting of its Commissions, Committees and Subsidiary Bodies. He may appoint one or more members of his staff to act in his place at such meetings.

Rule : 31. The Secretary General or a member of the Secretariat designated by him may, at any time, with the approval of the Presiding Officer, make to the Conference, Commission, Committee or Subsidiary Body, either oral or any written statements concerning any question under consideration.

Rule : 32. It shall be the duty of the Secretariat, acting under the authority of the Secretary General, to receive, translate and distribute documents, reports and resolutions of the Conference, its Commissions, Committees ; draft and circulate the records of the meetings ; be responsible for the safe keeping of the documents and records and perform all other work which the Conference may desire.

VII. LANGUAGES

Rule : 33. The working languages of the Organization are English and French. The host country shall make an effort, as far as possible, to arrange for the interpretation of the proceedings of the Conference and its Commissions and Committees in the two languages.

Rule : 34. In case of any extra-ordinary difficulty, the proceedings of the Sessions shall be conducted in one language, which is most widely understood by members of delegations participating in the Conference. In such a case, atleast one Address shall be delivered to the Conference in the second language of the Organization to preserve its status as a working language of the Organization. All documents as well as the Journal of the Conference shall be issued in the languages which are adopted as the working languages of the Conference.

Rule : 35. The delegates shall make speeches, according to their choice, only in one of the working languages of the Conference.

VIII. RECORDS AND REPORTS

Rule : 36. All reports and Documents having bearing on the business of the Conference shall, as far as possible, be kept at all Plenary Sessions at the Conference and made available to delegates, should the necessity arise.

Rule : 37.   The Report of the Conference shall consist of the Summary of the proceedings of the Plenary Sessions and the reports of the Commissions and Committees adopted by the Conference. This report shall be circulated by the Secretary General to Member Countries within six months, after the close of the Session.

IX. PUBLICITY OF MEETINGS

Rule : 38.   The Sessions of the Conference and meetings of its Commissions and Committees and Subsidiary Bodies shall be held in public unless the body concerned decides otherwise subject to any directions given by the Conference. The Secretary General shall decide whether any particular Session of the Conference, Commissions or Committee should be open to the Press.

Rule : 39.   When it is decided to hold a private meeting, all persons shall be excluded except the members of those delegations which are entitled to vote and such representatives and observers as may be specially invited by the body concerned to participate in the deliberations.

Rule : 40.   Any decisions taken at a private session of the Conference, its Commissions and Committees or Subsidiary Bodies shall be announced at the early public meeting of the body concerned.

X. CONDUCT OF BUSINESS

1. Quorum :

Rule : 41.   At the Plenary Sessions of the Conference, its Commissions and Committees, a majority of the Member Countries attending the Sessions, shall constitute the quorum.

2. Points of Order :

Rule : 42.   In the course of a debate any Member Country may raise a point of order and such points of order shall be immediately decided by the President.

3. Voting :

Rule : 43.   Each Member Country, shall have one vote in Conference or in any Commissions, Committees or Subsidiary Bodies. Such Member Country shall, however, have no vote in the Conference or any of its Commissions, Committees and Subsidiary Bodies if it has not paid its membership Contributions for the proceeding two financial years. The Conference may, however, permit the country to exercise its right to vote if it feels that the failure to pay the contribution was due to extra-ordinary circumstances and that the contribution would be forth-coming within prescribed time.

Rule : 44.   Decisions of the Conference shall be taken by a simple majority of the members present and voting. But a three-fourths majority of the members present and voting shall, however, be needed for making amendments to the Constitution and for suspending or amending and Rules of Procedure of the Conference. However, in no case, the number of members voting for the motion shall be less than one half of the members of the Organization.

Rule : 45.   The normal voting shall be by show of hands. But when the result of a vote by show of hands is in doubt, the President may take a second vote by roll call. The counting and recording of votes by show of hands or by roll shall be conducted by or under the supervision of the Conference Elections Officer, appointed by the Secretary General.

Rule : 46.   The Election of the Secretary General and members of the Executive Committee may be by secret ballot, if desired. Any other elections and decisions relating to individuals shall be voted by secret ballot whenever five or more members so request the President or if the latter so decides.

Rule : 47.   The ballot papers for a secret ballot shall be duly initiated by an authorised officer of the Secretariat of the Conference. The Election Officer shall be responsible for ensuring compliance with the requirement. For each ballot only one blank paper shall be given to each delegation entitled to vote.

Rule : 48.   The Secretary General shall be responsible for the safe custody of all ballot papers until the elected candidates take office or for three months after the date of the ballot, whichever is the longer period.

Rule : 49.   Any delegate or representative may challenge the result of a vote or election immediately after the result has been announced. In the case of a vote by a show of hands or roll call vote, should the result be challenged, the Chairman shall cause a second vote to be taken forthwith.

Rule : 50.   A secret ballot may be challenged at any time within three months of the date upon which it took place or until the elected candidate takes office, whichever is the longer period. Should a vote or election by secret ballot be challenged, the Secretary General shall cause the ballot papers and all relevant record sheets to be re-examined and shall circulate the result of the investigation, together with the original complaint, to all members of the Organization.

Rule : 51.   An officer of the Secretariat designated by the Secretary General who shall be known as the Election Officer, shall, with the assistance of a deputy or deputies, be responsible for the following duties :

(a) to ensure that the provisions of the Constitution and the General Rules of the Organization regarding voting and electoral procedures are correctly carried out

(b) to be responsible for all arrangements for voting and elections ;

(c) to advise the President of the Conference on all matters pertaining to voting procedures and mechanics ;

(d) to supervise the preparation of ballot papers and be responsible for their safe custody ;

(e) to report to the Chairman of the Conference the presence of a quorum before any vote is taken ;

(f) to maintain records of all election results, ensuring that they are faithfully recorded and published ;

(g) to undertake such other relevant duties as may arise in connection with voting and elections.

Rule : 52.   In the case of election of two or more persons, the persons obtaining the higher number of votes shall be elected. In the case of equal division of votes, a second vote may be taken, where necessary.

Rule : 53.   The Conference may limit the time to be allowed to each speaker and the number of times any delegate or representatives may speak on any question. When debate is limited and a delegate or representatives has spoken his allotted time, the President shall call him to order without delay.

Rule : 54.   The following motions shall have precedence in the same order over all other proposals or motions before the meeting, except a point of order ;

(a) to suspend the meeting ;

(b) to adjourn the meeting ;

(c) to adjourn the debate on the item under discussion ; and

(d) for the closure of the debate on the item under discussion.

Rule : 55.   Parts of a proposal or an amendment shall be voted on separately if a member requests such division, provided that, if objection is made, the question of division shall be decided by the Conference.

Rule : 56.   When an amendment to a proposal is moved, amendment shall be voted on first. When two or more amendments to a proposal are moved, the Conference shall first vote on the amendment deemed by the President to be furthest removed in substance from the original proposal and then on the amendment next removed therefrom and so on, until all the amendments have been put to the vote.

XI. APPOINTMENT OF THE SECRETARY GENERAL

Rule : 57.   After discussion at a private meeting, the Executive Committee shall submit for approval by the Conference its nomination or nominations for the post of the Secretary General of the Organization. It shall also submit at the time, a draft contract establishing the terms of appointment, salary and allowances of the Secretary General. The Conference shall consider their nomination or nominations and the draft contract at a private meeting and shall come to a decision, if necessary, by a secret ballot.

Rule : 58.   The contract shall be signed jointly by the new Secretary General and the President of the Conference acting in the name of the Organization.

XII. BUDGET AND FINANCE

Rule : 59.   The Conference shall at each regular Session :

(a)   examine and adopt the budget for the ensuing financial period ;

(b)   adopt the final accounts of the Organization for the preceding financial period, after having considered the report of the Executive Committee thereon ;

(c)   consider the report of the Secretary General on the receipt of contributions from Member Countries since the previous session ; and

(d)   on the recommendations of the Executive Committee, or on the request of a Member Country, transmitted to Secretary General not later than 120 days before the opening of the Session, re-examine the scale of contribution of Member Countries.

XIII. CONVENTIONS AND AGREEMENTS

Rule : 60.   The Conference may adopt the drafts of any Conventions or Agreements with any member country or any international organization.

Rule : 61.   The draft of such Convention or Agreement, shall be proposed by the Executive Committee and conveyed to the member countries by the Secretary General along with the documents on the Agenda of the Conference.

XIV. PROCEDURE FOR AMENDMENT OF THE CONSTITUTION

Rule : 62.   The Conference shall also consider the draft amendment or amendments to the Constitution proposed by the President, Vice-Presidents or the Secretary General in accordance with the provisions of the Article XIII Clause 2 of the Constitution provided these amendments have been previously communicated by the Secretariat to the members of the Organization atleast 60 days before the opening of the Conference.

XV. ELECTION OF MEMBERS OF THE EXECUTIVE COMMITTEE

Rule : 63. At each General Session, the Conference shall elect nine members who, with the President and the two Vice-Presidents, shall constitute the Executive Committee of the Organization.

XVI. RULES OF PROCEDURE; SUSPENSION AND AMENDMENTS

Rule : 64. No rule of procedure shall be suspended unless decided by the Conference by a two-thirds majority of Members present and voting.

Rule : 65. Amendments to rules may be made by the Conference by a simple majority of members present and voting but the number of members voting for a motion shall not be less than one-half of the number of members of the Organization. But no amendment shall be moved unless a hundred and twenty days notice for moving such amendment has been received by the Secretary General from the Member country. These amendments shall be communicated to the members by the Secretariat at least sixty days before the date of opening of the Conference.

B. THE EXECUTIVE COMMITTEE

I. MEMBERSHIP AND TENURE

Membership :

Rule : 1. The Executive Committee shall consist of twelve numbers, including the countries represented by the President and the two Vice-Presidents. The out going President of the Organization shall be an ex-officio member of the Executive Committee.

Tenure :

Rule : 2. The tenure of members of the Executive Committee shall be co-extensive with the General Session of the AARRO Conference.

II. ELECTION AND REPRESENTATION

1. Election of Members :

Rule : 3. The nine members of the Executive Committee shall be elected by the AARRO

Conference during its General Session.

Rule : 4. The election of the Executive Committee shall be held at the concluding Plenary Session of the AARRO Conference.

Rule : 5. The nominations for the election of members of the Executive Committee shall be made by the member nations latest by the third day of the opening of the Conference and shall be handed over to the President of the Steering Committee. Each nomination shall be made separately and duly proposed and seconded by two members of the Organization. The nominations shall also contain the consent of the member countries nominated for election. The Steering Committee shall consider the nominations and communicate them to the Conference for consideration and election.

2. Parity and Representation :

Rule : 6. In electing the members of the Committee, the Comference shall observe the rule of parity in distribution of seats among the two continents of Africa and Asia so that the numbers of members of the committee, which will include the President and the two Vice-Presidents, is divided equally and each continent has a representation of six members on the Committee.

Rule : 7. The Conference shall also give the widest possible representation on the Committee to the member countries by rotating the membership in turns among various countries in different regions of Africa and Asia.

III. SESSIONS

1. Chairmanship :

Rule : 8. The President of the Organization shall preside over the Session of the Executive Committee.

Rule : 9. In the absence of the President, one of the Vice-President, or in their absence, a member of the Executive Committee Selected by it shall preside over the sesion.

Rule : 10. The President shall have no vote during the Session of the Executive Committee but he may direct a member of the delegation of his country to vote in his place.

2. Frequency :

Rule : 11. The Executive Committee shall meet three times in between two consecutive Sessions of the AARRO Conference.

Rule : 12. It will hold its First Session at the venue of the Conference immediately after the close of the Conferance. The Second Session will be held sometime during the non-Conference years. The Third Session will be held immediately before the beginning of the Conference at its venue.

Rule : 13.   The Committee, during the First Session, shall appoint the auditors of the Organization for the current period.

Rule : 14.   The Committee during its Second Session, which will be major session, will review the progress of the approved programme of work of the Organization. It will finalize the dates and approve the provisional programme and Agenda of the next General Session of the Conference. It will also consider the Programme and Budget of the Organization for the ending period, and any other matters which need be brought for consideration before the next Conference.

Rule : 15.   The Third session of the Committee will finally consider all the matters to be referred to the next AARRO Conference.

Rule : 16   A Session of the Executive Committee shall also be convened by the Secretary General, upon a request from two-thirds of the members of the Executive Committee.

3.   *Quorum* :

Rule : 17.   Five members of the Committee shall form the quorum for a meeting.

4.   *Agenda* :

Rule : 18.   The Secretary General, in consulation with the President, shall prepare a Provisional Agenda of the Session of the Executive Committee and communicate it to the members not less than forty five days before the commencement of the Session. The documents pertaining to the Agenda shall also be despatched for circulation at least twenty five days before the commencement of the Session.

Rule : 19.   The members of the Committee may request the Secretary General, not less than twenty days before the commencement of the Session, to insert an items in the Provisional Agenda. The Secretary General shall circulate the revised Provisional Agenda to the members together with other papers.

5.   *Publicity and Participation* :

Rule : 20.   The Sessions of the Committee shall be held in private, unless decided otherwise by the Committee.

Rule : 21.   Any member country not represented on the Committee may also submit a note on any item on the Agenda and participate as an observer, in the meeting of the Committee.

6.   *Report* :

Rule : 22.   The report on the work of the Committee shall be communicated to all other members of the Organization. It shall also be submitted to the General Sessions of the AARRO Conference for approval and adoption.

IV. FUNCTIONS

1. *Matters Entrusted by the Conference* :

Rule : 23. The Executive Committee shall deal with all matters which are entrusted to it by the AARRO Conference and shall take steps to implement its decisions and policies. It shall also, between the Sessions of the AARRO Conference, act on its behalf as well as review the current activities of the Organization.

2. *Agenda, Programme and Budget* :

Rule : 24. The Committee shall propose the Provisional Agenda for the General Session of the AARRO Conference, drawing attention to specific policy issues which will require consideration of the Conference and make recommendations to the Conference on the Draft Programme of Work and Budget for the following period particularly with reference to :

(a) Content and balance of the Programme, having regard to the extent to which it may be proposed that existing activities be expanded, reduced in scope or discontinued.

(b) the extent of coordination of work between AARRO and other international organizations.

(c) priority to be given to existing activities, extension of such activities and to new activities.

3. *Administration and Finance* :

Rule : 25. The Committee shall :

(a) exercise control over the administration of funds and movable and immovable assets of the Organization ;

(b) report to the Conference on the financial position and the final audited accounts of the Organization ;

(c) advise the Secretary General on matters of policy affecting administration;

(d) approve transfer of budget allocation from one Head to the other ;

(e) approve the scale of salaries and the conditions of employment of the staff ;

(f) approve the auditors of the Organization.

Rule : 26. The Committee shall review, examine and wherever necessary approve any proposals of the Secretary General regarding short and long-term investments and make recommendations to the Conference on any modification in the scale of contribution and for the creation of a reserve fund or any special fund involving any additional financial implications to the member countries.

4. *Constitution*:

Rule : 27.   The Committee may consider and propose to the Conference any amendment to the Constitution of the Organization or the draft of an agreement or convention to be signed by the Organization with any member country or any international organization.

5. *General* :

Rule : 28.   The Committee may establish any sub-committee for advising on or reviewing of any technical or administrative or financial work and convene a seminar or constitute a working party for the study of any subject.

Rule : 29.   The Committee shall report to the Conference on its work emphasizing any policy matters for consideration.

V.   VOTING

Rule : 30.   Voting at the Sessions of the Committee shall be by show of hands, unless decided otherwise by the Committee.

VI.   RULES OF PROCEDURE

Rule : 31.   The Executive Committee shall adopt its own Rules of Procedure and voting.

Rule : 32.   An amendment to the rules may be proposed by a member of the Executive Committee provided sixty days' notice for making such an amendment has been received by the Secretary General.

C. PRESIDENT AND VICE-PRESIDENTS

I. ELECTIONS

Rule : 1. The office bearers of the Organization would be (1)   The President known as President of AARRO and (2) Vice-President of AARRO—Africa and (3)   Vice-President of AARRO—Asia.

Rule : 2. The offices of the President and two Vice-Presidents would be filled by election. Each regular General Session of AARRO Conference would elect these office bearers who shall be the heads of the delegations participating in the Conference, although the elections would be of the countries and not of individuals.

Rule : 3. The countries concerned would, after the General Session of the AARRO Conference, be approached to appoint finally, the persons who would be ex-officio.

Rule : 4. The nominees for the offices should at least normally be of the ranks of serving Minister of the Government or the heads of the Organization in the case membership is held not by the Government but by an Organization.

Rule : 5. The countries holding the offices would keep the AARRO Secretariat informed regarding any changes in respect of the offices held by the President and the two Vice-Presidents of AARRO.

Rule : 6. The office holders would function in an honorary capacity and shall hold office till new elections are held.

II. FUNCTIONS

Rule : 7. The President shall be the formal head of the Organization.

Rule : 8. The President shall preside over General Sessions of the AARRO Conference, the meetings of the Executive Committee and any other meetings and Conference of the AARRO.

Rule : 9. The President shall exercise, during the interval betweens the two Sessions of the Executive Committee, all the powers of the Executive Committee of AARRO. All decisions of the President shall, however, be placed before the next meeting of the Executive Committee for confirmation.

D. SECRETARY GENERAL

I. APPOINTMENT

1. *Nominations* :

Rule : 1. The nominations for the Post of the Secretary General shall be invited from among the member countries of AARRO, who would be requested to send these direct to the President of the Organization. The President would arrange to convene, as early as possible, a meeting of Executive Committee for considering the nominations and for making a suitable proposal.

Rule : 2. In case a meeting of the Executive Committee cannot be held within a reasonable period of time, the President might circulate the nominations received among the members of the Executive Committee for considering the nominations and for making a suitable proposal.

2. *Appointing Authority* :

Rule : 3. The Secretary General shall be appointed by the General Session of the AARRO Conference.

Rule : 4. In case any necessity arises, the President may make an interim appointment on the basis of the proposal of the Executive Committee.

3. *Terms and Conditions*:

Rule : 5. The Executive Committee shall draw up the contract containing the terms and conditions for the appointment of the regular as well as the interim incumbent of the Post of the Secretary General. The contract shall include the salary, allowances and any other privileges offered to him. The contract shall be presented to the General Session of the AARRO Conference for its approval.

4. *Contract* :

Rule : 6. The Contract shall be signed by the President, on behalf of the Organization, and the candidate who is appointed to the post.

5. Acting Secretary General :

Rule : 7. Pending the appointment of the new Secretary General or during the absence of the regular incumbent of the post, the senior most person in the Secretariat shall act as the Secretary General.

II. FUNCTIONS

1. Execution of Decision :

Rule : 8. The Secretary General shall be the Chief Executive Officer of the Organization and shall convene sessions of the Conference and the Executive Committee and any other Commissions, Committees and Sub-Committees, appointed by them and carry out the decisions taken by these bodies.

2. Direction of Programmes :

Rule : 9. He shall prepare, in the light of guidance given by the Conference at previous sessions, by Commissions or Committees of the Conference and by the Executive Committee, regional or other technical Conference, the draft programme of work and budget of the Organization and submit them to the Conference, after having consulted the Executive Committee.

Rule : 10. He shall have full powers and authority to direct the programmes and execute the policies of the Organization as decided by the Conference and the Executive Committee, and in conformity with the Rules of Procedure of the Organization, and shall also act on behalf of the Organization in all matters.

Rule : 11. He shall keep the members informed regarding the progress of the Organization in a suitable manner and shall present a comprehensive report on the financial, technical and administrative aspects of the work of the Organization at each General Session of the AARRO Conference.

Rule : 12. He shall, if he considers necessary, establish panel of experts or working party or parties to make a study of any subject which may be, in his opinion, useful for the members of the Organization.

3. Administration & Finance :

Rule : 13. He shall be responsible for the internal administration of the Organization and for the appointment and discipline of the staff.

Rule : 14.   He shall request and receive membership contributions and any donations or special contributions and be responsible for proper maintenance and submission of accounts and their audit by the auditors of the Organization.

4. Admission of Members :

Rule : 15.   He shall receive applications for admission to the membership of the Organization and take action in accordance with the provisions of the constitution. He shall also carry out all responsibilities with regard to any conventions and agreements entered into by the Organization with member countries and Organizations.

III. STAFF

1. Appointments :

Rule : 16.   The staff of the Organization shall be appointed by the Secretary General in accordance with the provisions contained in the budget and according to any directions in this regard by the Executive Committee. Selection and remuneration shall be made without regard to race, nationality, creed or sex. The terms and conditions of appointment shall be fixed in contracts concluded between the Secretary General and the members of the staff. Appointment to the posts of the Directors shall be made by the Secretary General, with the prior approval of the Executive Committee, which shall, when necessary, be obtained by circulation.

Rule : 17.   The Secretary General shall submit proposals to the Executive Committee on the scale of salaries and conditions of recruitment and service of the staff and on the general structure of the administrative and technical services of the Organization.

Rule : 18.   The Secretary General, with the approval of the Executive Committee shall promulgate such general staff regulations as may be necessary, including the requirements of declaration of loyalty to the Organization.

Rule : 19.   The Secretary General shall, in so far as may be feasible, arrange for public announcement of staff vacancies and shall fill vacancies in accordance with such competitive methods of selection as he may consider most suitable for various types of appointments. For posts, other than those in the General Service Category, the Secretary General shall invite names from all member countries and make his recommendation to the Executive Committee for its approval. In case of all other appointments, he shall make suitable arrangements for interview and, wherever desirable, test of candidates, and fill the vacancies in accordance with such competitive methods as he may consider necessary for various categories of posts.

Rule : 20.   The staff of the Organization be responsible to the Secretary General. Their responsibility shall be execlusively international in character and they shall not seek or recieve instructions in regard to the discharge thereof from any authority external to the Organization. The member countries undertake fully to respect the international character of the responsibilities of the staff and not to seek to influence any of their nationals in discharge of such responsibilities.

2. *Maintenance of Discipline & Dismissals* :

Rule : 21.   Subject to staff Regulations referred to in Rule 16, the Secretary General shall be free to act according to his own judgement in appointing, assigning or promoting members of staff. He shall also have full powers for their dismissal, except in the case of the Directors, where the approval of the Executive Committee shall be essential, which shall, when necessary, be obtained by circulation.

E. FINANCIAL RULES

1. *Applicability*

Rule : 1.   These rules shall govern the administration of the funds of the Afro-Asian Rural Reconstruction Organization.

2. *Financial Period*

Rule : 2.   The financial year of the Organization shall be the Gregorian Calendar Year but the financial period for purpose of drawing the Budget Estimates and incurring expenditure shall be four calendar years.

3. *Budget*

Rule : 3.   The budget estimates for the financial period shall be prepared by the Secretary General.

Rule : 4.   The estimates shall cover the receipts and expenditure for the financial period and shall be presented in U.S. Dollars.

Rule : 5.   The estimates of expenditure shall be drawn separately for administrative expenditure and for technical projects each, and will be accompanied by such explanatory statements as may be necessary to convey detailed information to the Conference.

Rule : 6.   The Secretary General shall submit the estimates to the Executive Committee for consideration during its second session.

695

Rule : 7.   The budget estimates as finalised by the Executive Committee, alongwith comments if any, by the latter shall be communicated to all member countries atleast sixty days before the beginning of the General Session of the Conference.

Rule : 8.   The budget estimates shall be considered and voted by the General Session of the AARRO Conference.

Rule : 9.   The Secretary General shall incur expenditure according to the provisions contained in the budget estimates voted by the Conference but, whenever necessary, he will propose any supplementary estimates to cover any emergent and unforeseen expenditure. These will be considered and approved by the Executive Committee during its second session and brought to the notice of the Conference during the General Session.

4.   *Appropriations* :

Rule : 10. The funds voted by the General Session of the Conference shall constitute an authorisation to the Secretary General to meet obligations and incur expenditure on purposes for which the amounts had been voted.

Rule : 11. The allocation of funds, although made separately for each financial year, shall be available to the Secretary General for meeting obligations and incurring expenditure during the financial period.

Rule : 12. The allocations shall be available to the Secretary General during the next six months following the end of financial period to which they relate to discharge any obligations and make payments for any goods supplied and services rendered during the financial period.

Rule : 13. At the end of the six months period mentioned in Rule : 12 the unspent appropriations, not utilised within the financial period, shall stand lapsed.

Rule : 14. The Secretary General may, if deemed necessary, effect the transfer of any allocations from one head of the expenditure to another head. Any transfers of allocations so effected by the Secretary General shall be brought to the notice of the Executive Committee during the following Session.

Rule : 15. The Secretary General may propose that any savings, which have been effected in the estimates of the expenditure, may be transferred to Reserve Fund which may be created by the Organization.

5.   *Funds* :

Rule : 16. The funds of the Organization shall be derived from the annual membership contributions by member countries, as also from other sources as mentioned in the Constitution.

Rule : 17. The membership contribution to be paid by each member country shall be fixed by the General Session of the AARRO Conference.

Rule : 18. The annual contributions to be paid by the member countries shall be based on the scale of contributions approved by the Conference.

Rule : 19. The membership contribution for each financial year shall be paid by a member country within sixty day of the conclusion of the previous financial year.

Rule : 20. At the beginning of each financial year, the Secretary General shall inform the member countries regarding the contribution to be paid for the current year and any outstanding payments which were not made by them during the preceding years.

Rule : 21. All contributions by member countries shall be made is US Dollars. In the case of the host country the contributions shall be made in the local currency. In exceptional cases, the Ex-Committee may permit a country to pay its membership contribution in any other convertible currency.

Rule : 22. The Secretary General shall bring to the notice of the Executive Committee, during its second session, the position of the receipt of contributions from member countries. The latter shall bring it to the notice of the Conference for proposing any system which may be followed to expedite the receipt of contributions.

Rule : 23. Any monies, apart from the membership contributions made by member countries and any others, shall be treated as miscellaneous contributions and shall be accepted by the Secretary General for expenditure on purposes specified by the donor and accepted by the Executive Committee.

Rule : 24. The receipt and expenditure of such miscellaneous contributions shall be made during the period for which they have been contributed by the donors.

Rule : 25. All monies belonging to the Organizations shall be kept in such bank or banks in the host country or outside as may be determined by the Executive Committee from time to time and the accounts shall be operated in such manner as may be decided by the Executive Committee.

Rule : 26. The Secretary General may, whenever desirable, make short term investments of monies, not needed for immediate requirements, in fixed deposits.

Rule : 27. All monies proposed to be transferred to the Reserve Fund of the Organization shall be reported by the Secretary General to the Executive Committee. These monies may be invested, thereafter, as long or short term deposits as decided by the Committee.

6. *Internal Control* :

Rule : 28. The Secrerary General shall establish, from time to time, in consultation with the auditors of the Organization, detailed rules of procedure in order to ensure effective adminstration of funds and exercise of economy in accordance with the Financial Rules of the Organization.

Rule : 29. He shall cause all payment to be made on the basis of supporting vouchers and other documents which ensure that services or goods have been duly received and that payment has not been made previously. He may designate the officers who will receive monies and incur obligations and make payments on behalf of the Organization.

Rule : 30. He shall maintain an internal financial control which shall provide for an effective day to day examination of financial transactions in order to ensure the regularity of receipts, custody and disposal of all funds and other resources of the Organization and the conformity of the expenditure with the appropriations voted by the Conference. He shall ensure that no obligations are met unless provision exist for them in the budget voted by the Conference.

Rule : 31. The Secretary General may, during one financial year, write off losses in cash or assets, provided that a statement of all such amounts written off is submitted to the auditors alongwith the annual accounts.

7. *Accounts* :

Rule : 32. Separate accounts shall be maintained of the Reserve Fund.

Rule : 33. The annual accounts of the Organizaton shall be presented in U.S. Dollars. Accounts records may, however, be kept in such currency as the Secretary General may deem necessary.

Rule : 34. The Secretary General shall present at each Session of the Executive Committee a statement showing the current financial position of the Organization.

Rule : 35. The annual accounts for the first calendar year of the financial period shall be submitted by the Secretary General to the auditors not later than 31st March following the end of the year to which they relate.

Rule : 36. The final accounts for the financial period shall be submited by the Secretary General to the auditors by March 31, following the end of the financial period.

8. *External Audit* :

Rule : 37. The Conference shall appoint a firm of chartered Accountants, operating in the host country, and in no way concerned with the Organization.

Rule : 38. The auditors shall perform such audit as he deemed necessary to certify :

(a) that the financial statements are in accordance with the books and records of the Organization.

(b) that the financial transactions reflected in the statements have been in accordance with the rules and regulations, the budgetary provisions and other applicable directives.

(c) that the securities and monies on deposit and on hand have been verified by certificate received direct from the Organization's depositories or by actual count.

Rule : 39 Subject to the directions of the Conference, the auditors shall be the sole judge as to the acceptance in whole or in part of the certification by the officials of the Secretariat and may proceed to such detailed examination and verifications, as they choose, of all financial records, including those relating to supplies and equipment.

Rule : 40. The auditors may test the reliability of the internal checks and may make such report with respect to that as they deem necessary.

Rule : 41. The auditors shall have free access, at all convenient times, to all books of accounts and records which are, in the opinion of the auditors, necessary for the performance of audit.

Rule : 42. The auditors, in addition to certifying the accounts, may make such observations as they deem necessary with respect to efficiency of the financial procedure, the accounting system, the internal controls.

Rule : 43. The auditors shall not, however, include any criticism in their audit report without first affording the Secretariat an opportunity to provide explanation to the auditors on the matter under observation.

Rule : 44. The auditors shall have no powers to disallow items in accounts but shall draw to the attention of the Secretary General for appropriate action any transaction concerning which they entertain doubt.

Rule : 45. The auditors shall submit their reports on accounts of the Organization for the first calendar year of the financial period to the Secretary General not later then April 30, following the year of the period to which the accounts relate.

Rule : 46. The Secretary General shall examine the accounts and the auditors' report thereon, and forward them to the Executive Committee alongwith his observations, and explanation, if any, for its considerations.

Rule : 47. The Executive Committee, in turn, shall forward these to the General Sessions of the AARRO Conference alongwith its observations and recommendation if any, for its consideration.

9. Delegation of Authority :

Rule : 48. The Secretary General may delegate to any officers of the Organization such of his powers as he considers necessary for the effective implementation of these rules.

10. General :

Rule : 49. These rules may be amended by the Conference in the same manner as provided for amendment of the Rules of Procedures of the Organization, pertaining to the Conference.

F. STAFF REGULATIONS

SCOPE AND PURPOSE

These Regulations embody the fundamental conditions of service and the basic rights, duties and obligations of the staff employed in the Secretariat of the Afro-Asian Rural Reconstruction Organization. They contain the broad principles of policy for the guidance of the Secretary General in the staffing and administration of the Secretariat.

I. DUTIES, OBLIGATIONS AND PRIVILIGES

Regulation : 1. The responsibilities of the staff of the Organization are not national but exclusively international. By accepting appointment they pledge themselves to discharge their functions and to regulate their conduct in the interests of the Afro-Asian Rural Reconstruction Organization.

Regulation : 2. All members of staff are subject to the authority of the Secretary General and to assignment by him to any of the activities or offices of the Afro-Asian Rural Reconstruction Organization. They are responsible to him in the exercise of their functions. In principle, the whole time of the members of staff shall be at the disposal of the Secretary General.

Regulation : 3. In the performance of their duties members of staff shall neither seek nor accept instructions from any government or from any other authority external to the Organization.

Regulation : 4. No member of staff shall, while serving the Organization, accept, hold or engage in any office or occupation which is incompatible with the proper discharge of his duties with the Afro-Asian Rural Reconstruction Organization.

Regulation : 5. Members of staff shall conduct themselves at all times in a manner compatible with their duties towards the Organization. They shall avoid any action and in particular any kind of public pronouncement which may adversely reflect on their status. While they are not expected to give up their national sentiments or their political and religious convictions, they shall at all times bear in mind the reserve and tact incumbent upon them by reason of their occupying a position in an international Organization.

Regulation : 6. Members of staff shall exercise the utmost discretion in regard to all matters of official business. They shall not communicate to any person any information known to them by reason of their official position which has not been made public, except in the course of their duties or by authorization of the Secretary General. At no time shall they, in any way, use to private advantage information known to them by reason of their official position. These obligations will not cease with their separation from service.

Regulation : 7. No member of staff shall accept any honour, decoration, favour, gift or remuneration from any government; or from any other source external to the Organization, if such acceptance is incompatible with his status in the Organization.

Regulation : 8. Any member of staff, who becomes a candidate for a public office of a political character, shall resign from the Secretariat before offering himself as a candidate for such an office.

Regulation : 9. The immunities and privileges allowed to the Afro-Asian Rural Reconstruction Organization by member governments are conferred in the interests of the Organization. These privileges and immunities furnish no excuse to members of staff for non-performance of their private obligations or failure to observe laws and police regulations. The decision whether to waive any privileges or immunities of the staff in any case that arises, shall rest with the Secretary General.

Regulation : 10. All members of staff shall subscribe to the following oath or declaration :

I solemnly swear (undertake, affirm, promise) to exercise in all loyalty discretion and conscience the functions entrusted to me as a member of staff of the Afro-Asian Rural Reconstruction Organization, to discharge those functions and regulate any conduct in the interests of the Afro-Asian Rural Reconstruction Organization only and not seek to accept instructions in regard to the performance of my duties from any government or other authority external to the Organization.

Regulation : 11. The oath or declaration shall be made orally by the Secretary General at a meeting of the Executive Committee by the Directors, Deputy Directors, Assistant Directors and Administrative Secretary before the Secretary General and in writing by other staff members.

701

II. CLASSIFICATION OF POSTS

Regulation : 12.   Appropriate provision shall be made by the Secretary General for the classificatio of posts and staff according to the nature of the duties and responsibilities requirec

III. SALARIES AND ALLOWANCES

Regulation : 13.   The salaries of the staff in the Directors category and those in the Genera category shall be determined by the Executive Committee on the recommendatio of the Secretary General provided that, for staff occupying positions subje to local recruitment, the Secretary General may propose salaries and allowance accordance with the best prevailing local practices and that for staff occupyin positions subject to International recruitment, the remuneration shall be propose according to the duty stations taking into account the relative cost of livin standards of living and related factors.

IV. APPOINTMENTS AND PROMOTION

Regulation : 14.   The Secretary General shall appoint staff members as required and according the provisions contained in the approved Budget for the period.

Regulation : 15.   The paramount consideration in the appointment, transfer or promotion of t staff shall be the necessity of securing the highest standards of efficienc competenance and integrity. Due regard shall be paid to the importance recruiting and maintaining the staff on as wide a geographical basis as possible.

Regulation : 16.   Selection of staff shall be without regard to race creed or sex. So far as practicable, selection shall be made on a competitive basis.

Regulation : 17.   Without prejudice to the inflow of fresh talen at the various levels, vacancie shall be filled by promotion of persons already in the service of th Organization in preference to persons from outside.

Regulation : 18.   Appointments for the posts of Directors and those in the Directors categor shall be for a period not exceeding five years but subject to renewal. Othe members of staff shall be granted either permanent or temporary appointments under such terms and conditions consistent with those regulations as th Secretary General may prescribe.

Regulation : 19.   The Secretary General shall establish appropriate medical standards whic prospective members of staff shall normally be required to meet befor appointment.

V. LEAVE

Regulation : 20.   Members of staff shall be allowed appropriate leave as prescribed in the rules.

Regulation : 21. In order that members of staff may take their leave periodically in their home countries, the Organization shall allow necessary travelling time for that purpose under conditions and definitions prescribed by the Secretary General.

VI. SOCIAL SECURITY

Regulation : 22. Provision may be made, if feasible, for the participation of members of staff in the AARRO Staff Pension Fund in accordance with the rules of that fund.

Regulation : 23. The Secretary General shall establish a scheme of social security for the staff, including provisions for health protection, sick leave and reasonable compensation, in the event of illness, accident or death attributable to the performance of official duties, acquiring or building a house for himself, payment of gratuity after retirement and/or separation from service etc.

VI. TRAVEL

Regulation : 24. Subject to conditions and definitions prescribed by the Secretary General, the Organization shall pay the expenses of members of staff and in appropriate cases, their dependents :

(a) upon appointment and the change of their duty station ;

(b) upon the taking of leave at home when authorised ; and

(c) upon separation from the service.

Regulation : 25. Subject to conditions and definitions prescribed by the Secretary General, the Organization shall also pay removal costs of personnal belonging of the members of staff :

(a) upon appointment and on the change of their duty station ; and

(b) upon separation from the service.

VIII. STAFF RELATIONS

Regulation : 26. The Secretary General shall make provision for staff participation in the discussion of policies relating to staff questions.

IX. SEPARATION FROM SERVICE

Regulation : 27. Members of staff may resign from the Secretariat upon giving the Secretary

General the notice required under the terms of their appointment.

Regulation : 28. The Secretary General may terminate the appointment of a member of staff in accordance with the terms of his appointment, or if the necessities of the service require abolition of the post or reduction of the staff, if the services of the individual concarned prove unsatisfactory, or if he is, for reasons of health incapacitated for further service.

Regulation : 29. If the Secretary General terminates an appointment, the staff member shall be given notice and indemnity payment in accordance with the terms of his appointment.

Regulation : 30. Normally, members of staff shall not be retained in active service beyond the age of sixty years. The Secretary General may, in the interests of the Organization, extend this age limit in exceptional cases.

X. DISCIPLINARY MEASURES

Regulation : 31. The Secretary General may impose disciplinary measures on staff whose conduct is unsatisfactory. He may summarily dismiss a member of the staff for serious misconduct.

XI. APPEALS

Regulation : 32. The Secretary General shall frame rules to deal with cases of appeal by the staff.

Regulation : 33. Any dispute which cannot be resolved internally, arising between the Secretary General and a member of the staff regarding the fulfilment of the contract of the said member, shall be referred for final decision to the Executive Committee of the Organization.

XII. GENERAL PROVISION

Regulation : 34. These Regulations may be supplemented or amended by the Conference, without prejudice to the acquired rights of staff members.

Regulation : 35. The Secretary General shall, from time to time, obtain approval of the Executive Committee for such staff rules and amendments thereto as he may make to implement these Regulations.

Regulation : 36. The Secretary General by virtue of the authority vested in him as the Chief Technical and Administrative Officer of the Organization may delegate to other officers of the Organization such of his powers as he considers necessary for the effective implementation of these Regulations.

Regulation : 37. In case of doubt as to the meaning of any of the foregoing Regulations the Secretary General is authorized to rule thereon subject to confirmation of the ruling by the Executive Committee at its next meeting.

SUPPLEMENTARY DOCUMENTS

(17) AGREEMENT FOR A PROGRAM OF MUTUAL COLLABORATION AND ASSISTANCE BETWEEN THE LEAGUE OF ARAB STATES AND THE AFRO-ASIAN RURAL RECONSTRUCTION ORGANIZATION, 1970

Adopted in New Delhi on November 20-22, 1970, at the Tenth Session of the Executive Committee of the Afro-Asian Rural Reconstruction Organization.

WHEREAS The League of Arab States, hereinafter referred to as the "LEAGUE" established to strengthen the close relations and numerous ties which link the Arab States, aims to promote close cooperation among the member states, inter-alia, (a) in economic and financial affairs, including commercial relations, customs, currency, and questions of agriculture and industry; (b) communications, including rail-roads, roads, aviation, navigation, telegraphs and posts; (c) cultural affairs; (d) social affairs; and (e) health problems; AND

WHEREAS The Afro-Asian Rural Reconstruction Organization, hereinafter referred to as "AARRO" was established by the African and Asian countries to, inter-alia, (a) launch concrete and wherever possible coordinated action to reconstruct the economy of their rural people and revitalize their social and cultural life; (b) to jointly discuss their problems and exchange views, ideas, information and experiences; (c) to formulate plans, devise means and take necessary action for the achievement of these objectives; AND

WHEREAS it is mutually expedient to establish general policies and procedure to follow in planning, developing and implementing suitable programmes in the spheres common to the League and the AARRO in order that such programmes may be carried out in the most effective way to attain their intended objectives and be closely coordinated with other related programmes either of the League or its members; or of AARRO or its members.

Therefore, The League and the AARRO have entered into an Agreement as set forth below and in Annexures (A and B) attached thereto.

Article I.   General Principles.

1.   The aims and objectives of the League insofar as these
relate to economic matters in the sphere of rural development as embodied in Article 2 of its Constitution; and the
aims and objectives of the AARRO as embodied in its Constitution. Preamble and Article I (both these Constitutions
attached with this Agreement as Annexures A and B) are hereby accepted by both parties as the basis for their mutual
collaboration and cooperation.

2.   All collaborative programmes shall be those that,
directly or indirectly, are included in the approved work
programmes of the two Organizations insofar as their member
and eligible member countries are concerned.

3.   All collaborative programmes shall be carried out with
all due regard to the sovereign rights of the respective
members of the two organizations and with their previous
consent which shall be obtained by the two organizations
jointly or severally.

4.   The parties to this Agreement hereby agree to exchange
timely information on the formulation, planning and implementation of the collaborative programmes.

5.   In determining the requirements for the formulation,
planning and execution and progress of the collaborative
projects, the two parties shall mutually agree regarding
the shares of each other to be provided from their own
resources or to be arranged by each from elsewhere.

6.   The two parties to this Agreement agree that the
greatest possible portion of the total cost of the agreed
investment or current expenditure on the programmed projects
shall be contributed by the beneficiaries, the parties acting
more by way of assisting the authorities concerned as far as
possible. This policy principle is a requirement of the
essential necessity of promotion of self-help principle among
the developing countries and their people. Therefore, as a
general rule, no project would be deemed eligible for mutual
collaboration unless it can provide an agreed minimum propor-
tion of the total cost of the project.

7.   Within the limits of resources available, the parties
to this Agreement shall endeavour to ensure that obligations
are discharged as expeditiously as possible.

8.   It is understood between the parties to this Agreement
that nothing in the Agreement shall be allowed to bind them
to enter into Agreement, within or outside the region, with
public or private bodies, international or national in character.

Article II· Technical Advisory Assistance.

1.   The League and the AARRO shall endeavour to render
technical and advisory assistance to each other or to their
members in the sphere of rural development and/or allied
areas, as and when required, subject to their budgetary
limitations or the availability of the necessary financial
and other resources.

2.   It shall be open to the parties to this Agreement to
ask, from each other, such assistance either on their own
or on behalf of their members, existing and future.

3.   Such technical and advisory assistance shall be furnished and received in accordance with the general principles
set out in this Agreement and with the relevant resolutions
and decisions of the competent authorities of the two parties
to this Agreement.

4.   Such technical and advisory assistance, may inter-alia,
consist of:

(a)   making available the services of advisors in order to
      render advice and assistance to or through the parties
      to this Agreement or their members;

(b)   organising or conducting seminars, training programmes,
      demonstration projects, expert working groups and
      related activities in such places as may be mutually
      agreed upon;

(c)   awarding scholarships and fellowships or making other
      arrangements under which the candidates nominated by
      the member countries of the two parties to this Agree-
      ment and approved by them, shall study or receive
      training;

(d)   preparing and executing pilot projects, tests, experi-
      ments or research in such places as may be mutually
      agreed upon;

(e)   providing any other form of technical advisory assistance which may be agreed upon by the two parties to
this Agreement in line with the general principles set
out above.

5. (a) Advisors who are to render advice and assistance
shall be selected by the concerned organizations in consultation with other parties concerned and they shall be responsible to the organization concerned.

(b)   In the performance of their duties, the advisors shall
act in close consultation with the authorities or the bodies
to which they may be assigned, and shall comply with instructions from the government concerned as may be consistent with
the nature of their duties and the assistance to be given
and as may be mutually agreed upon between the parties concerned.

(c)   The advisors shall, in the course of their advisory
work, make every effort to instruct any technical staff
that may be associated with them in their professional
methods, techniques and practices and in the principles on
which these are based.

6.   The parties to whom the advisors may be assigned shall
do everything in their power to ensure the effective use of
the technical advisory assistance made available.

7.   The parties to this Agreement shall consult together
regarding the publication, as appropriate, of any findings
and reports of the advisors etc., that may prove of benefit
to others and to themselves.

8.   The parties to whom the advisory technical assistance
might be provided would be persuaded by the concerned party
to this Agreement to the furnishing and compilation of all
findings, data, statistics and such other information as
will enable the parties to this Agreement to analyse and
evaluate the programmes of technical assistance, or their
results in the course of their implementation or of after
completion.

Article III. Administrative and Financial Obligations.

1.   The parties to this Agreement shall defray, in full
or in part, as may be mutually agreed upon, the costs
necessary to the rendering of technical advisory assistance
or to the formulation, planning and execution of any collaborative projects, which may be agreed upon from time to
time. These costs may include:-

709

(a)   the salaries and subsistence (including duty travel or per diem) of the persons assigned;

(b)   the cost of any other travel outside the country;

(c)   the costs of transportation of the persons during their travel to and from the point of entry into the country;

(d)   insurance (health and accident) of the assigned persons;

(e)   any other approved expenses.

2.   The parties to this Agreement shall be competent to mutually agree for the actual mechanics and procedures for the provision and administration of funds to facilitate collaborative arrangements.

Article IV. Facilities, Privileges and Immunities.

The parties to this Agreement agree that they shall endeavour to persuade the competent authorities in their respective members, existing and future, to accord to the staff of the two organizations, including advisors engaged by them to carry out the technical and advisory or other assignments, all facilities, privileges and immunities that are commensurate with their status and comparable to those enjoyed by persons of similar ranks or status of international organizations, during their stay in these countries.

2.   The parties to this Agreement agree to provide from time to time each other the names and other particulars of the persons for whom the facilities, privileges and immunities may be required.

Article V.

1.   This basic Agreement shall enter into force upon signature by the duly authorized representatives of the League and the AARRO.

2.   This basic Agreement may be modified by agreement between the two parties to this Agreement each of which shall give full and sympathetic consideration to any request by the other for such modification.

3.   This basic Agreement may be terminated by either party upon written notice of a period of SIX MONTHS to the other party, and shall terminate upon the expiry of this period .